OBJECT-ORIEN
JAVASCRIPT

BUILD MAINTAINABLE AND SCALABLE APPLICATIONS

OLIVER LUCAS JR

TABLE OF CONTENTS

Chapter 10

Preface

Welcome to "Object-Oriented JavaScript: Build Maintainable and Scalable Applications"! This book is your guide to mastering object-oriented programming (OOP) in JavaScript and leveraging its power to create robust, well-structured, and efficient applications.

JavaScript, often known for its dynamic nature and functional programming capabilities, has evolved significantly. With the introduction of ES6 classes and the growing complexity of modern web applications, understanding and applying OOP principles in JavaScript has become increasingly important.

This book takes a comprehensive approach, starting with the fundamentals of objects and prototypes and progressing to advanced topics like design patterns, modularity, and asynchronous programming. Whether you're a beginner to OOP or an experienced JavaScript developer looking to deepen your understanding, this book provides the knowledge and practical examples you need to succeed.

What You'll Learn

Core OOP Concepts: Master the fundamentals of objects, prototypes, classes, encapsulation, inheritance, and polymorphism in JavaScript.

Modern JavaScript Features: Leverage ES6+ features like classes, modules, and async/await to write clean and efficient OOP code.

Design Patterns: Explore common design patterns (Factory, Singleton, Observer) and learn how to implement them effectively in JavaScript.

Modularity: Structure your applications using modules and dependency injection to promote code reuse and maintainability.

Asynchronous Programming: Handle asynchronous operations seamlessly using promises and async/await within your object-oriented code.

Testing and Debugging: Write unit tests for your classes and learn debugging techniques to identify and fix issues in your OOP code.

Maintenance and Refactoring: Keep your codebase clean, efficient, and adaptable through regular maintenance and refactoring practices.

Who This Book Is For

This book is for JavaScript developers of all levels who want to:

Gain a solid understanding of OOP principles and how they apply to JavaScript.

Learn how to design and implement robust and maintainable object-oriented applications.

Improve their code organization and structure using modules and design patterns.

Master techniques for handling asynchronous operations in OOP code.

Write testable and debuggable JavaScript classes.

How This Book Is Organized

The book is divided into clear and concise chapters, each focusing on a specific aspect of OOP in JavaScript. The chapters build upon each other, providing a gradual progression from fundamental concepts to advanced techniques. Code examples and visualizations are used throughout the book to reinforce learning and demonstrate practical applications.

Join the Journey

I invite you to embark on this journey to master object-oriented programming in JavaScript. By the end of this book, you'll have the skills and confidence to design and build sophisticated applications that are maintainable, scalable, and ready to meet the challenges of modern software development.

Chapter 1

Objects: The Building Blocks of JavaScript

1.1 Understanding Objects and Properties

This chapter sets the stage for your journey into object-oriented JavaScript. We'll delve deep into the core concepts of objects and properties, ensuring you have a rock-solid foundation for the rest of the book.

1. What are Objects?

Real-World Analogy: Imagine a backpack. It has different compartments to hold various items like books, pens, a water bottle, and maybe even a laptop. In JavaScript, an object is like that backpack – a container that holds different pieces of information. These pieces of information are called **properties**.

Key-Value Pairs: Each property in an object has a **key** (the name of the compartment) and a **value** (the item stored inside). For example, in a `person` object, the key `firstName` might hold the value `"John"`.

Representing Entities: Objects are incredibly useful for representing real-world entities or concepts in your code. Think of a `car` object with properties like `make`, `model`, `color`, and `year`. This allows you to organize and structure your code in a way that mirrors the real world.

2. Properties: Data Associated with Objects

Data Types: Properties can hold various types of data:

Primitive Types: Numbers (e.g., `age: 30`), strings (e.g., `name: "Alice"`), booleans (e.g., `isEmployed: true`).

Complex Types: Arrays (e.g., `hobbies: ["reading", "coding"]`), other objects (e.g., `address: { street: "123 Main St", city: "Anytown" }`).

Accessing Properties:

Dot Notation: `objectName.propertyName` (e.g., `person.firstName`). This is the most common and convenient way.

Bracket Notation: `objectName["propertyName"]` (e.g., `person["firstName"]`). Useful when property names are dynamic or contain spaces.

Manipulating Properties:

Adding: `objectName.newProperty = value;` (e.g., `person.city = "London";`).

Modifying: `objectName.existingProperty = newValue;` (e.g., `person.age = 31;`).

Deleting: `delete objectName.propertyToDelete;` (e.g., `delete person.age;`).

3. Object Literals: Creating Objects

Syntax: Use curly braces `{}` to define an object literal. Inside the braces, you list the properties and their values in the format `key: value`, separated by commas.

Example:

JavaScript

```
const myDog = {
  name: "Buddy",
  breed: "Golden Retriever",
  age: 3,
  isGoodBoy: true
};
```

Visualizations:

Diagram: A simple diagram showing an object as a box with key-value pairs inside, visually representing how objects store data.

Real-World Mapping: A visual showing how a `car` object maps to an actual car, with arrows connecting properties like `color` to the car's paint and `model` to its nameplate.

Exercises:

Object Creation: Create objects representing various things: a book with title, author, and page count; a product with name, price, and description; a movie with title, director, and release year.

Property Manipulation: Write code to access specific properties of the objects you created, modify some of their values, and add new properties.

Data Transformation: Take an array of data (e.g., student names and scores) and transform it into an object where the keys are student names and the values are their scores.

1.2 Working with Methods and `this`

In this section, we'll explore how to add behavior to your objects using methods. We'll also demystify the sometimes confusing `this` keyword, which is essential for working with methods in JavaScript.

1. Methods: Adding Behavior to Objects

Functions Inside Objects: A method is simply a function that is stored as a property of an object. This allows objects to not just store data, but also perform actions.

Example:

JavaScript

```
const dog = {
  name: "Buddy",
  breed: "Golden Retriever",
  bark: function() {
    console.log("Woof!");
  }
};

dog.bark(); // Output: "Woof!"
```

Shorthand Method Syntax (ES6): A more concise way to define methods in modern JavaScript:

JavaScript

```
const dog = {
  name: "Buddy",
  breed: "Golden Retriever",
  bark() {
    console.log("Woof!");
  }
};
```

2. The this Keyword

Referring to the Object: this is a special keyword in JavaScript that refers to the "current" object. Inside a method, this refers to the object that the method belongs to.

Example:

JavaScript

```
const person = {
  firstName: "Alice",
  lastName: "Smith",
  greet: function() {
        console.log("Hello,  my  name  is  "  +
this.firstName + " " + this.lastName);
  }
};

person.greet();  //  Output:  "Hello,  my  name  is
Alice Smith"
```

Dynamic Context: The value of this is determined dynamically at runtime, depending on how the method is called. This can sometimes lead to unexpected behavior if you're not careful.

3. Common Use Cases of `this`

Accessing Properties: Use `this` to access other properties within the same object, as shown in the `greet` method above.

Modifying Properties: You can also use `this` to change the values of properties within the object.

JavaScript

```javascript
const counter = {
  count: 0,
  increment: function() {
    this.count++;
  }
};

counter.increment();
console.log(counter.count); // Output: 1
```

Visualizations:

Diagram: A diagram showing an object with both data properties and method properties, highlighting that methods are functions associated with the object.

`this` **in Action:** A step-by-step visualization of how `this` changes its value depending on how a method is called, illustrating its dynamic nature.

Exercises:

Adding Methods: Add methods to your previously created objects (book, product, movie). For example, a `book` object could have a `read()` method that logs a message like "You are reading [book title]".

Using `this`**:** Practice using `this` within methods to access and modify properties of the object.

Method Chaining: Explore how to chain methods together by returning `this` from a method, allowing you to call multiple methods in a sequence (e.g., `myObject.method1().method2()`).

By the end of this subtitle, readers will:

Understand how to define and use methods within objects.

Grasp the concept of `this` and how it dynamically refers to the object.

Be able to write methods that access and modify object properties using `this`.

Have a solid foundation for working with object behavior in JavaScript.

1.3 Object Literals vs. Constructors

Now that you're familiar with objects, let's explore the two primary ways to create them in JavaScript: object literals and constructors. Understanding the differences between these approaches will allow you to choose the best method for your specific needs.

1. Object Literals

Simple and Direct: Object literals provide a concise way to create a single object. You define the object's properties and methods directly within curly braces `{}`.

Example:

JavaScript

```
const book = {
  title: "The Lord of the Rings",
```

```
  author: "J.R.R. Tolkien",
  pages: 1178,
  read: function() {
    console.log("You are reading " + this.title);
  }
};
```

Singletons: Object literals create singleton objects, meaning you're creating a single, unique instance of that object.

2. Constructors

Blueprint for Objects: A constructor is a special function that acts as a blueprint for creating multiple objects with similar properties and methods.

new **Keyword:** To create an object using a constructor, you use the new keyword followed by the constructor function name.

Example:

JavaScript

```
function Car(make, model, year) {
  this.make = make;
  this.model = model;
  this.year = year;
  this.start = function() {
      console.log("The " + this.make + " " +
this.model + " is starting.");
  };
}

const myCar = new Car("Toyota", "Camry", 2023);
const anotherCar = new Car("Honda", "Civic",
2022);
```

Multiple Instances: Constructors allow you to create multiple instances of an object, each with its own unique set of property values.

3. Key Differences and When to Use Each

Feature	Object Literals	Constructors
Creation	Single object	Multiple objects (instances)
Syntax	`{ }`	`function ConstructorName() { ... }`
`new` keyword	Not used	Required to create instances
Use Cases	- Representing single, unique entities - Simple objects with few properties	- Creating multiple objects with similar structure - Complex objects with many properties and methods

Visualizations:

Literal vs. Constructor: A visual comparison showing how an object literal creates a single, predefined object, while a constructor acts as a template for creating multiple objects.

Blueprint Analogy: A diagram illustrating a constructor as a blueprint for a house, where each house built from the blueprint is a separate instance with its own characteristics.

Exercises:

Create Objects: Create objects representing different concepts using both object literals and constructors.

Compare and Contrast: Analyze the code you wrote for each approach and identify the differences in syntax and object creation.

Choose the Right Method: Given a scenario (e.g., creating a user profile, representing products in an online store), determine whether an object literal or a constructor is more suitable.

By the end of this subtitle, readers will:

Understand the difference between object literals and constructors.

Be able to create objects using both approaches.

Know when to choose object literals versus constructors based on their needs.

Have a deeper understanding of object creation in JavaScript.

Chapter 2

Prototypes and Inheritance

2.1 The Prototype Chain

In JavaScript, objects inherit properties and methods from other objects through a mechanism called the **prototype chain**. This concept is fundamental to understanding how inheritance works in JavaScript and is crucial for building efficient and reusable code.

1. Every Object Has a Prototype

Hidden Link: Every object in JavaScript has a hidden property called its **prototype**. This prototype is itself an object.

Inheritance: When you try to access a property or method on an object, JavaScript first checks if the object itself has that property or method. If not, it looks at the object's prototype. If the prototype doesn't have it, it looks at the prototype's prototype, and so on. This continues until the property or method is found or the end of the chain is reached (the `null` prototype).

2. Visualizing the Prototype Chain

Imagine a chain of objects linked together:

Object: Your initial object (e.g., `myDog`).

Prototype: `myDog`'s prototype (e.g., `Dog.prototype`).

Prototype's Prototype: The prototype of `Dog.prototype`, which is `Object.prototype` (a base prototype for almost all objects in JavaScript).

Null Prototype: The end of the chain, `Object.prototype` has a prototype of `null`.

3. __proto__ and `Object.getPrototypeOf()`

`__proto__`: In most browsers, you can access an object's prototype using the `__proto__` property. However, this is not a standard way and is generally discouraged.

`Object.getPrototypeOf()`: The standard and recommended way to access an object's prototype is using `Object.getPrototypeOf(object)`.

4. Example

JavaScript

```
function Dog(name, breed) {
  this.name = name;
  this.breed = breed;
}

Dog.prototype.bark = function() {
  console.log("Woof!");
};

const myDog = new Dog("Buddy", "Golden Retriever");

console.log(myDog.name);  // Output: "Buddy"
(found on myDog itself)
myDog.bark();  // Output: "Woof!" (found on
Dog.prototype)
console.log(Object.getPrototypeOf(myDog) ===
Dog.prototype); // Output: true
console.log(Object.getPrototypeOf(Dog.prototype)
=== Object.prototype); // Output: true
```

5. Benefits of the Prototype Chain

Inheritance: Objects can inherit properties and methods from their prototypes, promoting code reuse and reducing redundancy.

Efficiency: Methods and properties are stored only once on the prototype, saving memory and improving performance.

Dynamic Nature: Changes to a prototype are immediately reflected in all objects that inherit from it.

Visualizations:

Chain Diagram: A visual representation of the prototype chain, showing the links between an object, its prototype, and so on, up to the `null` prototype.

Inheritance Tree: A tree-like structure illustrating how multiple objects can inherit from a common prototype, highlighting the hierarchical nature of the prototype chain.

Exercises:

Explore Prototypes: Use `Object.getPrototypeOf()` to examine the prototypes of various built-in JavaScript objects (e.g., arrays, strings, functions).

Create a Prototype Chain: Define a constructor function and add methods to its prototype. Create instances of the constructor and observe how they inherit from the prototype.

Modify Prototypes: Change a method on a prototype and see how the change affects all instances that inherit from it.

By the end of this subtitle, readers will:

Understand the concept of the prototype chain and how it enables inheritance in JavaScript.

Be able to access an object's prototype using `Object.getPrototypeOf()`.

Recognize the benefits of the prototype chain in terms of code reuse and efficiency.

Have a solid foundation for understanding prototypal inheritance in the next sections.

2.2 Prototypal Inheritance in Action

Let's dive deeper into how prototypal inheritance works in practice and see how it enables you to create objects that inherit properties and methods from other objects.

1. Creating Objects with Shared Behavior

Constructor Functions: We use constructor functions to define a blueprint for objects with similar properties and methods.

Prototype Property: Every constructor function has a `prototype` property, which is an object that will be shared by all instances created with that constructor.

JavaScript

```
function Animal(name) {
  this.name = name;
}

Animal.prototype.eat = function() {
  console.log(this.name + " is eating.");
};

const cat = new Animal("Whiskers");
const dog = new Animal("Buddy");

cat.eat(); // Output: "Whiskers is eating."
dog.eat(); // Output: "Buddy is eating."
```

Shared `eat()` **Method:** Both `cat` and `dog` inherit the `eat()` method from `Animal.prototype`.

2. Extending Prototypes

Adding Properties and Methods: You can add new properties and methods to a prototype even after objects have been created from it.

JavaScript

```javascript
Animal.prototype.sleep = function() {
  console.log(this.name + " is sleeping.");
};

cat.sleep(); // Output: "Whiskers is sleeping."
```

Dynamic Inheritance: All instances of `Animal` now have access to the `sleep()` method.

3. Overriding Inherited Methods

Customization: An object can override an inherited method by defining its own version of that method.

JavaScript

```javascript
function Cat(name) {
    Animal.call(this, name); // Call the parent constructor
}

Cat.prototype = Object.create(Animal.prototype);
// Inherit from Animal
Cat.prototype.constructor = Cat; // Reset the constructor property
```

```
Cat.prototype.eat = function() {
    console.log(this.name + "  is  eating  cat
food.");
};

const myCat = new Cat("Mittens");
myCat.eat(); // Output: "Mittens is eating cat
food."
```

Specific Behavior: `myCat` uses its own `eat()` method, while still inheriting other methods from `Animal.prototype`.

4. Benefits of Prototypal Inheritance

Code Reusability: Avoid writing the same code multiple times by defining shared behavior on the prototype.

Efficiency: Methods are stored only once on the prototype, saving memory.

Flexibility: Objects can customize their behavior by overriding inherited methods.

Visualizations:

Inheritance Diagram: A visual representation of the inheritance relationship between `Animal`, `Cat`, and their prototypes, showing how methods are inherited and overridden.

Object Structure: A diagram illustrating how `cat` and `dog` have their own properties (`name`) but share the `eat()` method from the prototype.

Exercises:

Create a Hierarchy: Define constructor functions for different types of animals (e.g., `Bird`, `Fish`) that inherit from `Animal`.

Override Methods: Customize the behavior of specific animal types by overriding inherited methods (e.g., a `Bird` might have a `fly()` method instead of `eat()`).

Extend Functionality: Add new methods to the `Animal` prototype and observe how they become available to all animal types.

By the end of this subtitle, readers will:

Understand how to create objects that inherit from prototypes.

Be able to extend prototypes with new properties and methods.

Know how to override inherited methods to customize object behavior.

Appreciate the benefits of prototypal inheritance in terms of code organization and efficiency.

2.3 Extending Built-in Objects

While JavaScript provides a rich set of built-in objects like `Array`, `String`, and `Number`, you can actually extend their functionality by adding your own properties or methods to their prototypes. This can be a powerful technique, but it's important to understand the potential implications and best practices before diving in.

1. Adding Methods to Built-in Prototypes

Example: `Array.prototype`

JavaScript

```
Array.prototype.unique = function() {
  return [...new Set(this)];
```

```
};

const numbers = [1, 2, 2, 3, 4, 4, 5];
const uniqueNumbers = numbers.unique();
console.log(uniqueNumbers); // Output: [1, 2, 3,
4, 5]
```

Now Available: All arrays now have a `unique()` method to remove duplicate elements.

2. Potential Issues and Best Practices

Naming Conflicts: Avoid adding methods with names that might clash with future additions to the language. Consider using a prefix or a more unique name.

Maintainability: Extending built-in objects can make your code harder to understand and debug, especially if others are not expecting this behavior.

Compatibility: Your extensions might not work as expected across different JavaScript environments or libraries.

3. When to Consider Extending

Missing Functionality: If a built-in object lacks a method you frequently need, extending it might be an option.

Utility Functions: For common operations, it might be better to create standalone utility functions instead of modifying prototypes.

4. Alternatives to Extending

Composition: Instead of extending, create a new object that wraps the built-in object and provides the additional functionality.

Polyfills: For browser compatibility, use polyfills to provide missing features in older browsers without modifying built-in prototypes.

Visualizations:

Extended Array: A diagram showing an array object with the added `unique()` method on its prototype, illustrating how all arrays now have access to this method.

Composition Example: A visual representation of how composition can be used to add functionality without modifying the built-in prototype.

Exercises:

Add a Method: Extend the `String.prototype` with a method to capitalize the first letter of a string.

Create a Utility Function: Write a standalone function that achieves the same result as the method you added in the previous exercise.

Compare Approaches: Analyze the pros and cons of extending the prototype versus using a utility function.

By the end of this subtitle, readers will:

Understand how to extend built-in objects by adding methods to their prototypes.

Be aware of the potential issues and best practices associated with extending built-in objects.

Know when it might be appropriate to consider extending built-in objects.

Be familiar with alternative approaches like composition and polyfills.

Chapter 3

Classes: A Modern Approach to OOP

3.1 ES6 Classes: Syntax and Features

ES6 (ECMAScript 2015) introduced a new syntax for defining classes in JavaScript. While classes in JavaScript are built on top of prototypes, they provide a more familiar and structured way to work with objects, especially for developers coming from object-oriented languages like Java or C++.

1. Class Declaration Syntax

`class` **Keyword:** Use the `class` keyword followed by the class name.

Curly Braces: The class body is defined within curly braces `{ }`.

Constructor Method: The `constructor()` method is a special method that is called when a new object (instance) of the class is created. It is used to initialize the object's properties.

Methods: Other methods are defined within the class body to define the object's behavior.

JavaScript

```javascript
class Person {
  constructor(name, age) {
    this.name = name;
    this.age = age;
  }
```

```
  greet() {
     console.log("Hello, my name is " + this.name
+ ".");
  }
}

const person1 = new Person("Alice", 30);
person1.greet(); // Output: "Hello, my name is
Alice."
```

2. Key Features of ES6 Classes

Clearer Syntax: Classes provide a more concise and organized way to define objects compared to constructor functions and prototypes.

Constructor Method: The `constructor()` method simplifies object initialization.

Methods: Methods are defined directly within the class body, improving readability.

`this` **Keyword:** `this` behaves similarly to how it works in constructor functions, referring to the instance of the class.

Inheritance: Classes support inheritance using the `extends` keyword, making it easier to create hierarchies of objects. (We'll cover this in more detail in the next section.)

Static Methods: Classes can have static methods (using the `static` keyword) that belong to the class itself, not to instances of the class.

3. Example: Static Method

JavaScript

```
class MathUtils {
```

```
  static add(a, b) {
    return a + b;
  }
}

console.log(MathUtils.add(5, 3)); // Output: 8
```

Visualizations:

Class Structure: A diagram illustrating the structure of a class, including the constructor, methods, and how instances are created.

Comparison with Constructor Functions: A visual comparison of how classes and constructor functions achieve similar results but with different syntax.

Exercises:

Create Classes: Define classes for different concepts (e.g., `Book`, `Car`, `Product`).

Add Methods: Add methods to your classes to define their behavior.

Create Instances: Create instances of your classes using the `new` keyword and call their methods.

Use Static Methods: Define a class with a static method for a common utility function (e.g., a `DateUtils` class with a `formatDate()` static method).

By the end of this subtitle, readers will:

Understand the syntax for declaring classes in ES6.

Be familiar with the key features of classes, including the constructor, methods, and static methods.

Be able to create classes and instances of those classes.

Appreciate how classes provide a more structured approach to object-oriented programming in JavaScript.

3.2 Inheritance with `extends` and `super`

Inheritance is a powerful tool in object-oriented programming that allows you to create new classes (child classes) that inherit properties and methods from existing classes (parent classes). This promotes code reuse and helps you establish relationships between different types of objects. In ES6, JavaScript provides the `extends` and `super` keywords to implement inheritance in a clear and concise way.

1. `extends` **Keyword**

Creating Child Classes: The `extends` keyword is used in a class declaration to specify that the new class inherits from an existing parent class.

Example:

JavaScript

```javascript
class Animal {
  constructor(name) {
    this.name = name;
  }

  eat() {
    console.log(this.name + " is eating.");
  }
}

class Dog extends Animal {
  bark() {
```

```
    console.log("Woof!");
  }
}

const myDog = new Dog("Buddy");
myDog.eat(); // Output: "Buddy is eating."
(Inherited from Animal)
myDog.bark(); // Output: "Woof!"
```

Inheritance: The `Dog` class inherits the `name` property and the `eat()` method from the `Animal` class.

2. `super` **Keyword**

Calling Parent Constructor: The `super()` method is used in the constructor of a child class to call the constructor of the parent class. This ensures that the parent class's properties are properly initialized in the child class.

Accessing Parent Methods: `super` can also be used to call methods from the parent class within the child class.

JavaScript

```
class Cat extends Animal {
  constructor(name, breed) {
    super(name); // Call the Animal constructor
    this.breed = breed;
  }

  meow() {
    console.log("Meow!");
  }

  eat() { // Override the eat() method
```

```
      super.eat();  // Call the parent's eat()
method
      console.log(this.name + " is eating cat
food.");
   }
}

const myCat = new Cat("Whiskers", "Siamese");
myCat.eat();
 // Output:
// "Whiskers is eating." (From parent's eat())
// "Whiskers is eating cat food."
```

3. Benefits of Inheritance

Code Reusability: Avoid repeating code by inheriting properties and methods from parent classes.

Maintainability: Changes to the parent class automatically propagate to child classes.

Organization: Create hierarchies of classes to represent relationships between different types of objects.

Visualizations:

Inheritance Tree: A diagram showing the relationship between the `Animal`, `Dog`, and `Cat` classes, illustrating the flow of inheritance.

Method Overriding: A visual representation of how the `eat()` method is overridden in the `Cat` class, but still calls the parent's `eat()` method using `super`.

Exercises:

Create a Hierarchy: Build a class hierarchy for different types of vehicles (e.g., `Vehicle`, `Car`, `Motorcycle`, `Truck`).

Inherit and Extend: Create child classes that inherit from your base class and add specific properties and methods.

Override Methods: Override methods in the child classes to customize behavior.

Use `super`: Call parent constructors and methods using `super`.

By the end of this subtitle, readers will:

Understand how to use `extends` to create child classes that inherit from parent classes.

Be able to call parent constructors and methods using `super`.

Know how to override inherited methods in child classes.

Appreciate the benefits of inheritance in terms of code organization and reusability.

3.3 Static Methods and Properties

Static methods and properties belong to the class itself rather than to instances of the class. They are useful for utility functions, helper methods, or maintaining data that is relevant to the class as a whole.

1. Static Methods

`static` **Keyword:** Use the `static` keyword before a method definition within a class to make it a static method.

Accessing Static Methods: Static methods are called directly on the class itself, not on instances of the class.

Example:

JavaScript

```javascript
class MathUtils {
  static add(a, b) {
    return a + b;
  }

  static multiply(a, b) {
    return a * b;
  }
}

console.log(MathUtils.add(5, 3)); // Output: 8
console.log(MathUtils.multiply(2, 4)); // Output:
8
```

No this **Access:** Static methods do not have access to this because they are not associated with any specific instance.

2. Static Properties

Class-Level Data: Static properties are used to store cata that is shared by all instances of the class.

Example:

JavaScript

```javascript
class Counter {
  static count = 0;

  constructor() {
    Counter.count++;
  }

  static getCount() {
```

```
    return Counter.count;
  }
}

const counter1 = new Counter();
const counter2 = new Counter();
console.log(Counter.getCount()); // Output: 2
```

Access with Class Name: Static properties are accessed using the class name, similar to static methods.

3. Use Cases for Static Members

Utility Functions: Create helper functions that are related to the class but don't operate on specific instances (e.g., `MathUtils.add()`).

Factory Methods: Static methods can be used to create and return instances of the class.

Counters or Trackers: Maintain class-level data, such as the number of instances created.

Constants: Define constants that are relevant to the class.

Visualizations:

Class Diagram: A diagram showing a class with static methods and properties, visually separating them from instance members.

Static Method Call: A visual representation of how a static method is called directly on the class, without creating an instance.

Exercises:

Create a Utility Class: Define a class with static methods for common string operations (e.g., `StringUtils` with methods like `reverseString()`, `trimWhitespace()`).

Implement a Factory Method: Create a class with a static factory method that creates and returns instances of the class with specific configurations.

Track Instances: Add a static property to a class to keep track of how many instances of the class have been created.

By the end of this subtitle, readers will:

Understand the purpose and usage of static methods and properties.

Be able to define and call static methods.

Know how to use static properties to store class-level data.

Recognize common use cases for static members in object-oriented design.

Chapter 4

Encapsulation: Protecting Your Data

4.1 Data Hiding and Privacy

Encapsulation is one of the core principles of object-oriented programming. It involves bundling data (properties) and the methods that operate on that data within a single unit (the object). A key aspect of encapsulation is **data hiding**, which restricts access to an object's internal state, ensuring that the object's data is protected and maintained in a consistent way.

1. Why Hide Data?

Prevent Accidental Modification: Data hiding prevents external code from directly modifying an object's properties, reducing the risk of accidental or unintended changes.

Maintain Data Integrity: By controlling access to data, you can enforce rules and validation, ensuring that the data remains consistent and valid.

Reduce Coupling: Data hiding reduces dependencies between different parts of your code, making it easier to modify and maintain.

Abstraction: It hides the internal implementation details of an object, presenting a simpler interface to the outside world.

2. How JavaScript Achieves Data Hiding

No True Private Properties (Yet): JavaScript, traditionally, doesn't have access modifiers like `private` or `public` (though they are coming in future versions!).

Conventions: Developers use conventions to indicate that a property should be treated as private:

Underscore Prefix: Prefixing property names with an underscore (_) is a common convention to signal that a property is intended to be private.

Closures: Closures can be used to create private variables that are accessible only within the scope of a function.

3. Example: Using Conventions

JavaScript

```
class Person {
  constructor(name, age) {
    this.name = name;
    this._age = age; // _age is intended to be private
  }

  getAge() {
    return this._age;
  }

  setAge(newAge) {
    if (newAge >= 0) {
      this._age = newAge;
    } else {
      console.log("Age cannot be negative.");
    }
  }
}

const person1 = new Person("Alice", 30);
console.log(person1.getAge());   // Accessing through a method
```

```
person1._age = -5; // Can still be modified
directly (convention)
console.log(person1.getAge());
```

4. Future of Data Hiding: Private Fields

(Hash) Prefix: Newer JavaScript proposals introduce true private fields using a # prefix. These fields are completely inaccessible from outside the class.

Example:

JavaScript

```
class Person {
  #age; // Private field

  constructor(name, age) {
    this.name = name;
    this.#age = age;
  }

  getAge() {
    return this.#age;
  }
}
```

Visualizations:

Encapsulation Diagram: A diagram showing an object with its properties and methods enclosed within a capsule, illustrating the concept of encapsulation.

Access Control: A visual representation of how data hiding restricts access to internal properties, with arrows showing allowed and disallowed access paths.

Exercises:

Implement Data Hiding: Create a class with properties that are intended to be private. Use conventions to indicate their privacy.

Use Getters and Setters: Provide methods to get and set the values of private properties, allowing controlled access.

Explore Private Fields: If your environment supports it, experiment with using private fields (#) to enforce true data hiding.

By the end of this subtitle, readers will:

Understand the importance of data hiding and privacy in object-oriented programming.

Know how to use conventions and closures to achieve data hiding in JavaScript.

Be aware of the upcoming private fields feature and its benefits.

Be able to design classes that protect their internal data and maintain data integrity.

4.2 Getters and Setters

Getters and setters are methods that provide controlled access to an object's properties. They are essential for implementing encapsulation and data hiding in JavaScript, allowing you to enforce validation, perform calculations, or trigger actions when properties are accessed or modified.

1. Getters

Accessing Properties: Getters are methods that retrieve the value of a property.

get **Keyword:** Use the get keyword followed by the property name (without parentheses) to define a getter.

Example:

JavaScript

```javascript
class Person {
  constructor(name, age) {
    this.name = name;
    this._age = age;
  }

  get age() {
    return this._age;
  }
}

const person1 = new Person("Alice", 30);
console.log(person1.age); // Output: 30 (calls the getter)
```

Property-Like Access: Getters allow you to access a property using the dot notation (person1.age), even though it's retrieved through a method.

2. Setters

Modifying Properties: Setters are methods that allow you to set or update the value of a property.

set **Keyword:** Use the `set` keyword followed by the property name (with a single parameter) to define a setter.

Example:

JavaScript

```
class Person {
  // ... (constructor)

  set age(newAge) {
    if (newAge >= 0) {
      this._age = newAge;
    } else {
      console.log("Age cannot be negative.");
    }
  }
}

person1.age = 31; // Calls the setter
person1.age = -5; // Setter prevents invalid
value
```

Validation and Logic: Setters allow you to enforce rules and perform actions when a property is modified.

3. Benefits of Getters and Setters

Data Hiding: Control how properties are accessed and modified, protecting them from accidental or invalid changes.

Encapsulation: Bundle data and methods that operate on that data within the object.

Validation: Enforce rules and constraints on property values.

Calculated Properties: Calculate a property's value on the fly based on other properties or data.

Side Effects: Trigger actions or updates when a property is accessed or modified.

Visualizations:

Getter/Setter Flow: A diagram showing how a getter is called when a property is accessed and a setter is called when a property is modified.

Validation Example: A visual representation of how a setter can validate a value before assigning it to a property.

Exercises:

Implement Getters/Setters: Add getters and setters to your existing classes to control access to their properties.

Add Validation: Incorporate validation logic within your setters to prevent invalid property values.

Create Calculated Properties: Define a getter that calculates a property's value based on other properties (e.g., a `fullName` getter that combines `firstName` and `lastName`).

Trigger Actions: Use a setter to trigger an action when a property is modified (e.g., update a counter or log a message).

By the end of this subtitle, readers will:

Understand how to define and use getters and setters in JavaScript classes.

Be able to control access to properties and enforce validation using getters and setters.

Know how to create calculated properties and trigger actions with getters and setters.

Appreciate the role of getters and setters in encapsulation and data hiding.

4.3 Benefits of Encapsulation

Encapsulation is a cornerstone of object-oriented programming, offering numerous benefits that contribute to building robust, maintainable, and scalable applications. Here's a breakdown of the key advantages:

1. Data Protection and Integrity

Controlled Access: Encapsulation restricts direct access to an object's internal data (properties). By using data hiding techniques (like private fields or conventions) and providing controlled access through getters and setters, you prevent accidental or unintended modification of data.

Validation: Setters allow you to enforce rules and constraints on property values, ensuring that data remains consistent and valid. This prevents data corruption and maintains the integrity of your objects.

2. Code Maintainability and Flexibility

Reduced Coupling: Encapsulation minimizes dependencies between different parts of your code. Changes to the internal implementation of an object can be made without affecting external code that uses the object, as long as the public interface remains consistent.

Easier Debugging: When data is encapsulated, it's easier to identify the source of errors or unexpected behavior because you have a clear understanding of how the data is being accessed and modified.

Refactoring: Encapsulation makes it easier to refactor your code, as changes to the internal implementation of a class are less likely to have ripple effects throughout your application.

3. Code Reusability and Modularity

Modular Design: Encapsulation promotes modularity by grouping related data and behavior into self-contained units (objects). These objects can be reused in different parts of your application or even in other projects.

Abstraction: Encapsulation hides the complex implementation details of an object, presenting a simpler and more manageable interface to the outside world. This makes it easier to understand and use objects without needing to know their internal workings.

4. Increased Security

Information Hiding: Encapsulation helps protect sensitive information by hiding it within the object. This prevents unauthorized access or modification of critical data.

Reduced Attack Surface: By limiting access to internal data, encapsulation reduces the potential vulnerabilities that malicious code could exploit.

Visualizations:

Modular Building Blocks: A visual representation of how encapsulated objects act like modular building blocks, with well-defined interfaces that connect them together.

Data Protection Wall: A diagram showing how encapsulation acts like a protective wall around an object's data, preventing unauthorized access.

By the end of this subtitle, readers will:

Fully appreciate the benefits of encapsulation in object-oriented design.

Understand how encapsulation contributes to data protection, code maintainability, reusability, and security.

Be able to apply encapsulation principles to create robust and well-structured applications.

Recognize the importance of encapsulation in building high-quality software.

Chapter 5

Abstraction: Simplifying Complexity

5.1 Interfaces and Abstract Classes

Abstraction is a key principle in object-oriented programming that focuses on hiding complex implementation details and presenting a simplified view of an object. Interfaces and abstract classes are powerful tools for achieving abstraction in JavaScript (and other languages). While JavaScript doesn't have built-in support for interfaces in the same way as languages like Java or C#, we can achieve similar results using conventions and patterns.

1. Interfaces

Contracts: An interface defines a contract or a set of methods that classes must implement. It specifies *what* methods an object should have, but not *how* those methods should be implemented.

No Implementation: Interfaces in JavaScript don't have any method bodies. They only declare the method signatures.

Example (using a comment-based convention):

JavaScript

```
// Interface for a Shape
class Shape {
  // calculateArea(): number
  // calculatePerimeter(): number
}

class Circle implements Shape { // Not a keyword,
just a convention
  constructor(radius) {
```

```
    this.radius = radius;
  }

  calculateArea() {
    return Math.PI * this.radius * this.radius;
  }

  calculatePerimeter() {
    return 2 * Math.PI * this.radius;
  }
}
```

Benefits:

Enforces Consistency: Ensures that classes adhere to a specific structure.

Loose Coupling: Reduces dependencies between classes.

Polymorphism: Allows objects of different classes to be treated as objects of a common interface.

2. Abstract Classes

Partial Implementation: An abstract class provides a common base for a group of related classes. It can have both abstract methods (without implementation) and concrete methods (with implementation).

Cannot be Instantiated: You cannot create instances of an abstract class directly.

Example (using a convention to prevent instantiation):

JavaScript

```
class Animal {
  constructor(name) {
```

```
    if (new.target === Animal) {
          throw   new   Error("Cannot   instantiate
abstract class.");
    }
    this.name = name;
  }

  eat() { // Concrete method
    console.log(this.name + " is eating.");
  }

  move() { // Abstract method (no implementation)
      throw   new   Error("Method   'move()'   must   be
implemented.");
  }
}

class Dog extends Animal {
  move() {
    console.log("Dog is running.");
  }
}
```

Benefits:

Code Reuse: Provides common functionality to subclasses.

Flexibility: Allows subclasses to provide specific implementations for abstract methods.

Structure: Establishes a clear hierarchy of classes.

Visualizations:

Interface Diagram: A diagram showing an interface and multiple classes implementing that interface, highlighting the common methods.

Abstract Class Hierarchy: A diagram illustrating an abstract class and its concrete subclasses, showing the inheritance relationship and the implementation of abstract methods.

Exercises:

Define an Interface: Create an interface for a "Drawable" object with methods like `draw()` and `getColor()`.

Implement the Interface: Create classes for different shapes (e.g., `Circle`, `Rectangle`) that implement the "Drawable" interface.

Create an Abstract Class: Define an abstract class for a "Vehicle" with abstract methods like `start()` and `stop()`.

Extend the Abstract Class: Create concrete subclasses for different types of vehicles (e.g., `Car`, `Motorcycle`) that provide implementations for the abstract methods.

By the end of this subtitle, readers will:

Understand the concepts of interfaces and abstract classes.

Be able to define and use interfaces in JavaScript using conventions.

Know how to create and extend abstract classes.

Appreciate the role of interfaces and abstract classes in achieving abstraction and building well-structured applications.

5.2 Hiding Implementation Details

Hiding implementation details is a crucial aspect of abstraction in object-oriented programming. It involves keeping the internal workings of an object hidden from the outside world, exposing only what is necessary for other parts of the code to interact with it. This approach offers several benefits in terms of maintainability, flexibility, and security.

1. Why Hide Implementation Details?

Reduced Complexity: By hiding the internal complexity of an object, you present a simpler and more manageable interface to other developers. This makes it easier to understand and use the object without needing to know how it works internally.

Flexibility: You can change the internal implementation of an object without affecting other parts of the code, as long as the public interface remains the same. This allows you to improve, optimize, or refactor your code without causing breaking changes.

Loose Coupling: Hiding implementation details reduces dependencies between different parts of your code. This makes your code more modular and easier to maintain, as changes in one part are less likely to have ripple effects throughout the system.

Security: Hiding implementation details can help protect sensitive data and prevent unauthorized access or modification.

2. How to Hide Implementation Details

Access Modifiers (in some languages): Languages like Java and C# have access modifiers (e.g., `private`, `protected`) that explicitly control access to members of a class. JavaScript, traditionally, does not have these built-in access modifiers (though they are coming in future versions!).

Conventions: In JavaScript, we use conventions to indicate that properties or methods should be treated as private:

Underscore Prefix: Prefixing property names with an underscore (_) is a common convention to signal that a property is intended to be private.

Closures: Closures can be used to create private variables and functions that are accessible only within the scope of a containing function.

Interfaces and Abstract Classes: Interfaces and abstract classes define contracts that specify *what* an object should do, but not *how* it should do it. This hides the specific implementation details behind the abstraction.

Encapsulation: Encapsulation, as discussed earlier, bundles data and methods within an object, providing controlled access through getters and setters. This hides the internal representation of the data and how it is manipulated.

3. Example: Hiding Complexity

JavaScript

```
class Car {
  constructor(make, model) {
    this.make = make;
    this.model = model;
      this._engine = new Engine();  // Engine
implementation is hidden
  }

  start() {
      this._engine.start();  // Interact with the
engine internally
```

```
    console.log("Car started.");
  }
}
```

Hidden Engine: The `_engine` property and the details of how the engine works are hidden from users of the `Car` class. They only need to know how to `start()` the car.

Visualizations:

Black Box: A visual representation of an object as a black box, with only its public interface exposed.

Layered Architecture: A diagram showing how abstraction can be used to create layers of abstraction, with each layer hiding the complexity of the layer below it.

By the end of this subtitle, readers will:

Understand the importance of hiding implementation details in abstraction.

Know how to use conventions and techniques in JavaScript to achieve information hiding.

Be able to design classes that expose clear and simple interfaces while hiding internal complexity.

Appreciate the role of information hiding in building maintainable and flexible applications.

5.3 Designing for Flexibility

Designing for flexibility is a key goal in object-oriented programming. It means creating classes and objects that can adapt to changing requirements and be easily extended or modified without affecting other parts of the system. This is crucial for building maintainable, scalable, and future-proof applications.

1. Principles of Flexible Design

Loose Coupling: Minimize dependencies between classes. Changes in one class should have minimal impact on other classes.

High Cohesion: Group related data and behavior within a single class. This makes classes more self-contained and easier to understand.

Abstraction: Hide implementation details and expose only essential information through well-defined interfaces.

Polymorphism: Allow objects of different classes to be treated as objects of a common type, enabling flexible and interchangeable components.

Open/Closed Principle: Classes should be open for extension but closed for modification. You should be able to add new functionality without altering existing code.

2. Techniques for Achieving Flexibility

Interfaces and Abstract Classes: Define contracts that specify what methods an object should have, allowing for different implementations.

Composition over Inheritance: Favor composition (combining objects) over inheritance to create more flexible and reusable components.

Dependency Injection: Pass dependencies into objects rather than having them create their own dependencies. This makes it easier to swap out components or change their behavior.

Design Patterns: Utilize design patterns (e.g., Strategy, Observer, Decorator) to address common design challenges and promote flexibility.

3. Example: Flexible Payment Processing

JavaScript

```
// Interface for payment processors
class PaymentProcessor {
  // processPayment(amount: number): boolean
}

class StripeProcessor implements PaymentProcessor
{
  processPayment(amount) {
    // Stripe API integration
  }
}

class PayPalProcessor implements PaymentProcessor
{
  processPayment(amount) {
    // PayPal API integration
  }
}

class Order {
    constructor(processor)    {    //    Dependency
injection
    this.paymentProcessor = processor;
  }

  checkout(amount) {
    this.paymentProcessor.processPayment(amount);
  }
}
```

Interchangeable Processors: The `Order` class can work with any payment processor that implements the `PaymentProcessor` interface, making it easy to add new payment options without modifying the `Order` class.

Visualizations:

Flexible Architecture: A diagram showing a system with loosely coupled components that can be easily rearranged or replaced.

Plug-and-Play Components: A visual representation of how components can be plugged in and out of a system due to well-defined interfaces and dependency injection.

By the end of this subtitle, readers will:

Understand the importance of designing for flexibility in object-oriented programming.

Be familiar with principles and techniques for achieving flexibility.

Be able to apply these concepts to create adaptable and maintainable applications.

Recognize the long-term benefits of flexible design in software development.

Chapter 6

Polymorphism: Adapting to Change

6.1 Method Overriding

Method overriding is a powerful mechanism in object-oriented programming that allows a subclass to provide a specific implementation for a method that is already defined in its superclass. This enables you to customize the behavior of objects based on their specific types while still maintaining a common interface.

1. How Method Overriding Works

Inheritance: A subclass inherits methods from its superclass.

Redefinition: The subclass can choose to redefine a method that it inherited. This means providing a new implementation for that method.

Signature Match: The overriding method in the subclass must have the same name, parameters (number and type), and return type as the method in the superclass.

2. Example

JavaScript

```
class Animal {
  makeSound() {
    console.log("Generic animal sound");
  }
}
```

```
class Dog extends Animal {
  makeSound() {
    console.log("Woof!");
  }
}


class Cat extends Animal {
  makeSound() {
    console.log("Meow!");
  }
}


const animal = new Animal();
const dog = new Dog();
const cat = new Cat();


animal.makeSound();  // Output: "Generic
animal sound"
dog.makeSound(); // Output: "Woof!"
cat.makeSound(); // Output: "Meow!"
```

Specialized Behavior: Each subclass provides its own implementation of the `makeSound()` method, demonstrating polymorphism.

3. Benefits of Method Overriding

Customization: Tailor the behavior of objects based on their specific types.

Flexibility: Adapt and extend existing code without modifying the original superclass.

Polymorphism: Treat objects of different classes in a uniform way while allowing them to exhibit specific behaviors.

Maintainability: Changes to a subclass's overridden method don't affect other subclasses or the superclass.

4. super **Keyword in Overriding**

Calling Superclass Method: You can use the super keyword within an overriding method to call the superclass's version of that method. This is useful when you want to extend the behavior of the superclass method rather than completely replacing it.

JavaScript

```javascript
class Bird extends Animal {
  makeSound() {
    super.makeSound(); // Call the Animal's makeSound()
    console.log("Tweet tweet!");
  }
}
```

Visualizations:

Method Overriding Diagram: A diagram showing a superclass and subclasses with an overridden method, illustrating how the subclass method takes precedence.

Polymorphism Example: A visual representation of how different objects can respond to the same method call in their own unique ways.

Exercises:

Override Methods: Create a class hierarchy and override methods in subclasses to provide specific implementations.

Use `super`**:** In your overridden methods, call the superclass method using `super` to extend its behavior.

Polymorphic Array: Create an array of objects of different subclasses and call the overridden method on each object, observing the polymorphic behavior.

By the end of this subtitle, readers will:

Understand the concept of method overriding and how it works.

Be able to override methods in subclasses to provide specific implementations.

Know how to use the `super` keyword within overridden methods.

Appreciate the role of method overriding in achieving polymorphism and flexibility.

6.2 Duck Typing in JavaScript

Duck typing is a form of dynamic typing in which an object's suitability is determined by its behavior (the methods and properties it has) rather than its explicit type or class. It's a core concept in JavaScript due to the language's dynamic nature. The name comes from the saying, "If it walks like a duck and quacks like a duck, then it probably is a duck."

1. How Duck Typing Works

Focus on Behavior: Duck typing doesn't care about an object's inheritance or whether it implements a specific interface. It only cares if the object has the necessary methods and properties to fulfill a certain role.

Flexibility: This allows you to use objects interchangeably, even if they are not related by inheritance, as long as they exhibit the expected behavior.

2. Example

JavaScript

```javascript
function makeFly(obj) {
  if (typeof obj.fly === 'function') {
    obj.fly();
  } else {
    console.log("This object can't fly.");
  }
}


const bird = {
  fly: function() {
    console.log("Bird is flying.");
  }
};
```

```
const airplane = {
  fly: function() {
    console.log("Airplane is flying.");
  }
};


makeFly(bird); // Output: "Bird is flying."
makeFly(airplane);  // Output: "Airplane is
flying."
```

Different Types, Same Behavior: Even though `bird` and `airplane` are completely different objects, they both have a `fly()` method. Duck typing allows `makeFly()` to work with both of them.

3. Benefits of Duck Typing

Flexibility: Use objects interchangeably based on their behavior.

Reduced Coupling: Avoid rigid type dependencies, making your code more adaptable.

Simplified Code: Less focus on type hierarchies and more on what objects can do.

4. Duck Typing and Evolving Code

Adapting to Change: Duck typing makes your code more resilient to changes in object structures. As long as an object provides the expected methods, your code can continue to work even if the object's internal implementation changes.

Adding New Types: You can introduce new object types without modifying existing code, as long as the new types achere to the expected behavior.

5. Considerations

Runtime Errors: Since type checking is not enforced at compile time, you might encounter runtime errors if an object doesn't have the expected methods or properties.

Documentation: Clear documentation is essential to communicate the expected behavior of objects used in duck typing scenarios.

Visualizations:

Duck Typing Diagram: A diagram showing different objects with the same method, illustrating how they can be used interchangeably despite their different types.

Flexible Code Example: A visual representation of how duck typing allows a function to work with various objects that exhibit the same behavior.

Exercises:

Implement Duck Typing: Create a function that accepts an object and performs an action based on the presence of a specific method (e.g., a `quack()` method).

Use Different Objects: Call the function with objects of different types that have the required method, demonstrating duck typing.

Handle Missing Methods: Add error handling to your function to gracefully handle cases where an object doesn't have the expected method.

By the end of this subtitle, readers will:

Understand the concept of duck typing and how it works in JavaScript.

Be able to apply duck typing to write more flexible and adaptable code.

Recognize the benefits and considerations of using duck typing.

Appreciate the role of duck typing in dynamic languages like JavaScript.

6.3 Real-world Examples of Polymorphism

Polymorphism, meaning "many forms," is a powerful concept that allows objects of different classes to be treated as objects of a common type. This enables you to write more flexible and adaptable code. Let's explore some real-world examples of polymorphism to see how it's used in practice.

1. Shapes and Drawing

Scenario: Imagine a drawing application that needs to draw various shapes like circles, rectangles, and triangles.

Polymorphism: You can define a `Shape` interface with a `draw()` method. Each shape class (e.g., `Circle`, `Rectangle`) implements the `draw()` method in its own way.

Benefit: You can treat all shapes uniformly, calling `shape.draw()` without needing to know the specific type of shape.

2. Payment Processing

Scenario: An e-commerce website needs to support different payment methods like credit cards, PayPal, and Apple Pay.

Polymorphism: You can define a `PaymentProcessor` interface with a `processPayment()` method. Each payment gateway class (e.g., `CreditCardProcessor`, `PayPalProcessor`) implements the `processPayment()` method according to its specific logic.

Benefit: The website can handle different payment methods seamlessly without needing to know the details of each gateway.

3. User Roles and Permissions

Scenario: A web application has different user roles (e.g., admin, editor, viewer) with varying permissions.

Polymorphism: You can define a `User` class with methods like `canEdit()` and `canDelete()`. Each role class (e.g., `Admin`, `Editor`) overrides these methods to define its specific permissions.

Benefit: The application can enforce access control based on user roles without needing separate logic for each role.

4. Animal Sounds

Scenario: A simulation or game that involves different animals making sounds.

Polymorphism: You can define an `Animal` class with a `makeSound()` method. Each animal class (e.g., `Dog`, `Cat`, `Bird`) overrides the `makeSound()` method to produce its specific sound.

Benefit: You can call `animal.makeSound()` on any animal object, and it will produce the correct sound based on its type.

5. File Handling

Scenario: A program that needs to read and write data from different file formats (e.g., text files, CSV files, XML files).

Polymorphism: You can define a `FileReader` interface with methods like `read()` and `write()`. Each file format class (e.g., `TextFileReader`, `CSVFileReader`) implements these methods to handle the specific format.

Benefit: The program can work with different file formats in a consistent way, hiding the complexities of each format's parsing and processing.

Visualizations:

Drawing Application: A visual showing different shapes being drawn on a canvas using the same `draw()` method call.

Payment Gateway Integration: A diagram illustrating how different payment methods are processed through a common `processPayment()` method.

By the end of this subtitle, readers will:

Be able to recognize and appreciate polymorphism in real-world scenarios.

Understand how polymorphism is used to create flexible and adaptable systems.

See the benefits of polymorphism in various domains and applications.

Be inspired to apply polymorphism in their own object-oriented designs.

Chapter 7

Design Patterns in JavaScript

7.1 Common Design Patterns (e.g., Factory, Singleton, Observer)

Design patterns are reusable solutions to commonly occurring problems in software design. They provide proven approaches to structuring your code, making it more maintainable, flexible, and efficient. Let's explore some of the most common design patterns and how they can be implemented in JavaScript.

1. Factory Pattern

Problem: Creating objects directly within your code can lead to tight coupling and make it difficult to change or extend your application.

Solution: The Factory pattern provides an interface for creating objects, but allows subclasses to alter the type of objects that will be created.

Example:

JavaScript

```
class CarFactory {
  createCar(type) {
    if (type === 'sports') {
      return new SportsCar();
    } else if (type === 'sedan') {
      return new SedanCar();
```

```
        }
      }
    }
```

Benefit: Decouples object creation from the code that uses the objects, making it easier to add new types of cars without modifying existing code.

2. Singleton Pattern

Problem: In some cases, you need to ensure that only one instance of a class exists, and provide a global point of access to that instance.

Solution: The Singleton pattern restricts the instantiation of a class to a single object.

Example:

JavaScript

```javascript
class Database {
  constructor() {
    if (Database.instance) {
      return Database.instance;
    }
    Database.instance = this;
    // ... database initialization ...
  }
}
```

Benefit: Ensures that there's only one database connection throughout your application, preventing resource conflicts and maintaining data consistency.

3. Observer Pattern

Problem: You need to notify multiple objects about changes in the state of another object.

Solution: The Observer pattern defines a one-to-many dependency between objects, where one object (the subject) notifies all its dependents (observers) when its state changes.

Example:

JavaScript

```javascript
class Subject {
  constructor() {
    this.observers = [];
  }

  subscribe(observer) {
    this.observers.push(observer);
  }

  notify(data) {
        this.observers.forEach(observer   =>
  observer.update(data));
  }
}
```

Benefit: Decouples the subject from its observers, making it easy to add or remove observers without affecting the subject's code.

Visualizations:

Factory Diagram: A diagram showing a factory class creating different types of objects based on input parameters.

Singleton Diagram: A diagram illustrating how a singleton class ensures only one instance is created.

Observer Diagram: A diagram showing a subject with multiple observers, and the flow of notifications when the subject's state changes.

Exercises:

Implement a Factory: Create a factory class that produces different types of products (e.g., electronics, clothing).

Create a Singleton: Implement a singleton class for a configuration manager that stores application settings.

Build an Observer System: Design an observer pattern for a news publisher that notifies subscribers about new articles.

By the end of this subtitle, readers will:

Be familiar with common design patterns like Factory, Singleton, and Observer.

Understand the problems these patterns solve and their benefits.

Be able to implement these patterns in JavaScript.

Recognize situations where these patterns can be applied to improve their code.

7.2 Subtitle: Implementing Design Patterns with OOP

Object-oriented programming (OOP) provides a natural foundation for implementing many design patterns. The concepts of encapsulation, inheritance, and polymorphism lend themselves well to structuring code in ways that align with the goals of various design patterns. Let's see how OOP principles can be used to implement some common patterns.

1. Factory Pattern and OOP

Encapsulation: The factory class encapsulates the object creation logic, hiding the specific implementation details from the client code.

Polymorphism: The factory can create objects of different types based on input parameters, allowing for flexibility and extensibility.

JavaScript

```javascript
class ShapeFactory {
  createShape(type) {
    if (type === 'circle') {
      return new Circle();
    } else if (type === 'rectangle') {
      return new Rectangle();
    }
  }
}
```

OOP Benefit: The factory method (`createShape`) can return different types of shapes (e.g., `Circle`, `Rectangle`), which are all treated as objects of a common type (`Shape`), enabling polymorphic behavior.

2. Singleton Pattern and OOP

Encapsulation: The singleton class encapsulates its instance, ensuring that only one instance can be created.

Static Members: A static property (`instance`) and a static method (`getInstance()`) are used to manage the single instance.

JavaScript

```javascript
class Logger {
  constructor() {
    if (Logger.instance) {
      return Logger.instance;
    }
    Logger.instance = this;
    // ... logger initialization ...
  }

  static getInstance() {
    if (!Logger.instance) {
      Logger.instance = new Logger();
    }
    return Logger.instance;
  }
}
```

```
}
```

OOP Benefit: The constructor prevents external code from creating new instances, and the static `getInstance()` method provides controlled access to the single instance.

3. Observer Pattern and OOP

Encapsulation: The subject and observer objects encapsulate their own data and behavior.

Inheritance: Observers can inherit from a common `Observer` class or interface, ensuring they have an `update()` method.

Polymorphism: The subject can notify different types of observers without knowing their specific implementations.

JavaScript

```javascript
class Subject {
  // ... (subscribe, notify methods)
}


class Observer {
  update(data) {
    // ... handle updates ...
  }
}
```

OOP Benefit: The subject maintains a list of observers and notifies them through a common `update()` method, allowing for flexible and dynamic relationships between objects.

Visualizations:

Class Diagrams: Show how classes interact and inherit from each other in the implementation of design patterns.

Sequence Diagrams: Illustrate the flow of method calls and interactions between objects in a design pattern.

By the end of this subtitle, readers will:

Understand how OOP principles are used to implement design patterns.

See the connection between encapsulation, inheritance, polymorphism, and design patterns.

Be able to apply OOP concepts to create more effective and structured implementations of design patterns.

Appreciate the synergy between OOP and design patterns in building robust and maintainable software.

7.3 Choosing the Right Pattern

With a variety of design patterns available, it can be challenging to determine which one is best suited for a particular situation. Selecting the right pattern is crucial for effectively addressing design challenges and creating maintainable code. Here's a guide to help you make informed decisions when choosing design patterns.

1. Understand the Problem

Identify the Issue: Clearly define the problem you're trying to solve. What are the specific challenges or limitations you're facing?

Analyze the Context: Consider the context in which the problem occurs. What are the constraints and requirements of your application?

2. Consider the Pattern's Intent

Pattern Purpose: Each design pattern has a specific intent and addresses a particular type of problem. Familiarize yourself with the intent of various patterns.

Match Intent to Problem: Choose a pattern whose intent aligns with the problem you're trying to solve.

3. Evaluate the Consequences

Trade-offs: Every design pattern has trade-offs. Consider the potential consequences of using a particular pattern in terms of performance, complexity, and flexibility.

Balance Trade-offs: Choose a pattern that provides the best balance of benefits and trade-offs for your specific needs.

4. Favor Simplicity

Start Simple: Don't over-engineer your solutions. If a simpler approach can solve the problem effectively, there's no need to introduce complex patterns.

Introduce Patterns as Needed: As your application grows and evolves, you can introduce design patterns to address emerging challenges and maintainability issues.

5. Pattern Categories as a Guide

Creational Patterns: Deal with object creation mechanisms, trying to create objects in a manner suitable to the situation. Examples: Factory, Singleton, Builder.

Structural Patterns: Compose objects to form larger structures and provide new functionality. Examples: Adapter, Decorator, Facade.

Behavioral Patterns: Concerned with algorithms and the assignment of responsibilities between objects. Examples: Observer, Strategy, Command.

6. Example: Choosing Between Factory and Singleton

Factory: Use the Factory pattern when you need to create objects of different types based on certain conditions or parameters.

Singleton: Use the Singleton pattern when you need to ensure that only one instance of a class exists and provide a global point of access to it.

Visualizations:

Decision Tree: A visual decision tree that guides you through questions to help narrow down the appropriate pattern.

Pattern Comparison Table: A table comparing different patterns, highlighting their intent, benefits, and trade-offs.

By the end of this subtitle, readers will:

Be able to analyze a problem and identify suitable design patterns.

Understand the importance of considering the intent and consequences of patterns.

Know how to choose between different patterns based on their specific needs.

Appreciate the value of simplicity and avoiding over-engineering.

Be equipped to make informed decisions when selecting design patterns for their applications.

Chapter 8

Modular JavaScript and OOP

8.1 Modules and Encapsulation

Modules are a powerful tool for organizing and structuring your JavaScript code. They allow you to break down your application into smaller, self-contained units, promoting code reuse, maintainability, and encapsulation. Let's explore how modules and encapsulation work together in JavaScript.

1. What are Modules?

Independent Units: Modules are self-contained blocks of code that encapsulate related functionality. They can contain variables, functions, and classes.

Import and Export: Modules use keywords like `import` and `export` to control what parts of their code are accessible to other modules.

Benefits:

Organization: Break down complex applications into manageable units.

Reusability: Reuse modules across different parts of your application or in other projects.

Maintainability: Make changes to modules without affecting other parts of the codebase.

Encapsulation: Control access to the module's internals, promoting data hiding and security.

2. Encapsulation within Modules

Private Members: Variables and functions declared within a module but not exported are private to that module. They cannot be accessed or modified from outside the module.

Public API: Exported members (variables, functions, classes) form the public API of the module. This is the interface that other modules use to interact with the module.

Example:

JavaScript

```javascript
// myModule.js
const privateVariable = "This is private";


function privateFunction() {
  // ...
}


export class MyClass {
  // ...
}


export function publicFunction() {
  // ...
}
```

Access Control: `privateVariable` and `privateFunction` are encapsulated within `myModule.js`. Only `MyClass` and `publicFunction` are accessible from other modules.

3. Modules and OOP

Classes as Modules: A class can be considered a module itself, encapsulating data and methods.

Modular Design: Combine modules and classes to create a modular and well-structured application.

Example:

JavaScript

```javascript
// user.js
export class User {
  constructor(name, email) {
    this.name = name;
    this.email = email;
  }


  // ... other methods ...
}


// app.js
import { User } from './user.js';


const user = new User("Alice", "alice@example.com");
```

OOP and Modules: The `User` class encapsulates user-related data and behavior, and the `app.js` module uses the exported `User` class.

Visualizations:

Module Structure: A diagram showing a module with its private and public members, illustrating encapsulation.

Module Dependencies: A diagram showing how different modules depend on each other, highlighting the flow of imports and exports.

By the end of this subtitle, readers will:

Understand how modules promote encapsulation in JavaScript.

Be able to create modules with private and public members.

Know how to use modules to organize and structure their code.

Appreciate the benefits of combining modules and OOP principles for building maintainable and scalable applications.

8.2 Organizing Code with Classes and Modules

Classes and modules are complementary tools for organizing your JavaScript code. They work together to create a structured and maintainable codebase. Let's explore how to combine these powerful concepts effectively.

1. Classes for Encapsulation

Data and Methods: Classes encapsulate related data (properties) and methods (functions) into a single unit. This promotes data hiding and provides a clear blueprint for creating objects.

Example:

JavaScript

```javascript
class Product {
  constructor(name, price, description) {
    this.name = name;
    this.price = price;
    this.description = description;
  }

  calculateDiscount(percentage) {
    return this.price * (percentage / 100);
  }
}
```

Encapsulation: The `Product` class encapsulates product-related data and the logic for calculating discounts.

2. Modules for Organization

Grouping Related Classes: Modules can group related classes together, creating logical units within your application.

Namespaces: Modules prevent naming conflicts by creating separate namespaces for each module.

Example:

JavaScript

```javascript
// products.js
export class Product {
```

```
// ... (class definition)

}


export class Inventory {

  // ...

}


// app.js
import    {    Product,     Inventory    }    from
'./products.js';


const   product   =   new   Product("Laptop",   1200,
"Powerful laptop");
const inventory = new Inventory();
```

Organization: The `products.js` module groups the `Product` and `Inventory` classes, keeping product-related code together.

3. Structuring a Modular Application

Feature-Based Modules: Organize your code into modules based on features or functionality (e.g., `user.js`, `products.js`, `cart.js`).

Layer-Based Modules: Separate concerns into different layers, such as data access, business logic, and presentation (e.g., `models.js`, `services.js`, `views.js`).

Dependency Injection: Use dependency injection to pass dependencies between modules, promoting loose coupling and testability.

4. Benefits of Combining Classes and Modules

Maintainability: Changes to one class or module are less likely to affect other parts of the codebase.

Reusability: Classes and modules can be reused across different parts of your application or in other projects.

Scalability: Modular design makes it easier to add new features or modify existing ones as your application grows.

Testability: Classes and modules can be tested independently, making it easier to identify and fix bugs.

Visualizations:

Modular Application Structure: A diagram showing the organization of classes and modules within an application.

Dependency Graph: A visual representation of the dependencies between different modules in your codebase.

By the end of this subtitle, readers will:

Understand how to combine classes and modules to organize their code effectively.

Be able to structure their applications using feature-based or layer-based modules.

Know how to use dependency injection to promote loose coupling.

Appreciate the benefits of combining classes and modules for building maintainable and scalable applications.

8.3 Dependency Injection

Dependency injection is a powerful technique for achieving loose coupling between objects and modules in your code. It promotes modularity, testability, and flexibility by decoupling the creation and use of dependencies. Let's explore how dependency injection works and its benefits.

1. What is Dependency Injection?

Dependencies: In software development, a dependency is an object that another object relies on to function.

Injection: Dependency injection is a way of supplying or "injecting" those dependencies into an object from the outside, rather than having the object create them itself.

Example:

JavaScript

```javascript
class Car {
  constructor(engine) { // Engine is injected
    this.engine = engine;
  }

  start() {
    this.engine.start();
  }
}


class Engine {
  start() {
    console.log("Engine started.");
  }
}
```

```
const engine = new Engine();

const car = new Car(engine); // Inject the engine
dependency

car.start();
```

Externalized Creation: The `Car` class doesn't create the `Engine` object itself. It receives the `engine` dependency as a parameter in its constructor.

2. Benefits of Dependency Injection

Loose Coupling: Objects are not tightly bound to specific implementations of their dependencies. You can easily swap out dependencies without modifying the dependent object.

Testability: You can easily test objects in isolation by injecting mock dependencies.

Reusability: Objects become more reusable because they are not tied to specific dependencies.

Maintainability: Changes to dependencies have minimal impact on the dependent objects, making it easier to maintain and update your code.

3. Types of Dependency Injection

Constructor Injection: Dependencies are passed as parameters to the constructor of the dependent object (as shown in the example above).

Setter Injection: Dependencies are provided through setter methods on the dependent object.

Interface Injection: Dependencies are provided through an interface that the dependent object implements.

4. Dependency Injection and Modules

Modular Design: Dependency injection works we l with modules, allowing you to inject dependencies between different modules.

Example:

JavaScript

```javascript
// database.js
export class Database {
  // ...
}


// user.js
import { Database } from './database.js';


export class UserService {
    constructor(database) { // Inject Database
dependency
    this.database = database;
  }
}


// app.js
import { UserService } from './user.js';
import { Database } from './database.js';


const database = new Database();
const userService = new UserService(database);
```

Modular Dependencies: The `UserService` in `user.js` depends on the `Database` from `database.js`. The dependency is injected in `app.js`.

Visualizations:

Dependency Injection Diagram: A diagram showing how dependencies are injected into an object from an external source.

Loose Coupling Illustration: A visual representation of how dependency injection reduces coupling between objects.

By the end of this subtitle, readers will:

Understand the concept of dependency injection and its benefits.

Be able to apply dependency injection in their code using different injection techniques.

Know how to use dependency injection with modules to create modular and testable applications.

Appreciate the role of dependency injection in building flexible and maintainable software.

Chapter 9

Asynchronous JavaScript and OOP

9.1 Promises and Async/Await with Objects

Asynchronous operations are common in JavaScript, especially when dealing with tasks like network requests, file I/O, or timers. Promises and async/await provide powerful tools for managing asynchronous code in a more readable and maintainable way. Let's explore how to use them with objects and classes.

1. Promises and Objects

Methods that Return Promises: You can define methods within your classes that return promises. This allows you to perform asynchronous operations within your objects and handle the results using .then() and .catch().

Example:

JavaScript

```
class User {
  constructor(id) {
    this.id = id;
  }


  async fetchUserData() {
    return new Promise((resolve, reject) =>
  {
```

```
        // Simulate fetching user data from an
API
        setTimeout(() => {
            const userData = { name: "Alice",
email: "alice@example.com" };
            resolve(userData);
            // or reject(new Error("Failed to
fetch user data"));
        }, 1000);
    });
  }
}

const user = new User(123);
user.fetchUserData()
  .then(data => console.log(data))
  .catch(error => console.error(error));
```

Asynchronous Operation: The `fetchUserData()` method simulates an API call that returns a promise.

2. Async/Await with Objects

Cleaner Asynchronous Code: Async/await makes asynchronous code look and behave a bit more like synchronous code, improving readability.

Example:

JavaScript

```javascript
class Product {
  constructor(id) {
    this.id = id;
  }

  async fetchProductDetails() {
    try {
      const response = await fetch(`/api/products/${this.id}`);
      const data = await response.json();
      return data;
    } catch (error) {
      console.error("Error fetching product details:", error);
    }
  }
}

const product = new Product(456);
async function displayProductDetails() {
  const details = await product.fetchProductDetails();
  console.log(details);
}
```

```
displayProductDetails();
```

Async/Await: The `fetchProductDetails()` method uses `async/await` to handle the asynchronous fetch call.

3. Benefits of Promises and Async/Await

Readability: Asynchronous code becomes more readable and easier to follow.

Error Handling: Simplified error handling using `try...catch` blocks.

Maintainability: Code becomes more organized and easier to maintain.

Composability: Chain asynchronous operations more easily.

Visualizations:

Sequence Diagram: Illustrate the flow of asynchronous operations using promises and async/await within an object.

State Diagram: Show the different states of a promise (pending, fulfilled, rejected) and how async/await interacts with those states.

By the end of this subtitle, readers will:

Understand how to use promises and async/await within object methods.

Be able to write asynchronous code in a more readable and maintainable way.

Know how to handle errors in asynchronous object methods.

Appreciate the benefits of combining promises and async/await with object-oriented programming.

9.2 Handling Errors in Asynchronous Code

Asynchronous operations in JavaScript, such as network requests or file I/O, are prone to errors. Robust error handling is crucial to prevent unexpected behavior and ensure the stability of your applications. Here's how to handle errors effectively in asynchronous code, especially when working with objects and classes.

1. Try...Catch Blocks with Async/Await

Synchronous-like Error Handling: Async/await allows you to use familiar `try...catch` blocks to handle errors in asynchronous code.

Example:

JavaScript

```javascript
class DataService {
  async fetchData() {
    try {
      const response = await fetch('/api/data');
      if (!response.ok) {
        throw new Error('Network response was not ok');
      }
      const data = await response.json();
      return data;
    } catch (error) {
      console.error('Error fetching data:', error);
```

```
        // Handle the error, e.g., retry, show
an error message, etc.
    }
  }
}
```

Error Handling: The `try` block encloses the asynchronous operation. If an error occurs (e.g., network error, invalid JSON), the `catch` block catches it.

2. Promises and `.catch()`

Chaining `.catch()`**:** When working with promises, you can use the `.catch()` method to handle errors that occur during the promise chain.

Example:

JavaScript

```javascript
class UserService {
  getUser(id) {
    return fetch(`/api/users/${id}`)
      .then(response => {
        if (!response.ok) {
          throw new Error('User not found');
        }
        return response.json();
      })
      .catch(error => {
```

```
        console.error('Error getting user:',
error);
        });
    }
}
```

Error Handling: The `.catch()` method at the end of the promise chain handles any errors that occurred in the preceding `.then()` blocks.

3. Custom Error Classes

Specific Error Types: Create custom error classes to represent specific types of errors in your application. This allows you to handle different errors in a more targeted way.

Example:

JavaScript

```
class AuthenticationError extends Error {
    constructor(message) {
        super(message);
        this.name = 'AuthenticationError';
    }
}


// ... in your asynchronous code ...
if (!user.isAuthenticated) {
    throw new AuthenticationError('User is not
authenticated');
```

}

Custom Error: The `AuthenticationError` provides a specific error type for authentication failures.

4. Error Handling Strategies

Retry: Retry the failed operation after a certain delay.

Fallback: Provide a fallback mechanism or default value in case of an error.

Logging: Log errors to a file or service for debugging and monitoring.

User Feedback: Display an informative error message to the user.

Visualizations:

Error Flow Diagram: Illustrate how errors propagate through asynchronous code and how they are handled.

Error Handling Strategies: Visualize different error handling strategies, such as retrying, fallback mechanisms, and logging.

By the end of this subtitle, readers will:

Understand the importance of error handling in asynchronous code.

Be able to use `try...catch` blocks and `.catch()` to handle errors in promises and async/await.

Know how to create and use custom error classes.

Be familiar with different error handling strategies and when to apply them.

Be equipped to write robust and reliable asynchronous code that handles errors gracefully.

9.3 Designing Asynchronous APIs

When building applications that involve asynchronous operations, it's essential to design your APIs with asynchronicity in mind. This ensures that your APIs are responsive, efficient, and provide a good user experience. Here are some key considerations for designing asynchronous APIs in JavaScript, especially when using objects and classes.

1. Promises and Async/Await

Return Promises: Methods in your classes that perform asynchronous operations should return promises. This allows the caller to handle the results (or errors) using `.then()` and `.catch()` or `async/await`.

Example:

JavaScript

```javascript
class OrderService {
  async placeOrder(orderDetails) {
    return new Promise((resolve, reject) => {
      // ... asynchronous order processing logic ...
      if (orderSuccessful) {
        resolve(orderConfirmation);
      } else {
        reject(new Error("Order failed"));
      }
    });
  }
```

}

Asynchronous API: The `placeOrder()` method returns a promise, making it an asynchronous API.

2. Callback Functions (Traditional Approach)

Pass Callbacks: If you're working with older code or libraries that don't use promises, you might need to use callback functions to handle asynchronous results.

Example:

JavaScript

```
class FileService {
   readFile(filename, callback) {
      // ... asynchronous file reading logic
...

      if (readSuccessful) {
         callback(null, fileContent); // First
argument is error (null if no error)
      } else {
         callback(new Error("Failed to read
file"));
      }
   }
}
```

Callback-based API: The `readFile()` method accepts a callback function that will be called with the result or error.

3. Event Emitters

Publish/Subscribe: For scenarios where you need to notify multiple parts of your application about an asynchronous event, consider using event emitters.

Example:

JavaScript

```javascript
const EventEmitter = require('events');


class         NotificationService         extends
EventEmitter {
  sendNotification(message) {
    // ... asynchronous notification sending
logic ...
    this.emit('notificationSent', message);
  }
}
```

Event-Driven API: The `NotificationService` emits a `notificationSent` event when a notification is sent. Other parts of the application can subscribe to this event.

4. API Design Considerations

Clear Documentation: Clearly document the asynchronous nature of your API and how to handle results and errors.

Progress Updates: For long-running operations, provide progress updates to the caller through events or callbacks.

Cancellation: Allow callers to cancel asynchronous operations if possible.

Timeouts: Implement timeouts to prevent indefinite waiting for asynchronous operations.

5. Choosing the Right Approach

Promises/Async/Await: Preferred for most modern asynchronous APIs due to readability and ease of use.

Callbacks: Consider for compatibility with older code or libraries.

Event Emitters: Suitable for event-driven architectures and scenarios with multiple subscribers.

Visualizations:

API Call Sequence: A sequence diagram showing the interaction between a client and an asynchronous API, including the use of promises or callbacks.

Event Emitter Diagram: A diagram illustrating how event emitters can be used to communicate asynchronous events between objects.

By the end of this subtitle, readers will:

Understand how to design asynchronous APIs using promises, async/await, callbacks, or event emitters.

Be able to choose the right approach for their specific needs.

Know how to document and communicate the asynchronous nature of their APIs.

Be equipped to design responsive and efficient asynchronous APIs that provide a good user experience.

Chapter 10

Testing and Debugging Object-Oriented Code

10.1 Unit Testing for JavaScript Classes

Unit testing is a crucial practice in software development, especially when working with object-oriented code. It involves testing individual units of code (like methods in a class) in isolation to ensure they function correctly. Here's how to effectively perform unit testing for JavaScript classes.

1. Why Unit Test Classes?

Identify Bugs Early: Unit tests help catch bugs early in the development process, making them easier and cheaper to fix.

Ensure Correctness: Verify that each method in your class behaves as expected, increasing confidence in your code.

Improve Design: Writing testable code often leads to better design and more modular classes.

Facilitate Refactoring: Refactor your code with confidence, knowing that your unit tests will catch any regressions.

Documentation: Unit tests serve as living documentation, demonstrating how your classes are intended to be used.

2. Choosing a Testing Framework

Popular Options: Jest, Mocha, Jasmine are popular JavaScript testing frameworks. They provide tools for writing tests, running them, and reporting results.

Example (Jest):

JavaScript

```javascript
// myClass.js
class MyClass {
  add(a, b) {
    return a + b;
  }
}

module.exports = MyClass;

// myClass.test.js
const MyClass = require('./myClass');

describe('MyClass', () => {
  let myClass;

  beforeEach(() => {
    myClass = new MyClass();
  });

  it('should add two numbers correctly', () => {
    expect(myClass.add(2, 3)).toBe(5);
  });
});
```

Test Structure: Jest uses `describe` blocks to group tests and `it` blocks to define individual test cases.

3. Testing Key Aspects

Constructor: Test that the constructor initializes properties correctly.

Methods: Test each public method with various inputs and expected outputs.

Edge Cases: Test edge cases and boundary conditions to ensure your methods handle unexpected inputs gracefully.

Error Handling: Test that your methods throw errors appropriately in exceptional situations.

4. Mocking Dependencies

Isolation: When a class depends on other classes or modules, use mocking to isolate the class under test.

Mock Objects: Create mock objects that simulate the behavior of dependencies, allowing you to control their responses and focus on testing the class's logic.

5. Test-Driven Development (TDD)

Test First: Write tests *before* writing the code, clarifying requirements and guiding the implementation.

Red-Green-Refactor: Follow the TDD cycle: write a failing test (red), write the code to make it pass (green), and then refactor the code to improve its design.

Visualizations:

Test Coverage Report: Visualize the lines of code covered by your tests, ensuring comprehensive testing.

Test Suite Output: Show the output of a test runner, highlighting passing and failing tests.

By the end of this subtitle, readers will:

Understand the importance of unit testing for JavaScript classes.

Be able to choose a testing framework and write effective unit tests.

Know how to test constructors, methods, edge cases, and error handling.

Be familiar with mocking dependencies to isolate classes under test.

Appreciate the benefits of test-driven development (TDD).

Be equipped to write testable code and ensure the quality of their object-oriented JavaScript applications.

10.2 Debugging Techniques for OOP

Debugging is an essential skill for any developer, especially when working with the complexities of object-oriented code. Here are some effective techniques to help you identify and fix bugs in your JavaScript classes and objects.

1. Browser Developer Tools

Console Logging: Use `console.log()` to inspect values, track execution flow, and identify potential issues.

Log object properties: `console.log(myObject)`

Log method return values: `console.log(myObject.myMethod())`

Log intermediate values within methods.

Breakpoints: Set breakpoints in your code to pause execution and examine the state of your objects and variables at specific points.

Step through code line by line.

Inspect variables and call stack.

Debugger Statement: Insert `debugger;` statements in your code to trigger the debugger at specific locations.

2. Specialized Debugging Tools

IDEs: Most modern IDEs (Integrated Development Environments) have built-in debuggers with advanced features like:

Conditional breakpoints

Watch expressions

Variable modification during debugging

Debugging Extensions: Browser extensions can provide enhanced debugging capabilities, such as:

Visualizing object relationships

Inspecting prototypes and inheritance chains

3. "Printf" Debugging

Logging Statements: Strategically place `console.log()` statements to track the flow of execution and the values of variables.

Focus on Key Areas: Concentrate logging in areas where you suspect the bug might be.

Temporary Logging: Use comments to easily add or remove logging statements as needed.

4. Rubber Duck Debugging

Explain Your Code: Explain your code line by line to an inanimate object (like a rubber duck). This can help you identify logical errors or inconsistencies.

Verbalization: The act of verbalizing your code forces you to think through the logic more carefully.

5. Debugging Strategies

Isolate the Problem: Narrow down the scope of the bug by systematically eliminating potential sources.

Test with Different Inputs: Vary your inputs to see if the bug is related to specific data or conditions.

Simplify the Code: Temporarily remove or comment out parts of your code to see if the bug persists.

Check for Common Errors: Be aware of common OOP-related bugs, such as:

Incorrect `this` context

Method overriding issues

Prototype chain problems

6. Debugging in Asynchronous Code

Promises and Async/Await: Use `console.log()` or breakpoints within `async` functions and promise chains to track asynchronous operations.

Asynchronous Stack Traces: Browser developer tools often provide ways to inspect the asynchronous call stack to trace the flow of execution in asynchronous code.

Visualizations:

Debugging Workflow: A flowchart illustrating the steps involved in debugging, from identifying the bug to verifying the fix.

Debugging Tools Overview: A visual overview of common debugging tools and their features.

By the end of this subtitle, readers will:

Be familiar with various debugging techniques for object-oriented JavaScript code.

Know how to use browser developer tools and IDE debuggers effectively.

Be able to apply debugging strategies to identify and fix bugs in their classes and objects.

Be aware of common OOP-related bugs and how to avoid them.

Have the skills and confidence to tackle debugging challenges in their object-oriented JavaScript applications.

10.3 Maintaining and Refactoring OOP Code

Object-oriented programming (OOP) offers many benefits for building maintainable software, but like any code, it requires ongoing maintenance and occasional refactoring to keep it clean, efficient, and adaptable. Here's a guide to maintaining and refactoring your object-oriented JavaScript code.

1. Why Maintain and Refactor?

Code Rot: Over time, code can become less organized and harder to understand, especially as features are added or modified.

Technical Debt: Accumulated code rot can lead to technical debt, making it more difficult and costly to make future changes.

Maintainability: Regular maintenance and refactoring keep your code clean, readable, and easy to modify.

Performance: Refactoring can improve the performance of your code by optimizing algorithms and data structures.

Extensibility: Well-maintained code is easier to extend with new features.

2. Maintaining OOP Code

Consistent Style: Follow consistent coding conventions and naming patterns throughout your project.

Meaningful Comments: Add clear and concise comments to explain complex logic or non-obvious behavior.

Documentation: Maintain up-to-date documentation for your classes and methods.

Version Control: Use a version control system (like Git) to track changes and collaborate effectively.

Code Reviews: Conduct code reviews to catch potential issues and ensure code quality.

3. Refactoring OOP Code

Identify Code Smells: Recognize common code smells that indicate potential problems, such as:

Long methods

Large classes

Duplicate code

Complex conditional logic

Refactoring Techniques: Apply refactoring techniques to improve your code, such as:

Extract Method: Break down long methods into smaller, more focused methods.

Extract Class: Move related data and methods into a new class.

Introduce Polymorphism: Replace conditional logic with polymorphism to make your code more flexible.

Remove Duplicate Code: Consolidate duplicate code into reusable methods or classes.

Refactoring Tools: Utilize refactoring tools provided by your IDE or code editor to automate common refactoring tasks.

4. Refactoring and Testing

Unit Tests as Safety Net: Unit tests provide a safety net during refactoring, ensuring that you don't introduce regressions or break existing functionality.

Refactor with Confidence: Refactor your code incrementally, running your unit tests after each change to verify that everything still works correctly.

5. Refactoring for Performance

Identify Bottlenecks: Use profiling tools to identify performance bottlenecks in your code.

Optimize Algorithms: Improve the efficiency of your algorithms and data structures.

Reduce Object Creation: Avoid unnecessary object creation or use object pooling to reuse objects.

Lazy Loading: Load data or resources only when they are needed.

Visualizations:

Code Rot Illustration: Visualize how code can become tangled and complex over time without proper maintenance.

Refactoring Example: Show a before-and-after comparison of code that has been refactored, highlighting the improvements.

By the end of this subtitle, readers will:

Understand the importance of maintaining and refactoring OOP code.

Be able to identify code smells and apply refactoring techniques.

Know how to use unit tests to support refactoring.

Be aware of performance considerations when refactoring.

Be equipped to keep their object-oriented JavaScript code clean, efficient, and maintainable over time.

www.ingramcontent.com/pod-product-compliance
Lightning Source LLC
LaVergne TN
LVHW052056060326
832903LV00061B/987

Not Impossible!

Not Impossible!

✦

How Our Universe May Exist Inside of a Computer

by G. Wells Hanson

iUniverse, Inc.
New York Lincoln Shanghai

Not Impossible!
How Our Universe May Exist Inside of a Computer

iUniverse, Inc.

For information address:
iUniverse, Inc.
2021 Pine Lake Road, Suite 100
Lincoln, NE 68512
www.iuniverse.com

ISBN: 0-595-31332-9 (pbk)
ISBN: 0-595-66296-X (cloth)

Printed in the United States of America

This book is dedicated to my wonderful children, daughter Tammi and son Adam. It is also dedicated to the memory of my only brother, Jarl, who from my first day was my mentor in all things, and whose existence ceased on an unhappy July afternoon in 1997. And finally it must be dedicated to my parents, long gone, who gave me life and much more, and for which I am deeply appreciative.

Contents

Acknowledgements

I would first like to express my deepest appreciation to my wife, Anne, already a published author, for her knowledge and in home assistance, for her input in designing the cover, and without whose extended tolerance, and continuous motivation to complete the book (and get a job), this manuscript may never have reached completion. I would like to thank Meta Stanchik for her considerable encouragement of, and input into this project. I would also like to thank her mother, Loraine Steinpreis, for her professional suggestions and corrections to the early manuscript. Finally, I want to thank Madonna Swanson for her insightful criticisms, which ultimately helped shape the book into its present form, and for her continuous spiritual bombardment.

Introductions

○ ○
All great truths begin as blasphemies.

—*George Bernard Shaw*

Chapter 0
Into The Rabbit Hole

○ ○

An invasion of armies can be resisted,
but not an idea whose time has come.

—Victor Hugo

If you've never considered that the world could be other than as you perceive it, this book is likely to jolt you. It is truly going to rock your world. It is going to be a roller coaster ride like none you have ever taken, certainly not for the faint of heart. There will be times when you will not believe what you are seeing, and you will want to get off and run away. Not only are you going to be badly tossed about (and perhaps bruised), but as you ride, you will see the world around you change in very strange ways. As if you were peering through water, you will see your reality, your truths, and knowledge begin to waver. It will at first seem to shimmer, like in the movie *Contact* when Ellie reaches out with her fingertips and touches the fabric of her reality. At times, your disbelief and incredulity will convince you that what you are seeing is completely false. Don't let it! As you press onward, all realities will suddenly cease as if your roller coaster has run off the end of its tracks over a huge and bottomless abyss, but it is much worse than that. There will be no abyss, no bottom, nor will you see the other side. You will have sailed into incomprehensible nothingness, no roller coaster, no space to sail through, nor anywhere to fall. As the book approaches the end, the vague outlines of a possible new reality will begin to take shape for you, but you will not be seeing this new reality with your eyes. Your eyes will be of no use here. In this reality, there will instead be a place for your mind, and by then your mind will have developed new senses, senses better than your eyes.

Some people think that there is a greater consciousness to which we all contribute and that we receive many of our ideas from it. Hardly a new idea, the con-

3

cept surfaces relatively frequently, and in the scientific arena of all places. It is usually mentioned when more than one person makes the same scientific advance at the same time. Examples of this phenomenon are when Darwin and Wallace both came up with the theory of evolution independently, and when Newton and Leibnitz both came up with the methods of The Calculus at the same time. Whatever its cause, the phenomenon is not that unusual. In fact, several of the more startling ideas in this book could very well be coming from some greater consciousness, for all I know. I say this because while I have been developing these ideas independently for well over thirty years, iterations of them are currently surfacing everywhere, suggesting they very well may be ideas whose time has finally come.

Unfortunately, the public as a whole has not been adequately prepared for these ideas. One of the reasons is that almost a century ago now, with the advent of quantum physics and the abstraction of science to mathematics, science took a turn that made it so incomprehensible that very little after that point actually made it into the public awareness. The public hears bits and pieces every now and then that are out of context and utterly mind boggling, so these ideas are experienced as curiosities and then forgotten. The vast majority of the non-scientific public is nearly a century behind in its beliefs and knowledge of science and the related philosophical implications. They have no way to make sense of the unbelievable picture that is forming of the universe as the puzzle pieces begin to fall into place.

The worlds introduced in this book will thus be startling and new to many readers, although some of these ideas have been around for a long time, a few of them for a very long time, even thousands of years. So why attempt a popular book with ideas that have previously been locked away in dusty old philosophy texts? One reason is that these ideas are resurfacing, particularly in the popular media such as movies like *Dark City*, *What Dreams May Come*, *Total Recall*, *Contact*, and the *Matrix* series. All of these movies demonstrate in their own way the theme that ***our perception of the world, as opposed to the real world, are two very different and distinct things***. It will be most beneficial if readers have seen and understood these movies.

The significant idea here is that the universe we experience, the universe we know and love, is, in many ways *not real*. In each movie mentioned above, the world as experienced by the characters is very different from what reality actually turns out to be, and it is necessary for the portrayed characters to understand this before they can make sense of their worlds. Several of these movies project the seemingly impossible idea that what we perceive as *the real and material world is an illusion*, and in fact does not exist in the form we experience it. Astonishingly, this is one of the ideas that has been around for several thousand years, even iterated by Plato in his *Republic*. In order to make sense of what they will see in this book, it will be very important for readers to grasp and understand the theme that the real world, as opposed to our perception of it, are two different things, and may be quite different.

I will be relying quite heavily on the readers' understanding of at least the first *Matrix* movie as it provides a nearly ideal environment in which to explore the ideas that will be introduced in this book. In Chapter 5, I will explain the movie to the readers so that they thoroughly understand the perplexing phenomena the movie exhibits that still confuse so many. Readers will benefit greatly from renting and watching the movie again prior to reading this chapter. The earlier the better.

One very interesting question not addressed in the movie is, "If there were physicists living in the matrix, what would they find when they probe the foundations of their virtual (computerized) reality?" Like Neo, we will be plugging ourselves into a matrix-like environment, and we will explore the physics that must exist in this computerized world. We will see what they see, what their experiments reveal about the physics that they find, and what they can and cannot tell about the computer in which they are imbedded. Can they determine that their experiences of their world are really computer generated? Can they deduce that the bottom level of the world they are testing is computerized? When they investigate the nature of the fundamental particles in this virtual reality, will it be evident that they are computer generated particles instead of real? How many levels of the subatomic world does this computerized reality support, and very importantly, what do they find at the *very bottom* level? Besides a physicist, we will also imbed a computer scientist, a neuroscientist (brain researcher), and a metaphysicist into this computerized world and will examine the revealing phenomena they discover as well.

We will also look at how we too might create a virtual universe inside of a computer, and how to then *create* a *real* physicist (like us) within this universe from the material of that computerized universe, as opposed to a plugged in physicist. We will see some fascinating algorithms, i.e. programming techniques, that a computer would likely use to create that physicist's experience of a real world, from fundamental particle effects to time. Very importantly, we will see the methods needed to harmonize and coordinate the events of such a massively complex universe so they would all fit together flawlessly. Finally, *we will see the many ways that these are similar to what physicists are actually finding in our world*!

Section One, *The Nature of Knowledge*, is designed to help shake readers loose from their reverie of believing in absolute knowledge. Most of us live our lives confident in our knowledge of the world around us. In order to enjoy this book, however, readers must be able to entertain the possible truth of ideas that utterly contradict their everyday notions of reality. We will examine in a friendly way what *truth and reality* really are, and humanity's attempts to achieve these. Additionally, we will examine the surprising implications of what knowledge really is, and apply these insights throughout the rest of the book to the universe we know. One of the more common feelings that the reader will be experiencing during this book is incredulity and outright disbelief, and without the benefits of reading Section One, I believe many readers will far too willingly put the book down prematurely, with no comprehension.

Section Two, *What's the Matter With Matter?*, introduces readers to some of the weird and incomprehensible discoveries that science has made about the universe. These weird phenomena will illustrate how the world as we experience it is not the way the world actually is. Further, it will introduce the exploration into how the *material world* as we know it somehow doesn't even exist, and into how this is possible. Readers will then learn some of how a universe works to prepare them to understand the computer programming of a universe undertaken in section four.

Section Three, *The Matter of Mind*, visits how information gets into the brain, and how the brain as an *information system* itself represents this information using just networks of neurons. It demonstrates the gaping abyss between information as represented in the brain and its representation in the mind, i.e. our experience. It revisits from Section Two the difference we found between the real universe, and our experience of it, and explains how this phenomenon happens, and thus how it is possible that the world, as we know it, does not exist. It concludes by exploring the fascinating mysteries of the mind and some of their implications.

Section Four, *How to Make a Physicist*, examines some of the strategies a *programmed* universe will need to work inside of a computer, and some of the properties of universes in general. We will then create the universe, and create a physicist from the actual (virtual) material within this computerized universe. We will examine how he interacts with his universe, and what he will and can find out about it. We will then discuss what it would take to give him a mind and some apparently implied relationships of the mind to the universe.

Section Five, *The Computerized Universe*, ties together all previous sections, and points out the myriad ways that the strategies used by the physical universe we live in are similar or identical to those necessary in our programmed universe.

It reveals that approximately two dozen of the relativistic and quantum phenomena that seem so mystifying to us, actually occur naturally in a virtual universe *programmed into a computer*. Even the quantum itself turns up as an artifact of programming a universe inside of a computer. It also introduces the recent suggestion that quantum physics appears to be based on information theory, and generally proposes the paradigm that the immaterial universe, the universe we live in, is some sort of fabulously universal information system.

The material of this book crosses several branches of science and philosophy, including physics, computer science, neuroscience, and metaphysics. Popular science books are rather appropriately aimed at science junkies and science groupies. This book, however, attempts to bring to a non-science oriented portion of the public the astonishment of the esoteric developments that exist at the most advanced frontiers of humanity's intellectual and scientific endeavors. This is not an easy thing to do. If I take a friend by the arm, and looking them in the eye, tell them that the material world they live in does not exist (as this book does), I'd be lucky if they accommodate me with a nod or an "uh-huh, sure." If I'm really lucky, they may think the concept is cool and want to believe it, but they still have no idea how it's possible. It is the primary point of this book to show them how it is possible to cross this gigantic chasm, to show them how to get from one side to the other, with this and several other equally unbelievable notions.

The material in this book is not only aimed at the nonscientific public but at the professionals too, so it is imperative that it sustain a high degree of accuracy and validity. On the one hand, I am trying to give the uninitiated reader some way to comprehend and grasp the gist of material that is mind twisting even to people advanced in these fields. To do so, I have had to occasionally resort to simplification and metaphor. Where I have illustrated a concept in this manner, I have tried to preserve the general truth of the supporting facts, but I must request that the professionals in these fields identify with the overall validity of the conclusions. Happily, I have found that the majority of the time the material can be conveyed factually in an easy and understandable manner.

This book is more though than just an *objective overview* of the arcane developments in science and philosophy. While by no means comprehensive, it airs additional speculations and viewpoints, some of which I support with varying degrees of conviction, some original, and some even contradictory. I have done my best to distinguish between dogma and speculation. If it is unclear, however, the reader is best advised to consider it to be speculation. You will not progress too far into this book before you discover that dogma is ***all** speculation anyway*.

So let me introduce myself. Along with some formal training in physics and mathematics, my education is in computer science, and I have spent a decade and a half sporadically pursuing machine intelligence down my own path, with some success I might add. (A small portion of it shows up later in this book.) I am certainly what one might call a science junky and have been investigating and observing nature and my world since well before school age. I developed a strong interest in philosophy in my early teens, which I have retained throughout my lifetime. For two and a half of my college years, my hands were privileged to participate in the creation of the subatomic particle detector (D0) that eventually revealed the existence of the last and final quark, the *top* quark, at Fermilab in 1994. I feel very privileged to have had the opportunity to contribute to that effort, and to have associated with the scientists involved.

I consider myself to be not only a deep thinker, but a free thinker, with a willingness to break mindset that has given my imagination the freedom to roam the rarely explored regions out at the very fringe of human thought. It is my hope that the reader will find these fringe ideas not only mind bending, but exciting, perhaps like drugs, without the drugs. I have to acknowledge, though, that today's youth was born into an environment so predominated by computers that many ideas in this book involving information systems that I find startling and mind stretching may be almost presupposed by them.

In the end, I think of myself as just a Virginia country boy. But if country boys are nothing else, they are necessarily earthy. As a kid, I used to walk behind a horse drawn plow and break up the clods of dirt in our freshly plowed field with my bare feet, and that's about as down to earth as one can get. My thinking tends to be earthy, and I hope it has found its way into my writing. I think every idea contained herein must be dirt simple, and I have tried to expose this simplicity to the reader. If I can understand it, you can understand it. I am basically just a barefoot country boy after all.

Between the covers of this book is juxtaposed knowledge from several distinct but *now* obviously related realms of knowledge. According to Edward de Bono, when information is laid out in new relationships, people are going to see connections that they didn't see before. It is my hope that the ideas presented will stimulate creative thought and new insights in others as well, perhaps in disagreement with mine. I could ask no greater reward.

At this point, I must warn the non-technical readers that you may not be able to just skim the material, reading a few selected words from each paragraph the way you would a novel, or a directive from your boss at work. While the book is non-technical, it is based on mental images that will be new to many and that must be available to your mind to comprehend later conclusions. To build these images, I have resorted to simple and hopefully interesting descriptions, but descriptions nevertheless, and I am not sure that there are many extraneous sentences in the book that don't contribute or may be skipped. This book does not just talk about the possibilities. It actually *demonstrates* how they are possible, which requires a considerably deeper discussion, and deeper reading. Consequently, the usually non-technical reader may find that an hour or two of reading flat knocks them out, so I have done my best to make the material easy and entertaining. To these reader, my suggestion is to take it slow, and don't try to read too much at a sitting.

Apologia to scientists:

Humanity seems of late to want to compare the universe to a computer, or more properly, an information system of some kind. Some of us, scientists in particular, initially began to notice similarities some time ago, and we have been talking about it for literally decades, even if only in small voices. The arts have picked up on those voices recently, amplifying them considerably. Scientists have begun to speak openly of some aspects of the universe as information related, going so far as to estimate the *computing power* of the universe. Still, no one is quite ready to commit to the idea that our universe is somehow a computer, and I think the reason is because it is not at all evident how to get from here to there, how to get from our perceived everyday material spatial world, to the notion that it is somehow plausible that we live as information inside of a computer. So this book is going to take the plunge, take as a working hypothesis the idea that the universe is an information system, and hew a *possible* path through the intervening wilderness. This path may not be the only or the best path. Much like the leader of a lightning bolt searching for a path to ground, this book will occasionally explore several potential paths, though it is beyond the scope of this book to investigate all potential pathways.

A book that ends up where this one does runs the risk of not being taken seriously, but as far as this author is concerned, the book is a serious attempt to explore serious ideas. In order to achieve its goal, this book enjoys a freedom of mind that few scientists practice regularly, the freedom to speculate, and then pursue those speculations to logical ends far beyond the boundaries of what is usually considered judicious. The results are, therefore, not the hard science with which scientists normally entertain themselves, but I think the results are of enough interest that they should be examined.

Untested ideas must be stated somewhere initially, and to explore them and their consequences, one must build on them as if they are acceptable notions. I repeatedly ask the reader to rely on his or her imagination in order to proceed. Although it is not uncommon that scientific advances have occurred by using *thought experiments*, this is not what science usually does, so some may be uncomfortable proceeding this way. As with any work of philosophy, if you read the last chapter first, you will know where the author is going, but you will have no understanding or acceptance of how that conclusion was reached. One can neither legitimately accept nor reject that conclusion without reading the intervening material. This book is as much about the journey, the discovery of a pathway, as it is about the destination.

This book is quite literally an exercise in puzzle solving, the pieces coming from philosophy, computer science, brain research, and physics. If the puzzle contains 1000 pieces, I imagine at this point I am only trying to fit in 20 or 30, maybe fewer. Many of these pieces will be in the wrong place, some upside down. At times, I will be looking for pieces to answer a certain question, pieces lying in plain view, but not recognizing them. I am sure that many readers will instantly spot some solutions that I did not see. I'm hopeful that astute readers will thus see and apply material in the book to areas left unsolved. The reader is, therefore, encouraged to participate in piecing this puzzle together.

Because I want the general, nonscientific reader to reach the end of this book with some idea of how the conclusion was reached (or just reach the end of the book), much of the description of the physics will seem elementary to physicists to the point of being metaphorical. As an example, I have used the concept of *light rays* when referring to the relativistic behavior of light, because it is simple and sufficient to grasp the behavior of light at that level. The professional physicist will almost certainly experience a desire to see such concepts described in *real* terms. The same will be true of professionals from other branches of science and philosophy. I really do need the professionals in these fields to appreciate the difficulty of making these concepts available to the general reader.

I am a software engineer by vocation, with avocations of AI research and philosophy, and while I consider myself well versed in the philosophy of quantum physics, it is possible that I may have missed a subtle aspect, or two, of quantum phenomenon. There is a considerable breadth, though, to the approach taken toward the issues addressed in this volume, and I doubt that any single inaccuracy will prove critical.

There is a great deal more to be found in this book than just that which is summarized in the final chapter. In the end, I think the sum of the material will affect the intelligent reader in three ways. By the time they have completed the book, readers will have spent enough time contemplating the mysteries of the mind to at least take the mind seriously as something that exists and stands in some relationship to this universe. Second, I think the reader will have loosened his death grip on the idea that the material world needs to exist, and it is my hope that many will be prepared to relinquish this belief completely. Finally, I think the reader will be ready to at least cautiously entertain the idea that many characteristics of our information systems show up in our scientific, quantum description of the universe.

Section 1
The Nature of Knowledge

o o o o o o o o o o o o o o o o o o o o o o o o o o o o o o o o o o

...and he will be the more learned,
the more he comes to know himself for ignorant.

—Cardinal Nicholas of Cusa, 1440

Chapter 1
The Uncertainty of Certainty

○ ○

We are fascinated by being wrong.
It teaches us about ourselves.
Not only are there things we don't know,
but the things we do know can be wrong.

—*Richard Price, The Future of Spacetime, 2002*

Knowledge! What is knowledge? Humanity has been thinking about knowledge since…well…since the beginning. Even in the book of Genesis of the Bible, our human story pretty much starts with the attainment of knowledge. Before Eve sampled, and then coaxed Adam to bite from the fruit of knowledge, life must have been pretty dull around Eden. Happier perhaps, blissfully ignorant, but none too exciting. They certainly exhibited none of the mental abilities that we cherish today as uniquely human. Imagine, Adam walks around in his lovely Garden of Eden, looks around at the pretty flowers, eats sweet fruits every now and then, and, every now and then, visits Eve. End of story! That's it…and for eternity. I'm not sure they saw this as paradise. No wonder Eve gave him the fruit. Way to go Eve! We'd have never amounted to anything otherwise.

Actually, while we weren't looking, the very mental traits that got us bounced out of Eden have become our proudest heritage, our identity as humans, considered by many to be that which distinguishes us from the animals. We canonize those who are curious, can think outside of the box, succeed by breaking the rules, or who test high in school. Our Summa Cum Laude's are draped in robes of great dignity and decorated with symbols of high honor. While we weren't looking, our kids, like Eve, started giving apples to their teachers, now symbolizing the passing of knowledge as a *good* thing, not an evil. And now that we've entered the information age, knowledge is everything!

Unfortunately, the Bible story also captures that there is a downside to the attainment of knowledge. With knowledge, all too frequently, comes that painful loss of innocence. Facts by themselves are lifeless things, but when they turn up pitted against a piece of cherished knowledge, they can feel painfully and ruthlessly cruel. Many of us as children, for example, experienced the stinging pain of deception upon being told that our belief in the benevolent and loving Jolly Old Saint Nick was, in fact, incorrect.

The uncertainty of common knowledge:

Yes, knowledge can be incorrect, and much worse, knowledge that we have come to cherish can be incorrect. Knowledge can be false, and of the many evils associated with false knowledge, the necessary pain of letting it go is certainly one of the most frequently experienced. We are destined to be painfully expelled from our dreamy Garden of Eden over and over again, every time we find ourselves *treasuring* a piece of information that turns out to be false. So where does the evil lie here, in the new fact, or in the false knowledge? Perhaps, as adults, it lies in our *indulging* ourselves in false knowledge in the first place. Certainly when we do so we can *expect* to get burned. Every one of us who has ever been drawn into a debate knows that if they enter the debate with incorrect facts, they can expect to be painfully embarrassed before the audience.

So how does one avoid acquiring misinformation, or at least avoid becoming attached to false information? We obviously wouldn't become attached to information we knew was false beforehand. We acquire information from so many different sources. It looks like one would have to research everything they were ever told, heard on the news, read in a book, saw on TV or commercials, on and on. This is surely an impossible task.

The recognition of this problem has actually been around for many centuries. The great French philosopher and mathematician, René Descartes, thinking about this very question decided that the only possible way to deal with this reality was to take *NO* fact as absolute. Always reserve a certain amount of doubt, even if small, about any information you harbor. You can *never* achieve a state where you can be 100% sure of yourself he reasoned. In more earthy terms, since you can never be *absolutely* sure, try to avoid staking your life on anything you *think* you know for sure. And try never to fall in love with *anything* you know, or you are quite likely setting yourself up for a broken heart.

Okay. So, if you couple the fact that few of us ever check the information that daily bombards us, with the fact that some of it almost certainly has to be wrong, it seems there is a horrifying potential that misinformation is being passed around among us. Could this be possible? Wouldn't we see evidence of it if it were? What we in fact by default do is rely on those knowledgeable among us to catch the error and raise the alarm. Unfortunately, this doesn't work very well. The problem is that those knowledgeable voices just don't carry very far, and humanity is so vast. You end up seeing only the perpetuation of the misinformation, and almost never the correction printed at the bottom of page 28. This does indeed happen to us. We end up accepting information as true simply because it is common knowledge and because it's evident that everyone else accepts it. Well, all too frequently, *common knowledge can be wrong*.

The following are some examples that have nailed me in the past. Although spread over my lifetime, I remember them for their surprise factor. Each one I found difficult to believe when I first heard it, some very difficult. For a couple of them, I can even tell you where I was and what I was doing. One of them I found deeply disturbing and am still tending to my rationalization. Without exception, my mind absolutely *refused* to believe them at first. For each one, I discovered anew how *difficult* it is to let go of knowledge just because it is common knowledge. For each one, I experienced again how difficult it is to accept what at first seems to be the impossible.

We are cresting the first little rise of our roller coaster ride and are poised at the brink of that first drop. For some of you, if you already know all of the following examples, it will be no drop at all. For others it will be a huge rush. Some will hold their hands high in the air and thrill at the freedom of letting go. But for some, it will be difficult, angering, even terrifying to let go of old and trusted knowledge, and implicitly along with it, the familiar facts they were so sure of. I want you to notice if this difficulty happens to you. It did me, and I share these examples with you because I too was one who had picked up false knowledge from the sea of *common knowledge* surrounding us.

If you're like most people, you know a few of the Biblical stories such as Adam and Eve, and Samson and Delilah. One thing you almost certainly know is that on that fateful day in the Garden of Eden, Eve, and then Adam took bites from an *apple*, the forbidden fruit of knowledge. I always thought it was an apple, anyway. Well, it wasn't an apple! At least the Bible doesn't say it was an apple. Do you believe it does? If so, do you believe me when I tell you that it doesn't? Are you skeptical of what I'm telling you? Perhaps you even think I'm a total wacko. But surely, you say, *everyone* knows it was an apple, and of course you're right about that. The fact is, however, that the Bible never mentions an apple, yet this piece of misinformation is so pervasive in our culture that our children give apples to their teachers, it shows up in countless literary references, and even turned up as the *correct* answer on a literature *CLEP* exam I took in college. (**Genesis, Chapters 2 & 3**)

Has this rattled your belief in *common knowledge* a little? Let's try that other well-known Bible story mentioned above, Samson and Delilah. If you're like me, you certainly know that in the story, Samson lost his great strength when Delilah cut off his long hair. What if you're now told that *Delilah never cut Samson's hair?* Surely, you say, you can't be expected to buy that! Everybody knows Delilah cut off Samson's hair. Again, there at least, you're right. Just about everybody does know this, but that's the whole point. In the story, Samson indeed lost his great strength when his hair was cut, but it wasn't cut by Delilah. (**Judges 16:19**)

Enough already with the Bible. Let's look for some other interesting pieces of common knowledge that are out and about and that you might harbor. You very likely believed at some point in your life that eating food high in cholesterol is bad for you. Perhaps you still do. Every other food label aimed at the health conscious claims to be low or no cholesterol. I spent years depriving myself of foods I loved, because they were high in cholesterol. Most of us even know why it's bad. It raises our blood cholesterol, which in turn ends up on the walls of our arteries, etc. What if I tell you now that this is all a myth? The fact is that there is **no** research indicating that it is harmful for you to eat high cholesterol foods. All the research concludes that *eating cholesterol has no effect* on your blood cholesterol levels. Apparently, if someone could flavor cholesterol to taste like chocolate, eating a pure cholesterol bar would be *healthier* for you than eating a candy bar.

The first time that I heard that this was a myth was in 1992. I was reading a book review about a book (written by a doctor) that made the astonishing claim that cholesterol in your food was not harmful...that it was all media hype. I didn't believe it for a second, and angrily dismissed it. My impression was that this guy was probably just trying to get his name in print, and that he was dangerously irresponsible and dishonest. Poor guy! It turns out that he was being honest, responsible, and factual. (**Dr. Robert Buist (1992). *The Cholesterol Myth.* South Africa: Pan Macmillan**)

Later in the mid 1990's, the scientific/medical community convened an investigation into how this misinformation had become so pervasive and wide spread. They concluded that existing research did not support the conclusion that eating cholesterol was harmful, and laid the whole responsibility on the media. Unfortunately, though, the correction was (figuratively) printed at the bottom of page 28 and most of the world missed it. Many foods out there are still labeled *low choles-*

terol. Whoever is responsible, shame on them! Look at what they've put us through with this misinformation.

The people who initially promoted this misinformation would defend themselves by saying that common sense seemed to imply that it was true. We now see that *common sense can be wrong* as well as common knowledge. One is tempted to call it all a premature speculation.

What do you know about HIV (Human Immunodeficiency Virus) and AIDS (Auto Immune Deficiency Syndrome)? Did you know that HIV causes AIDS? Well, guess what. The fact is that HIV has never been proven to be the cause of AIDS. The key word here is "proven." There's a lot of research going on aimed at stopping HIV from infecting people, so a lot of very bright and knowledgeable people are obviously making the assumption that HIV does cause AIDS. However, it's against the law to inject someone with HIV to actually prove that it is the cause of AIDS. Perhaps a more surprising fact is that the link between AIDS and HIV is weak enough that *many of the world's governments do not accept HIV as the cause of AIDS*, including many of the world's countries hardest hit by AIDS. Should we be opening our minds to the possibility that HIV may not be the cause of AIDS? Should we at least make an effort to hear what these dissenters have to say before we make personal commitments to our own point of view?

Here's another one that got me a few years ago. A lot of people find this one offensive. In fact, it seems everybody finds it offensive, including me. I am, therefore, including it basically against everyone's good advice, so be warned, but I'm including it because it serves to make my point in two ways. One is that sometimes we do indeed find the truth to be offensive, and I'm afraid that some of what I'm going to ask the reader to imagine in this book, they might find offensive. It's really not so surprising that reality can be offensive. Just about everything that criminals do is offensive to the right-minded, but it is real, and its offensiveness makes it no less real. Also I include this example because I found it to be so *counter to my common sense*, and much of what I will ask the reader to imagine in this book will violate everyone's common sense. So brace yourselves.

In the spring of 1978, the *New Woman* magazine contained an article concerning the wonderful benefits some women experienced after being forcibly, even brutally raped. That's right. The real thing, not the behind closed doors, consenting adults thing, but the "totally against her will" type of rape. Naturally, a pitched battle of reader's letters raged all summer long, and to my disbelief, many of the letters coming from rape victims actually supported the premise of the article. They said things like they were so glad it happened to them, that it showed them their place in life, that it was the best thing that could have happened, things like that. Referring to their rapist, many women sang their praises. Can you believe it? I guess the fact here is that unless those letters were fabricated, some women do indeed perceive forcible rape to have been a positive experience. *(New Woman Magazine, spring & summer issues, 1978)*

Actually, I have to add a personal addendum here. I believe that the explanation for this phenomenon is not that these women somehow liked it, but quite the opposite. I have seen the identical phenomenon occur in men who have been overwhelmed by *extreme force and fear.* In one case, the guy was beaten half to death by a gang, losing teeth, broken bones, etc., and afterwards he sang their praises! It's an uncomfortable and astonishing thing to witness. It appears that our brains have an automatic safety switch that's activated when things become horrifying enough, and which enforces the rule that "if you can't beat them, love them." And isn't this the same phenomenon captured in George Orwell's book *1984*? "Rats!"

Here's another one that got me in 1997. Do you believe that the Branch Davidians of Waco, Texas fame were a far out religious cult with perverted and deviant sexual practices as portrayed by the media at the time? Further, do you believe that the U. S. Govt. *didn't* commit and cover up *major* atrocities prior to, even during the Davidians' incineration? Do you believe that the Davidians were something other than just *very good people*, better even than you and me, just trying to be righteous? A great deal of evidence to the contrary has surfaced since the Davidian's immolation, much of it exposed in the 1997 *Academy Award* nominated documentary *WACO—The Rules of Engagement.* If you're one who enjoys being shocked and thoroughly surprised, by all means, rent this tape from your local video store. There are other good documentary tapes on this topic too, but you might want to start with this one because of its credentials. Besides its *Academy Award* nomination, it won the IDA Feature Award 1997, and for you diehards out there, it got "Two Thumbs *Way* Up" from *Siskel & Ebert.* Live a little. Rent it! *(Documentary: WACO—The Rules of Engagement)*

Here's one I've seen surprise some people. Do you believe that King Arthur and the Knights of the Round Table lived in medieval England? I think they put him around 500 AD? It turns out that King Arthur and his Knights of the Round Table, as portrayed by Sir Thomas Mallory, never existed at all. Most academic scholars on the subject do accept his non-existence as fact, although some think that the myth may have been started around a Roman general from that time period. His story is of historical importance as it introduces new social and civic ideas to the world, but apparently no such person ever lived, and he's pure myth. I hope this doesn't disappoint you too much.

Here's kind of a tame one. Almost everyone will recognize this as a picture of an atom.

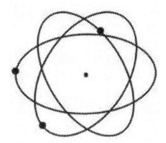

The fact is that an atom looks nothing like this. This is what the atom was believed to look like up until 1915, during your great-grandparents era, maybe before! If this is your idea of an atom, then you are nearly a century out of date in your understanding and beliefs about the physical universe. What an atom and the modern universe really are will be tackled in the second section of this book, *What's the Matter With Matter?* Some of the knowledge and beliefs you will be asked to relinquish in that section will be much more mind bending than anything you are experiencing here. An atom is in fact something so strange that the human mind just doesn't have the ability to picture it at all.

This one amazed me a decade ago. Any of us who, even peripherally, follow the gun control debate in the media know how overzealous the NRA is in its single-minded crusade to prevent any and all gun control. Are you ready to believe that the NRA actually *supports* a great deal of gun control? That's right! They even frequently work with legislators *proposing new* gun control legislation if you can believe it. As a major example, the NRA always supported the "Brady Bill" *in its instant background check form,* now called the National Instant Check System (NICS). The NRA supported, even strenuously pushed for, NICS in the early 1990's. If you find this hard to believe, you might find it an interesting exercise researching and discovering just how you were successfully deceived. *(http:// www.nraila.org/)*

Finally, the last one! Who do you think was the first President of the United States of America? Did somebody say George Washington? Sorry. Although this is common knowledge, once again common knowledge has failed. The *very first* **President of the United States** of America was John Hanson (no relation). He was elected by Congress in 1781, served for the one year then required under the Articles of Confederation, and played a great part in making the presidency what it is today. The Articles of Confederation were the original document that defined the United States of America for the first eight years after the revolution. The Constitution was later created to repair deficiencies in the Articles of Confederation. When I was a kid, I had several delivery jobs in the Washington, D. C. area, and frequently had to travel John Hanson Hwy that extended out of eastern D. C. into Maryland. When my brother informed me that John Hanson was actually the first president, I, of course, couldn't believe it. (I don't know how he found out.) He was a really remarkable guy, John Hanson. You might check him out. Actually, there were *six more* presidents elected by Congress. George Washington in fact, was the eighth President of the United States of America, but the first under the newly implemented Constitution. (**http://www.marshallhall.org/hanson.html**)

(During my research, I discovered that there is yet another contender for first president other than George Washington. The following site asserts that one Samuel Huntington was really the first president. http://virtualology.com/)

Hopefully you found those examples to be fun and interesting. While your impression may be that I wanted you to believe them all on your first pass, I neither expected nor hoped for that. What I'm hoping for is that you found at least one of them *very difficult* to believe, and that now you are observing in yourself what the mind does when confronted with information that is impossible to accept. One of the more common reactions is that you almost certainly dislike, or are angry with this author right now. You will be thinking that he is a fraud and a charlatan. Your mind is creating reasons for him to have said the things he did, reasons that are certainly less than noble. Is it the Bible ones, the rape one, or perhaps the President one? If it's the Waco or NRA ones, your mind is most likely telling you that he must be prone to conspiracy theories. If you are thinking these things, or feeling these ways, then I have accomplished exactly what I wanted to accomplish, because you see, *this is exactly the way I felt too* when I encountered this information initially.

In an attempt to prepare you for these examples, I have suggested several points. One emphatic point is that *all that stuff you think you know just isn't necessarily so*. Right now, no matter how unpleasant, it is imperative that you open up your mind to the possibility that the above information is correct. You don't have to accept it as fact yet. *Just open your mind to the possibility* that it's true. This is the hardest part anyway!

Another point is that we really do receive *misinformation* from the world around us. According to Descartes' wisdom, we should know better, and never allow ourselves to be completely certain of the things we see, hear, or read, no matter from what source. I have done my utmost to ensure that the above information is accurate and factual, but according to this wisdom, it's possible that I am incorrect with some of my facts too. If this is the case, I will just have to console myself that I have inadvertently made my own point! You really should verify them for yourself!

And I sincerely hope you found this all to be great fun! This little ride is just getting under way.

History has shown us that many of the beliefs that a society or culture holds may be flat wrong. Clearly, however, this can be deduced from the fact that every culture, current or otherwise, harbors beliefs that conflict with other cultures, so of course they can't all be right. Just think of the cultural differences between the U. S. and, say, Afghanistan. A good question at this point might be "Just how then does a culture even work or function if it harbors erroneous beliefs?" The answer is that these cultures still function just fine because their erroneous beliefs make no real difference. Many of the mistaken beliefs espoused above make no difference to our society at all, while others do. As long as they don't make any real difference, everything is fine. However, occasionally they do make a difference, and the consequences to a society may be serious. It is much easier to look back into history and identify the erroneous beliefs that prevailed earlier, than it is to spot the ones that we are certainly harboring now.

The belief that the Earth, and thus humanity, dwelt at the center of the universe prevailed throughout our history until, remarkably, just a few hundred years ago. Did this erroneous belief have any serious consequences to humanity? Not really. Only I suppose if one considers the stress and strife our ancestors endured when they had to relinquish this cherished belief.

How about the belief that the Earth was flat, which also was *common knowledge* throughout most of our human history? Apparently some educated people had access to the knowledge that the Earth was round ever since the Greeks showed it to be so several thousand years earlier. This was not what the common man believed, however, until relatively recently. All of us have heard the stories about Columbus' crews wanting to turn back for fear of falling off the edge of the Earth. What a bunch of dummies, we think to ourselves. We were born knowing better! Actually, in their defense, it is not a trivial thing to demonstrate that the Earth is round if one excludes airplanes, satellites, and pictures from space as of course our ancestors did. You might want to try to figure out how you would go about determining that the earth is round, given only their resources.

Medicine sports a rich history of mistaken beliefs, many with serious consequences, at least to the suffering patients. They did things like saw/drill/hack holes in people's skulls to let out the evil spirits that caused migraines, or attach leeches to people to suck out their diseased blood when they fell ill. Of course, these almost certainly had the beneficial consequence that many fewer people complained of having headaches, or admitted to feeling ill. (If these remedies were implemented today, a statistical follow up study would surely show a dramatic decrease in these problems.)

Then there was the belief in witches that had serious consequences to the several hundred thousand people, mostly women, who were burned alive, or in a few lucky cases hanged. Remarkably, many of these victims believed it all themselves and suffered their horrific deaths believing they were purifying themselves with fire.

Then there are the extreme cases where a whole society collapses because of mistaken information or a mistaken belief. The collapse of the Aztec culture is an example of this. The Aztecs believed that the Spanish explorer Cortez was a god returning to take his rightful place on the throne. Based on this belief, Montezuma, the ruling king, turned the throne of the Aztec Empire over to Cortez. Cortez and his men then proceeded to kill Montezuma and to ransack and destroy their empire.

(Oops! The preceding paragraph was written based on my research of the Aztecs, Montezuma, and Cortez. I have since been advised by a knowledgeable acquaintance that although the above rendition is *common knowledge*, it is false! Fascinatingly, according to this source:

> *"This section is really interesting because it is false information about false information. The story of the Aztec god who was to return and who Cortez is supposedly mistaken for was written after the Spanish successfully conquered the Aztecs. Prisoners taken back to Spain were forced to write the Codex that depicts the return of a God who looked like Cortez. The Spanish conquered the Aztecs by entering into an alliance with the surrounding cities because the neighboring peoples hated the Aztecs and were more than willing to help the Spanish defeat them. This is interesting because the Spanish purposefully created misinformation that has successfully made its way into our history."*

Do you see how *difficult* it is to be certain of our knowledge!)

There are several points that I hope the reader got from all of this. One is that accepted *common knowledge* is very unreliable and can easily lead us into believing things that are absolutely false. We have no way of knowing what parts of it are right and what parts of it are wrong, particularly if it is the kind that has little consequence. There is no exaggeration here. Most of the time we can't even identify where we got these ideas. We just believe it because everybody else does.

The other thing I hope you experienced is how surprisingly difficult it can be to accept that a piece of engrained common knowledge is wrong. I know how preposterous some of the above statements may have seemed to you initially, maybe still. I know, because for each one of them, I was there myself.

So the real point is this. I want you to now know that it's *possible* that knowledge you have held your entire life can be wrong! The prevailing wisdom suggests that you assign at least a small percentage of *uncertainty* to everything you think you know for *certain*. While this may seem like all a game to you up until now, this is really in deadly earnest. I want you to have felt the incredulity and difficulty of letting go of information that you are attached to, and I want you to be aware of these feelings so that when you feel them again later on in the book, you will not give in to them. If you are really going to survive this roller coaster ride, you have got to learn how to ride it, how to stick to your seat no matter how hard it rattles and shakes you. Consider this a foreshadowing of what is to come. You are going to be asked to relinquish far more deeply engrained knowledge than appeared above. You will in fact be asked to give up as false much of the most fundamental stuff you learned about the world in the very first months and years of your life as an infant. We will be playing catch-up for a whole century of lost science, and as alien as this stuff will feel, we must walk through it, for what we are facing dead ahead is far more alien still.

The next four chapters will continue the process of preparing you for what is ahead. If the earlier metaphor of Adam and Eve holds, then this is all about losing your innocence, but hey, there are times when losing your innocence can be fun, right? So let's get on with it. We've got a long way to go.

Chapter 2
Truth & Reality

o o o o o o o o o o o o o o o o o o o o o o o o o o o o o o o o o o o o

Pretty much all the honest truth-telling
there is in the world is done by children.

—*Oliver Wendell Holmes*

If we are driving and become lost, some of us will pull into the nearest gas station or convenience store and get directions. The directions we receive may be good, or they may be bad. If they are good, we will end up getting to where we want to go, but if they are bad, we will end up somewhere where we don't want to be. No one asking for directions wants to receive bad information.

If we invest in the stock market, our goal is to increase the value of the investment. If we are not professional investors ourselves, we are well advised to seek advice from those who are. The advice we receive may be good advice, in which case our money will increase, or it may be bad, in which case we will lose money. No one investing in the stock market wants to receive bad information.

If we are going to embark on the journey of understanding the world we live in, we want to base our understanding on the most accurate information available. If it is good information, the conclusions we draw from it are likely to be true. If it is not good information, we will draw false conclusions about the world. To the greatest extent possible, we want our information to be *true* knowledge of the *real* world.

We saw in the last chapter how difficult it is to be certain about the information we receive from the world around us. Methods have been developed that dramatically improve the odds of the *truth* and *reality* of the information we receive when we investigate our world. We will now examine these ideas, and methods, more closely.

The *ideas* of truth and reality:

Truth and *reality* are close cousins. If one looks in the dictionary to discover what they are, one will find the same words used to define both, words like *factual*, *actual*, and of course *true* and *real*. The dictionary isn't much help, though, if one wants a definition that they can actually use to determine what is true, what is real, and what isn't. So how do we tell if something is real or true? As you may suspect after only a moment's thought, this question leads straight out to deep and dangerous water where only the most powerful swimmers frolic. But we will at least get our feet wet, splashing around a little at the shallow edges, and get some sense of what it feels like.

Let's ask ourselves some questions about just *reality* first. What does it take for us to call something real? What are some things that aren't real? How do we know that dreams aren't real? Or do we? I hope the reader will agree that before something can be called real:

1) **It must exist.** Now this may seem like a strange question, but how do we know if something *exists* or not?

2) **It must have some effect**. By effect, I mean there must be some way to *detect* it. It must reflect light so we can see it, or in the case of very clean plate glass, it must be impenetrable to our nose and forehead when we accidentally walk into it. If we're claiming it is some specific thing, it must have the effect(s) of the thing we are claiming it to be. If we are claiming a *door* is real, then it must have the effect of a door and not a solid wall (or a plate glass window). In other words, for a duck to be real, it must walk, quack, and act like a duck. If something has these effects of a duck, then the duck exists and is real. If it has some other effect, but not the effect of a duck, then we know it exists, but we don't yet know what it is. Having a *detectable effect* is a fundamental requirement for something to *exist*.

3) **Its effect must be consistent**. While *consistent* is a very big and important word in the world of reality and truth, at this point we take it to mean simply that something continues to exist *without change*. In order for a duck to really be a duck, it must be a duck consistently. It must stay a duck. If someone makes a stack of sandwiches out of it, its material still exists, but it's not a duck anymore. It didn't stay a duck, and the duck *doesn't exist* anymore.

4) **It must be demonstrable**, i.e., you must be able to show somebody that it is real. While you may be perfectly happy that something is real and privately enjoying its existence, it has value only to you unless you can convince others that it's real too. The condition where something is real to you but is not demonstra-

ble to others is sometimes called schizophrenia. The *demonstrable* requirement is of course closely related to numbers 1, 2, and 3 above. For a duck to be demonstrably a duck to others, it 1) must exist, 2) must walk, quack, and act like a duck, and 3) must continue to do so every time you show it to somebody else.

If something we perceive has these four qualities, we will all agree that it's real.

Now what about something like dreams? Are dreams real? If you think that dreams aren't real, anyone certainly has a perfect right to ask you to explain *how you know* they aren't real? You should try to answer this question. It's not so easy, but if you look for how dreams fail to pass the above four rules, it's not too hard. Dreams belong strictly to the realm of our *experience*. We all agree that we *experience* dreams, but unfortunately, nothing in the dream exists outside of the dream. We can't *demonstrate* (#4) our dream to other people for one thing. If we dream about a duck, we can tell people about it, but we can't actually show them the duck. "But wait a minute," you say. What about this? What if we consider the dream world and the waking world to be two different worlds, two independent realities? I can demonstrate a dream world duck to dream world people just like I can demonstrate a duck in this world to people in this world. Then isn't the dream world duck by definition *real*, at least in the dream world?

Oops! I say, haven't we gotten a bit far from shore here? Don't you feel we might turn around now? Well, I suppose. We can say, however, that dreams are overall remarkably **in**consistent. You may be dreaming about a duck one moment, and the next moment it becomes your little brother, or it's now not there at all. So my take is that dreams fail to be real even in the dream world on the consistency requirement (#3). A dream world duck just doesn't stay a duck, even in the dream world.

Just thinking about dreams, though, has opened up a whole new kind of reality to us. We all agree we have dreams. So *there is such a thing as a dream*. Dreams do *exist* (#1), and existence is the number one requirement to be real. *Something* is real about a dream. If it's not the dream itself that is real, then what is it about a dream that is real? Something *exists*! If we had a dream, we did have an *experience*. That is, we *experienced* the dream, and it's the *experience* that existed. The *stuff* we experienced *in* the dream, the content of the dream, didn't exist but the *experience* itself existed, and if it existed, then according to #1, it meets the number one requirement to be real.

Now I'm sure some of you saw that I just glossed over a whole bunch of problems, so this deserves at least a little more clarification. For one thing, when I said above that "We all agree we have dreams," did I just make up a whole new rule for reality that says something like:

5) If we all agree on something, then it's real. We already know that a major point of the first chapter was to show that *this isn't a reliable rule.* Everybody *can* be wrong.

What then gives us the confidence to say that dreams exist? In a nutshell, what happened is that we just jumped up a rung of the reality ladder into another realm, into the world of *experience.* Our *experience* of the world is to the world what a *big screen* is to a movie. Without your experience of the world, you have no world at all. And without the movie screen, you have no movie at all. You have to *experience* the world in order to know of it, and there has to be a screen of some kind for you to experience (see) a movie.

We can even carry the analogy another step and say documentaries, which attempt to portray reality on the screen, are like experiencing the real world, and fiction or cartoons shown on the screen are like experiencing dreams. In both cases, reality or fiction, *the screen exists independently of the movie*, and we see the movie on it, even in the case where the stuff shown isn't real. The screen has a reality of its own, a higher reality than the content of the movie, quite independent of what is being shown on it. And the act of *experiencing* has a reality of its own, one level higher than the content of what's being experienced, real world or dream.

The *realm of human experience* comes with its own set of philosophical problems, but we're going to leave those to the whiz kids to argue about. This book is going to assume that you and I, and even schizophrenics, do indeed have experiences. We are going to take as fact that experiences exist, that you experience the taste and yellow of mustard; that you experience the sensations of hot and cold; that you experience your dreams at night; and that you experience the presence of the love of your life. If the whiz kids come up with a different answer, then we're in real trouble and this book is moot, because the rest of this book relies very heavily on, and will explore more deeply, the existence of experience. For that matter, not just the rest of this book, but the rest of your life depends *heavily* on your experience. As with the movie screen, if your experience of *your* life ever goes away, there's no more show.

With all this talk about *reality*, the concept of *truth* has been left on the back burner. Truth and reality are closely related, but there are some not-so-subtle differences that need mentioning. Foremost is that *truth* doesn't apply to ducks. A duck can be real, but it can't be true. Truth **does** apply to **statements** about ducks, and here's the connection between *truth* and *reality*. If the *statement* about the duck says something that is *real*, then the statement is *true*. If there is a real blue duck in front of you, and you point at it and say, "that duck is blue," then you have uttered a *true* statement. If the reality is that the duck is brown, on the other hand, you have uttered a *false* statement. If a statement is true, we call it a *fact*. In the first chapter, I laid down several hopefully surprising facts, i.e., statements intended to be true. Taking the first one as an example, the Adam and Eve/apple one, if you look in your Bible (as I hope you did) and no apple is mentioned as claimed, then the statement is true and it is a fact. On the other hand, if you opened your Bible and it does indeed refer to an apple as the fruit of knowledge, then the statement is false and it is not a fact. A huge branch of philosophy, which incidentally includes mathematics, has built up over the last several thousand years that concerns itself with the principles of determining the truth or falseness of statements. This is called "logic" of course, and while still incomplete after *several thousand years* of work, it is certainly one of humanity's greatest cerebral achievements.

Determining truth and reality:

What is it that makes truth and reality so interesting in the first place? Why is it bad to tell a lie? It has to do with knowledge, and it has to do with the reliability of knowledge. And the reliability of knowledge has to do with the reliability of results of actions we take based on that knowledge, that is, accuracy and fulfillment of expectations. Every action we take is based on the knowledge we have, from how to stay alive on the freeway, to how much salt to put in the casserole. Even how to make a date. Hopefully, that knowledge is knowledge of the *real* world. If some poor farm boy grows up isolated from girls, and goes off to college with the expectation that acquiring sex with a woman is achieved the same way the rooster did in the hen house (which is highly unethical by human standards), he's not likely to procreate successfully in this lifetime, even if he does get out of jail. His knowledge does not reflect the real world, and his expectations based on his actions will not be fulfilled. These are the reasons why truth and reality are important, and these are the reasons it is of such interest.

From a very early age, we learn to determine what is true and what is real. We absolutely have to. We have to learn all the mundane realities like crying causes milk, we and the bars of our crib can't occupy the same space at the same time, and as we get older, how not to hurt ourselves in a thousand different ways. As we get older still and are allowed into potentially dangerous environments, like out in traffic, we are literally saving our lives with every step we take. We have to know what is real!

So how do children learn what's real and what isn't? They certainly don't compare everything they encounter against the list of four points above. Children learn from *experience*. There's that word again, and that's the same "experi" as in "*experi*mentation." They don't care if the philosophers are arguing about what's real and what isn't. They need to know what's real, and they need to know it now. Nature is an unforgiving mistress. Children learn that they cannot walk through walls, that fire is hot, that milk is sweet, and that spankings hurt, and they learn it all from experiencing, and experimenting with, the world around them. Little children are true scientists, hard wired apparently to test reality in every way, touching that hot burner, tasting that Drano, and lighting that match, all to experiment with reality. They learn that dreaming they can fly, no matter how hard they wish it, doesn't make it happen in the real world. They want the facts, man, just the facts. We continue to rely on our experience and experimentation for the rest of our lives, but as we get older we get really confused, confused in ways that children don't. You never hear someone say, "Man, that three year old is really in denial!" Children just don't know how to deny reality, only adults. Among other problems, as we get older we develop *preferences* for and against certain facts. Children's minds are wide open to all facts. (Could this be why the news media runs down to Mrs. Anderson's second grade classroom to find out what the children think every time there's a world crisis?) We'll explore a few of the difficulties we adults develop to determining truth and reality shortly.

It wasn't until relatively recently in human history that an attempt was made to set down *procedural rules* to reliably determine what is real and what isn't. When it was done, it turned out to have a lot in common with what our kids are hardwired to do already. It's pretty straightforward really. In it's simplest form, it says that "If something is real, *then just show me*" (rule #4), and by "show," we frequently mean with an experiment, just like the kids do. This is necessary to eliminate the claims of the schizophrenics and other well meaning people whom, for whatever reason, get it wrong. Sounds pretty simple and reasonable, doesn't it? It is primarily this requirement that distinguishes science from other methods of determining reality, and it is thus called the *scientific method*. Of course, once again, the brainiacs will quickly drag this all out into deep and difficult waters, so here's a slightly enhanced version of the scientific method, to give you a feel for it. It in effect says:

1) Someone's claim that something is real is called a *hypothesis*, and is not accepted as real until it has been *shown* to be real. That is, just show me! To show that it is real;

2) A hypothesis must be *testable*. That is, there has to be a way to tell if it's real or not. People can actually claim things to be real that *aren't testable*. If it's not testable, then there's no way to test if it's real or not, so there's no way to determine that it's real, and suppose two people claim two different things to be real, but *neither* is testable. There's no way to determine which one is right and which one is wrong unless they're testable. They can't both be right. A hypothesis, therefore, must be testable before it can even be determined if it's real or not. The competing hypotheses as to the origin of the universe, which is such a hot potato from time to time, is a fine example. Many of these are not testable, and until they are, none can be accepted as real *under the scientific method* and must remain hypotheses. What makes a hypothesis testable anyway?

3) The test must *make a prediction* as to the outcome of the test that can be looked at and verified as real. If I'm hypothesizing that a blue duck is real, then I have to produce a blue duck to verify this hypothesis. While this is fine for ducks, it won't work for many hypotheses of great interest, because often there is nothing to hold up and look at. These are the hypotheses that provide an explanation for, or propose a system behind something that is already known to exist. Once again, the different hypotheses of the origin of the universe makes a good example. We know the universe exists, but it's not possible to actually *look* at something like a cause.

For a simplistic demonstration of this, let's go back to our blue duck, and propose two competing hypotheses for its cause, explaining how it came to be blue. One person proposes the hypothesis that the duck was born blue, while somebody else thinks it more likely that somebody dyed it blue, like the Easter ducks from when I was a kid. Until we perform some experiments to determine whose explanation behind our blue duck is correct, neither can be considered correct. Both hypotheses are happily testable in this case, since either the blue dye or the naturally occurring pigments would be detectable in a laboratory. Both hypotheses make the required *prediction*, that is, one predicts that blue dye will be found while the other predicts that natural blue pigment will be found. Both hypotheses can be considered testable hypotheses, and it is possible to determine if one of these is the true cause of our duck's blueness. To show that a hypothesis is true, it has to be testable. That is, it must propose a test, and make a prediction as to the result of that test.

Many readers will have noticed that the word "theory" did not show up in my representation of the *scientific method* when they know darned well that it should have. If they know this much, then they also know that the word has two different meanings in common usage. The word is sometimes used to mean a *hypothe-*

sis, as when one says that "One *theory* is that the duck was dyed blue." Or the word is sometimes used to refer to a body of knowledge that has already been accepted as real, as in Einstein's Theory of Relativity, or quantum theory.

The two uses of the word "theory" do have a certain aspect in common that should be pointed out. In both cases, they are used to represent ideas that are allotted at least a small degree of *uncertainty*. Yes, this is the same uncertainty that I urged the reader in Chapter 1 to assign to everything they have contentedly accepted to be 100% real and true. Science lives in the interesting realm of knowledge that is *never* considered 100% absolutely positively certain. The reason is that it is almost a daily occurrence for new hypotheses to be overthrowing old theories.

Under the scientific method, there is no final word. It's like the street fighting gunslingers of the old American West. It seems there was always a faster gun, and everybody at least had the right to try. This resulted in a continuously faster gunslinger being number 1. In sports, the same sort of playoffs result in only the best teams ever making it to the championship, and in science, it results in continuously more accurate and better theories. Even the above two mentioned theories that I said have been accepted as *real,* necessarily retain a degree of uncertainty. While Einstein's Theory of Relatively elegantly accounts for much known phenomena in the universe, and quantum theory also accounts for much known phenomena, the two theories have a point where *they contradict each other*, so they can't both be 100% right and real. It is known that modifications will have to be discovered, or even a whole new system discovered that unites the two bodies of knowledge and removes the contradictions.

While the scientific method as a formalized procedure for determining what's *real* is relatively new to the scene, methods of logic for determining the *truth of statements* began appearing several thousand years ago. Probably the most useful thing to come out of logic is the proof. Some might even say that the proof is the whole point of logic. The proof is kind of an exciting thing. With a proof, you can show some things to be true (or not) without resorting to the experiments and demonstrations required above. Well, almost. To prove something in logic, we have to at least *start out* with true statements, called *premises*, whose truth depends directly on what is real. Once we have a set of *true statements* to start with as a foundation, all manner of new statements, called conclusions, can be shown to be true.

The process of arriving at the *conclusion*, starting from the *premise* statements, is called *reasoning*. If the premises are all true, and the reasoning is done correctly, then the conclusion is guaranteed to be true too. We human beings pretty much don't do anything without a reason, so whether or not we realize it, we reason, and thus use logic all the time. Sometimes we don't have very good reasons, and sometimes we don't reason very well, but what can I say. We try. Then again this is not formal logic either. The whole point of formalizing logic is of course to make sure that it's done correctly and that the conclusions are *always* true and reliable.

A quick example of early formal logic is the time worn syllogism about men and Socrates. Remember, if the two premises are true, then the conclusion must be true too. It goes like this:

Premises:

    All men are mortal.

    Socrates is a man.

Conclusion:

    Therefore, Socrates is mortal.

Think about those two premises for a second. Do you see how the conclusion **has** to be true if the premises are true? Because the conclusion was reached using logic based on true premises, it had to be true, and the Greeks didn't have to verify this with an actual experiment. (Of course we know they did anyway.)

The Greeks and Egyptians of several thousand years ago did a great deal to advance formalized logic, applying it in a useful way to the world around them and developing it in mathematics. The Egyptian Euclid took just 5 true premises concerning geometry and, using logic and reasoning, proved a new set of conclusions. These conclusions, since they were *proven* to be true, could then be added to the original premises, and it was then possible to prove new conclusions using his newly proven bunch of premises. This process was repeated over and over until he had built up a huge body of knowledge (Euclidean Geometry), all proven to be true, because each intermediate step had been proven, all based on the truth of *just the original five premises.* Today all mathematics is done this way. No new knowledge is allowed into a body of mathematics until it has been logically proven to be true, and once proven, a statement can then be reused in the process of proving new conclusions.

Remember that there is a close connection between truth and reality. If all the statements that Euclid had logically proven were really true, then each one must say something about the world that is *real*, else it wouldn't be true. In effect, the Greeks and Egyptians applying logic to knowledge were able to deduce a great deal of *true* information about the *real* world without ever getting out of their chairs. This was an astonishing thing! They could figure out what was real without having to do an experiment, without having to see it, and before they had seen it with their own eyes. The more they tried it, the more their confidence in their logic as a method of determining reality increased. They began to see that logic was somehow deeply connected to the functioning of the real world, that in some way, logic must be driving the real world, since somehow everything derived by logic was real. They began to see logic as a reality in itself, as *reality itself*, in some inexplicable way hidden behind the scenes but nevertheless the basis for the universe. To try to account for this, they proposed another universe, a non-material invisible, bodiless universe that *was* reality, and they called it Logos. Logos was, and still is, a beautiful thing. It had an exquisite perfection unattainable in the material world of our experience. It was beautiful and it was pure, and many of them fell in love with its *perfection* and cherished it. And they cherished it to the exclusion of knowledge that was true and real, but that did not seem to fit their arbitrary idea of beauty and perfection.

Oh, the sin of it all. A whole new Garden of Eden from which we had to be expelled. This idea, this requirement for *perfection*, turned out to be extremely seductive and tenacious, and endured in one form or another for roughly 2000 years, and it did a lot of damage. The problem was not with the beauty or reality of logic. In fact, as previously pointed out, logic is the foundation for all of mathematics today, and believe it or not, the idea of an abstract non-material universe like Logos is still very much alive today. The problem came from the arbitrary requirements for *perfection* that now excluded grubby old hands-on *experiments* as a source of determining reality. Following that brilliant burst of Greek and Egyptian cerebral advancement, the method of experimentation to determine reality took nearly a 2000 year hiatus, and the "perfection" rule, zealously enforced by authorities, played a major part. It was the slow recognition of the need to test claims of reality that finally broke humanity out of the Dark Ages, and the idea of the scientific method took hold.

We now recognize the need for both *experiment* and *logic* in the determination of reality, and many sciences today are divided into the two specialties of experimental science and theoretical science respectively. The role of the theoretical sciences is to generate *hypotheses* using mathematics and logic, and the role of the experimental sciences is to show if they actually are *real* or not using experiments to test them…but this street runs both ways. If some unexpected phenomenon is discovered experimentally, it is not until a rigorously logical explanation has been developed for it that we can claim to understand it. Armed with both techniques the world broke out of its stagnation, and has advanced dramatically in the last several centuries.

Problems and Pitfalls:

Gradually as we mature, we human beings start developing preferences for certain knowledge, and of course, against certain knowledge. Facts quit being just useful and powerful things that we gather in all their bounty, and start taking on a certain value to us. Facts it turns out, start giving us pleasure, or causing us pain. You can probably assign every new fact to a pain/pleasure scale where say, zero is neutral, 10 is very pleasurable, and −10 is very painful.

Painful   Neutral   Pleasurable

−10   0   10

| | | | | | | | | | | | | | | | | | | | | | | |

Fact values on the pain/pleasure scale

When this begins to happen, a whole new kind of reasoning begins to take over the way our brains work, a reasoning that has nothing to do with truth and reality. If someone tells us something we like and enjoy hearing, we accept it very readily and without the scrutiny it deserves, but if someone tells us something we don't like to hear, we may reject it outright simply because we don't like it. We might even give ourselves away by saying something like, "I don't want to hear it!" It matters not at all that it might be a useful fact. What comes to matter is whether or not we like it.

This pain/pleasure value system is certainly humanity's biggest obstacle to accepting raw truth and reality. If we accept too much information that isn't true, and reject too much information that is true, we end up living in a kind of fantasy world, a fantasy world that we find pleasurable and become very attached to. We then have to constantly defend our private little Garden of Eden from painful offending facts. We all do this to some degree. We can't help it. It's truly human nature. It's the only way we remain sane, to be a little bit insane. However, if we want our personal universes to be anywhere close to what is real and true, we have to stay alert to our desire to reject information that is uncomfortable to us just because it is uncomfortable.

One result of this is that we all end up living in worlds that are different from everybody else's. We all see the world differently, have different philosophies, different preferences, different dislikes, etc. We spend a great deal of our social energies learning each other's preferences, and then treading carefully around each other's dislikes. If we all see it differently, this means that at most, *only one of us has it completely right.* Now there's a disturbing thought. Actually, it's even worse than that. As you will see in the next chapter, it is certain that none of us have it completely right. I imagine if we ever do achieve machine intelligence, the machines will be able to accept all facts painlessly, and will all end up with the same philosophies, same preferences, etc. Since their reality will include all of those dirty little facts we can't bear to hear, we'll hate it. (There's a sci-fi story in there for somebody.)

Another result of our resistance to accepting unpleasant facts is that it makes it very difficult to change a society's beliefs once they have become dogma. We all have heard about poor old Galileo who, circa 1630, was convicted of heresy and excommunicated from the church for championing Copernicus' Sun centered solar system. Actually, Copernicus himself, a century earlier, had a little more savvy about the whole thing. Knowing that the church authorities would take offense, he withheld the publication of his theory until his death in 1543. Galileo actually got off pretty light, though, all things considered. Thirty some years earlier there was a Dominican named Giordano Bruno who got more of it right than either Copernicus or Galileo. He not only realized that the Earth orbited the Sun, but that the Earth was just a planet, that the stars were actually suns too, just very far away, and that *neither* the Earth nor the Sun was at the center of the universe. The authorities of the period found his (real) ideas to be so counter to their arbitrary idea of God's *perfection*, that in 1600, they had his soul purified by fire and burned him alive. Apparently during the Inquisition, this was not an uncommon event at all.

Does this all sound to you like a condemnation of the Church of the period? Not at all! This is about the people involved. This is about us. We all want to do something like what they did when someone tells us something that threatens our most cherished beliefs, and if people have the power, then this is what they do. Our silly little value system can be a dangerous thing. It cares not one whit for truth and reality. Truth and reality are not its concern. Its concern is maximizing our comfort and minimizing our discomfort with our place in the world. And like the church, science isn't immune either. Scientists who should know better may still develop strong emotional attachments to certain theories and hypotheses. The infighting and backbiting that can go on can be astonishingly intense, even bitter. Thank goodness we live in an era, at least temporarily, where the authorities don't literally kill us for being wrong. *Or for being right!*

Personal Truths:

With all of this interference from our little value systems, we each end up with our own personal view of the universe. We start out as children eagerly accumulating knowledge about the world, but this process of building our personal view of the world diminishes with time. By the time we're in our twenties, we have developed a pretty good overview of how we think the world works, and it's beginning to affect what facts we'll entertain as real. While we do still eagerly pursue the details about the universe, the foundation for our worldview has already formed by then.

Somewhere in our thirties, though, our willingness to even modify our worldview to conform to new facts ceases. Our, until now, malleable universe hardens. "Enough!" we say. "Henceforth, I will expect all new facts to conform to the universe as I see it. If they don't, I will find a way to make them." And we do find a way. Suddenly we become very defensive about our personal worldview. Ten years earlier, we recognized that some of the answers our elders were feeding us were totally crap. There was just no way we could make them make sense. Now when asked, we find ourselves reciting their same litanies, expectant that they have somehow become sensible explanations. It doesn't matter whether your worldview happens to be based on religion or science. None of us seem to be totally exempt from this phenomenon. The best we can do is be aware, and not to give in to that tendency within ourselves.

Another casualty of this is that it further diminishes our already stunted ability to identify what we *don't know*. It is a tricky thing, identifying when we don't know something, and way too few people become adept at it. In our quest for knowledge, identifying when we don't know something is at least as important as identifying what we do know. As with our kids, "I don't know" should certainly remain the most frequently used answer in our repertoire of answers. We would like to know, we wish we knew, or we feel we can't afford to appear not to know, so we come up with some answer when in reality we aren't at all sure, or we haven't got a clue. Remember in the movie *Contact* when Ellie asks the little kid if he thinks life exists elsewhere in the universe, and the kid shrugs and says, "I dunno." Ellie, nodding her head for emphasis replies, "Good answer!" She's right. It's a hard answer to give, even when it is the right answer. The majority of adults would almost certainly have given some answer reflecting what they want to believe, rather than what they actually know about life in the universe. If you're afraid you'll appear stupid by answering, "I don't know," just practice tilting your nose up and saying in your best elitist accent, "Despite my considerable efforts, I've been unable to reliably make that determination at this time." Me, I prefer the kid's answer.

Like our personalities, our worldview develops largely as the result of two roughly equally influential forces. The first is the brain we are born with, and its apparently hardwired predispositions. Some kids are just born bad, and some kids are just born little angles. That kind of thing. We all know cases. The second factor is what we learn from the *experiences* we have in life. (There's that word again.) Our experiences are drastically colored by our aforementioned hardwired predispositions, which guarantees that no two people ever have the same experiences, even when they're exposed to the same events. If our little angel is abused as a child, chances are they'll grow up with low self esteem and a learning disorder, whereas if our little devil is abused as a child, they could grow up to be a serial killer. This is just the old *nature vs. nurture* dichotomy you may have heard about, where *nature* is the hardwired brain you were born with, and *nurture* is the life experiences you are exposed to. Anyway, between the two of them, we are guaranteed, each of us, to pass through a very unique life. None of us lives the same life, and as our lives slice their way through time and space, we all experience our own unique cross section of the world. This means we all end up different and with different viewpoints on things, and with different worldviews.

The flip side of this is that each of us has an extremely limited viewpoint as compared to the whole body of people as a group. Our personal worldviews, the sum total of our lifetime of experiences, are necessarily very limited. None of us sees the whole picture, but just a limited slice of reality. There's an ancient very worn out story about five blind men who are taken by the hand and led up to an elephant to determine what it is by feeling it. Of course, each one grabs a different body part and arrives at a different conclusion of what an elephant is like. The first one grabs its trunk, and determines that the elephant is long and thin like a snake. The second grabs an ear, and determines that the elephant is thin and flat, like a big leathery leaf. A third grabs a leg, and determines that it is more like the trunk of a tree. The fourth encounters its broad side, and determines that it is broad and solid like a wall. The story has the potential to be considerably more interesting than it is, but you get the picture. They each got it very wrong, because none of them experienced more than a tiny portion of the whole.

Despite our each having different worldviews, there are deep areas of consensus among us as to the foundations. Some of these we are aware of, but many we learned so early in our life that they are simply a part of the way the world is, and we are unaware of them. These are no less than the actual way we see the universe we live in. Unfortunately, though, not even our deepest areas of agreement may be taken as absolutely true, but are built on shifting sands. Not only may they differ from culture to culture, and from religion to religion, but in any given culture, they slowly change over time. We shall visit some of these different universes in the next chapter.

Chapter 3
Paradigms and Personal Universes

○ ○

…could thou and I with him conspire
To grasp this sorry scheme of things entire,
Would not we shatter it to bits—and then
Remould it nearer to the heart's desire!

—*Omar Khayyam*

Everything that we think is true, everything that we think is real, is an inhabitant of our thoughts and is thus uniquely personal. Our minds fit these thoughts together in cohesive ways, fitting them together to create a unified whole that we individually consider sensible. This structure we build from our facts, this unified whole, then takes on the properties of truth and reality itself, and it is most natural for us to consider it to be real if we do indeed find it to be a sensible construction. This unified whole is a construction of our minds, and if we are going to understand the truth and reality of the external universe we live in, we have to also understand the nature of this process, of this unified whole.

Paradigms:

What is a paradigm? A paradigm is something that is behind our worldview. It is so fundamental, that sometimes we aren't even aware of it. It is the foundation that the stuff we are aware of sits on, but it is more than that. It is also the framework, the structure, which determines how the details of our worldviews fit together. A paradigm is a way of imagining what is going on behind the scenes. Paradigms give us the ability to *represent* what is going on in the universe. There is a current paradigm. There is always a paradigm. Our current paradigm is the way we currently imagine that the world works.

For example, one of the more common notions of how the universe works is the modern *mechanistic* worldview. By this I mean we largely see the daily happenings of our universe as governed by *cause and effect*. While the idea of cause and effect has been around since the beginning of time, it is only relatively recently that we have learned to apply it to just about every detail of the universe. For example, not too long ago many happenings, like the motions of the planets, or illnesses, were thought to have other causes, i.e., spirits, fates, gods, essences, etc. Now it is more common to think that the planetary motions are *caused* by the laws of motion and the law gravitation, that the Sun's heat is *caused* by thermonuclear reactions, and that illnesses are *caused* by microbes and other wee things, rather than demons as was once thought.

This *mechanistic paradigm* even made it possible to account for the process of life itself. Up until about 150 years ago, it was still common to believe that life required some unknown *essence* that was non-mechanistic. As chemistry, medicine, and physics advanced and we discovered that all life on earth is based on carbon, the essence of life was believed to inhabit the element carbon somehow. When carbon was finally shown to be just as lifeless as any other element, many accepted that no such essence was required, that there was no essence of life after all, that it was all just mechanistic. The atoms and molecules that make up living organisms dance on their own. While highly intricate and specialized, their activity turns out to be every bit as mechanical as planetary motion or the drive train in your car. Very importantly, this new paradigm, this mechanistic view of life, had a major advantage over the essence of life idea. It opened up the potential to manipulate the life process itself, creating the possibility of inventing new medicines, discovering, mapping, and manipulating genes, perhaps even creating life in a test tube.

Do you see how the mechanistic paradigm gave us a handle with which to manipulate the process of life? When life was thought to result from some sort of unknown essence, we had no handle that would touch it. There was no way to get to it. The *essence of life* idea itself had sprung from an even earlier, more primitive, paradigm. What ever that one was, it must have been quite weak. Perhaps up until then, there had been no good way to account for the difference between living and non-living objects. The essence of life idea, when it took hold, must have given the people of the period a wonderful sense of clarity and power. Now they had a way to account for the difference between living and non-living. Both the life essence and the mechanistic paradigms are different ways of accounting for the phenomenon of life. *A paradigm is a way of accounting for the observed phenomena in the universe.*

A paradigm is the background for a way of looking at the world. It forms the context for all of our explanations and theories. A paradigm has much in common with a theory in that both provide an explanation for observed reality, but a paradigm is usually much more all-encompassing than a theory. Also, theories are more specific and usually explicitly formalized, whereas a paradigm is rarely formalized, and indeed may be hiding as unconscious assumptions about the universe. Having said that, the reality is that the distinction between theories and paradigms is quite smeared. There are theories that are so broad that they effectively act as paradigms, and the term *paradigm* is now sometimes showing up applied to rather narrow, explicitly stated theories.

Humanity's Paradigms—a (really!) brief history of *Western* thought:

Humanity's ancestors have been through any number of paradigms during our long history. In his book *Masks of the Universe*, Edward Harrison describes some of the different ways that our ancestors have seen the universe to be at different times in our history. Each of these universes, to the people of the period, was *the* universe. What Harrison is calling universes, I have extracted as the paradigms below. The names I am using for these different paradigms are based on the names Harrison used for his various *Masks of the Universe*.

While there are other, equally fascinating histories of thought that we could trace, e.g. Eastern thought, our brief summary of Western thought will suffice here to demonstrate the concept of humanity's paradigms.

The Magical Paradigm:

No one will ever know for sure, but it is supposed that our most primitive paradigm was probably the magical paradigm. Long before civilizations appeared, there would have been a time when the world, and the activities and actions in it, were completely unexplained. The flying birds, swaying trees, and crashing thunderstorms simply had no explanation. The feeling of wonder and awe that these early peoples experienced must have been very similar to the feeling of wonder we experience watching the unexplained acts in a magic show today, only magnified many times. It was *all* magic to them! In fact, it was probably not thought that there even ought to be an explanation at all.

It must have been an incredible leap of genius that first came up with the idea of a *spirit* as the mover of things. Anyway, at some point, the objects and activities of the universe came to be animated by spirits, and the concerns and emotions of these apparitions mirrored ours. They had their likes and dislikes, angers and jealousies, just like us. This is because we created them from the world we were familiar with, the only spirits we knew, and they were of course us. Our control over this universe, our handle so to speak, came by way of charms, spells, incantations, sorcery, etc. This understanding of the universe would have seemed like the end all to the peoples of this period. No further or deeper understanding of the world was necessary or even possible.

The Mythical Paradigm:

Human beings are great at generalizing. We see *similarities* in things, and begin immediately to lump them into categories. In the above magical universe, our ancestors saw the similarity in things that moved, vs. things that didn't, and lumped them all into the categories of things having spirits, and things without. At some point, they began to see similarities in the responsibilities of the myriad spirits that they had created to animate the world, and they lumped them into new and more generalized categories. Spirits were now fewer, but more powerful. A single spirit was now responsible for the success of the hunt, rather than all the separate bear, antelope, deer, pig, spear, bow, and arrow spirits. Another spirit was responsible for the fertility and fecundity of the tribe. Another was responsible for the weather, another the seasons, the Sun, the Moon, volcanoes, on and on. These eventually became generalized even further, and evolved into the early gods.

Once again, our paradigm was strongly influenced by the familiar world of our experience, and these mythological entities were emotionally just like us too. Or more accurately, as their powers grew, this time they were modeled after our kings and queens. Our control over this universe was, therefore, now more in the form of appeasing the gods, often in the form of honoring them with ceremonies, gifts, and sacrifices. Keep them smiling, and they would keep us around. This understanding of the universe seemed like the end all to the peoples of this period, and no deeper understanding was necessary or imaginable.

It seems that every early culture, on every continent, went through its own version of this paradigm. Many reached only some intermediate stage that included both spirits and gods, but around the Mediterranean and the Near East, some cultures evolved to believe in all-powerful gods. Each nation had its own god, and they continuously warred against each other. The material of the world now became dead and devoid of spirits, all power having been removed to the various gods. This paradigm is known as the mythical paradigm, because looking back from our current paradigm, all of those spirits and gods are now seen as myths. The well-known Greek and Roman mythologies are of course great examples that sprang from cultures with versions of the mythical paradigm.

The Geometric Paradigm (or The universe according to Aristotle):

The matter of the world was now spiritless and dead. It still moved, but no longer at the will of an occupant spirit. All the various gods merged into a single almighty god. Arrows still flew true, or otherwise, and the celestial bodies still moved around the heavens, but spirits and gods no longer moved them, so a new explanation was needed.

Between roughly 600 BC and 200 AD, the study of the now inanimate world and universe flourished, and early science and mathematics was born. The four pure essences of matter were *discovered*, earth, water, air, and fire, of which all matter was believed to be composed. It was discovered that the motions of the celestial bodies could, astonishingly, be accounted for by applying the power of their newfound logic, mathematics, and geometry. To explain the observed motions of the Sun, Moon, planets and stars, they invented systems of rotating transparent crystal spheres, spheres within spheres, and spheres attached to spheres that each celestial object was attached to. The Aristotelian universe, with its perfect rotating spheres, was geometric and harmonious…and understandable. For the first time in human history, the universe was discovered to be comprehensible to our mind without the actions of intervening spirits

The Aristotelian universe, with its perfect spheres, soon became incorporated into the new monotheistic religions emerging at this time. The earth stood still at the center of the universe. Above the earth were the spheres of each celestial body, and above that, the sphere of heaven. The system became connected to a divine plan, and that implied divine *perfection*, or at least our idea of it 2000 years ago. Our handles into this paradigm were our minds and our logic and mathematics, with their newly discovered ability to describe divine perfection. This understanding of the universe seemed exquisitely perfect to the peoples of this period, beyond anything previously imagined possible, and no deeper understanding was necessary or possible.

The Medieval Paradigm:

Over the next thousand plus years, Aristotle's universe was brought into harmony with Islamic, Judaic, and Christian beliefs. Matter once again became animated. All matter moved according to God's will now. The celestial objects, rotating in their perfect spheres, were moved by angels. Earth, standing quite still at the center of all the goings on of the universe, was the home of humanity, mortal vessels for the immortal souls. Within the bowels of the Earth was Hell. Between the Earth and the lunar sphere was purgatory. The lunar sphere was guarded by angels, and was the gate to all higher spheres. Then came the planetary and Sun spheres and the crystal clear sphere of the stars. Beyond the stellar sphere was the bright blue firmament of heaven that you can see till this day just by going outside and looking up, and beyond that, the empyrean, a realm of purest fire where God dwelt. Created and blessed by God, the universe's heavenly perfection was verified by the perfect spheres from which it was composed. It's beautiful geometry, originally invented merely as a method to describe the universe, now carried far more weight, and was applied as a *proof* that this paradigm was real.

Through it all, the belief in the rational design of the universe remained. Applying logic, this design could actually be proved. Humans could understand its geometry and its purpose. This universe could be understood by everyone. There was no question that the Earth stood still. It was plain to see. One could actually look up and see the bright blue firmament of Heaven. Our control over this paradigm was largely through prayer and piety, but very importantly too, through the recognition that we human beings could understand, and thus manipulate, the workings of the world. And our understanding provided us with a handle into it. As a result, mechanical contrivances began to proliferate, including complex geared mechanisms that mimicked the motions of the heavens. From these efforts, the mechanical clock was invented in the 13th century. This understanding of the universe, with its geometric perfection and divine plan, seemed like the end all to the peoples of this period, and no deeper understanding was necessary or even possible.

The Infinite Paradigm:

In this paradigm, and following no small amount of stress and strife, the crystal spheres are gone. The Medieval paradigm had fallen because it had totally neglected to take into account that God's powers were infinite. It had been limited to humanity's arbitrary and pitiful idea of *perfection*, and now the world exploded with new knowledge. The Sun is now the center of the solar system. The universe is infinite and the stars extend to infinity. The Earth, planets, and all matter move according to the mathematical laws of motion. With the discovery of the law of gravity, it was now possible to prove mathematically that the universe was infinite, thus mathematically proving the infinity of God. God was infinite and everywhere, continually at work maintaining the order of the universe.

The regularity of the clock-like mechanisms that had been invented to mimic the universe turned out to result from the mathematics behind it. All of nature, all of God's handiwork, worked like mathematical clockwork. It now became possible to *deduce* detailed facts about the world from observing God's handiwork. Our mathematical handle into this paradigm was extremely tight fitting, and our control became much more powerful than in any previous paradigm. This paradigm, with its precise ability to account for the actions of nature, seemed like the end all to the peoples of this period, and no deeper understanding was necessary or imaginable. There was a difference now, though, from earlier paradigms. The door had been opened to free inquiry, and the scientific method had come into its own as a method of determining and verifying reality.

The Mechanistic Paradigm (The age of reason):

This paradigm is base on the clock-like regularity and mathematics discovered in the earlier paradigm. However, the notion that God is continually at work maintaining the order of the universe is replaced with the new idea that God created the universe mechanically perfect, set it into motion, and since that time it has been running on its own. Once created and set in motion, like a clock (or the tongue-in-cheek claims of the Maytag repairman), the universe requires no further maintenance. The workings of the universe could now be studied as a field of its own, and were not caused by God's continual interference. The universe consisted of self-running systems, on autopilot so to speak. The laws of God became the laws of nature and science was (re)born.

In the quest for reality and truth, science and religion had been one and the same field until now. In the 1800's, the word *scientist* entered our lexicon. The universe became purely mechanical. All change became describable using cause and effect, and God the Creator was no longer needed to cause any change other than the very first nudge that started it all, known as the First Cause. The belief prevailed that all the goings on of the universe could now be explained with reason and science, and that with these tools, the human mind could solve all riddles of nature.

It became evident that humanity itself was a Johnny-come-lately on this planet and to the universe, and with God only responsible for the First Cause, a new *mechanistic* explanation was required to account for humanity's inevitable existence, our existence. Evolution and survival of the fittest arose to fill the bill. The tools of the new mechanistic paradigm made it possible for the first time to solve the riddle of life itself. Humanity, which with the fall of the Medieval paradigm had been painfully displaced from the center of the universe, now became of little more importance to the universe than mold on the crust of an ordinary planet circling a mediocre star on the outskirts of a 100 billion starred galaxy among billions of such galaxies. Armed with the myriad new branches of science using the scientific method, and the rapidly advancing fields of logic and mathematics, our grip on, and control over reality became nearly absolute.

The search for reality and truth has now split into two branches, science and religion, each of which keeps a close and wary eye on the other. Religion continues on, providing a paradigm for those things not covered, or coverable, under the scientific branch, largely our spiritual affairs and beliefs, but religion and science have by no means separated completely. Religion has always had to make, always has made, and always will make necessary adjustments to accommodate new and verified discoveries about the universe. On the other side, many scientists retain religious and spiritual beliefs. It seems that nearly every great scientist retains some religious or spiritual interpretation of his beliefs. Like Yin and Yang, and all of its dualistic implications, these two branches crave to reunite. Is it possible that one day they will come to embody the same realm of knowledge, and become one again?

In summary, all paradigms have several things in common:

1) Paradigms are largely about representing the universe, and they provide people with some way to represent, and think about, the universe. They provide us with a mental model of how things work. This determines the methods we choose to manipulate, control, and research the world around us.

2) Each succeeding paradigm is based on something already known to us, usually ideas developed in the previous paradigm. Human beings can only imagine things in terms of what they already know, and paradigms are no exception. In the earlier paradigms, the spirits and gods that moved the world were *copies* of us. In the later paradigms, each succeeding paradigm was largely *copied* from some creation or invention that became familiar during the previous paradigm, the clock mechanism for example.

3) Each paradigm seems like the last word to the people in it. Within any paradigm, the end of all knowledge seems to be in sight, and it is impossible to imagine a new paradigm before the basis for it has formed, that from which it will be copied. For example, it would have been nearly impossible to imagine a universe that worked like clockwork before the invention of clocks.

The above discussion of paradigms may have left the reader with the impression that all people living during the time of a particular paradigm adhere to that paradigm. This is definitely not the case. People are now spread across many different paradigms and probably always have been. I have personal friends who are Deists as from the mechanistic paradigm, and other friends who are Theists, as from the earlier paradigms. I know people who are undecided, and people who don't care. There is apparently some number of people who have gone all the way back to the magical paradigm, practicing witchcraft and forming covens, and of course there are Creationists who largely adhere the ideas of the Infinite paradigm. None of us adheres purely to a single paradigm, but for the most part mixes and matches parts from many paradigms.

It would be a rare individual, though, no matter what their preferred paradigm, that doesn't accept the power of the scientific branch of the Mechanistic paradigm while they watch TV, fly in an airplane, or work on a personal computer that is equivalent to the super computers of a decade ago. Nearly all the wonders and conveniences of the modern world flow from this Mechanistic paradigm, and include radio, automobiles, penicillin, electricity and electrical appliances, satellites and space travel, stereos, CDs, and cell phones. This book will, for the most part, be following the recent events occurring down this branch, the scientific branch. There are some amazing ideas stirring down this trail that we will be examining.

Paradigm shifts and advances in knowledge:

So where do new theories and paradigms come from in the first place? (Most of what will be said in this section applies equally well to both theories and paradigms.) In almost every case, a new theory or paradigm results from the activities of the scholars of that period. All ages have their scholars. Apparently, since primitive times all the way up until the present, there have been people who have found time to sit around and think about things. Of course, there aren't a whole lot of people who feel this need. Pretty much just the whiz kids who, for some unknown reason, need to make sense of the microscopic details of it all. I guess what I'm saying then is that every age has had its whiz kids. Even the cave men and women must have had their whiz kids. After all, the average IQ back then was 100 just like it is today. We tend to think of them all as dummies compared to us, but who of us today could survive a week in their environment? *Ayla* was something of a whiz kid, come to think of it, for those who've read Jean M. Auel's *Earth's Children*[R] series. Anyway, like *Ayla*, these people are frequently in trouble with the societies they live in. It's almost as if they spend their spare time looking for weaknesses and holes in whatever paradigm is prevailing and cherished in their age.

So far, no paradigm has withstood their constant scrutiny and sniping. As time goes by, enough problems and holes accumulate in any paradigm that the difficulties begin to suggest a new solution. A new paradigm then eventually suggests itself that fits the facts better than the existing paradigm.

When this happens, we have a problem. While the thinkers were cloistered away in their little cloisters and abbeys, all of us non-scholars were out there happily going about our daily lives without a care believing, say, that we're living at the center of the universe and that the world is flat, while the scholars are now aware that we're not even close. The scholars now have the unenviable job of letting the rest of the world know that what everyone has believed all their lives is all wrong. A *paradigm shift* is imminent.

Changing paradigms is a painful thing, so painful in fact, that they generally occur gradually, and only over several generations. It is not easy to let go of the universe you know and love, and that has always worked just fine for you, to be replaced by something new and alien that you can't even understand. This is as true for the authorities who are running the world as it is for the common folk. It is especially difficult if you're over thirty-five and have locked into your beliefs, and the people who run the world are *always* over thirty-five. As we saw earlier, frequently somebody has to die.

The paradigm shift from the Medieval Paradigm to the Infinite Paradigm is one of the better examples. We have already mentioned the difficulties experienced by Copernicus, Giordano Bruno, and Galileo, and this shift took well over a century to complete. The scholars of this period were faced with having to decide between two totally different paradigms. On the one hand, they had the paradigm with the Earth at the center of the universe and the multiple crystal spheres within crystal spheres that had been adopted by the European and Near Eastern religions. On the other hand, the Infinite Paradigm had the Sun centered solar system with the Earth and all the planets were in orbit around the Sun. It was not easy for the scholars of this period to decide between the two competing paradigms. We will not go into the details of the myriad problems they were confronted with, but generally, the problem was that neither one of the paradigms solved all of the problems that had arisen. Neither one matched the observed motions of the celestial bodies perfectly.

We now know that the Sun centered theory won out in the end, but the problem was that the early version of the Sun centered theory required the celestial bodies to move in *perfect* circles, which didn't match the observations. They had a hard time letting go of their arbitrary idea that God in all his perfection had created the universe to use perfect circles. The old Earth centered system had compensated for this problem by attaching little rotating spheres to the big spheres, setting some of the spheres off center, etc., etc.

This difficulty with the Sun centered theory wasn't remedied until the mathematician Johannes Kepler, using the extraordinarily accurate observations of one Tycho Brahe, discovered that the planet's orbits were actually (imperfect) *ellipses* that could be calculated mathematically. Kepler was a contemporary of Galileo, only living in Germany. He got himself excommunicated too, only from the Lutherans.

In the mean time, when there are two competing theories that are equally good, how does one decide between them? A related question had been addressed centuries earlier by one William of Occam. In his efforts to sort between multiple explanations of things, he had arrived at the conclusion that *"it is foolish to accomplish with a greater number what can be done with fewer."* In other words, if two competing explanations are equally accurate, but one is horrendously complex and difficult to use, and the other one does the same thing, but is easy to use, go with the simpler. This principle of conceptual economy became known as Occam's Razor. In the information age, this might be rephrased so as to say that if two computer programs do the same job, but one is difficult to use and the other is user friendly, go with the one that is more user friendly. William of Occam had unknowingly anticipated a principle of the computer age, and we adhere to this version of his principle today as common sense.

As it turned out, the Earth centered crystal spheres system had become horrendously complicated and difficult to use, so the Sun centered theory, even though imperfect itself, offered the simpler solution, which gave it a great appeal. This simplicity, and Occam's Razor, kept it alive long enough for its correct version, with the elliptical orbits of planets, to be discovered.

I think that most of us have experienced something very close to a paradigm shift when we were kids. As children, we simply do not have the intelligence to understand many things about the world, and our parents and guardians, out of kindness, come up with alternative explanations. Then again, sometimes they give phony explanations just to make life more interesting for the kids. Eventually, as we mature, we are forced to drop these explanations and replace them with the real adult world version. Examples of these might be the Sand Man, the Tooth Fairy, the Easter Bunny, and Santa Claus. Let's follow the *Santa Claus theory* as the source of our Christmas presents as an example of how an old paradigm collapses and is replaced by a new superior explanation.

As children, many of us were told that on Christmas Eve Santa Clause rides down from the North Pole in his flying sleigh, pulled by flying reindeer, lands on our roof, comes down our chimney, and places our gifts underneath the Christmas tree. Like society's whiz kids, as we get older and begin to gather information about our world, we begin to wonder such things as, "how does a fat man get down that little chimney?", "can reindeer REALLY fly?", "how does Santa visit everybody in our town all in one night?", "who are these Santa's standing on every other street corner, and in every department store." Parents attempting to keep the explanation alive must resort to ever more complex explanations: "he's really an elf," "Santa's reindeer have magic power," "all those other Santas are just his helpers," etc. In the end, the explanations become extraordinarily complex and unlikely, until it finally becomes too complicated to be maintainable or believable to the maturing child, and the whole thing crumbles, to be replaced by the much simpler if less exciting explanation that your parents put the presents under the tree. Ditto the Easter Bunny. Ditto the Tooth Fairy. At some point, the requirements to support these ideas become unrealistic and preposterous. This is where the rationale behind Occam's Razor comes from.

There was a paradigm shift that occurred in the last half of the 1800's, which we need to examine. This one occurred without fanfare, basically only in the scholarly community, and it became evident that it had occurred only after it had happened.

By the mid 1800's, it had long been apparent that mathematics and logic fit to reality like a key fits to a lock, giving us an extremely powerful handle into manipulating and modeling the phenomena of the universe. It gradually became apparent, though, that as the mathematics became more and more advanced, it was providing us with a view into a universe that was beyond the human capability to imagine. Once again, that which was designed to mimic reality worked so well that it was moved from an artifact of one paradigm to the foundation for the next paradigm, and became itself the description of reality.

Mathematics was now used not only to describe known reality, but to even generate descriptions of new and unknown realities. An early example of this was the phenomenon of magnetic and electrical forces that somehow caused action in objects without contacting them, i.e., action at a distance. Scientists initially tried to envision what was going on by imagining tubes of force that reached across space from one object to the other. When these turned out to be untenable, they were replaced by the idea of force fields, which is how we frequently represent them to this day. But the idea of a force field is today recognized to be a completely artificial construct, its only purpose being to give us humans some way to imagine, to picture, electromagnetic force. The mathematics, though, never faltered. It was right on and worked perfectly all along, whether human beings could muster up a mental picture of what was going on or not. In fact, the mathematical solution of the electromagnet force problem produced the surprising and unexpected bonus of explaining light, further verifying the *rightness* of the pure mathematics.

By the beginning of the 1900's, it was inescapable that the mathematics was accurately describing a universe that was based more on logic and mathematics than on our idea of the material world we lived in. Once again it became apparent that there was a reality behind the real world that was immaterial and invisible. We had gone full circle, and arrived back where the Greeks and Egyptians had been 2000 years earlier. Only now we were far more advanced than they. Just for fun, the great mathematician Cauchy made something of a *nonsense* change to one of Euclid's original five premises. (You will recall from Chapter 2 that for a logical *conclusion* to be true, the *premises* it's based on must be true.) Cauchy changed the premise that *parallel lines never meet* to the premise that *parallel lines do eventually meet at infinity*. Another great mathematician, Georg Riemann, then proceeded to create a new body of geometry, a kind of nonsense geometry where all conclusions still followed logically from the premises, and that contained the nonsense conclusion that space itself could be curved. At least the logic and mathematics worked. Einstein based his theory of relativity on this new geometry, and introduced us to a universe where time passes at different rates, and the length of a yardstick varies depending on how fast you are traveling. All of this fell out as predictions of the logic and mathematics. This nonsense geometry was correct after all. It was our, and Euclid's, common sense idea of the universe that was wrong. This paradigm, the paradigm that formal logic and mathematics provide a more accurate window into reality than our common sense *experience*, became known as the Formal Paradigm. With the advent of the utterly incomprehensible quantum physics, the Formal Paradigm became assured.

The Formal Paradigm differs from all the other paradigms we have examined in one remarkable way. One of the purposes of all those other paradigms was to provide us with a way to mentally model the universe, a way to actually imagine what was going on. This is not the case with the Formal paradigm. We can no longer imagine what is going on behind the phenomena we observe. We still have a model, but it's a mathematical model now, not a mental model, and unless you're one who understands higher mathematics, you have no model at all. Even those who do understand the math are left feeling dissatisfied and like they don't understand, because there is no way to describe what is going on in terms that are familiar and comfortable to the human mind.

Knowledge as philosophy:

No knowledge it seems is absolute. The pursuit of knowledge is a very human activity, and thus the bodies of knowledge we create are very man made things. If societies are separated and both develop bodies of knowledge in the same fields, they will not come up with the same representations. One example is music. We in the West feel that our A through G harmonic scale is the way all music should be written, but our friends in the Middle East and the Far East both came up with very different ideas of music. Medicine too. When acupuncture and other Eastern ideas of medicine were introduced into this country several decades ago, we literally experienced culture shock. Their approach to medicine seemed to be little more than herbs and spices applied with magic, and it seemed impossible that it could have merit. Then of course, there's African and Native American medicine. Spirituality is another example. Humanity has come up with dozens of religions, and Eastern religions are nothing like ours. Then there are languages. Not only did every tribe of humanity come up with a different language, but they came up with varying syntaxes, and even different sounds to use to communicate. Not only do languages use different alphabetic sounds, but the native Mongolians actually speak some of the time while sucking breath in instead of out, and the Clack language out of Africa interjects tongue clicking and clacking as part of their speech.

Humanity is winging it. We're doing the best we can do, which is pretty good, but that implies that there is room for something better, and apparently there is. It doesn't seem to matter how smart we are, there's always somebody smarter. It's a disconcerting phenomenon that no matter what the political party of your choice, there's a brilliant someone from the other party who can reason you out of your choice. (Not that we let that affect us.) No matter how good we are, there's always plenty of room at the top for a faster gun. It takes almost no imagination to imagine a rather ordinary space alien who's twice as smart as our smartest human being. If our top IQ is around 200, then doesn't that mean there is such a thing as an IQ of 400, or 4000? Humanity can produce no better minds than those who have made it to the top of our Judicial branch of government. In this case, I'm referring to the nine justices who sit on the Supreme Court of the United States. These are the *Best* of the Best of the best, and yet they regularly disagree. When the controversial election of George Bush over Al Gore made it to the Supreme Court for a final decision, they were split as closely as possible down the middle. Our best people make their best decisions and best rules for us to live by, but those people are out front and flying by the seat of their pants. And when our best and brightest are debating it, it's called philosophy.

A lot of people have spent a lot of effort on trying to define what philosophy really is. If the word *philosophy* connotes anything to most people, it connotes an indefiniteness or uncertainty to the subject under discussion. Those of us who worship at the *Church of Reality Now* sometimes tend not to take philosophers too seriously. The primary image conjured up is one of a bunch of hopelessly brilliant people who are busy disagreeing over a subject so abstract that they can't find a worldly experiment to resolve their disagreement. And once in awhile they say things that really don't make much sense to the rest of us earthlings. I was reading recently where some philosophers have reached the conclusion that communication between people is impossible. That's right! It turns out to be logically impossible for minds to *communicate* with each other. Then they turned around and *communicated* this new insight to the rest of us. Duh! Do you think they should have thought about it a little longer before saying anything?

I found it somewhat disconcerting when I went to sign up for a course in Logic in college, only to discover that I had to take it through the Philosophy Dept. I wanted to learn logic, not the *philosophy* of logic. The fact is, however, that logic, and indeed all knowledge, is considered philosophical at its foundations. If one pursues an education in a field to the ultimate level, one is granted a PhD, that is, a Doctor of *Philosophy*. They are now a philosopher. Logic is philosophy, and mathematics is based on logic. And physics' iron grip on reality is based on mathematics. Mathematics and physics, it turns out, are pure philosophy.

It's hard to imagine mathematics as possessing the uncertainty that we designate to philosophy. Almost everyone would agree that the numbers and arithmetic that we learned in elementary school are fundamental and absolute, but actually they're not. We must remember that there are other quite different representations for numbers. The most familiar of these is the Roman Numerals. With Roman Numerals, Euclid was able to invent geometry, and Archimedes was able to solve the riddle of *pi*. They must have felt that Roman Numerals were the end-all in the world of mathematics and in number representation. Roman Numerals had their problems, though, including no good way of doing arithmetic. Try adding MCMVC to MLCCCVC using the rules of ordinary arithmetic, and you'll find you can't do it strictly by following the rules. When the zero of our current decimal numbering system came into full usage in India, our present form of arithmetic became possible, but this is still a man made invention, and it is not necessarily the end-all of numeral representation. In fact, there are almost certainly better ways, as the Arabic numeral system (as it's called) that we use today has some problems in representing the real world too.

One problem is that the wonderful zero, which made our current system of arithmetic possible in the first place, has some behavior that is not like a number at all. You can add, subtract, and multiply with it, but you can't divide with it. It is literally true that the result of dividing by zero is any number at all, including but not limited to infinity. Now infinity is not even considered a number. Maybe it should be. Anyway, with our current system, division by zero is an illegal operation, and when it occurs out of necessity, which it does, the result is said to be undefined. That means you can't do it, but when it happens anyway, you can't use the result. Not a very elegant representation of the behavior of the universe if you ask me. While we're on the subject of numbers, we might as well point out that most people don't even know what a number really is, even though we think we do. We count with numbers, write numbers, do arithmetic with numbers, so we know very well how to use numbers. We think we understand numbers, but this *feeling of understanding* is nothing more or less than our *feeling of familiarity* with numbers. Very few actually even wonder how a number represents a quantity.

The numbers you bandy about so adroitly are really just a short hand way of writing a polynomial. For example, the number 432 is really just the list of the coefficients of the polynomial $4X^2 + 3X + 2 = 432$, where the solution for X is the base for a number system. In our case X = 10. All of the rules that make addition, subtraction, multiplication, and division so easy come from the characteristics of polynomials, and to think the Arabs came up with this thousands of years ago...but of course, *Algebra* is an Arabic word after all. If our numbers are based on a representation this complex, there must be other complex ways to represent quantities. Come to think of it, logarithms is very nearly just such a system. Logarithms can be based on 10 just like our ordinary numbers, but its easier to base them on the number 2.7182818284...the *transcendental* number "*e*" that is infinitely long and can't even be written down. If you didn't understand these last few lines, don't worry about it a bit. The point of all this, which I'm sure you get, is to show that simple numbers are nowhere near as simple as they seem. No wonder it's all considered philosophy.

Physics is based on mathematics. To most people, the mathematical description of reality used by physics is no description at all. Where did this come from in the first place? The answer, in part at least, is related to the requirements of the scientific method. In the scientific method, remember, if something is going to attain the status of *real*, then it has to be testable, and the result of the test has to be predicted correctly by the hypothesis or theory. It turns out that about the most convenient type of prediction is something that can be measured, and measurements are almost always in numbers. As a simple example, two kids circa 1960 might predict that each of their hot rod cars is more powerful than the other guys. The test they devise to decide who's right is to see whose car will go from 0 to 60 the fastest. The result of each test is the time *measurement* of how long it takes their car to go from 0 to 60, which is a number. The prediction each made is that his time measurement will be a smaller number than the other guy's, and the one with the smallest number wins. Whether someone is testing the strength of gravity by measuring the speed of falling objects, or testing the strength of the electrons field by measuring its curved path in a magnetic field, the results are numbers, and any useful theory must predict these *numbers* accurately, and that requires mathematics. And that's why physics nowadays is all mathematics.

So physics ends up describing reality almost entirely in terms of things that can be measured. It's a lucky thing that there really aren't so many things that can be measured. In fact, remarkably, there are only three. These are time, location, and weight (or mass), and that's about it. Most other quantities that we bandy about are based on just these three. Speed for example, which was so important to those kids of the sixties, is really a combination of the location measurements and time measurements, i.e., 60 miles per hours tells us that a car will change its *location* by 60 miles in the *time* period of 1 hour. It, therefore, takes two measurements to determine someone's speed, a *location* measurement and a *time* measurement.

The fact that all physical description, that everything in the universe from the macro universe to the micro universe, from quasars to quarks, must all be based on so few measurable realms is at the root of a great philosophical debate right now about what physics really is. Are these three measurable realms of time, space, and mass the only things that are even knowable to us in the physical universe? Just looking out the window, my experience of the world certainly seems to be far richer than this. As measuring instruments, though, the rods and cones in my eyes are strictly limited to measuring the cascading effects of only these three quantities. This measurement information is converted into nerve impulses on the optic nerve and then travels from my eyes into the low levels of my brain. As it works its way up through many levels of information processing to my higher mental processes, how does this information, these measurements, get translated into this rich experience that we all have? But I digress. This will be discussed much more thoroughly in Section 3, *The Matter Of Mind*. The point here is that physics is far more philosophical than you may have realized.

Somewhere around a century ago, physics broke from the bonds of the material world and became what many would feel is pure philosophy. As already mentioned, in the last half of the 1800's, physics experienced a paradigm shift from the Mechanistic paradigm to the Formal paradigm. With this shift, the mathematics moved from being simply a useful tool to describe the world, to become the greater reality itself. The material world, the world of our experience, the world that we can imagine, was left behind, and somehow became just a high level mental artifact of the low level micro world and the mathematics that was behind it all. This Formal paradigm, this adherence in the pure mathematics as *the* description of reality, opened the door for yet another paradigm shift at the beginning of the 1900's. This was the discovery/invention of quantum physics.

What the mathematics of quantum physics was telling us, was and still is utterly impossible to imagine. The objects of quantum physics, the particles from which our world is composed, do not have unique identities, do not always exist in specific places or at specific times, may proceed into multiple futures simultaneously, may be multiple places at the same time, can appear on the other side of a wall without going through it, and seem to have insider information about what another particle is doing a billion miles away. The ancient and common idea of cause and effect, so intuitive to us and brought to its greatest fruition in the Mechanistic paradigm, has had to be discarded. Nothing is caused at all. We are no longer able to predict exactly what will happen in a given situation, no matter how well understood. We can only say that one prediction will occur with one probability, and another prediction will occur with another probability.

This paradigm has the interesting characteristic that no one has yet come up with a way to think about this universe, to picture it mentally, although the mathematics work *perfectly*. The whiz kid physicists have come up with well over half a dozen different possible models, but the more imaginable ones, those most friendly, the more concrete ones, are slowly being eliminated. We are being left with the ones that are completely abstract, that are based on nothing material at all. Of course, strict adherence to the Formal paradigm, with its utterly abstract representation of the universe, would have predicted this. While mathematics and physics seem to be bedrock reality to us, their foundation is inconceivable to us. They are in fact pure philosophy.

The concept of paradigms is a scary thing. The very existence of so many fallen past paradigms demonstrates that we are not always right about how we perceive the universe. With a little contemplation, it implies to us that we, almost certainly, can never be right about our interpretation of the universe. With our Formal and quantum paradigms, it seems to us that we have achieved the ultimately correct model. Of course, that is precisely what they believed in every one of those earlier paradigms. No better paradigm was imaginable or possible.

Obviously, the fact that we cannot imagine a better paradigm carries no weight at all. No one in any of the earlier paradigms could imagine any future paradigm. All future paradigms were based on ideas that hadn't occurred yet. From within it, there is no way to distinguish our current paradigm as more permanent than any other paradigm. As knowledge progresses within a paradigm, it has always led to a new paradigm, and our knowledge is most definitely progressing. It seems impossible that our current paradigm won't one day succumb to a truer paradigm like all paradigms before it.

Our current paradigm is just one more paradigm in the long chain of paradigms. Our paradigm is not the final paradigm, not yet the one true paradigm. Our current paradigm will one day be challenged by another, more real paradigm. But when two paradigms clash, how do we decide which one is the more *real* one? What makes one description of reality better than the other one? **We always hope that the new one is better because it is at least closer to the real reality, while the older one has been proven false**. The truth is that one is superior only because it describes phenomenon and predicts measurements more accurately than the other. Or perhaps it is chosen for other pragmatic considerations, such as, one is simpler or easier to use than the other (Occam's razor). Now here's a startling idea. Even though two paradigms may be mutually exclusive, if they both predict reality equally accurately by the scientific method, it doesn't matter at all that one is real and one isn't. If we decide on one using Occam's razor, say, we simply can never know if one is more real than the other. If we adhere to the scientific method and both make the required testable predictions, and if both predictions are found to be true, then we simply have no way of knowing. (The various interpretations of quantum physics exhibit exactly this characteristic.) We have chosen other pragmatic methods to help us decide, but these methods in the end rely on such ideas as which is the simplest, or more user friendly. If both achieve the same accuracy, then we simply have to accept the one that is the easiest to use. Paradigms are not selected on their truth. Our paradigms and theories can never achieve more than a *most useful* representation of reality, and in the end are chosen for pragmatic reasons. Indeed we may switch back and forth between different representations several times before settling on one, or moving on to another completely different representation that achieves greater accuracy, discarding the originals. The two competing theories of the wave nature, and the particle nature of light is just such an example, and both were eventually subsumed in the wave/particle duality idea of complementarity.

The scientific method dictates that to find reality, we must test our hypotheses against their predictions in the real world. You'll recall that the hope was that matching our predictions to reality would provide us with a way to determine reality. After several centuries of experience, we have discovered that it's not so simple after all. Over and over we have created paradigms that appear to provide exquisite matches to experience and experiments, only to discover that this requirement soon yields an even better fitting paradigm. Are we doomed to repeat this experience *ad infinitum*? It is a disconcerting thing to contemplate that there may be no end to it at all, that there never will be any ground, a one true and final reality, to stand on.

Our current knowledge is simply a representation of reality that fits the facts the best we can do. All of the sciences, medicine, mathematics, etc., all rest on a philosophical foundation that is nothing more than "It works better than anything else we have had before *now!*" Science is only as far as it is and is never complete. Our body of knowledge will continue to grow. Old ideas will be discarded in favor of new ideas that explain better what the world is really like. These new ideas themselves will eventually fall. Our current scientific explanation is simply the best-fit model that we have achieved up to this point, a model that will eventually fail.

Our current knowledge is not absolute and will in fact appear more and more naive as generations stretch into the future several centuries. Just a hundred years ago, the world was quite a different place. No one yet knew for sure even whether atoms existed. In fact, popular opinion at the time was running against them. Thomas Edison was inventing his light bulb, but no one yet knew what electricity was. Just two hundred years ago the now primitive steam engine was a futuristic dream still 30 years away. They didn't know what light was, and atoms had not yet even been proposed as a contemporary hypothesis. Only five hundred years ago, people believed that the sky above us was full of rotating crystal spheres to which were attached the Sun, Moon, and the rest of the cosmos.

As we look back at our ancestors, we must also realize that to our descendents of a hundred years in our future, our current knowledge will appear surprisingly incomplete. Two hundred years from now we, and our knowledge, will appear to them as astonishingly primitive and naive. Five hundred years from now, the world of humanity will look back on us, compassionately I hope, as utterly primitive and hysterically naïve, even total idiots. There's no escaping this. The only certainty concerning our current knowledge is that eventually it will be entirely replaced with alternate, and to us, utterly unimaginable explanations. The frontier of science passes beyond old representations, leaving them behind as (sometimes laughable) historical markers, and replacing them with often esoteric new ones. All of those earlier paradigms tell us that despite our best efforts, we humans are not always right in our knowledge. In fact, they tell us we have never been right in our knowledge. Uncertainty is certain.

And this book is not exempt. As time passes into the future, one, two, five hundred years, more and more of the facts, ideas, and speculations iterated herein will fall and be replaced with new interpretations and new paradigms. I suspect that the observation discussed in this chapter, that paradigms are temporary interpretations of reality and that we are forever destined to look back on ourselves as primitive, will at some point be the lone surviving truth. I suspect that that notion will in the end turn out to be the truest utterance of this document, and will most likely end up the last fact standing.

As with people living in all paradigms, it may seem impossible to the reader that our current paradigm should ever fail. Is it possible, for example, that our current notion of the solar system with the Earth and planets circling the Sun can ever become subsumed or antiquated? Yes, it is! Not only will this book show how the current paradigm might fail, but also it will propose a new one. It is one purpose of this book to try to imagine what the next paradigm might be.

Chapter 4
Understanding and Thinking

○ ○

When logic and proportion
Have fallen sloppy dead
And the White Knight is talking backwards
And the Red Queen's "off with her head!"
Remember what the dormouse said:
"Feed your head..."

     —*White Rabbit—Grace Slick—Jefferson Airplane*

Understanding and modeling:

What is understanding? What does it mean when we say we understand something? Is understanding related to paradigms? Will computers ever be able to understand?

You will recall from the last chapter that paradigms, whether accurate or inaccurate, gave us a way of understanding the universe we live in. They gave us a way to think about the universe, a way to represent it in our minds. With our paradigms, we had a way to *model* the universe, and we could account for all of its characteristics and actions with our model. Sometimes the model was concrete, as with the rotating crystal spheres. Sometimes it was totally abstract, as with Logos or the mathematical representation, and sometimes it was kind of in between, as when the spirits were running it all. Given any of those earlier models, we were able to provide explanations for what we saw going on in the universe. One requirement then, for *understanding* to occur, is that we have a mental model that fits together with, and explains or accounts for what we experience.

As far as computer understanding goes, is *having a model* the only requirement to our saying that a computer understands something? All *good* computer programs work from a model. In fact, the computer program may very well qualify as a model itself, but this model is simply a mimic of the model in the programmer's mind. Sometimes it is a copy of the model the programmer uses to understand, but more often it is a collection of methods, rules of thumb, and tricks that the programmer employs to reach a desired end, and that have nothing to do with reality. This is called a *heuristic*, and you will be seeing this word again. A heuristic is not so distantly related to a paradigm in that both may be thought of as models, but heuristics are freed from the requirement that their model be real. (Then again, paradigms haven't done so well being real either.)

Some people thinking on this have arrived at the conclusion that understanding is something so human that no matter how intelligent our computers behave, they will never truly be able to understand anything. Not the way humans do. This may well be true if what they are talking about is the *feeling of understanding* that we humans *experience*. Then the larger question is simply, "Will our machines ever have *feelings*?" If not, computers will never understand, but they will never *not understand* either, since the feeling of not understanding something is at least as strong as the feeling of understanding. But understanding, while first and foremost to us humans is a feeling, is also very much more than a feeling, and the rest of what it is, is quite achievable with machines.

When we think we understand something, we are experiencing a *feeling*...feeling like we understand, of course. Let's try some examples. Let's say you hit the light switch and the light doesn't come on. Do you feel like you understand why? Most people would say that this isn't what they expected to happen, so they don't yet understand, although they have some ideas what the explanation might be. Suppose now you look into the problem and find that the light bulb is burned out. Do you *now* feel like you understand why the light didn't come on? Of course you do. You would not *expect* the light to come on if the bulb is burned out. So minimally, *expectation* is involved with our feeling of understanding. The expectation in this case is simply the prediction our model is making.

How about this one. I show you a rather ordinary one-inch rock and I place it on the table in front of you. The instant I release it, it falls rapidly upward and crashes onto the ceiling where it settles without moving. Do you feel like you understand what is happening? Hopefully not! I wouldn't. My model of the world predicted something entirely different. So we now retrieve the rock from the ceiling and I hand it to you. You feel a small force of the rock pushing upward in your hand, and when you release it, it again falls rapidly upward and crashes onto the ceiling. If you were at this point asked to explain how or why the rock is behaving this way, you would be unable, and would readily state that you don't yet understand.

As an interesting aside, I actually have a very clear adolescent memory of reading an article in the Washington Post of the discovery of a mineral that had this anti-gravity characteristic of falling upward. It was in the early 1960's I believe. Of course, it's hard now to believe that the Washington Post would print such a thing, so perhaps I read it in the Washington Daily News or the Washington Star, two now defunct newspapers of that period. The events from way back then do lately seem to be shifting around, quietly changing themselves bit by bit from my precision memories. Then again, maybe just last night I dreamed the memory of reading that article, and it's the memory of the dream of the memory I'm remembering.

Now suppose I take the rock, leave the room, and return moments later carrying a light weight two-inch cardboard box, which I show to you, and place on the table in front of you. The instant I release it, it falls rapidly upward and crashes onto the ceiling where it stays without moving. Now do you feel like you understand what just happened? After thinking on it for a moment, you say, "Aha!" Of course you understand. You know perfectly well that I must have put the rock in the box and that caused it to fall to the ceiling, so now you smugly feel that *feeling of understanding*. If I retrieve the box and show you the rock inside of it, everything is fine. Your *new* mental model, your new explanation worked, and your feeling of understanding is assured. Now though, if I open the box and there's no rock in it, the feeling of understanding disappears and we're back to scratching our heads and feeling that we don't understand. We now at least have a handle on your feeling of understanding so that we can turn it on and off at will.

Anyway, our experience of understanding is first and foremost a feeling, but the question becomes, "what's going on when we experience this feeling?" What are the circumstances we're in that cause this feeling to occur? What is the difference in the state of the information in our heads when we feel we don't understand, versus when we feel we understand?

The first thing that jumps out at us is that understanding occurs when the behavior of something is what we *expect*. As long as everything is going along the way we expect it to, then there's nothing we don't understand. We have a mental model of the world and it's working just fine. Everything that the world is doing is matched and accounted for in our model. But as soon as our model of the world fails to account for something, that is, as soon as something *unexpected* occurs, our feeling of understanding toggles to one of not understanding, and we go about looking for the cause of the unexpected behavior. Then when we find the cause, the unexplained behavior reverts from something unexpected to something expected. Our mental model, which includes things like burned out light bulbs, once again accounts for the world, so now the feeling of understanding reoccurs.

If we look at the example of the anti-gravity rock hidden in the box, we see that despite the fact that we *never understood* what was going on with the rock, we still experienced the feeling of understanding when the box fell to the ceiling. Once the behavior of the rock became a *familiar* concept to us, that *familiarity alone* was sufficient to make us feel we understood the behavior of the box when it did the same thing. The behavior of the box could now be accounted for by putting the rock in the box, even though the behavior of the rock itself was never accounted for, or understood at all.

The *feeling of understanding* then, in the end, is a rather shallow and not very profound thing. All that is required is that something be accounted for in terms of things that are simply already familiar to us, in terms of things we already know. And it's not so difficult to program a computer to account for computer things, that is symbols, in terms it already has. There is no deep knowledge required. *Explanations* and *definitions* both work this way. They duplicate the event or word respectively in concepts that are already familiar to us. The familiar concepts themselves do not have to be deeply understood, just familiar. Indeed, if each component concept itself needed to be understood, it too would need to be understood in terms of familiar components, and we would immediately be confronted with needing an infinity of levels of understanding to understand anything. Of course, searching for the next lower level of understanding is exactly what scientists are for. That's what they do, and the fact that there may well be infinite levels of understanding is what they call job security.

The requirements for understanding something are that it be represented to us in terms that are familiar to us, in concepts that are known to us, that are already part of our model. Once we become aware of something new under the sun, once it has been *cognized*, it is automatically added to our model of the world. Once we are familiar with a rock that falls to the ceiling, anything else with the same behavior will be *re-cognized* and understood as similar to our rock. In fact, the act of recognition is the act of identifying where something already fits in our mental model. Our new feeling of familiarity is our signal that our mental model has duly noted and incorporated this new behavior, and indeed, the *expected* behavior of this rock henceforth has now become to fall to the ceiling. We would now be surprised if it didn't!

If someone else comes along with something new that behaves this way, we immediately recognize it as similar to our rock, and put it in the same now familiar class, that is, the class of things that fall upward. If someone brings in a chunk of metal that exhibits this behavior, we describe it as *like* the rock, only made out of metal this time. Everybody who knows about the rock will immediately have a good grasp on the characteristics of the new object. We describe and understand things in metaphors, similes, and analogies. We compare the characteristics of new things to the characteristics of things that we already know and are familiar with. Importantly, in the example above of the metal object, the description included not only the *similarity* to what was already familiar to us, but also what was *different* about it too. It included the piece of information that it differed from the rock in that it was made out of metal this time.

Similarity and difference:

As you will see, pretty much all knowledge is handled in our brains using *similarity* and *difference*, hereafter referred to as *sim/dif* for short, and it saves us humans huge amounts of brainpower and memory. Each group of things that are similar we need represent in our brains only once, all only as a single mental thing. We do this by creating categories for similar things, and everything in the category shares the common characteristics. What is so important about mental categories is that we only need to represent this *category* in our brains once.

The list of categories is endless in itself. Some examples are *dogs, animals, cars, appliances, families, numbers, stars, books, lips, and legs.* In your personal life, you will realize that for any one of these categories, there are dozens to hundreds of unique instances that you know of. Let's take the category *cars* for example.

There are probably a dozen or so actual cars that you personally know by sight at this time. You know what a car is. Try to think for a minute of all the different things that a car is, its characteristics that are common to all cars. It has tires, doors, windows, a steering wheel, seats, rearview mirror, license plates, an engine, an accelerator, brakes, uses fuel, and that's just the beginning. All cars are *similar* in these ways. Now think of two different cars that you personally know of, and think how these two cars are *different*. Just ask yourself how you know that they are *different* cars? Mostly what you'll think of is just color and vehicle type. One's red and one's blue, and one's a sedan and the other's an RV.

The cars may differ in many other ways too, but the point is, we save ourselves the effort of thinking of hundreds and hundreds of details by first of all identifying their similarity category, and only then identifying how they are different.

The similarities are embodied in the knowledge that they are both cars, versus a car and a house, say. The differences are that one is a red sedan, and the other is a blue RV. Similarity and difference, sim/dif, have allowed you to create a useful description of either car very quickly and efficiently.

Imagine for a moment the mind of some poor brain damaged individual who can no longer identify the categories of the things that he encounters. He would see your two different cars as two completely different things. For each one, he would have to memorize that it had tires, doors, windows, a steering wheel, an engine, etc. For each one, he would be surprised to discover that it had seats, a rearview mirror, and license plates. He would never realize that they were cars, or even that they were *similar*.

We categorize things according to their *similarities* endlessly. Categories within categories, level after level. You will notice that all of the above characteristics of the car category are themselves categories of things. Tires, doors, and windows are types of things, categories for things, not the specific instance of a thing itself. Tires are divided into a myriad of sub-categories—radial, 4 ply, all terrain, etc. Each of these categories embodies characteristics that are similar/ common to every tire in that particular category. Categories are so important to us as mental energy savers that we largely think in categories. Last night on the news there was a story of a university coed in Tempe, AZ who was struck and killed by a car traveling so fast that it knocked her in two. Now while you probably want to dwell on the gruesome image of the coed for a minute (which is itself a category by the way), let's get back to the car. All we know about it is that it was a car, and some of the things we know about the category *cars* is that they're fast and heavy and can be extremely destructive to an unfortunate human body. For contrast, imagine for a moment that the news story had said that she had been struck by a piece of Styrofoam. We use the car category as a means of doing a quick lookup of the characteristics of cars that are important to this situation. We completely gloss over all of those other characteristics mentioned above. We don't care about its tires or its rearview mirror. We barely glance at our car category and it is sufficient to create an *understandable* mental scene. We don't need a mental image of the specific car. Thinking in categories based on similarities is a hugely efficient way of thinking.

With all this discussion of the usefulness of identifying *similarities*, where does the other half of sim/dif, the *differences*, fit in? In the end, the idea of differences may be even more important than the idea of similarities. As pointed out when thinking of those two cars you know above, it's really by their differences that you know them. These are the characteristics that distinguish them from other cars. If there are no differences between two cars, then it's impossible to tell them apart, and they lose their unique identities. Of course, for two totally identical cars to lose their identities, they would have to lose their *different* locations in space too. Then they would both be the same car sitting in the same spot. Now there's a thought. Maybe that car over there is really a whole bunch of identical cars all sitting in the same place-time in space-time. The point is that if there are no differences, absolutely no differences whatsoever, then the two objects do not have unique identities, and in the macro world at least, this makes them the same object.

Can something like this ever happen? In a way. While no two distinct cars may ever suddenly become one car with the same identity, in the world of information this can happen, and your mind and brain are definitely information handling systems, as are computers. It's easy to imagine two people talking about two distinct objects while not realizing it is actually the same object. During the discussion, in each of their heads they are representing two similar but distinct objects. When they discover that they are talking about the same thing, their minds will have to merge the two objects into a single object. Imagine two ladies sitting, discussing their respective husbands over tea. They have known each other for years from their lady's club meetings, but have never met the other's spouse, and each is maintaining a mental image of her husband as well as the other lady's husband. Then one day they come to find out that their husbands are/is a polygamist(s), and they both have the same husband. Their distinct images of their respective husbands will now have to be merged into one person. Of course, this is only able to happen in information systems, which our minds happen to be, where objects don't have any real existence but are represented only as information.

Similarities as abstractions:

We derive our categories for things by noticing what is *similar* among objects in the world around us. We look out there at all those things that have feathers, and we see that among the objects having feathers there are many different kinds, and we create a mental category for feathered things and call it birds. Then we remove all *actual* instances of birds from our mental object, and let it be an empty object that stands for all birds. This is called an abstraction. The abstract mental object of *bird* does not refer to any specific bird, but contains the empty component subcategories that are common to all birds. When we do encounter a real world bird, we recognize it as an *instance* of this abstraction of things with feathers.

As before, all of those *subcategories* that make up the bird category are abstractions too. For example, the sub-category of *feathers* is a category abstracted from identifying what is similar among those objects we pluck off of birds. The abstract object in our minds for the category *feather* represents all feathers, but contains no representation of any single instance of a real world feather, so feathers is an abstraction too, which represents all feathers. So is feet, and eyes, and bill, and wings. All of the *components* of the bird abstraction are *abstractions* too.

In a real world instance of a bird, each of those component abstractions themselves take on a real world instance. To have a real world instance of a bird, it must have real world instances of eyes, a bill, feet, wings, a head, feathers, etc. An abstraction then is in many ways a list of more abstractions. The abstractions in the list are components of the higher level abstraction, of the parent abstraction. And of course, each component abstraction is a list of its own component abstractions. Down and down we go. We apparently could descend down into these components of components almost endlessly.

Following down just one thread of the components of a bird for example, we might go down from bird to feather, to fibers of the feather, to proteins that compose the fiber, to amino acids that compose the protein, to molecules that make up the amino acid, to atoms that make up the molecules, to protons, to quarks. And who knows if this is the bottom? Each one of these is an abstraction for something that actually exists, and is a component of the abstraction above it, but most of us would stop at the feather for all practical purposes. As an aside, I should note that as we descend down the above chain of abstractions, the abstractions themselves become more and more mathematical, until somewhere around the atom level our mental pictures fail and the only representation we have of them is mathematical.

Abstractions and words:

With the myriad words I have given and then called abstractions, some readers may be thinking that all of the words in our language may be abstractions, and they would be just about right. But what about proper nouns that we use to refer to real world instances of something, to a specific thing. If we know somebody named Edith, and we refer to her by uttering *Edith*, then we are not referring to Edith's category, say woman, but the real world *instance* of Edith. In this case, we are referring to an instance of the abstraction *woman*, and we say that the abstraction has been instantiated. So we have words that refer to *instantiated* abstractions, rather than to the (*uninstantiated*) abstraction itself. For the most part, though, our words represent just the abstractions of real world things, and this in not limited to just nouns, but extends to verbs and prepositions, etc. The verb *to run* refers to an abstraction of what it is to run, to anyone or anything running, not one specific instance of someone running. The preposition *between* refers to all instances where something is in between other things, not one specific real world instance.

Our *words* represent the concepts we have, and most of them are abstractions. Obviously, there is a close relationship between abstractions, words, and concepts. We think in concepts. In the most general sense, *concepts* are everything we experience in our heads, whether it's our concept of Edith, or our concept of a bird. And if we want to communicate a concept to someone else, we have to find the *words* that describe it to them. It would be very hard to think of a concept that we have that we cannot find the words to capture it, to represent it. If I could think of one, I couldn't tell you what it was because there would be no words to describe it. There's a flip side to this, however, and that is that we get virtually all of our concepts that we use for thinking from our words. And this means that our language largely dictates to us what concepts we will have, that is, what we *can* think. Is it possible that there are concepts that we cannot have in our native tongue, but maybe in some other language? There are a lot of languages out there, and there are a lot of words that just don't translate from one language into another. Each language contains concepts that are much more easily expressed in that language than in some other languages.

As a demonstration of how the words we know dictate what concepts we can have, years ago when I was a firefighter, we were called to a natural gas leak where a backhoe digging a trench had ruptured a gas line. When we returned to the station, one of the other firemen was telling me that in the dirt at the end of the ditch there was a spot where the ground was on fire with a "*fire that was cold.*" He was amazed and had never seen anything like this before. I had seen it too, and recognized it as the flaring and sparkling laser spot that the backhoe operator had been using as a guide. This particular firefighter, though, had no knowledge of lasers, so he had to use the only words and concepts he had available to describe it. Out of all of his life's experiences, what the thing that he was seeing most resembled to him was *fire*, only it was *cold*. Sim/dif.

Sim/dif and existence:

The word *duck* is of course an abstraction for a certain kind of bird. A duck has feathers, wings, and a bill like all birds. These are a few of the things that make it *similar* to other birds and qualifies a real world duck to instantiate the bird abstraction. But it also has things that are *different* from other birds, and these are the things that qualify it as being a duck, vs. a cardinal say. Let's say to qualify as a duck it must walk, quack, and act like a duck. Ducks waddle when they walk, so we'll say that *waddling* is walking like a duck. *Quacking* needs no further description, and *acting* like a duck, let's abbreviate that idea to swimming. In this case, if we see a real world instance of a bird, and it waddles, quacks, and swims, then we have a duck. *Sim/dif*, similarity and *difference*, have come together again to give us a workable description of the duck object we have stumbled onto.

Now back in Chapter 2 we used these very characteristics of a duck to determine that it *existed* at all. We said that walking, quacking, and acting like a duck are the *effects* it had, by way of which we even knew that a duck existed. Now most people may not usually think of these things as effects. If someone were to ask you to name some sort of effect that a duck could have, you'd probably think of its effect on the ecosystem or something, but in fact, walking, quacking, and acting like a duck are effects too. The thing that is being affected in this case is of course your mind. That's where thinking, understanding, and abstractions take place after all. That's where the concepts of waddling, quacking, and swimming are being activated. Seeing a duck causes these *effects* to happen in our minds, and our mind identifies these characteristics as belonging to the duck abstraction. All the characteristics that we think of as making up a duck can be thought of as the effects it has in our mind when we perceive them, and this is true for all of our abstractions.

Now a duck interacts with the world it lives in, and the way it interacts is by way of the effects it has on the world. It affects the water it lands in by causing ripples. It affects the air it flies through by causing vortexes. It affects the light that hits it by reflecting different colors. (Which in turn reaches and affects the rods and cones in your eyes.) It affects a finger that presses on it by pressing back. It is by its effects that we detect it, that we are able to know it is there at all. Imagine for a minute that it neither reflected light nor pressed back against your finger. Light would pass right through it and it would be invisible. Your finger would pass right through it and you'd never be able to feel it. It's starting not to exist, and if it loses all of its effects, we won't be able to detect it at all and we can rightly say with no consequence that it doesn't exist at all. If we can't detect it, it has no effect on us, and it literally makes no *difference* to us whether it exists or not...and this idea extends to everything in our universe. If it has no effect, it literally makes no *difference* to the universe, or to anything in the universe, whether it exists or not.

Now very interestingly, we have just extended our idea of sim/dif from the effect real world objects have in our *mind*, to the effect objects have on each other in the physical world. Take a billiard ball for example. One of the effects of a billiard ball is that it is very hard. Hardness is really a measure of resistance to penetration, so saying it's very hard is really saying that it has the effect of being very impenetrable, **and this effect only affects objects that have a *similar* quality.** One billiard ball affects another by causing it to ricochet off of it when one clicks them together. If one attempts to click a billiard ball against a rubber ball, the rubber ball is less resistant and is indented, but the billiard ball not at all. Ditto a marshmallow. Water has even less resistance and if you drop a billiard ball in water, the water still offers some resistance but the billiard ball passes through. Air has even less of the hardness effect, and thus barely affects the billiard ball at all. Outer space has *no hardness*, no resistance, and consequently has no effect on the billiard ball. *Only objects with **similar effects** affect each other.* To detect a billiard ball using its hardness effect, one needs something else that has at least some hardness too.

The same is true for detecting an electron, which is detected by its electrical force. It has no effect on a neutron that sports its own but different force, the strong nuclear force, but the electron does affect the proton, which sports an electrical force. In fact, it becomes apparent that this interactive effect becomes *the very definition of similarity.* That is, it's only because they affect each other that it can be said that they have a similarity. If a new particle comes along that is affected by the electron, we say that it has an electrical property too, and thus it is in this way *similar* to the electron. What's really true is simply that there is some way that they affect each other. The concept of *similarity* captures that they have an interactive *effect*. This describes the *similarity* part of how *sim/dif* applies to interacting objects, but what about the *difference* part of *sim/dif*?

The difference part is pretty easy actually. Think back to the example of the two cars that you are familiar with. They were *distinguishable* from each other by their *differences*. And the duck was *detectable* because of the *difference* it made to the light it reflected that reached your eyes, and the *difference* it made to your finger when you pressed on it. The electron is *detectable* because of the *difference* it makes on the proton, and other electrically charged particles. The *difference* is nothing more nor less than the *interactive **effect*** itself that something has on the world around it. Several times now we have stated that having an *effect* is the criteria we use for determining that something *exists*. If something doesn't make a *difference*, then it simply doesn't *exist*, and this is the same as saying that something only exists as its effect. It has to make a difference in something in order to have an effect on the world around it that makes it detectable.

This is also true for the effects things have on your mind and perception. To have an effect on your perception, they must make a difference in it. They must change it somehow. You only detect a duck flying against the sky because of its *difference* from the sky. If it made no difference, you wouldn't see it. Now we have already said that your brain creates abstractions of things based on the similarity of things, and that all of these similarities between things are abstractions too. For example, the abstraction for *bird* is composed of the abstractions for feet, wings, bills, etc. We have already seen that abstractions are abstractions of the effects that something, say a duck, has on your mind, and we have just seen that effects are really differences. Putting all this together, abstractions are really abstractions of the differences that real world objects, say ducks, make in your mind. At the same time, though, we also said that abstractions were like a list of all those characteristics that were *similar* among the objects represented by the abstraction.

Don't let this confuse you. An abstracted mental category is created from the effect of something on your mind, from the *difference* that something made. But several objects may all have the *same* effect, make the same difference, and this is how they are similar, and this is what triggers the abstraction in the first place. So quite literally, several objects, say a blue car and a red car, may make *similar differences*. This mixing of similarity and difference only gets confusing because our unconscious brain is so nimble and adept with them, that it is constantly working with differences in differences, differences in similarities, similarities of differences, and similarities of similarities. As long as we don't try to consciously think about it, our brains aren't confused at all.

When I first began thinking about the concepts of similarity and difference, I came to the table imagining that whatever else they were, they were opposites. If someone had asked me what the opposite of *similarity* was, I would have replied immediately that *difference* was the opposite. Upon scrutiny, though, they aren't opposites at all. They both refer to the interactive effect one thing has on another, the same interactive effect. In its simplest form, it appears that similarities identify realms, and differences are actual values on realms, but this all becomes very confusing very quickly. For example, the realm on which the measurable differences occur that evince the electromagnet realm, is always a different realm, frequently the realm of location. It becomes even more confusing, almost indecipherably confusing, in that frequently realms themselves may be compared for differences.

But the only way we know of anything is by the difference it makes. Let's think about that. That means that the only information we ever get about the outside world is not from knowledge of the object itself, but from the difference it makes, and this goes for that electron as well as what's going on in your head. Now a "difference" is kind of an abstract thing. It is not the thing itself, but the way the thing affects the world around it, the disturbance that it makes. The only information we get about that cardinal sitting outside the window is the disturbance it makes in the light that strikes it. You actually never see the cardinal, only the disturbance it causes in the light it reflects. The only information we can get about an electron or a proton is the disturbance that one makes on the other. We have no *direct* evidence that the electron exists. We call the disturbance that it makes an electron. We have no *direct* evidence that the cardinal exists either, only the disturbance it makes. It turns out that the idea of direct evidence is a fallacy. All information about the world is indirect whether cardinals or electrons. All information is only of disturbances. When these disturbances are sensed by our senses and make it all the way into our brains, the *group of neurons* they activate become the symbols themselves that represent this information. These symbols are then sorted according to sim/dif and our minds, whatever they are, decode them into the symbols we experience. Then, somehow, we *experience* seeing a cardinal.

Symbols:

Now these symbols in our brains, these patterns of activated neurons, include our abstractions, and as we saw earlier, our abstractions are very closely linked to our words. We in fact use words as tags or labels for our abstractions. We use words as tags or labels for our *instantiated* abstractions as well, words like *Edith*, or *that cardinal*. Words in fact act as tags or labels to any and all of our mental concepts. Words are a way of reducing all of those abstractions, all of those networks of activated neurons, each concept we have, to a single reference point. It's a handle with which we can instantly locate and pull up vast amounts of information associated with that concept. When we see or hear the word *pumpkin*, we immediately think of the orange gourd, Halloween, and everything else associated with it. When we see or hear the word *Elvira* we immediately think of that sultry, sexy, ghoulish vamp from TV, her décolletage, and everything else that comes with her. (Or at least I do.) A word, in fact, is a symbol for all that it stands for. When I type words on this page, each word has a vast amount of mental information behind it, and with just a few letters, I can make what is happening in my mind happen in yours too.

A *symbol* is something that stands for something else. It is not the thing that it stands for. The words "cherry pie" is the symbol for that wonderful baked object that comes out of an oven and tastes delicious. There's a big difference between an actual cherry pie and its word symbol "cherry pie." If one were trying to communicate in sign language, one might hold up a cherry pie and point at it when one wanted to say something about a cherry pie. If we needed to actually have every object we were talking about in order to refer to it, communication would be very awkward and difficult indeed. We, however, can talk about things because we have words that act as symbols for those things that we want to talk about. Another symbol familiar to us is our flag, which in the United States at least, stands for the people, the *freedom* from excessive governmental control over us, and the ideals that are the United States. Another symbol is money, which is the symbol for the value and worth of such things as work and property. The paper and ink that is money itself has no value at all, and the study of why a worthless piece of paper can symbolize value is the concern of economics.

Symbols are so convenient to use, that we use them a great deal in thinking. Many people claim to think in words, and only minimally reference the massively complex concepts or abstractions behind the words while thinking. The existence of these massively complex concepts, which the word symbols represent so simply, is what is behind many thinkers believing that computers will never achieve true understanding. They are what give meaning and relevance to our words. Without them, we are left with simply meaningless symbols.

These thinkers believe that a computer, which is programmed to simply manipulate words and language correctly (called a Turing machine), might appear to an observer to have intelligence and understanding, but without access to the concepts behind the words, there is no intelligence or understanding. I agree…but now you're confused because I stated quite explicitly earlier that I thought understanding (sans the human feeling) was quite achievable by machines. The only conclusion you can make from this is that I believe that those complex concepts behind the words can be programmed in, and programmed to work just like they do in our minds. The trick will be of course programming those abstractions, and abstractions within abstractions. Discovering the structure and representation of knowledge is a difficult task, but major insights have occurred in the last decade or so. Many of these have been captured and implemented in the latest object oriented programming (oop) languages.

The world as symbols:

No matter how deep we look, information about things is represented by something else, something other that the thing itself. Remember that we are only able to detect objects by the difference they make in some realm like light, from the disturbances they cause. Most disturbances we detect are more accurately characterized as a collection of disturbances, but this collection may be considered a single disturbance for most practical reasons. The myriad light rays reflected from a cardinal is a fine example. The point is that this disturbance becomes a symbol that represents the cardinal. The light reflected from a cardinal and traveling toward your eye is not the cardinal itself, any more than the *word cardinal* is the cardinal itself. Both represent the cardinal, and are symbols for the cardinal, i.e., neither is a cardinal itself. Information about something it turns out is always just a symbolic representation of, or for, that thing. It is never the thing itself.

Information is always conveyed by way of symbols. The symbols may be disturbances in light waves, disturbances in protons, activated networks of neurons, or just words for something, but it is never the thing itself. At some point, the thing itself begins to shimmer, to lose its reality. Its reality becomes suspect if we realize that we never directly perceive it, never know it directly. All we ever know of is only a disturbance that we attribute to something being there. The brain then takes all the information it receives through the senses, and converts that already symbolic information into new representations, new symbols, which it proceeds to manipulate. These new symbols are simply our perceptions of the world, and this is what we call thinking.

Mathematics is all symbols too. All those numbers, plus and minus signs, equals signs, and parentheses are just marks on a piece of paper. The numbers are symbols for quantities, but are not the quantities themselves. The old Roman Numeral III actually uses three lines to represent the quantity three, but most symbols for numbers are just marks. Learning to do mathematics was considered hard by many of us who had to take algebra in high school. (At least it was for me.) It required lots and lots of thinking, and it wasn't easy thinking. It had to be figured out. There was so much understanding required. It, therefore, was something of a surprise to me to realize that algebra can be performed correctly without any thinking at all. Algebra, and indeed all of mathematics and arithmetic, does what it does by symbol manipulation. Symbol manipulation involves nothing more than changing one set of symbols to another set of symbols according to certain rules. One does not even need to know what the symbols stand for or why they are doing it.

That mathematics can be reduced to simply dumb symbol manipulation was marveled at centuries ago, but it has really become obvious with the advent of computers and hand held calculators. As a child, you spent a great deal of time memorizing those old now familiar addition and multiplication tables. What you were really doing was memorizing the *symbol conversion tables* that are used for addition and multiplication. If you saw the symbol pattern, 2 x 3, you would follow the rule to look in the row marked **2** and column marked **3** of the multiplication table, and you would discover the symbol **6** sitting there. You then memorized the first ten rows and first ten columns of this table, and after a lifetime of *familiarity* with it, you feel like you *understand* why, but actually you don't really care. All you really care about when somebody asks, "what's 7 x 8?" is coming up with the symbol **56**. A computer is able to do multiplication too by looking up the symbol conversions in the multiplication table without ever knowing why, or even knowing what a number is. Of course, it can perform algebra and all higher mathematics in a similar way. It looks for certain combinations of symbols, and when it finds one, it uses some rule to convert it to a new combination of symbols. In the end, all mathematics can be reduced to its symbols and its manipulation rules, changing one pattern of symbols into another pattern of symbols.

In order to capture the sheer mindlessness of this idea, Douglas Hofstadter, in his book *Gödel, Escher, and Bach, An Eternal Golden Braid,* called it all just *typographical operations*. Imagine for a minute a newspaper typesetter machine that does nothing but set type for a printing machine. In principle, this machine could easily be set up to replace certain patterns of letters and numbers when encountered with other letters and numbers. To it, there is no meaning behind the marks it makes whatsoever. Yet this machine can in principle perform any and all mathematical operations.

Now for the last several centuries, scientists using the scientific method, and measurements, have been reducing just about all of science to mathematics. Things like quantum physics are pure mathematics with no mental foothold in our ordinary world at all. The only thing we know about quantum physics is what its mathematics tells us, but mathematics, at its base we now realize, is simply symbol manipulation. That means that these symbols and their rules of manipulation have somehow captured the universe as described by the Formal paradigm and quantum physics.

It is something of a surprise, then, to discover that the objects and behavior of the universe too can be reduced to symbols and rules of their manipulation. Any time a new phenomenon of physics is discovered, the race is on to discover how it can be represented, duplicated, using just the rules of symbol manipulation, and when we have succeeded, we say that we *understand* it, that we have a model for it.

We have seen several examples of how new methods, developed to mimic reality in one paradigm, take on a greater reality and become the foundation for the next paradigm. Will symbol manipulation become the basis of reality in our next paradigm? A few centuries ago the clock mechanism provided the foundation for the clockwork like mechanistic paradigm. Will the typesetter machine become the new mechanism that best describes the universe? Has it already?

That symbol manipulation is becoming recognized as important to our description of reality shouldn't come as too great a surprise if you think about it. After all, that's exactly what we are doing in our heads all day long. Our mind creates symbols for the universe from the Morse code like dots and dashes it receives as encoded information from our sense organs, and we begin learning the behavior of these mental representations on the day we're born. Mathematics and our minds both manipulate the world as symbols. What *is* surprising (and scary) about it all is that the two don't always agree, and this begs the question, "Which one is the more real?" Which set of symbols is the real reality, the ones we perceive in our minds, or the ones we represent with mathematics? We will be examining these differences much more deeply shortly.

This difference between our mental and mathematical representations of the world is nowhere experienced more profoundly than when physics students are first exposed to it. As people learning modern physics move from their daily frame of reference to the scientific one, from their mental representation to the mathematical logical one, they frequently experience a sensation of oddness. Not only does what they are learning seem very strange, but the reasons behind it become unintuitive. Events occur the way they do in the scientific frame of reference for the simple reason that it would be *illogical* for them to happen some other way. Things happen the way they do because the logic and the numbers declare that they will. The word *because* loses much of its use here, except for referring to principles of logic. The student is moving from the visual, mentally representable universe, to the imageless, abstract one. He is moving to the Formal paradigm where the principles of reality are just the rules for manipulating symbols.

When one has represented something with symbols, one has made an abstraction. The Formal paradigm has moved away from the material world as we are familiar with it, and represents it with symbols, largely mathematical. Although these symbols are man made, many have felt throughout history that they somehow represent the truer reality. They represent a greater reality that exists *behind* the reality of our familiar material world. It was the explicit realization that this process of abstraction was possible, and was actually occurring, that led the ancient Greeks to imagine Logos. The classic example demonstrating this is the principles abstracted from geometric figures, say the triangle.

The Pythagorean Theorem states that for a right triangle, the sum of the squares of the two shorter sides equals the square of the hypotenuse, the longest side. This is a principle that is derivable using pure logic and which is represent-able in symbols as the simple formula, $A^2 + B^2 = C^2$. Now this formula is *perfectly* true only for a perfect right triangle. If the triangle is just *almost* perfect, then the result of applying the Pythagorean Theorem is just *almost* true. It is a close approximation in this case. Well, the kicker is that the perfect right triangle doesn't exist in our real world. With our exquisite technology, we can come within microns of drawing one, maybe even better, but it will never quite be per-fect. And of course, 2000 years ago when they first pondered this, their best trian-gles would have been hopelessly crude by comparison. The idea of a perfect right triangle was quite obviously an *abstraction*. The space in front of you is full of them, but they are imaginary, and have no materiality at all. Yet astonishingly, there are logical principles derivable from this imaginary, non-material world thing, e.g. the Pythagorean Theorem.

There are no perfect principles that apply perfectly to an imperfect real world triangle. Our material world triangle comes to seem just a crude model of this abstract idea. If one asks which came first, the perfect triangle, or the crude real world triangle modeled on it, one is left with the feeling that the abstraction came first, that it is the more basic and has the greater reality. It's not an easy thing to do at first, to let go of the *real* world, and envision an abstract world as the more real.

Now here's a thought. What if we force ourselves to realize that the real world, the one we're used to in our heads, is only represented as mental symbols too, just like the mathematical one. This removes some of the conflict, doesn't it, if *every-thing*, real world as well as triangles, is actually imaginary? This is not a new idea. In fact, this is a basic concept of Zen Buddhism. Zen apparently wants us to bring ourselves to the state of *enlightenment* by way of endless indecipherable rid-dles and head games, but let me save you the trouble. Their endgame is the real-ization that the only things one knows about the world is what one is conscious of. And consciousness is mind. That which makes it into your mind is all that it is possible for you to know. In other words, for each one of us, it's *literally* **all in our mind**!

Chapter 5
Information Based Realities

The rabbit hole went straight down like a tunnel for some way, and then dipped suddenly down, so suddenly that Alice had not a moment to think about stopping herself before she found herself falling down what seemed to be a very deep well.

— *Alice in Wonderland—Lewis Carroll*

Virtual realities:

You walk into the video arcade and discover that there's a new video game in town, one that requires you to put on a helmet. It sounds exciting, so you decide to try it. As you put the helmet on, you notice that there are miniature video screens in front of each eye and built in earphones. You feed your hard earned money into the yawning slot, and suddenly the virtual reality world comes to life.

You are standing on a barren volcanic plain with far off mountains. A pterodactyl soars in the distance. You can hear it screeching as it searches for prey on the ground below. You realize that you are out in the open, completely exposed if it turns and comes flying your way. As you swing your head to look to the left, the motion sensors in the helmet sense your movement, and the driving computer pans the view to the left on the little screens you're viewing. A few yards off you see a huge animal fece, with a pair of sunglasses and a sneaker imbedded in it. Suddenly you hear a noise off to your right so you swing the helmet all the way right. The computer obligingly pans the view all the way to the right for you matching your head's movement. There's a tyrannosaurus rex several hundred yards away. It has obviously just spotted you and is turning to come after you, clearly intent on turning you too into a tyrannosaurus turd. You are caught off guard. This is happening too fast. You weren't ready for this yet. It's not fair at all, but this makes no difference whatsoever. The virtual reality tyrannosaurus is now bearing down on you. You turn left to run away and stupidly encounter the safety restraints. It's too late. You don't know how to run, and don't have time to figure out how. You're still trying to figure out how to work this damn thing when you see the giant teeth close (painlessly) on you and your world goes dark. Suddenly big red letters appear in your head. They say, "*Yum! Yum! Enter money to play again.*"

This is roughly the capability level of virtual reality today. The idea is to use computers to generate as close as possible in you an experience in a pretend world, a world generated by the computer. Currently, the computer is pretty much only capable of giving you the visual and audible portions of this experience. Of course, to be a *totally* realistic experience, it would have to minimally include the rest of your senses as well. One day, if virtual reality improves enough, you might smell the reeking animal dropping before you see it, and you might feel the agony as the giant teeth tear you open as the game ends.

The problem is that the other senses are beyond our current capability, and perhaps always will be. The ability to produce every possible odor seems unrealistic, and to convey the sense of taste at all, one would have to put the taste source in their mouth. This all presumes that we actually need to *create* the odor or the taste, and then use our own sense organs, like our nose or tongue, to sense it.

The information from our sense organs is transmitted from the sense organs to the brain via nerves. The optic nerve, for example, transfers the visual information received in the eye back to the brain where it is perceived as vision. This suggests a potentially different way of getting computer generated sensory information into the brain. If one could tap into the optic nerve, the computer could stimulate it directly to carry the visual information to the brain, without having to put it out on miniature screens that the eyes then convert to visual information on the optic nerve. The same is true for all of our other senses as well. By tapping into the nerve that carries taste information to the brain, the computer could electronically generate the sensation of every possible taste in your brain and bypass your tongue and taste buds completely. Of course, this would all require some kind of surgery to get you all wired up. Once wired, if this became a standard, all you would have to do is plug yourself into to the next video game to experience a completely realistic virtual reality that could control *all* of your senses.

In 1997, David Deutsch authored his prize-winning book, *The Fabric of Reality*, in which he compares our Formal paradigm reality to a virtual reality, much like the virtual reality described above, only infinitely superior. It is so superior, in fact, that it's the one we *call* reality. In a chapter appropriately entitled *Virtual Reality*, he describes a futuristic scenario of being able to plug a human brain directly into a computer so the computer can activate the senses by directly stimulating the sensory nerves without having to resort to little TV screens and earphones. He even includes a picture of a reclining man with a cable running from the back of his head to a near by computer.

The matrix:

Soon after that, the movie *Matrix* was released, which was also based on a similar scenario, i.e., people plugged directly into a virtual reality computer. (I do not know which of these efforts began first, or if they were developed independently.) In this movie, the people don't know it, but their real bodies exist in pods filled with liquid. Tubes inserted into their throats provide them with nutrients and air, but they are of course completely unaware of this. In order to make this work, cables are plugged into their brains, spinal cords, and elsewhere that provide all of the sensory input to their sensory nerves, overriding all other senses coming in from the sense organs of their real bodies. They cannot see the world of their pods, nor feel the liquid they're submerged in, because their senses are overridden by the computer. This gives the computer the access it needs to itself supply the complete span of sensory experience to their brains and minds. The computer then provides them with artificially generated sensory input based on a completely artificial world, a virtual reality. They see, hear, feel, smell, and taste a completely nonexistent, complete world.

All the millions of people in the pods are networked together, just like office computers today. In today's office networks, the network server, the master computer, sends information to any computer in the office. The receiving computer then processes the information, and sends its response back to the master computer. This information in turn is then processed at the master computer and the result sent back to the office computer. Back and forth, each processing and responding to the information sent by the other.

In the Matrix environment, the master computer sends sensory information to the brain of any person in their pod. That person then reacts to this new sensory input, and their reactions are picked up by the computer plug-ins and sent back to the master computer. For example, the master computer may send someone the visual sensory information of a stick flying at him. The person sees a stick flying at him, so he throws up his arm to protect himself. His motor impulse attempting to throw up his arm is intercepted by the plug-ins, so in the pod the arm never moves, but the computer receives this information, calculates the correct movement of the arm, and sends back the sensory information of the arm moving. The person actually sees and feels his virtual arm moving just the way he thought he moved it, moving up to block the stick. The person cannot tell that his real arm, the arm on his body in the pod, never moved. He saw and felt his arm move in the virtual reality after all. He is actually driving the virtual body in the virtual reality through the computer as if it were his own body. The computer intercepts his actions, and applies them to the virtual body for him. The fact is, what he is perceiving as his body, and indeed his entire material world, doesn't exist at all, but he doesn't know the difference.

Besides maintaining the whole virtual environment, say a city, the master computer maintains a virtual body for each person in the pods, and this virtual body is completely controlled by the brain and mind of the person in the pod as if it were their own. If they look in the mirror, they see a being they take to be themselves. In fact, neither the mirror nor their being exist, but are generated in their brain by the driving computer. In the movie, the being that they see and control is a carbon copy of their body in the pod, but in fact it need not look like them at all. It need not even be human for that matter.

They see, hear, and converse with other people. These other people they see are the computer generated images of other people also in pods plugged into the computer. The minds of the people in the pods are able to interact with one another physically and via conversations passed through the computer in the virtual environment. The computer continuously keeps track of where everyone is and what everyone is doing in the virtual world, and keeps everyone supplied with this sensory information in real time. If you see a friend of yours, you are able to walk your virtual body over to them and shake each other's hand. The computer has sensors buried deep within your brain via the plug in the back of your head, so when you go to speak to your friend, these sensors pick up the motor impulses that would ordinarily generate speech in your body. The computer then processes them, moves your pharynx, larynx, and mouth accordingly, and sends out the audio sense of hearing your words and voice to everyone within hearing distance. The seeming material manifestation of these people, indeed the entire material world you experience, doesn't exist at all. And there's absolutely no way for you to tell the difference.

Or is there?

What about science? In our world, it is the job of scientists to first determine the behavior of the world, and second to explain why and how it behaves the way it does. What will the scientists find when they run their experiments in the virtual reality? Remember that the master computer that generates everything they perceive will be producing the results of the experiments too, and then sending them the sensory information of these results. The humans they meet on the street need be little more than empty shells that the computer is manipulating, but we will assume that the computer universe mimics our universe to a much deeper level than that. When a pathologist performs an autopsy on someone, instead of a hollow shell they will find a body filled with organs, composed of cells made from proteins, etc. People will die from virtual hearts that fail, and virtual cancer, just like in our world. When brain researchers open someone's skull and insert electrodes into the exposed brain, that virtual brain will be composed of bundles of neurons, the activity of which is closely related to what the person in the pod is feeling and thinking. But just how deep down will the virtual world go? *There will be a bottom level* below which the virtual reality does not need to go.

The same is true for physics. Will scientists discover that all matter is composed of atoms? If so, what will the experimental results coming out of the atom smashers show? Will they find protons, neutrons, and electrons, or will the computer not bother to go that deep? The behavior of matter need not even be consistent in the virtually reality like it is in the real universe. As we saw in the movie, the computer can even alter the immediate past to allow it to create a different future. Remember the deja vu scene with the black cat. And what about computer science? The computers themselves will be composed of virtual stuff that is itself computer generated. Will the computer scientists be able to detect anomalies in the basic operations of their computers that reveal that their computers are themselves computer driven?

When examining the foundations of their reality, scientists will discover characteristics that are artifacts of its computerized origins. Will the clues they find as to the structure of their reality allow them to deduce that they are inside of a computer generated, virtual reality. These and other questions will be addressed further throughout the book.

It is imperative to understanding much of the rest of this book that the reader has a good grasp on the behavior and consequences of living in a virtual environment like that mentioned in David Deutsch's book *The Fabric of Reality*, and as portrayed in the movie *Matrix*. To bring the reader to this understanding, I have selected several scenes from the movie *Matrix* that frequently are not understood, and will provide the explanation for the reader's edification.

In the movie the *Matrix*, the virtual reality that is created by the computer is called the Matrix. When we say that a person is *in the Matrix*, it means that they are plugged into the computer and they are conscious only of the computer generated virtual reality. Everything in the Matrix is generated by the computer.

FAQs:

How did they get the girl with the white rabbit on her shoulder to lead Neo to the nightclub?

Remember that Neo is plugged into the Matrix, so his world is being generated by the computer. With their computer system in the Nebuchadnezzar, Morpheus' crew is able to tap into the Matrix and watch what is going on. They knew that the girl with the white rabbit on her shoulder was coming to his door and that they were going to invite him to a nightclub. This allowed them to tell him beforehand to "follow the white rabbit," and for Trinity to herself enter the Matrix and be waiting for him at the nightclub.

How did they make his mouth disappear?

Remember, this is a virtual reality. The computer is controlling everything about his virtual body, including his working mouth when it is working. The computer simply switched his mouth to one that perhaps had grown shut and then continuously provided him with this sensory feedback.

How did Neo have the experience of having the bug implanted into his abdomen and then in the middle of the experience find himself waking up?

The Matrix is a computer generated virtual reality, not the real world. The computer controls all of his sensory input, and thus his experiences, and it simply switched his sensory input from the experience he was having to the experience of just waking up in his own bed.

How did taking the red pill allow Neo to exit the Matrix?

Morpheus explains that the red pill is part of a trace program designed to disrupt Neo's input/output signal so they can pinpoint his location. Remember first of all that at that point they are still inside the Matrix, that is, they are experiencing a virtual reality. Neo's real body is still in his pod. This Matrix computer is keeping track of everybody in the Matrix, and knows what he or she is doing. Morpheus and gang have the capability of tapping into the Matrix program using their own computers, so what they have done is started a little independent program that scans for someone taking this particular red pill. Remember, the pill is represented in the computer as information too. When their program, which is searching for someone taking their red pill, finds that someone, it causes the Matrix to start relinquishing control of that person's body and brain to the trace program. The person experiences those parts of his body for which i/o has been interrupted, for which he is no longer receiving sensory input from the Matrix, as cold and silvery. When the Matrix program has lost all contact with Neo, it then auto-disconnects his apparently dead body from the system, and flushes it away to where Morpheus and the Nebuchadnezzar are now waiting to retrieve him.

How come Neo can learn new skills and information so fast?

The plug-in in the back of his head is meticulously interconnected throughout his brain, and is able to run his experience of training on any subject at super high speeds. The computer is not limited to the information transfer speeds of the everyday material world where a class might be spread over ten or twelve hours, and over a semester.

How can they be so much stronger in the Matrix than they actually are?

The plug-in in the back of their head intercepts the motor impulses that the brain is sending to the arms and the legs. This impulse is then received at the Matrix master computer and converted into the actions that the person's virtual body takes. In the real world, a person's strength is limited by his brain impulse and the actual strength of his muscles that must be built up, but in the Matrix, it is simply limited by the brain generated impulse that the Matrix computer receives. If someone learns to send motor impulses as if he is much stronger than he is, the computer will cause his virtual body to behave accordingly, and in the Matrix, the effect the computer generates will be that he is very strong.

How can they learn to move so much faster in the Matrix than in the real world?

The brain has learned from a lifetime of experience that the material world body's arms and legs only move so fast. This need not be the case in the Matrix since the computer will cause the arms and legs on the virtual body to move as fast as the brain now dictates. Their speed of motion is no longer limited by material reality. When one realizes this, he can learn to move much faster, potentially as fast as his brain can generate the motor signals. If a person has an extremely fast brain, he may reach speeds that resemble computer speeds.

Why are the phones necessary for them to get out of the Matrix?

It is possible for the members of Morpheus' team to enter and exit the Matrix. They have their own plug-in system that they can use to plug themselves in and then exit back out again. This private system of theirs that can tap into the Matrix needs to locate them within the Matrix system before it can extract them, or safely delete them, from the Matrix. The few phones known to their system are similar in function to that of the red pill, and provides their computer a means of locating their information in the Matrix computer. It locates them in the Matrix by using these few select telephones, which is why they need to be connected by one of the few telephones that their system knows about. It then deletes them safely from the Matrix.

Why do they die if their virtual body dies?

The plug-in in the back of their heads is intimately connected throughout their brains and bodies. The Matrix computer is able to cause their deaths and stop all nervous system activity in the real body when the virtual body dies, thus causing death in the material body itself.

Why do people not die then in their practice environment?

Their practice environments were programmed by themselves and were not plugged into the Matrix. So their practice virtual reality was programmed so that the environment itself would not cause deadly trauma to the virtual body, as when they programmed the street in such a way that a falling body would bounce rather than splatter. Also, I'm sure they simply programmed their practice environments not to kill the real body if the virtual body should die.

What are the sentient beings?

In the movie, the Matrix contained sentient beings that were not connected to human bodies anywhere, but were in fact simply Artificial Intelligence programs. They were of course not limited to the constraints of the real world, and were able to move at computer speeds and with extreme strength. They can move as fast as bullets, for example, because the computer moves both them and the bullets. The flip side of this is that they are limited to only that which their program provides them. Humans on the other hand have no such limitations and this is why Neo was eventually able to outperform them. These programs had minds and feelings just like people, a phenomenon that is not elaborated further in the movie. The minds of the rest of the virtual people in the movie are of course provided by the minds in the bodies in the pods.

How does the kid bend the spoon?

In the movie, it is possible for a mind to control more than just his body. One way that this might occur is that if the computer plug-ins are tightly enough coupled to a persons brain, what the mind imagines may be picked up by the computer and actualized in the Matrix just like a person's motor responses. If the kid is able to somehow communicate to the computer that he is perceiving the spoon bending, the computer will obliging send out the sensory information of the spoon bending. This ability obviously occurs only rarely in the brains plugged into the Matrix.

How does Neo take control of the sentient, and how does he become all powerful in the Matrix?

Neo obviously has the same ability as the kid bending the spoon to send his perceptions to the Matrix computer, only more so. The Matrix computer then dutifully recreates his perception in the virtual reality. He would, therefore, be able to take over the sentient by first perceiving himself doing so. The computer would then assign him the sentient's program along with all of its computer resources.

Why do the mouths in their real bodies bleed when they are, say, struck in their virtual mouth in the Matrix?

I dunno. This phenomenon is not occurring in the matrix, but in their real world bodies. Or is it perhaps because, unknown to us, their *real* bodies are actually virtual bodies too, only in the next higher level virtual universe?

Later in the book we will be referring to a virtual reality environment very similar to that referred to by David Deutsch and the movie *Matrix*. It will be somewhat simpler though than the *Matrix*. It will not be run by machines fulfilling a malevolent purpose. In fact, it will be almost identical to that envisioned by David Deutsch that runs the universe at a very low microscopic level, and all higher level phenomena result from this lower level. There will not be unexplained Artificial Intelligence sentient beings in it. In fact, it will not include or require Artificial Intelligence at all. People in it will not have extraordinary strength, speed, or powers, like the ability to bend spoons. It will in fact be a rather ordinary universe (if there is such a thing). It will be a dumb programmable computer, although *infinitely* more advanced and powerful than today's computers, and it will attempt to mimic our universe as closely as possible.

This futuristic virtual reality will serve several purposes for the reader. We will be following creatures who "live" inside of it, who are studying the nature of their virtual world, and we will see what weird results their investigations and experiments reveal about it. And we will use it to discover some of the programming considerations that are required to program a working universe inside of a computer.

Section 2
What's the Matter With Matter?

○ ○

...when a person is forced to change a basic belief or viewpoint, the brain undergoes a series of nervous sensations equivalent to the most agonizing torture.

—Sidney Madwed

Chapter 6
The Strange Universe

Not only is the universe stranger than we imagine,
it is stranger than we can imagine.

—*Sir Arthur Eddington, (1882–1944)*

Matter:

What is matter? Matter is the *stuff,* the substance in the world around us. It is, for the most part, the stuff we can *feel* and *see*. It is the chair you're sitting in. It is the cardinal sitting outside the window. Your physical, human body is composed of matter, as is the body of your mate. It is the Earth itself, the Moon, the Sun, the stars. It is everything we feel and see. Sometimes matter is hard to see, or you can't see it at all. In this case, we have to know it's there by feel. That plate glass window that we walked into earlier is one example. The air is another.

> Who can see a hurricane force wind?
> Neither you nor I.
> But when it knocks you to the ground,
> you *feel* it passing by.

There is another common way to detect matter, and that is by its weight. This is also the way we tell how much matter we have. Joe Sumo over there who weighs 300 pounds has three times as much matter in his body as Buttercup, his poor little 100 pound wife. He's also three times as big, but size alone is not always a good indicator of the amount of matter in an object.

Even though they have the identical size, a one inch cube of gold weighs about 20 times as much as a one inch block of wood. That means there's about 20 times as much matter inside of a piece of gold as there is inside of an equal sized piece of wood. Scientists who want to know how much matter is in an object don't use its *weight* directly like we do, but something called *mass* that is closely related to weight. Just like weight, Joe Sumo still has three times the mass of his diminutive wife, Buttercup. For the sake of accuracy, we will henceforth for the most part refer to the amount of matter in objects as its *mass*. So gold has about 20 times the *mass* of wood for equal sized pieces.

As an aside, gold has so much mass that it's *almost twice as heavy as lead*, and thus is a pain in the rear to move around. When you see those guys handling those big ingots of gold on TV...nuh-uh. They'd be struggling much more than is usually portrayed, if they could move them at all. Imagine the comic relief these movie writers are passing up having frustrated robbers, say, at first thinking that the gold had been glued down, then discovering that they have to resort to extraordinary means just to move their loot. Just ten or fifteen of those big ingots in the trunk of their getaway car would blow the tires, break the springs, and in the right car, raise the front wheels off the ground and up into the air. Imagine them standing there, hands on hips, trying to figure out what to do now.

Besides its weight, mass gives us two other ways to measure the quantity of matter in an object. These are its momentum and its gravitational attraction. If we send our cube of gold flying into a wall at 100 miles/hr, it will hit the wall much harder than the block of wood flying at the same speed. In fact, it will hit the wall 20 times harder. Measuring this gives an accurate measure of the mass of an object. The other means of measuring an objects mass is to measure its gravitational force. Most people already know that the bigger an object, the greater its gravitational force. The gravitational attraction of the Earth for example, is about six times greater than that of the Moon, because the Earth is much bigger, much more *massive* than the Moon.

Our cube of gold has a gravitational attraction too on objects around it and although small, very precise instruments have been created that can measure it. Doubling the size of our cube of gold will double the mass in it, and also double its gravitational attraction. Since two objects attract each other gravitationally, one convenient method of measuring their mass is to put a spring between them and measure how much the spring is compressed as their mutual gravitational attraction pulls them together.

This is of course a description of how your bathroom scale works, so whenever you step on your bathroom scale, what's really being measured is the gravitational attraction between you and the Earth. An objects *weight* is just its gravitational attraction to the planet you're standing on, and of course varies from planet to planet. Because Joe Sumo is three times as massive as Buttercup, his attraction to the Earth is three times greater than hers, and the measurement of his weight will be three times greater.

As for the matter in the world around us, it is possible to break, crush, grind, powder, and otherwise divide any particular kind of matter into a smallest possible piece. That is, there is a smallest possible piece into which any kind of matter can be divided, glass for instance, and still be a particle of glass. The ancient Greeks hypothesized that this was the case (although they never proved it), and called this smallest possible particle of matter the atom. We call them *molecules* and *atoms* today, molecules being made up of aggregates of atoms.

Among his many accomplishments, Einstein was one of the people who helped prove *finally* that atoms *exist* circa 1905. It was obviously no simple task demonstrating that atoms exist since it took the brilliance of someone like Einstein to do it, and the reason is that atoms are so incredibly tiny. They are so much smaller than light waves that they can't reflect light, which is how we see things, so we can't see them even with a microscope, because microscopes use light. As pointed out earlier, the only way we know that something *exists* is by some *effect* it has, so if it doesn't reflect light, we need some other effect by which to detect it. The one used by Einstein was a well known phenomenon called Brownian motion. If one looks through a high-powered microscope at very tiny particles, they are seen to jiggle and dance about, called Brownian motion. Einstein was able to prove mathematically that this jiggling was caused by the impact of atoms and molecules bouncing off of these extremely tiny particles, thus demonstrating that atoms and molecules actually exist.

Interestingly, sciences like chemistry and physics had relied on the ideas of atoms and molecules for some time prior to 1905. Even though no one had proved they existed, scientists knew full well that the microworld worked as if they existed, and the mathematics that described the microworld used the concepts of atoms. Just because the mathematics of atoms worked well, however was not sufficient to assume that they really existed, and the idea was circulating that the *mental model* of atoms was just a mental crutch to help us imagine what was going on, and that atoms didn't need to exist at all. You will recall that this had recently been the fate of the idea of tubes of force that allowed the mind to imagine forces like gravity and magnetism acting at a distance. So there was something of a paradigm conflict in progress between those who thought atoms were real and those who thought that atoms were just imaginary. The staunch atomist Ludwig Boltzmann poor soul, mistakenly believing that he had lost, committed suicide over it all. You will note that this is in fact a conflict between the atomist and the Formal paradigm. The Formal paradigm recall elevates the mathematics to the highest reality and doesn't require the material reality of atoms at all.

If there's a lot of space between the atoms and molecules of a substance, that substance is compressible. Most solids and liquids are only very slightly compressible, because their atoms and molecules are very close together already, but gases, like air, are very compressible because their atoms and molecules are not held to each other and can be very far apart. If you compress the molecules of a gas until they are close enough together, the gas too will become a liquid, and will not compress much further. The compressed gases of liquid oxygen (LOX) and liquid nitrogen can be found at most hospitals, and liquid carbon dioxide can be found in CO_2 fire extinguishers. Examples that are perhaps closer to home are butane lighters, propane, and LPG (liquefied petroleum gas), which are all gases compressed until their molecule are very close together and they become liquids.

For convenience, we frequently divide the universe into two areas of consideration, the microworld and the macroworld, based on size. The microworld encompasses everything that is very, very small, smaller than large molecules, about the size of the atoms and smaller. The macroworld encompasses everything larger than molecules, on up to the size of the universe itself. Molecules bridge the microworld and the macroworld, some being small enough to be considered microworld, and some being so large as to be considered macroworld. There is another reason besides just size for creating this division, though, and that is that these two parts of the universe exhibit strikingly different behavior. The behavior of the microworld is dictated by the realm of quantum physics, which can be wonderfully unintuitive. The macroworld on the other hand is the universe we live in and are familiar with, since our bodies fall within the range of being bigger than molecules, and smaller than the whole universe.

There is one other characteristic that marks the division between the macroworld and the microworld, and that is that the macroworld is all that we perceive. We are unable to perceive microworld phenomena, and their effect must be elevated to macroworld before we can detect them. That is the only way we know of them.

The strange macroworld:

But its not just the microworld that can behave wonderfully unintuitively, but the macroworld as well, especially when one considers what the math is telling us must be true. This section is going to introduce the reader to the odd behavior of the macroworld, but is by no means going to force you to wade through a whole bunch of boring physics. On the contrary, it will display only what's weird, strange, and interesting about the macroworld. This chapter is called *The Strange Universe*, after all.

The first couple of examples are also going to demonstrate *very briefly* what I mean when I keep saying that it all drops out of the math and logic. It's there only for illustrative purposes and after these two examples, there's no more math…so don't despair. I don't want you to memorize or learn any of this. All I want you to do is enjoy the stuff that feels weird to you, and particularly anything that seems impossible to you. I think it's important that I emphasize this. Some of what you're about to see will seem *impossible* to your mind! Your first impulse will be to feel that you don't understand it. Don't let this stop you or even slow you down. It's not so much that you don't understand it as it is that your mind is unable to twist that way, that you're normal. My advice is to try to learn to enjoy the sensation of discovering that something is true that seems impossible to the normal human mind.

One of the first oddities of the universe that was realized is that there is no such thing as what you might call a *permanent place*, or even a *same place*. By this I mean that you can never claim from one moment to the next that something is in the same place that it was. I know you are sitting there reading this and thinking you are in the same place you were a moment ago, but you're not. The place you're sitting is actually moving very rapidly. The Earth is turning at 1000 miles/hr at the equator, or closer to 700 miles/hr if you're located near the mid latitudes. The Earth is orbiting the Sun at 60,000 miles/hr. The Sun is orbiting the center of the Milky Way galaxy, and all the galaxies are moving in space relative to each other. Everything in the universe is moving relative to everything else, and it turns out there is no place, no spot out there, not even in principle, that is staying in the *same place*.

That's not yet the good stuff, however. The fact is that there is not only no thing out there that is staying in the same place, *there is no spot out there in space that is staying in the same place*. Now at first you might think that it should be possible to go back to the same place you were, say, one second ago, but that's not possible either, and it's not just because we don't have a way to figure out where we were or how fast we're moving. It turns out that there is no such absolute place in the universe as where you were one second ago.

We've all had the experience of sitting in a stopped vehicle when we suddenly realize that everything around us has started to move, only to discover a moment later that it was us that was moving. The first impression it turns out, the impression that everything else was moving, has a certain legitimacy to it. The way our minds deal with the chaos of everything moving is to always consider ourselves to be at rest and consider everything else to be in motion. Since, as you'll see in a moment, it turns out that locations in space are really arbitrary, it doesn't matter if you consider yourself in motion or standing still, so it's quite convenient to consider yourself to be sitting in the same place from one moment to the next even though there's really no such thing. The common terminology for all this, that there is no such thing as a constant place in space, is to say that there is no such thing as *absolute space*.

Now I've been harping for some time how it's the mathematics that force us to accept all the weird stuff that's being discovered, so let me demonstrate how that happens here with a really simple example. If you don't like math, then don't worry about it, but you might want to just read along anyway since I'm doing my best to make it fun and easy.

A car on the interstate traveling at 80 miles per hour will go how far in one hour? (Everybody goes 80 these days, right?) Since *80 miles per hour* means the car will travel 80 miles in one hour, the answer is that the car will travel 80 miles. Now, how far will the same car travel in two hours? You multiply your original answer by 2 and come up with 160 miles as your new answer. Now how far will a car going 71 miles per hour go if he drives non-stop for 12 hours. To get this answer, you multiply how fast the car is going by how many hours he drives, that is 71 x 12, and you come up with 852 miles. This method of solving the problem can be captured in the statement that

> the distance traveled by a car equals its speed multiplied by the travel time.

This can be reduced to what's called the distance formula, i.e.,

$$distance = speed \times time$$

To find the distance something traveled, simply multiply the speed by the travel time. This is nothing but the old distance formula you saw in middle school or high school, and it's all we need to demonstrate the lack of absolute space.

So let's take our driver off the interstate and put him driving a spaceship in outer space where he can relax back in his chair, put his feet up on the console, and watch what's going on outside. Now, since there is no such thing as absolute space, he feels like, and can legitimately consider himself to be sitting perfectly still and not moving at all. Now just like the on interstate, let's add another spaceship driver going the other way, and let's say he's traveling the other way at

68 miles per hour, a speed that, coincidentally, means he is moving at *100 feet per second*. But since there's no absolute space, there's no way to tell who's sitting still and who's moving, so this new driver also has the right to consider himself as sitting perfectly still. The first thing that happens as the two spaceships are approaching each other is that they each think that they are the one sitting perfectly still, and that the other guy is approaching at a speed of 100 feet per second. And of course they're both right, but when we apply our little distance formula, it has an interesting consequence.

Let's say that in his perpetual boredom, one of the drivers has taken up the habit of bouncing a tennis ball off of the floor, always bouncing it in exactly the same spot, and timing it so that each bounce hits the floor exactly one second apart. Now to him, he's not moving, so his speed is zero, and if we use the distance formula to see how far the spot where he is bouncing his ball has moved, we get the trivial result from *distance = speed x time* that

$$distance = 0 \text{ x } 1 \text{ sec,}$$

so distance = 0. In other words, the place where he is bouncing the ball hasn't moved at all and is always in the same place…but what about the other guy. He thinks he's the one who's standing still and the bouncing tennis ball is traveling past him at 100 feet per second, so applying our little formula from his point of view as to where the spot the ball bounces, he gets

$$distance = 100 \text{ x } 1,$$

so the distance between two bounces is 100 ft, and is not the same place at all. You see that the two points that are the *same place* for one guy are *100 ft apart* for the other guy, and this is how the mathematics shows us that there is no such thing as a same place, or absolute space for everybody. As you can see, ***it's all relative*** to where you're sitting and how fast the other guy's moving, so this became known as the *Principle of Relativity*, which is not yet to be confused with Einstein's *Theory of Relativity*.

There's something very different about the two universes these guys perceive. In one, the spot where the ball bounces is the exact same place, and in the other it's two different spots 100 feet apart. It's almost as if each of us drags our own universe around with us, our own space, so everybody lives in slightly different universes. At this point, do you observe your mind refusing to accept this? If you feel this is a little too weird to accept, you're in good company. Sir Isaac Newton, the guy who came up with the laws of motion, knew that this was a consequence of his work, but could simply never buy it. His mind, pretty much like the rest of us, was just too conditioned to perceiving the universe as absolute space. It seems like no matter how hard we try, or how ingenious we are, it's just about impossible for any one of us to get it all completely right.

Now awhile later, by the second half of the 1800's, James Clark Maxwell was coming up with his equations of electromagnetic radiation, which finally explained what light was. Once again, the math came up with a fascinating prediction. The prediction was that a light ray traveled at 186,000 miles per second, but here's the weird part. It didn't matter how fast you were moving, or how fast the other guy was moving. The formula said that unlike the bouncing tennis ball, everybody would always perceive the same light ray to be traveling at 186,000 miles/sec no matter who was moving or who was standing still. No matter which ship you were in, you would both see a light ray to be traveling at 186,000 mi/sec. Now let me show you why this is weird.

We'll take our two drivers again and make them jet fighter pilots this time. Now jet fighters have guns that shoot at each other, and guns have gun barrels and bullets. When a gun fires a bullet, what happens is that the gunpowder behind the bullet explodes, violently accelerating the bullet down the length of the gun barrel to a very high velocity, perhaps 4000 feet per second (or about 2,700 miles per hour). Now this all happens inside of the gun barrel, so if the gun barrel is sitting still, the bullet will come out at 4,000 ft/sec, but if the jet fighter and its gun barrel are already traveling at Mach I, which is about 1,000 ft/sec, the bullet will still be accelerated in the barrel by an additional 4,000 ft/sec, and will now come out traveling at 5,000 ft/sec. Furthermore, if the jet fighters are both coming straight at each other while they are shooting, each traveling at 1,000 ft/sec, they will be approaching each others bullets at an additional 1,000 ft/sec, so they and the bullets will impact at 6,000 ft/sec. We don't yet have jets that will travel as fast as the bullets that they fire, but if we ever do, those jets will be able to accelerate and catch up to or even pass any bullets that they fire.

Now the weird thing is that this addition of velocities doesn't happen with light. Light somehow manages to always keep its speed just exactly 186,000 mi/sec different from your speed, no matter what your speed is. If you try to fool it by changing your speed, light seems to change its speed right along with you so that it's still moving at 186,000 mi/sec. Let's take these guys out into space, now with their space fighters that shoot high powered laser beams. (Laser beams are made out of light of course.) So now they're both flying straight at each other at 100,000 miles/sec, say. If one fires his laser, and if lasers acted like bullets, the beam should leave traveling 186,000 mi/sec faster than his fighter, or 286,000 mi/sec. The other guy who's approaching at an additional 100,000 mi/sec should see the laser beam coming straight at him at yet an additional 100,000 mi/sec or 386,000 mi/sec...but this doesn't happen with light like it does with bullets. Somehow light's speed is always adjusted to just 186,000 mi/sec for every observer no matter how they're moving. Instead of seeing the beam leave his laser gun at 286,000 mi/sec, the first pilot sees it leave at a mere 186,000 mi/sec. And instead of seeing the beam approaching his ship at 386,000 mi/sec, the second pilot sees it approaching only at 186,000 mi/sec. Maxwell's equations say that no matter how fast you or the other guy is moving, both of you, each of you, will always perceive the same light beam to travel at 186,000 mi/sec. If a pilot fires his laser and then accelerates to try to catch up to the beam, no matter how much he accelerates he will always see it still pulling away from him at 186,000 mi/sec, as if the light were accelerating too. Now if you followed the above discussion, this may seem impossible to you, and therefore, you feel the need for further explanation. Sorry. The explanation is in the mathematics of Maxwell's equations. Just try to hold onto the idea that no matter how you are moving or how fast you or someone else is going, everyone will see light to be traveling at 186,000 mi/sec.

Needless to say, this was really hard for a lot of people to swallow, and the latter half of the 1800's was spent trying to figure out how this could be so. This phenomenon was finally verified by an experiment conducted by a couple of whiz kids named Michelson and Morley. As odd as this was, though, there was something even stranger that dropped out of it, and that was that there was now something wrong with time. As hard as it was for scientists to give up the idea of absolute space, they now had to give up the idea of absolute time for everybody.

Absolute time is basically the simple idea that time passes at the same rate for everybody, but now it had to be accepted that time doesn't pass at the same rate for everybody. If you and someone else are traveling at different speeds, it turns out, *for each of you, the other guy's clock is running slower than yours.* That's not a misprint! For him, your watch will run slower than his, and for you, his will run slower than yours. No kidding. Now don't bail on me! This all drops out of the mathematics and logic, and has been thoroughly verified in the last 100 years. If your mind has difficulty grasping this, that's fine. There are many good books available that demonstrate this phenomenon fairly easily. But I will show you that something is going wrong with the idea of time, that absolute time can't be right, just by going back to our simple little distance formula and plugging in the speed of light.

You will recall that with the loss of the idea of absolute space, two people moving relative to each other could no longer agree on the distance between two events (like a bouncing tennis ball). Just to make the numbers easy, let's say one person determines the distance between two events to be 186,000 miles, while another person determines the two events to be twice as far apart, i.e., 372,000 miles. Let's make the events little explosions in space of some kind, and let's have the second event triggered when the light beam from the first explosion reaches it. Since both people have to see the light beam travel the distance at the same speed, i.e. 186,000 mi/sec, they will each see the time it takes for the same light ray to travel the distance as different. To illustrate, the *distance a light ray travels* according to the little distance formula is:

Distance = speed (of light) x time
Observer #1 sees the distance as 186,000 = 186,000 x time—so time = 1 sec
Observer #2 sees the distance as 372,000 = 186,000 x time—so time = 2 sec

So now not only is the distance between the same two events not the same, but the time each observer perceives passing between the same two events is different too. The first observer will see the two events as one second apart while the other will see the same events as two seconds apart. Clearly something is going wrong with absolute time, just like it did with absolute space. This all of course turned out to be true, but the point is that it first showed up as a consequence of the logic and math, and only later was verified by experiment.

◆   ◆   ◆

For the mathematically curious reader only:

(This segment is not essential to the remainder of the book and may be skipped.)

I was quite surprised to discover that I could fairly simply derive Einstein's Theory of Relativity formula for calculation of time dilation using just our little distance formula, and the Pythagorean Theorem. Here's how. Let's go back to our guys in the spaceships who are passing by each other in outer space, but let's get rid of the bouncing ball and replace it this time with a bouncing pulse of light. To envision this, imagine each pilot has a ten foot high vertical tube with perfect mirrors on each end that simply keeps a little short pulse of light bouncing back and forth between the mirrors once started. This will drive his clock, and each bounce will be one tick of the clock. This clock will tick very fast—about one hundred million ticks per second.

Now, that is what each one sees in his own spaceship, because each one thinks he's the one sitting still and of course his tube is going nowhere, but this isn't what he sees when he looks over at the other guys spaceship which is passing him. The other guy is moving past at a high rate of speed so he sees the other guys tube as moving by very fast also. If he were able to take a series of (very) high speed photos of the other guys light tube as it passed, it would look something like this. Let's say the ship with its tube is moving left to right.

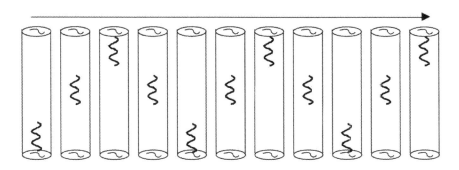

Now you will notice that for an observer, in his own ship a light pulse only has to travel the ten feet from the bottom of his tube to the top of his tube to traverse from the bottom mirror to the top mirror, a distance we will call **A** below…but this is not what he sees over in the ship going past him. In the time it takes that light pulse to travel up the tube, he will see the tube move to the right a distance we will call **B**, and *he will see that light pulse travel a diagonal distance from the bot-*

tom to the top mirror. We will call this diagonal line **D**. We are saving the letter **C** for its traditional meaning, which is the **C**onstant speed of light.

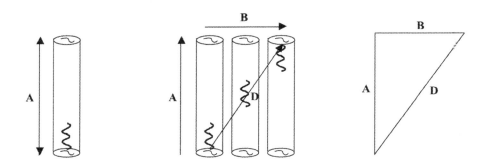

Now you will notice that our distances **A**, **B**, and **D** all form a right triangle, so all we have to do now is put them together and apply our little distance formula and the Pythagorean Theorem.

We said earlier that each pilot sees his time as different from the other guy's, so what we want to calculate here is the length of each clock tick, that is, the difference in times it takes light to bounce from the mirror at the bottom of the tube to the mirror at the top. A pilot will see his own pulse travel only the distance **A**, while he will see the other pilots pulse travel the distance **D**, which is significantly longer than **A**. Since the *speed* of the pulses (the *speed of light*) is by law seen to be the same for both pulses, our pilot will see the other guy's pulse take longer to traverse the tube (the hypotenuse **D**) than his own, since the other guy's pulse has to travel farther. We want to discover the formula that will give us the ratio of these two different times given the velocity of the other guy's spaceship. Let's let t_1 be the time it takes the pulse to travel the stationary tube, **A**, and let t_2 be the time it takes a pulse to travel the diagonal, **D**. Then the ratio of the other guy's time to our time is t_2/t_1. Now we want to get our distances **A**, **B**, and **D** into terms of time and velocity, and we can do this by simply plugging them into our little distance formula $d = st$.

The distance **A** is how far a pulse of light will travel in the time t_1 traveling at the speed of light, represented by our constant C.

So for distance **A**, $d = st$ becomes $A = C\,t_1$.

The distance **B** is how far the other guy's spaceship will travel in time t_2 traveling at whatever his speed is, we'll call his speed V, for velocity.

Here, for distance **B**, $d = st$ becomes $B = V\,t_2$.

The distance **D** is the distance light travels in the time t_2, so **D** = C t_2.

But **D** is also the hypotenuse of the triangle, so the Pythagorean Theorem says that

$$\mathbf{D}^2 = \mathbf{A}^2 + \mathbf{B}^2.$$

Substituting in the squares of the above distance formula equivalences gives

$$C^2\, t_2{}^2 = C^2\, t_1{}^2 + V^2\, t_2{}^2.$$

Gathering t_2 expressions on the left gives $C^2\, t_2{}^2 - V^2\, t_2{}^2 = C^2\, t_1{}^2$.

Factoring out t_2 gives $t_2{}^2(C^2 - V^2) = C^2\, t_1{}^2$.

Dividing through by $t_2{}^2$ gives $C^2 - V^2 = C^2\, t_1{}^2/t_2{}^2$.

Dividing through by C^2 gives $(C^2 - V^2)/C^2 = t_1{}^2/t_2{}^2$.

Reducing the left side gives $1 - (V^2/C^2) = t_1{}^2/t_2{}^2$.

Taking the positive square root gives $\sqrt{(1 - (V^2 / C^2))} = t_1 / t_2.$

Inverting and changing sides gives $t_2 / t_1 = 1 / \sqrt{(1 - (V^2 / C^2))}$

This is the formula from Einstein's theory of relativity for the ratio of t_2 to t_1.

To find t_2, multiplying both sides by t_1 gives $t_2 = t_1 / \sqrt{(1 - (V^2 / C^2))}$

You will notice that as V goes to C, the denominator on the right goes to zero, so the other guys time interval, t_2, goes to infinity. Clearly, the other guy's time would stop relative to us as his velocity approached the speed of light, that is, the ticks of his clock would get slower and slower and finally cease to tick if his time interval becomes infinitely long.

It is interesting to note that much of this relationship from Einstein's Theory of Relativity is embedded in the Pythagorean theorem discovered from abstracting imaginary perfect triangles over two thousand years ago. The only thing new is the knowledge that the speed of light is a constant for all observers. While Pythagoras could not have foreseen the Theory of Relativity specifically, I'm certain he would tell us that he felt the depth and power of the truth he had captured in his abstract theorem.

◆   ◆   ◆

Einstein was, of course, one of the big players in figuring all this out, and this is all a part of his Theory of Relativity, which is highly mathematical, and the mathematics of Relativity predicts, or demonstrates, some other highly unintuitive phenomena.

After this, the math behind the phenomena we will be examining gets a lot harder, **so we won't be doing any more math** henceforth. I just wanted to give the reader the flavor of what I mean when I speak of the math predicting the phenomenon, so the rest of this won't be so involved. Just remember that the phenomena we will be examining are all a consequence of the mathematics and logic.

Before we get into more of the weird stuff about the universe, let's list the weird stuff we just saw previously. For two people moving relative to each other, we saw that:

- There is no such thing as a same place
- They will measure different distances between the same two events
- Light always travels at 186,000 mi/sec relative to every and any observer
- Time runs more slowly for moving people than for stationary people
- The other guys clock always appears to run slower than yours

Notice I said that this all applies to two people moving relative to each other. That's where the word *relativity* comes from. The following phenomena that we will be examining are also a result of relativity. Here are some more.

The length of space shortens in the direction something or someone is moving.

This is related to what we said earlier about there being no absolute space. Two people moving relative to each other will not only disagree on the distance between two points, but they will each see the distances shrinking for the other guy. As the other guy approaches closer and closer to the speed of light, all of his distances in the direction of his motion will get closer and closer to zero. At the speed of light, there would be no length in the direction of motion. One interesting thing about this is that not only do distances between objects shrink, but the objects themselves shrink in the direction they are moving.

Matter shrinks in the direction it is moving.

The faster an object goes, the shorter it gets. It's hard enough to imagine space shrinking, but it is really hard to think of matter shrinking, of rulers themselves becoming shorter. We think of matter as containing stuff, of containing material stuff that doesn't shrink or that can only be compressed so far. It's as if their whole universe becomes thinner and thinner in the direction of their motion. At the speed of light, objects would have zero thickness. As we will see, though, it never quite reaches zero width, but it can come so close to zero as speed approaches the speed of light that it's hard to tell the difference. It can even become thinner than a single atom.

Time will stop for a person moving at the speed of light.

As he goes faster and faster, his time slows down more and more, until at the speed of light, time stops. If he could go faster than the speed of light, his time would reverse and run backwards.

The trouble is that there is something else about the universe that prevents him from ever quite reaching the speed of light. That something is the well known formula, $E = mC^2$, associated with relativity. (No more math, I promise.) In this formula, E is for energy, m is for mass, and C is the speed of light. There are a whole bunch of things that are implied by this formula.

The faster an object moves, the heavier it gets.

Energy and mass are proportional the formula says. That means simply that as one increases, so must the other. If one decreases, so must the other, and energy is related to the speed of an object. For example, a car moving 60 mi/hr has a lot more energy than a car moving at 30 mi/hr. Making something go faster increases its energy, and if energy increases, so must its mass the formula says. This means that as something or someone goes faster and faster, it not only gains more and more energy, but it gets heavier and heavier. It is, therefore, possible to make that earlier block of wood twenty times heavier, as heavy as the same sized cube of gold, simply by pushing it to a fast enough speed. Somewhat paradoxically, as it's becoming heavier and heavier, we're going to observe it becoming thinner and thinner, that is, smaller and smaller.

An object can never reach or exceed the speed of light.

It turns out that it is impossible for something or someone to reach or exceed the speed of light. As an object approaches the speed of light, its mass increases right off of the scale and goes to infinity, i.e. it's infinitely heavy. To accelerate an object that last little bit to reach the speed of light would, therefore, require infinite energy to do it. Infinite energy is not available, so it simply can't be done. This also is what prevents something from exceeding the speed of light, and thus prevents it from ever going backward in time.

The faster an object moves, the stronger its gravity becomes.

An object's gravitational force also increases with its speed. As an object's speed increases, its mass increases, and mass remember is responsible for an objects gravitational force. It is, therefore, possible to accelerate our little block of wood to a speed so close to the speed of light that it will have the same mass and gravitational force as, say, the Earth itself. I read a science fiction story when I was a kid, *The Wailing Asteroid* I believe, which even went one better. Some aliens were trying to destroy our solar system by sending some objects through it at velocities so close to the speed of light that the gravitational forces would be so great that they would tear the Sun, the Earth, the whole solar system apart. This possibility falls out of the mathematics too.

Time is a fourth dimension.

The dimension of time can be thought of as very similar to a space dimension. We perceive space as consisting of three distinct dimensions, each one of which is perpendicular to the other two. Time can be considered a fourth dimension that is perpendicular to all three of our perceived space dimensions. Our brains are constructed in such a way as to experience the three spatial dimensions as space and the fourth dimension as time. It is virtually impossible for our brains to conceive of four spatial dimensions, but it is great fun trying. A common trick is to drop back a dimension, represent our space as just two dimensions instead of three, and then imagine time as the third dimension instead of the fourth. When this is done, one way to picture all this is that we and our space are flying through the time dimension at the speed of light. There are lots and lots of fun amateur level books out there that play with understanding the fourth dimension. Some of the phenomena are quite astonishing.

Space dimensions and time dimensions are swappable.

As we and our space dimensions speed through the fourth dimension at the speed of light, we are already traveling at the maximum speed limit. Any speed given to a person or object in our three space dimensions would then mean that their total speed would exceed the speed of light. What happens in this conception that prevents us from exceeding the speed of light is that the time dimension of the moving object tilts into the space dimensions in the direction of motion, and the space dimension begins to become its new time dimension. At the speed of light, the dimension in the direction of motion would totally become the objects new time dimension. But to the observer of the moving object, that new time dimension is still a space dimension, and the observer's time dimension has become one of the objects space dimensions. For the speeding object, one of its original space dimensions has become its time dimension, and its original time dimension has become one of its three space dimensions.

The rear end of a moving object appears before it reaches you.

As a speeding object is approaching you, it appears to you to be tilting out of your three space dimensions and into another dimension into which you cannot see, your current time dimension. As the object's space tilts, this tilting process appears to rotate the object in such a way that it begins to appear that it is traveling more and more sideways. As the object's speed becomes more pronounced, so does the rotation. As this happens, the rear end of the object appears to rotate toward you, the observer, and you begin to see the back end of the object before it reaches you.

It's possible for a single event, someone's birth or death say, to occur twice in your lifetime.

Think of someone you care about who is far away from you right now, the farther the better. They are doing something at this instant, that is, *right now* they exist and are doing something. Try to imagine what they are doing right now. The real point of this is that you and that person have the same "*right now.*" There is such a thing for you and them called *right now*, but under relativity, when those dimensions begin to tilt into and out of shared space and time dimensions, your idea of *right now* tilts too. It turns out that if you are to accelerate away from your current location at a great acceleration, you can tilt your current *right now* backwards into the other persons past, or into their future, depending on which direction you go. It is, therefore, possible for you shortly after someone's birth to accelerate away thus tilting your *right now* to a time when their birth had not yet occurred, and their birth would occur again some time later. The same is of course true of someone's death. Shortly after their death, you could tilt your *right now* back to a time before their death had occurred, a time when they are alive.

Space can be curved.

A straight line is a one dimensional object, but a curved line is a one dimensional object that is curved in a second dimension. A flat plane is a two dimensional object, but the surface of a sphere is a two dimensional object that has been curved through a third dimension. The surface of the Earth is an example. It turns out that three dimensional space can likewise be curved in a fourth dimension, and it turns out that our three dimensions of space are curved in a fourth dimension. It is hard for a being to tell that one set of dimensions are curved in a higher dimension, but there are ways. Remember how our ancestors had difficulty telling that the surface of the Earth was curved. If the Earth were really flat, a person traveling in a straight line would never have ended up back at the starting place. So one way for them to tell that the surface was curved into a sphere was for Magellan to sail off toward the West, and arrive back to where he started coming in from the East. Imagine an explorer going to the effort to travel in a perfectly straight line. If he (magically) returned to his starting place, he would know that his straight line really wasn't straight at all but was curved in another dimension.

Light bends when it passes a massive object.

Now it turns out that light usually travels in a straight line, but when a light ray passes a hugely massive object like our Sun, the line that the light ray follows bends. But light has to travel in a straight line, so how can this be? What's going on, at least according to the math and logic, is that the light is indeed traveling in a straight line, but in a four dimensional space. If we could somehow expand ourselves up one dimension into four dimensional beings, the light would once again appear to travel in a straight line, but our three dimensional space is curved into four dimensional space, and down here in three dimensions light appears to travel in bent lines. Einstein again. This is the basis of his General Theory of Relativity.

Gravity is caused by curved space.

It turns out that the phenomenon of gravity too results from the curvature of our three dimensional space in a fourth dimension. That light bends in a gravitational field reveals that that supposed field is really a curvature of three dimensions in a fourth. The same bending of the path of a light ray occurs in the path of an object passing another massive object, only it's even more evident. This all implies that as the Earth orbits the Sun in what appears to us to be a near circle, it's actually traveling in a straight line in four dimensional spacetime. Here the ideas of gravitational fields and gravitational force are replaced with, and shown to result from, geometry itself.

Space can fold back on itself.

Since space can curve and bend in higher dimensions, if it bends enough we would call it a fold. What this means is that some place in space very far away may actually be very close to us across a higher dimension. A crude example might be the surface of the Earth again. Traveling on the two dimensional surface of the Earth, Bejing and Washington D. C. are twelve or thirteen thousand miles apart, but they are much closer across the third dimension through which the surface is curved. In this case, that would be a path through the Earth, which is a distance of only about eight thousand miles. Now imagine a beach ball made into a globe of the world but only half full of air. If one pushes Washington D.C and Bejing together with their finger tips, they are so close together that they almost touch. It is theoretically (mathematically) possible to traverse these shortcuts across the universe if they exist, and thus travel to very distant locations in the universe by traveling only a short distance across a fold in another dimension. These theoretical shortcuts between two locations in space through another dimension are called *worm holes*, and are understandably popular as a means of travel to science fiction writers.

Two twins may age at completely different rates.

This is the so called twin paradox with which you are likely familiar. What it refers to is the phenomenon that one person can accelerate away from the Earth and taking a different path through spacetime, may return to the Earth having aged much less than someone else, say his twin brother. It's usually portrayed as two twenty year old twins waving goodbye to each other as one enters his space-ship, and then in the next frame the returning twin, now twenty-five years old, is shaking the shaking hand of his 80 year old brother who's barely able to hobble up on his cane.

The universe is expanding.

The mathematics of Einstein's Theory of Relativity said, astonishingly, that the universe must be expanding. No one had ever imagined such a thing, or wanted to, so Einstein introduced an artificial fudge factor into his equations just so they wouldn't say that the universe was expanding. A decade or so later the astrono-mers peering out into space through their big shiny new telescopes saw that everything in the universe was flying apart at incredible speeds. The universe was indeed observed to be expanding. Eating humble pie, Einstein had to pull his fudge factor back out of his equations, calling it the worst blunder of his life. Although unbelievable at the time, his original mathematics had been right all along.

Space is stretching.

Everything in the universe is moving apart at high speed, but they aren't really flying apart through space. What's going on is that space itself is expanding. Remember earlier how we talked about space shrinking in the direction of motion? Well, space can stretch too, and that's what the universe is doing. You can think of it as kind of like blowing up a balloon. Hopefully the metaphor ends there, though, and the universe isn't going to pop if it gets too big.

The universe started with a big bang.

When the universe was first observed to be expanding, it appeared as if it were flying apart, as if from the result of a gigantic explosion. One astronomer opposed to the theory, sarcastically referred to it as the *big bang*, and to his cha-grin, the name stuck. If one runs the expanding motion of the universe backwards in time, it all ends up as a single point smaller than the tip of a needle. All of the matter and energy of the universe was compressed into this tiny point, which expanded violently 12.7 billion years ago to become the vast universe we observe today. This is what we today refer to as the big bang theory of the creation of the universe, and it is now the prevailing scientific theory. Considerable evidence has accumulated to support it, and several *predictions* made by the theory have been verified as true. Remember from Chapter 2 that one requirement for a theory to be considered true is that it make predictions that can be verified as true.

Distance is shrinking.

Whoa! Didn't I just say that space is expanding, or stretching? Is it possible to both shrink and stretch? It turns out that distances shrinking and space stretching have a lot in common. If space is expanding, what is observed is that the distances between the galaxies in outer space are increasing. This means simply that as each day passes there are more and more miles between the galaxies…but this will also happen if the distances of space are shrinking. In this case, the measure of the mile is just getting shorter and shorter so we measure more and more miles between galaxies. Some say that this is the more accurate description of what is really happening, that is, distances are shrinking rather than space is expanding. How big is the universe then? Did we start shrinking when the universe was as big as a basketball, say, and we're just all very microscopic, and getting more microscopic all the time? Or did we start shrinking when the universe was zero size? In this case, the big bang was an implosion instead of an explosion, and we are all somehow smaller than nothing…and getting smaller. As usual, there's no way to imagine it.

There may be multiple universes.

Our universe is composed of some number of dimensions, as will be discussed when we examine string theory in a moment. Apparently, however, universes themselves can be floating around in yet higher dimensions, so there may be more than one universe floating around out there.

Universes can collide.

A new theory has surfaced recently that is competing with the big bang theory as a description of the origin of our universe. It says that our universe was created when two other universes collided. Apparently, this can spark a new universe, and this theory is being taken seriously. It isn't quite right yet. It's got some major malfunctions just like Copernicus' original theory of the Sun centered solar system, but also like Copernicus' theory, it has some characteristics that indicate that it's onto something, that it's on the right track. This theory originally sprang from some whiz kids studying higher dimensional *membrane theory*, and quickly became known as *brane* theory for short. Then someone found a legitimate way to call it the *p-brane* theory, and because physicists have so few ways to amuse themselves, this may be the name that sticks.

Human beings may one day create universes.

As our knowledge of physics and the universe increases, some people are speculating that humans may some day have the ability to spawn a universe or two. This may all sound kind of grandiose, but the *mathematics* of quantum physics indicate that a universe can spring into existence for no good reason out of absolute nothingness. We know by now that it's not a wise thing to ignore the mathematics, and that a universe can spring from nothing certainly takes care of the problem of resources. I suppose that means that the sum total of everything in a universe adds up to nothing. It's a little bit disconcerting to realize that if we can do it, so can some other being, and that our universe might just be some alien kid's high school science project. I hope there's plenty of time to go before he/she graduates.

The universe may end at any moment.

There's a lot of interest as to whether the universe will go on expanding forever, or if one day it will stop, reverse direction, and all fall back together disappearing into that infinitesimal point from which it sprang, called the *big crunch*. There is another way, however, that it may all end. The same quantum physics that predicts that it is possible for the universe to spontaneously spring from nothing also predicts that it is possible for the universe to simply spontaneously cease to exist at any moment. It's all a matter of probabilities. It may be that we and the universe are destined to exist forever, or destined to end in the next twenty minutes. Of course, if this is the way it is to be, we will simply never know it happened.

The universe consists of at least ten or eleven dimensions, possibly more.

Physics right now is an aggregate of several incomplete theories that neither fit together cleanly nor completely cover all holes. You are already aware of the inconsistencies between relativity and quantum physics. Physicists have been busy for some decades now looking for a unified single theory that will cover it all, sometimes referred to as TOE, or the Theory Of Everything. One blossoming theory that is considered to be the most promising by many is called string theory. In this theory, all matter is composed of vibrating one dimensional strings that are tightly curled in a higher dimension. These strings have zero thickness so they are utterly immaterial, and thus have no mass either. In fact, *that which we perceive and measure as mass results from the way these strings interact*. It turns out so far that the most promising model requires ten or eleven dimensions to make it work.

All those microworld things that we call particles are composed from these vibrating nothings. This is a new paradigm based primarily on the mathematics of geometry, a new model of what's behind it all, and it is correspondingly much more powerful than the paradigms that it is replacing. It promises to subsume relativity and quantum physics, to explain the seemingly arbitrary masses of the subatomic particles, as well as the seemingly arbitrary strengths of the forces of nature. In this paradigm, the laws of nature are turning out to result from the geometric properties of dimensions, space and time.

Some matter barely interacts with other matter and is barely detectable.

The neutrino is one variety of the fundamental particles, like electrons, protons, and photons, but unlike electrons, protons, and photons it just barely interacts with the other matter around it. High energy electrons and protons traveling at extreme velocities can be stopped by a few blocks of concrete, and high energy photons can be stopped by a few more blocks of concrete, but neutrinos pass through concrete literally like it isn't there. In fact, they pass right through the Earth almost as if it isn't there. A block of matter the size of a million Earth's would stop only a tiny percentage of these elusive pieces of matter.

Most of the material of the universe we can neither see nor feel.

Way back at the beginning of the chapter, I said that matter is the stuff that we can see and feel. Apparently, I lied. It has recently been discovered that there is a lot more matter right around us than meets the eye, and we can neither see it nor feel it. One property of this strange stuff being that it doesn't interact with (reflect) light, it has been dubbed *dark matter*. If we can't see it or feel it, then according to chapter 4 we need to find some other effect that it has in order to say that it exists, in order to consider it real. How do we know it's there at all? In this case, we know it's there by its gravity.

Astronomers looking out into space have discovered that galaxies, including our galaxy the Milky Way, move in strange ways that cannot be explained by the gravity of the stars, planets, and interstellar dust and gas that can be detected. In fact, it turns out that the ordinary matter that is detectable, the stuff like us, our world, and the stars, is only a fraction of the matter out there. Some estimate that our type of matter is less than four percent of the matter around us. This means that perhaps more than ninety six percent of the matter in the universe is dark matter. It doesn't interact with matter in any way that we know of except gravitational attraction, which is extremely weak. It is here among us, passing through us and around us, but it doesn't interact with our bodies and we have no senses to detect it. We don't know anything about this matter, like if it's organized into dark matter atoms or something. We don't know if it's organized in ways that can support something like life or mind, a fanciful idea that leads to an even more fanciful idea that if great civilizations have evolved there, then we could be surrounded by them as they passed through and around us undetected at this very moment.

Matter isn't as hard as you think.

Matter in our every day experience can only be compressed to a certain point and then can't be compressed any further. For the most part, as atoms and molecules are pressed together, they reach a point where they simply can't be compressed further…but this turns out to be because of the rather piddly forces that we're able to apply. Stars, that may have many millions of times more mass than the Earth, create gravitational forces so great that matter can be compressed together much more compactly. During their energetic lifetimes, stars create enough energy to balance and prevent these crushing forces from succeeding, but at the end of their life cycles as the energy diminishes, these crushing gravitational forces can become dominant. Dead or dying stars can end up in one of several compressed states.

The Sun is expected to end up as what's called a *white dwarf* about five billion years from now. In this case, its gravity will have compressed it to about a millionth of its current size and its matter will be millions of times heavier and more compact than gold. A single teaspoon of material will weigh more than and contain more material than an aircraft carrier. Some stars bigger than our sun will end up crushed smaller still as neutron stars. Their material is compressed into a sphere roughly the size of Manhattan Island and are of unimaginable density. These are the pulsars that astronomers have discovered that pulse radio beacons into space around ten to a hundred times per second. If a star is big enough, it may end its life by collapsing into a black hole. In this case, the gravitational force becomes so strong that the crushing force can't be stopped by matter at all, and it is crushed to zero size, right out of existence. All that's left behind is the huge gravitational field, kind of like the grin from the vanished Cheshire Cat.

You are a star child (whether you want to be or not).

Stars start out composed mainly of hydrogen and helium, which are the smallest two atoms. They generate their huge energies through the process of putting these little atoms together to make bigger and bigger atoms, a process called nuclear fusion. Yes, that's the same process humans have captured to create the hydrogen bomb. Many stars at the end of their life cycles, and in the process of becoming those compressed forms above, actually explode first as novas and supernovas, in the process both blasting these newly created bigger atoms back into space and creating even bigger atoms during the explosion itself. This is how the other ninety elements are created, those besides hydrogen and helium.

The only atoms that formed in the universe after the big bang were hydrogen and helium so originally there were only these two elements. Then the first generation of stars exploded blowing the first round of heavier elements out into space. This all later condensed into second generation stars most of which have now also exploded returning their heavier atoms back into space too. We're now 12.7 billions years into the process, and our sun, it turns out, is a third generation star and thus formed from the material blown into space by both the first two generations. The planet Earth, in fact, is completely composed of the heavier atoms that were formed inside of the first two generations of stars. And that includes you and the material in your body as a resident participant in the Earth's ecosystem. You are quite literally composed of star stuff.

The Stranger Microworld:

The matter of the macroworld is composed of aggregates of the minute particles of matter of the microworld. As mentioned earlier, there is a smallest particle of any given substance of our macroworld, so there is such a thing as a single particle of, say, water or gold. These particles are the atoms and molecules and are exceedingly small, on the order of ten million to the inch. But why stop here at the atoms? It turns out that atoms are aggregates of several other kinds of particles, the protons, neutrons, and electrons, and it turns out that protons and neutrons are also made up of aggregates of particles called quarks and gluons. During the past century, it turns out that hundreds of different microworld particles have been discovered and cataloged.

In the early part of the 1900s, when the atom was finally established to exist, it was first discovered to be composed of a dense nucleus made of protons and neutrons with electrons in orbit around the nucleus. Here is the way the atom was visualized to be at that time.

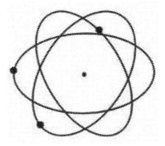

Very naive view (solar system-like) of an atom

Almost immediately it was realized that this visualization was impossible, because it didn't fit the facts of the way atoms absorb and emit light. After that, things got complicated. The atom turned out to be difficult to visualize at all, so apparently for this reason, this is the last picture of the atom that was popularized to the public, and this is thus how most people picture the atom to this day. So, what happened?

What happened is that microworld particles turned out not to be particles as we know particles. We think of particles as tiny specks of matter, and by matter I mean matter like we're used to, matter that you can see and feel, but in the microworld matter is much different. For one thing, those electrons and protons turned out not to be just littler pieces of matter, of material stuff. One simplified way of thinking of them is just as little places in space that have certain characteristics, certain effects on the other nearby places in space that makes them detectable. For example, an atom may be thought of as a minute region of space that attracts other atoms, emits photons, etc. An electron is likewise a little *place* that walks, talks, and acts like an electron. Protons and neutrons likewise. (And of course a duck can be considered to be just a region of space too) Sometimes those particles are not so little regions of space, but may be extended over much larger regions of space. The following graphics are several more attempts to actually picture an atom, roughly in chronological order, but keep in mind that these images are really attempts to portray certain *effects* that these little *regions* have.

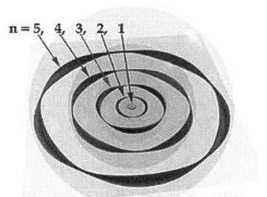

Niels Bohr - Louis de Broglie atom, 1924

Early wave representation of the electron shells of an atom

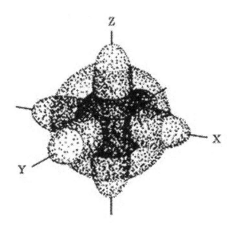

High Probability Regions for Electrons of an Atom

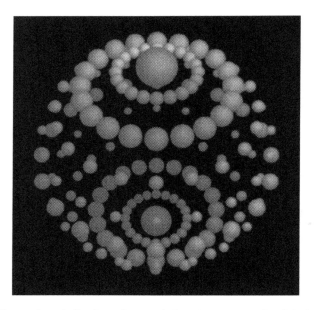

tridimensional display of one of the eigenstates (n=8,l=6) of the Hydrogen atom

http://www.lactamme.polytechnique.fr/Mosaic/
Copyright (c) 1994–2004 Jean-Francois Colonna.
Copyright (c) 1994–2004 France Telecom R&D and CMAP/Ecole Polytechnique.

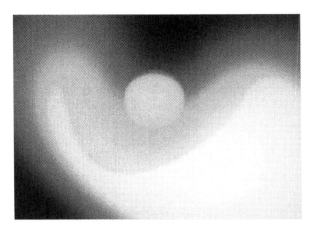

**tridimensional display of a linear superposition of 6
eigenstates of the Hydrogen atom**

All of the above pictures are attempts to represent characteristics of the atom, not what it actually *looks* like. You'll see in a moment that we can't picture what it looks like. Look again at the last picture. See how some regions are more definite than others. These regions really represent regions of probability density of where some effect will be detected, in this case where the electron will occur. The very lightly shaded regions represent a very low probability of the electron being there and the much denser regions represents a much higher probability.

Now here's the really interesting part. The electron doesn't exist as a particle at all until somebody actually tries to detect it. In the meantime, while everybody is leaving it alone, it exists as a wave distributed over space, which is what the picture is trying to represent. That may not look like what you usually think of as a wave, but *mathematically* it is described as a wave, and that is the shape of that particular wave. It may not be knowable whether this wave has any reality or not beyond its mathematical power of description. We can't actually detect it. Every time we look it turns into a particle and all we detect is the particle. And all this is true for all of those other so-called particles too; electrons, protons, neutrons, etc. They all exist as very immaterial, perhaps nonexistent probability waves most of the time, and then when they need to act like a particle, that wave collapses onto a minute point and they act for an instant as a particle. Then they immediately dematerialize again into a probability wave until the next time it needs to have the effect of a particle, and the wave will again instantly and momentarily collapse to a single point.

Now this is what the mathematics tells us is going on, and it has been determined to be true by experiment to a very high degree of accuracy, but there are two great mysteries created here for scientists, and us, to think about. One is "what exactly is the particle when it's not being a particle, i.e., when it exists only as a wave?" The other is "what is it that suddenly makes a particle need to act like a particle, that is, what makes the wave collapse to a point?" How does the particle know when to act like a particle and not a wave? Scientists have been researching, and arguing over these two mysteries for three quarters of a century now, since about 1925. Many scientists have believed that this couldn't be right, that there had to be a more complete and satisfying explanation of the microworld than this. Einstein himself argued that this description was incomplete and that there had to be a more concrete reality behind it. Niels Bohr, another great mind of the era, disagreed and championed the idea that it was a complete description, that this is the way the microworld really is. The philosophical debates that raged for several decades between Einstein and Bohr are some of the most exciting in human history, and helped narrow the mystery to the deceivingly simple question of just what can and cannot be known about the universe. Bohr believed that this description of the microworld was all that could be known, and that there was no other reality or materiality behind it. Einstein believed that there was something more realistic behind it all and that more could be known about this reality. So far, Bohr's interpretation has been born out in every respect, and Einstein's in none.

In the end, and importantly, it all comes back to *information*. Just what is it possible to know about reality? What part can we know, and what parts are we just imagining are there, since we can never detect it? Let's take that probability wave for example. It is nothing but a mathematical description, a bunch of symbols on a piece of paper that happen to predict accurately what we observe. Is there something real about it? Does it have some sort of physical reality? Is it some sort of real wave, or is it just a *heuristic*, a convenient but meaningless mathematical model that predicts accurately what we will observe in our experiments? Does that mathematical model capture something real that is going on, or is it itself somehow the bottom line?

Remember back from Chapter 3 that the scientific description of reality is mathematical because science works with measurements, and measurements are numbers. Predicting experimental results then boils down to predicting what those measured results will be, and being numbers this requires mathematics. Remember too how we said that there are only three things we can measure about the world, and that these are time, space, and mass. Well, these are not quite the same things in the microworld as you will see shortly, in fact they're quite different. Again, it's all about what we can and cannot know about the microworld, in this case, what information we can retrieve with measurements. We're actually quite limited as to what we can detect.

So here are some of the things the mathematics tells us about the microworld, that is, what we can, and have observed to be true. Once again, you will find much of this difficult or impossible to comprehend. And once again, rather than let this be a cause for despair, try instead to enjoy the feeling of amazement.

Let's repeat the interesting phenomena that we have just seen:

- Particles exist not as particles but as extended regions of a probability wave when no one is looking.

- Somehow, the particle wave knows to collapse to a point only when somebody looks.

The world isn't described by cause and effect anymore.

In the world we are used to, cause and effect rules. This is the Mechanistic paradigm that has held sway now for several centuries. When billiard balls collide at just the right angle, the balls bounce off of each other and go exactly where the player mentally calculated that they would (if he's good). That is, the player can *cause* the billiard balls to go where he wants. This is not what happens in the microworld. Remember, instead of miniature billiard balls, these particles exist as spread over whole regions. When someone looks, the particle can manifest itself anywhere within this region. Two colliding particles, therefore, are not constrained to traveling in precise directions or at precise speeds, but may next manifest themselves anywhere within a region of probability, each point having a certain probability that the particle will appear there. These probabilities are represented mathematically as a wave. The *cause and effect* method of calculating where a particle will be exactly is now replaced by a *probability* that a particle will appear at a variety of locations within regions.

Heisenberg's uncertainty principle.

Obviously where a particle is going to show up when somebody looks becomes uncertain, but this is *not* to be confused with Heisenberg's uncertainty principle. Remember from way back that we can only know that something exists by some effect it has on the world around it. If it doesn't have an effect on something, if it doesn't disturb something, we have no way of knowing it was there, but the particle's interaction with the world necessarily disturbs the particle itself too. This leads to an inability to determine certain information about the particle, *even when you look.*

There are many types of information that are disturbed, but they all come in pairs. For example, it is impossible to determine a particle's *location* exactly and at the same time determine its *motion* exactly. Imagine a blind man trying to gather information about the location and movement of billiard balls on a billiards table during a game by touching the balls as they move. As a ball is rolling along and he touches it with his fingertip, he finds out right exactly where it is, but he has now utterly disturbed how it is moving. For him to determine its motion, he would have to touch it somehow so lightly as to not disturb its motion, but he would have to continue touching it over some interval to determine how fast and the direction the billiard ball is moving. In this case, though, he would not have observed the billiard ball in an exact location, but over an interval of its motion. He can know then, either where it is exactly and be uncertain how it's moving, or he can know how it's moving, but not have an exact location of where it was.

In some ways, we're like blind people trying to probe what's going on down in the microworld, and in the process of trying to get information, disturbing the heck out of it. Another information pair that is disturbed by looking is *energy and time*, that is, you can either know its energy measurement, but not what time you measured it, or you can know when you measured it, but not its exact energy.

Particles don't really have exact locations.

Now this sounds like a rehash of the uncertainty principle, but actually it's an elaboration. In the billiard ball example above, the billiard ball actually exists as a ball, and it actually has a certain velocity in a certain direction. Physicists have arrived at the conclusion that this is just not so for particles. Particles simply don't exist in an exact place or move with an exact motion. Physicists have determined that a particle exists in a combined motion/position state, and that it's the method of how we probe the microworld that will determine what we see. The result we get back from one method of looking is a location. The result we get back from another method of looking is a motion, and interestingly, there are in-between ways of looking. What we see then is a smeared particle with an uncertain motion. Once again, the same sort of uncertain existence holds for the combined time/energy measurements. So what exactly is this thing that we are probing that we have always up until now thought of as a particle? No one knows, frankly. Many attempts have been made to envision it, but in the end none have held up. All we know about it is what the mathematics and our instruments tell us about it, and the only thing the mathematics tells us is the probabilities of what our probing instruments will read when we try to look. All we can know is the effect this thing has on our measuring instruments, and the effect our measuring instruments have on it. We are being forced to abandon our notion that we can envision what is going on behind it all, and of course, *envisioning what's behind it all* is our definition for a paradigm.

Particles don't really exist at exact times.

This follows from the above comparison of the energy/time uncertainty with the location/motion uncertainty. If the energy of the particle is measured, the time of the measurement is uncertain. Conversely, if the time of the measurement is known exactly, the energy is uncertain. The physicists have concluded once again that it doesn't really exist in an exact state of either, but is in a combined energy/time state. The result we get once again depends on the measuring instrument we use to look.

Particles spin strangely.

Particles spin on an axis. This is known because they exhibit angular momentum, which is the kind of momentum we find in spinning objects. Whatever they are doing, though, it's not spinning like an ordinary macroworld object. For example, some of them have to be flipped over twice in order to reverse the direction of their spin. Whatever dimensions are like in the microworld, they're not like our macroworld three dimensions. And just in case that's not strange enough for you, a quantum particle can spin in opposite directions simultaneously.

Particles pursue multiple futures simultaneously.

The probability wave predicts that the particle could appear any number of places at a given moment. But life doesn't stop in the microworld just because nobody's looking and collapsing the wave onto a point. The fact is that the wave evolves very quickly over time. It may be that if the particle is on one side of the wave it will interact with another particle next to it there. This changes the wave to include the effect of that interaction forever after. Or it may be that the particle is on the other side of the wave and thus interacts with yet a different particle over there. This opposite possibility too is included in the evolving wave after that. Each of these is a distinct future that the particle may pursue. If the wave isn't collapsed onto a single future, the wave continues to evolve farther into these multiple futures, each one of which will spawn multiple futures of its own. We will not know which future path the particle actually took until the wave is collapsed. Then all the others are abandoned but one, the one we detect. All possible futures of a particle evolve simultaneously, and the wave predicts the probability of each being the one discovered when somebody looks.

History can be changed for a particle.

As a wave evolves down multiple futures, the futures become multiple potential histories. Physicists have set up experimental apparatus that can be altered from one configuration to another well after an experiment has begun and a particle has begun its journey through the apparatus. Basically, in these experiments a particle can start out following a single path, or two possible future paths, simultaneously. The split occurs at the very beginning, at the first instant of the experiment. Amazingly, the choice of path can be affected by the arrangement of detectors at the far end of the experiment, that is, the detectors at the other end determine how the particle will travel long before the particle gets anywhere near the detectors.

Now, this is strange enough, but it gets stranger. Long after the experiment has begun and the path of the particle has necessarily already been established and it is well underway, if the detectors are rearranged, it will change the path that the particle had decided to take. It's a little bit like closing the barn door after the horse is stolen, and now having the horse not having been stolen at all. There doesn't seem to be a time limit as to how far back in time you can go to change these historic paths *as long as the wave hasn't been collapsed onto a definite outcome.* The path of light traveling for billions of years from distant quasars can be set by how we detect it here on earth. In other words, we can go back and determine which history this light will have from billions of years ago by choices we make here and now on earth.

Particles don't have unique identities.

When we look at the billiard balls on a pool table, there's no doubt about the identity of the balls. The eight ball is the eight ball and we'd better not get it mixed up with the one or the fifteen. This just doesn't hold for particles in the microworld. They no longer occupy explicit places in space, they overlap, and they seem to fade into and out of existence as necessary. Now all particles of a given kind, electrons say, are exactly the same, basically indistinguishable. Instead of a pool table covered with distinguishable balls, imagine a table covered with eight balls. Now all of a sudden it's getting difficult to tell them apart, but they still have unique identities, determinable from their locations if nothing else. But what happens if they lose their distinct locations the way microworld particles do. Imagine that when nobody's looking they turn into waves that spread out over the pool table, overlapping and intermingling their waves into one single blob wave. The next time somebody looks and they all turn back into eight balls again, there is no longer a way to tell which one was which. In fact, the ones that are seen now really aren't the identical ones that were there earlier. Between times that anybody looks, they take on kind of a group identity and sacrifice their individuality.

Particles can materialize on the other side of a wall without going through it.

A particle may dematerialize on one side of a wall and instantly materialize on the other side without traveling through the wall. It's all up to that probability wave. The wave can pop up in multiple disconnected places at once, including on the other side of a wall without ever extending through the wall. When a particle does this, it's called *tunneling*. It happens so frequently, that is the probability of a particle doing this is so high, that the phenomenon has been harnessed to create a type of electron microscope called a tunneling electron microscope. Those old material walls just aren't what they used to be. As an aside, it turns out that this can happen to big macroworld objects too, including your grandmother or even you since we are just aggregates of this microworld stuff. There really is the very distinct possibility that you could suddenly find yourself sitting outside in the yard, or in the parking lot. Unlike the microworld objects, though, where the probability is relatively high, the probability of it happening to a macroworld object drops to such a miniscule value that it is unlikely to ever occur even once in many many lifetimes of the universe.

Space is packed solid with particles that don't really exist.

Microworld particles can be created from nothing, from space, it turns out, and are called virtual particles. The trick is once created to stay created though. Apparently it takes a certain minimum amount of energy for a virtual particle to stay created and only extremely rarely is this energy available. If the energy isn't available when a particle is created, it wastes no time in winking back out of existence. If the energy is available when a virtual particle winks into existence, then it becomes real and stays around as a real particle. In fact, that's where all the particles come from. The vacuum of space is literally jam packed and seething with these virtual particles. If they don't stay around, how do we know that they were ever there at all? Well, first of all they showed up in the mathematics of course. But our definition of existence requires that they have some effect on the world around them that makes them detectable, and indeed their effect has been detected.

Particles seem to be connected across any distance of space.

Two particles that have interacted, that is, have mingled their waves, retain aspects of their newly shared identity across any distance of space. What this means is that interacting with one of the particles at some time later under the right circumstances will also interact with the other particle too, and instantaneously, even though it could be on the other side of the universe by now. Distance just isn't a consideration in this case.

It may be our mind, or consciousness that collapses the wave.

We have no idea what the mind or consciousness are, but they seem to be present whenever the wave is collapsed. In fact, so far they are the only things anyone has come up with that are uniquely present every time the wave collapses. No matter what we do, we observe and experience only one of the possibilities predicted by the wave function. The wave may predict the probabilities of a thousand different possible observations, but we will experience only one of these. This single outcome becomes real, becomes a permanent, definite element of our history, and then the next wave starts spreading out from that point. In our macroworld, only a single definite reality exists. What collapses the wave, and if it's mind that does it, is surely one of the biggest and most important questions confronting science today.

The multiverse as an alternative to the universe.

There is an alternative explanation of the collapsing wave that is just barely imaginable that works and that must, therefore, be taken seriously. That is that the wave never does collapse to a single outcome, but that all those different outcomes actually **all** exist somehow. Each different outcome represents a new universe, and the competing universes **all** exist. As the observer of these events, we human beings too split into myriad entities. One of us exists in each universe, and thus observes only a single outcome of the so called wave. I say *so called*, because the wave in this case becomes simply the mathematical result of the interactions between all of the different universes. The up side of this hypothesis is that the interactive mind is no longer required as the explanation of what collapses the wave, and in fact the wave doesn't exist. The wave mathematics is in this case explained. The down side is that we are left with infinities, infinities upon infinities of universes. How can all those infinities of universes actually coexist? This reality, if it is one, has been dubbed the *multiverse*.

Particles exist in many different kinds of space besides just our three dimensional space.

Space is composed of dimensions. There are three of them in the space we can imagine. These three dimensions are all related in that they represent the three coordinates necessary to specify the location of something; that is, they compose the realm on which locations are specified. Physicists call this *location space* or *configuration space* to distinguish it from other spaces that they deal with, for example *phase space*. These other spaces are called spaces because they too have dimensions that specify values on their realms. It is convenient to think of the values in these strange spaces as specifying locations in these spaces. Our senses do not sense these other spaces, and our minds do not represent them to us as space, like it does with location space. Perhaps if it did, we would perceive them as the same sort of space we perceive our location space to be.

What has been described here are some of the phenomena predicted and observed under the discipline of quantum physics. Quantum physics 80 years ago was not, and still is not an easy thing to accept.

The very first person to stumble onto any inkling of quantum physics was Max Planck in 1900. The *mathematics* of the physics of the time predicted that the light emitted from a heated object would suffer a fate that physicists were calling a "violet catastrophe"...*but it didn't*! This was one time that the mathematics was wrong...because the physics was wrong. We all know that as an object is heated it first begins to glow red, then orange, then yellow, and finally when hot enough it will glow blue. If you've ever had a fire in the fireplace, or even a campfire, you have seen flames (hot gas) that glow with these different colors. Now in order to make the mathematics fit the facts, Max Planck was playing around with alternatives and discovered if he limited the possible energies of the atoms to integers, (1, 2, 3, etc.), rather than continuous energies, he could avoid the violet catastrophe and make the results come out to match the results of experiment.

Now this was a *ridiculous* and completely unacceptable idea to physicists (including Planck himself), since it is exactly like saying that a baseball can travel 70 mph, 80 mph, 90 mph, or even 100 mph; but it can't travel at speeds in between these numbers. Speeds like 83 mph or 95 mph are prohibited. As startling as it was, though, it turned out to be the correct mathematics. Planck called these integer packets of energy "quanta." This is where the word for *quantum* physics comes from. Max Planck manipulated the math to fit the facts and never really accepted it as the true or correct interpretation of what was really going on. Einstein too.

Even though Einstein never accepted much of quantum physics, he won the Nobel Prize for his contribution to it's creation, not for his Theory of Relativity, and not for his proof that the atom existed. He won it for his explanation of the Compton effect, which relied on Planck's idea that the energy of the photon was quantized. But Einstein, to his last, argued vigorously against the probabilistic explanation provided by quantum physics. One of his more well known opinions is that (paraphrasing) *God does not throw dice*. Max Planck too resisted the idea until his death lamenting, "...that new scientific theories supplant previous ones not because people change their minds, but simply because old people [scientists] die." He at least recognized that even though unacceptable to him, this new reality might be correct. Although quantum physics was here to stay, Einstein never was able to relinquish the idea that his "gut" beliefs were correct, or that his intuitive beliefs might not be the way the universe actually was.

Chapter 7
The Immaterial Microworld

What I am going to tell you about is what we teach our physics students in the third or fourth year of graduate school... It is my task to convince you not to turn away because you don't understand it. You see my physics students don't understand it... That is because I don't understand it. Nobody does.

—Richard P. Feynman, QED, The Strange Theory of Light and Matter, (1918–1988)

Is anybody home?:

From somewhere back in our history starting about the time that we became human, we and our ancestors have been searching for truth and reality. Each one of those earlier paradigms originated as an attempt to understand the universe more accurately than the paradigm that preceded it. All of our sciences, all of our religions, have been attempts to hone in on the ultimate truth, the one true reality of *what's behind it all.*

With the advent of the scientific method, this pursuit became not only more precise, but increasingly more volatile. The incessant inflow of new knowledge requires that our view of reality be updated more frequently now. New paradigms endure for barely a century if that, depending on where we rather arbitrarily draw the lines. The scientific method with its requirement of rigorously testing hypotheses and theory against reality guarantees that each new description of reality will ever more closely approach the limit of the final absolute reality. Each new theory predicts the experimental measurements even more accurately than the theory it replaces. So where has all this precision brought us?

For the first time in human history, ***we have no idea at all of what reality is like***! The up side, though, is that for the first time we know this for sure. As our methods and descriptions became ever more accurate, it became ever more evident that the reality we are measuring, in both the macroworld and the microworld, is very, very different from the reality we experience. With our scientific method, we have addressed the need to be *sure* of our knowledge, and one sure piece of knowledge that it has led us to is that we know we don't know what reality is...***for sure***. As far as understanding what's behind it all, we seem to have returned to the Magical paradigm, and we are starting over.

Actually, ever since the advent of the scientific method several hundred years ago, it was evident that, in a way, we were indeed returning to the Magical paradigm. With the Magical paradigm, there was no known explanation behind what was being observed. The implication after all of applying the scientific method to our continued investigations is that we aren't at the bottom level yet, that we don't yet know what's behind it all. Otherwise, we wouldn't need a method by which to proceed with our search. We wouldn't still be searching. So there has always been an unexplained bottom level upon which the rest of physics has stood.

Physics has never even had an understood foundation. Is it inevitable that this should always be the case, that there never can be an end to it all, a bottom level on which it all rests, and that explains it all and needs no further explanation? A completed physics is certainly easy to imagine, and has of course been what physicists had imagined would be the outcome all along. In fact, it was believed by some circa 1900, that it was close. In this case, the belief was that the atom, which was composed of the proton and electron, was the bottom. The proton and electron were thought to be "real" particles. They were the bottom level of the particles and they, and the atoms they composed, were the matter out of which all else was constructed. It certainly seemed feasible that the bottom level, the foundation, would turn out to be something material and real, as opposed to formless, immaterial mathematics and logic.

Quantum physics, roughly speaking, is a body of mathematical methods and practices that predict with exquisite accuracy what results we can expect to observe from experiments, and as you already know, it predicts them as probabilities. By itself, *it does not provide us with an interpretation* of what's going on behind the mathematics, or behind our experiments. Mathematics as you will recall can be reduced to just dumb symbol manipulation, just mindless typographical operations. This is a most unsatisfying situation for physicists who like to feel that they understand what's going on, so they have made several attempts to provide interpretations of what the mathematics of the microworld is telling us.

One school believes that there still might be some way that there is something *real* behind it all. They are, therefore, called the *realists*. By *real* they mean *something* along the lines of macroworld particles that have definite attributes, such as definite location and energy even while we're not looking. This is the kind of reality we perceive in the ordinary world familiar to us, and their motivation is to extend at least some of this ordinariness into the microworld. This is the kind of reality that up until 1925 all physicists imagined as composing the microworld. The realists are looking for some way that the microworld can consist of real, definite objects, particularly while no one is looking.

They have long ago, though, had to relinquish the requirement that these particles be conceptually similar to microscopic versions of material macroworld particles. Clearly they are not. They will settle at this point for something, aspects and attributes actually, that have a definite existence in between times that someone looks. This would restore some ordinariness to the little particles, and it would mean that all those indefinite probabilities were simply the result of our ignorance of what is really happening behind the scenes. But they still recognize the need for the wave to put limits on a particle's aspects, its location say.

Since one particle's wave necessarily mingles with and affects the wave of a neighboring particle, and since this mingling thereafter must stretch across any distance of space, then two particles must constantly somehow stay in contact and instantly communicate their respective attributes so that they may remain consistent with each other. And, of course, that wave must still somehow let particles walk through walls. At some point, the requirements for the behavior of these *real* particles becomes so un-ordinary that little is gained by adhering to the realist's requirement. After all, the motivation was to preserve ordinariness down at the microworld level. Nevertheless, the desire to project some ordinary, familiar aspects of the macroworld into the unobservable microworld is so strong that as mentioned earlier, many of quantum theory's originators never relinquished this hope and belief in their lifetimes.

But we are confronted again with the problem of paradigms. There are several different schools of thought out there, several different paradigms, as to how to interpret what's going on in the microworld, the realists being just one school. If we have several paradigms, each of which describes the world *exactly*, which one do we choose? According to Occam's Razor, we should choose the one that's the simplest, the most practical or user friendly. The problem here is that they are all identical in the way they're applied, i.e., they all use the same mathematics. If the realists calculate the outcome of some experiment, and a different school calculates the outcome of the same experiment, the calculations, the marks we see on the paper, look identical and are indistinguishable.

We cannot apply Occam's Razor here because none is simpler or easier than another. In principle and practice then, we can choose whichever one is the friendlier to our minds, but here again, none of them are really very friendly. They all require that we use the mathematics of the wave and accept instantaneous action at a distance. So let's say we pick one. We say to ourselves, "Ok, this one is the way I'm going to think about it in my head from now on." We've settled the issue for ourselves, but after a while we find that it's not a very satisfying solution. That's because we still haven't convinced ourselves that the one we've chosen is the "right" one, and that's because it's nothing more than an *unfounded* belief. There's just no way to tell which is the right one. There's no test we can apply that will distinguish one from the rest. We're back to the problem of proposing hypotheses that cannot be tested and validated as true or false. And if you remember from chapter 2 on the scientific method, if a hypothesis is not testable then there's no use in entertaining it at all, because there's no way of ever knowing whether it's valid or not.

For the better part of a century now, the *realists* have been hoping that somehow all this quantum uncertainty was all going to turn out to result from ignorance on our part as to what's behind it all. They have been devising ways that some sort of *ordinary* reality can be behind the observed phenomena. Now one thing this all implies is that there is another school that *did* relinquish the idea that there was some sort of ordinary matter behind it all and indeed this is the case. In fact, what has come to be called the *orthodox interpretation*, or the *standard interpretation*, believes that it is neither useful nor possible to attempt to even consider what is *real* in the microworld. The orthodox interpretation stops at the mathematics, saying that since this is all we can possibly know then this is all there is. They believe that *since we cannot know more than we do*, then there just isn't any sense worrying about if there's anything more behind it or not. They believe nature is telling us that *there isn't anything more*, there is no hidden reality behind it. To them, we have reached rock bottom, and the mathematics is it. I suspect they are aided in no small part by the difficulty of accepting the weirdness of what that reality would have to be if it existed. So far the discovery of *ordinariness* that the realists have been hoping for just isn't happening. The advance of the *orthodox interpretation* has been relentless, powerful, and so far unassailable.

According to the *orthodox interpretation* particles do not have definite attributes at all, like location, when not being looked at, but that's not the end of it. The attributes that a particle turns out to have, result partly from what measurement apparatus we use to look with. This happens because all the entangled particle waves of all the particles of the measurement apparatus then also become part of the particle's wave. And that includes the observer, i.e. us.

The measurement instrument, and we ourselves, are composed of this microworld stuff after all. If this realization is carried to its logical conclusion, this means that what attribute we see is what we look for. What we human beings see and measure is usually location, but quantum particles do not have inherent properties prior to being observed. This implies that something is wrong with our very idea of location in the microworld. These waves we have been imagining don't even exist in location space, but instead, location space is a result of the measurements we perform. We measure location, because that's what we look for.

In the orthodox interpretation, *atoms and particles are not things*, and they are not real waves either, not in any ordinary sense, because waves exist in, and take up space. It turns out that space somehow *results* from our observing them. Location, and thus space is an effect they have, an observable effect. A particle's attributes do not exist inherent in the particle itself, but are our perception of the effect produced by the experimental arrangement. The deepest *real* thing that *we* can know is the measurement instrument itself, and don't forget that the measurement instrument is composed of these microworld phantoms too.

In the orthodox interpretation, the observer *chooses* (not necessarily *free* choice) what the microworld seems to be like by what attributes s/he looks for. With the introduction of *choice* into the schema, choice plays a role in what the universe is we see. If the wave potentials for a particular observation haven't been collapsed onto a single outcome for billions of years, all those ancient potentials apparently still exist, and we can collapse them back to even billions of years ago by a *choice we make now*. We have seen that this ability to choose which of the wave potentials we want to see not only can reach back and affect reality across time, but can reach out across all space as well. This ability of the observer to choose and thus cause certain aspects of the microworld to become real has been referred to as observer created reality, or OCR, and it has some interesting implications. One of them was expressed early on by one of quantum physic's founders, Erwin Schrodinger. It goes like this.

A particle's probability wave contains the potential for many possible futures, and apparently all of the futures proceed forward until one is chosen and the wave collapses all the way back to its beginning. Now the final detection, that is the final observational effect, can be and is *amplified* into a macroworld event by our measuring instrument that we experience. (We couldn't know of it otherwise.) If our measuring instrument is working away and no one is looking at it, it apparently has not collapsed the wave to a single outcome until somebody looks, so the measuring instrument itself is in multiple states of measuring all possible states. Now for simplicity, Schrodinger imagined a wave with only two possible potential results, and he imagined a measuring instrument, say a Geiger counter, which would measure only these two possible potentials and take one action if one outcome was measured and a quite different action if the other outcome was measured. Once again, if nobody is looking, the wave, which now includes all the particles of the Geiger counter itself, is progressing forward through both futures and taking both potential actions at the same time. They of course aren't real(ized) until somebody looks.

Now just for the thrill of it the action he imagined his Geiger counter taking was the release of a small quantity of poisonous gas, and just to get everyone's attention, he imagined taking the whole thing and sealing it in a box along with some unfortunate cat. The situation then is that while nobody's looking, both of the potential futures proceed to conclusion. In one future, the cat is happily alive, but in the other future the cat is most certainly dead. This is famously known as the "Schrodinger's cat" experiment. Since up until now nobody has opened the box and looked, the $64,000 question is "is the cat dead, is it alive, or is it somehow in both states until some future time when somebody opens the box and looks?" Of course, the only way to find out is to look, but this will assuredly collapse the wave onto a single outcome, so no matter what we do we will observe only one outcome or the other. So the answer is that we don't know, and it appears that we can never answer this question by looking.

Now you have already seen that when two particles interact, what's happening is that their probability waves merge to a single comprehensive wave that now predicts the probabilities for a pair of particles, vs. two single particles. As more and more particles interact, the waves of all of these particles merge into a single wave, and their probabilities become *entangled*. Macroworld objects, like measuring instruments or even you or me, are composed of huge groupings of particles that are all interacting, and thus macroworld objects are also governed by conglomerated probability waves. As mentioned earlier, though, as the group of particles becomes larger, the probabilities are greatly reduced and become extremely limited, so we only see macroworld objects behaving in very definite and predictable ways, not tunneling through solid walls for instance.

We have also seen that once a particle's wave has become entangled with another particle's wave, they remain entangled even if they separate by great distances. As more and more particles in the universe interact, more and more particles become entangled, and more and more of the universe becomes entangled into a seamless whole. Remember for instance, all of the atoms that compose the Earth and our bodies were created inside of stars which have exploded, so the material of our bodies is entangled with a great quantity of other material that is now dispersed throughout the Milky Way galaxy. Then again, if the Big Bang is correct, all matter was interactive at the very beginning, in which case all matter in the universe must participate in one single entangled wholeness of some sort. In this sense, the universe is a completely connected whole, truly a *universe*.

Mind and matter:

For millennia now, philosophers who worry about things like the difference between matter and the mind have been arguing about whether we have free will or whether everything we do is predetermined. Now it seems pretty obvious to most people that they do have free will, since they seem to happily go about their daily business doing what they choose to do. The problem is that if the details of the world are determinant, that is, governed by something like cause and effect, then each little thing that happens is caused by something before it, so events can be described as long chains of cause and effect, where the last effect becomes the cause of the next effect. In this case, every event large or small becomes predetermined. If you think about it, each one of us becomes pretty predictable to those who know us very well, so maybe the feelings we have that drive our free will are more predetermined than we realize.

As physics developed and mathematics' iron grip tightened on our description of the world, predetermination became more obvious than ever. Now the down side to this is that our bodies and particularly our brains are governed by these very laws of nature, so it began to appear that each event that occurred in our brains occurred automatically and predictably, that is, as a result of the previous event in our brains. When the neurons are activated that make us feel hungry, they automatically activate the next set of neurons that make us get up and look for food. One set of neuron impulses sets off the next set of impulses, and in this case our conscious minds, which appear to us to make the decision, would have nothing to do with it. We would be like robots. Free will in this case is an illusion. The brain does its thing totally automatically and consciousness is just along for the ride. We think we make decisions and take deliberate actions, but this must all be an illusion if determinacy rules in the depths of our brains.

A couple of decades ago some researchers actually found a way to test this. One of the experiments they did was to wire up subjects so they could monitor the electrical activity in their arms. Then they asked the subjects to intently watch a clearly marked rotating disk and at some point to move their arm. The subjects were then asked to reveal the position of the disk at the point they acted to actually move their arm.

What the researchers found was astonishing. They found that the wired up arm internally prepared to move about a quarter to half a second *before* the subject even decided to move the arm. Now this is exactly what one would expect to find if consciousness is in fact just along for the ride and free will is only an illusion. The conscious decision to move the arm was a Johnny-come-lately to the physical act that was already well under way. At first glance at least, this looks like the death knell for free will. But there's a way out.

Enter quantum physics and the wave function. Earlier it was pointed out that macroworld objects, like Schrodinger's measuring device, proceed forward down multiple potential futures just like microworld objects, and these futures are collapsed onto a single outcome when someone looks. Now there's been a lot of discussion as to whether the mind, whatever that is, is involved with collapsing the wave to a single outcome, so for the sake of argument, for a little while let's suppose that the mind is involved. And let's recognize that the brain itself is an object composed of massively wave entangled particles, and that it may, therefore, proceed down multiple futures just like a Geiger counter or any other measuring device or macroworld object. This seems to suggest the possibility that at any given moment the brain is pursuing multiple potential futures, some of which could be moving the arm, and others in which the arm doesn't move.

So let's say that the mind really is involved with collapsing the wave to a single outcome, so at some point in each of the experimental subjects their mind chooses to move the arm. *Now* what would the researchers expect to find? The history that the moving arm outcome would collapse onto would have to be the brain and nervous system state where the arm had prepared to move. The *history* of a collapsed result will always be consistent with that result, so if this interpretation holds up, quantum entanglement has at least temporarily breathed life back into the predetermination/free will debate. Also if this holds up, it will be the best indication so far that the mind is involved in the wave collapse. No measuring instrument or macroworld object narrows the gap between the mind and the wave collapse closer than the brain itself.

In this interpretation, the human being, and his brain in particular, becomes one with the wave of the measuring device, and the wave collapse is somehow caused by the mind collapsing the wave of the brain. One somewhat interesting implication of this idea is that if it is true, the mind interacts with (has an effect on) the brain, and this suggests the possibility that the mind has at least a small amount of independence from the brain. This will all be considered much more deeply in Section 3, *The Matter of Mind*, where I attempt to demonstration (and believe successfully) that just such an independence appears to exists.

Interpreting the microworld:

Another quite different school is the multiverse school introduced earlier that holds that the wave never does collapse onto a single outcome, but instead all outcomes are realized. In the multiverse interpretation, there are infinities upon infinities of complete universes, and it is continuously multiplying by more infinities every second. This interpretation too precludes our everyday interpretation of space and materiality. There just is no way in our materialistic viewpoint of the world that there can be even two universes existing coincidentally. Materiality prohibits that. There's just no room. In the multiverse, your body and mind split into an infinite number of human beings right along with the universes so any one of your beings follows only a single thread and thus has only a single history. In the multiverse, every *possible* universe achieves existence, no matter how improbable. Believe it or not, this multiverse interpretation has considerable appeal among physicists and is fairly well taken. The reason is that the multiverse avoids the wave collapse problem altogether and thus avoids the unknowns (like the mind) associated with what causes it to happen.

As it turns out, none of the different interpretations permit us to imagine a microworld composed of material particles. The orthodox interpretation believes there is no lower level of reality behind it at all, no materiality, and that the question is necessarily moot since we can simply see no deeper. The hope of the realists has been that the wave is just a statistical description of what the particle aspects are doing. They want to believe that something *real* exists the whole time, not just as a potential, and that there are real but hidden causes for the particle to go where it goes. This is the only interpretation that preserves any aspects of ordinariness at all, but it necessarily adheres to the same unintelligible observed phenomena, the same mathematical description as the other interpretations. The multiverse interpretation, for its part, spawns infinities of universes every moment. None of the interpretations allow us to imagine anything like *substance* as we know it at the level of the microworld, and there is not even any such thing as *space* in the microworld.

In the end, the microworld is unobservable to us. It is below the realm of anything we can sense directly. It is for one thing simply way too small. In order to know it exists at all, we have to find ways for it to affect us, and all we can know about it are its effects. We can never see or detect a particle directly. We are destined only to know its effects. We can never see the microworld, the *ground* that the macroworld stands on, only the effects and the mathematics that predict those effects.

How can it be that we can say that we're not even certain that there is anything behind the mathematics that we might call stuff, or substance? It has to do with how we find out what we know about the microworld.

There reaches a point below which we cannot go for any particular method of physical inquiry. Before Janssen invented the microscope in 1590, we had no way to detect the world of the "wee beasties" as Leewenhook described them when he first peered into the microscope. All the effects that germs and single celled creatures caused were attributed to other, usually ephemeral things. Life was thought to result from some essence, and disease was thought to be caused by demons. That sort of thing. A century ago the atom was not known to exist, and the battle was raging as to whether there was anything *real* behind the effect of the atom, or whether the bottom level was the mathematics. As we have seen, eventually the atom was proven to exist.

During recent times, the battle has been raging as to whether there is anything real behind the quantum mathematics or whether it is all just the mathematics and logic. One might be tempted to conclude from these examples that like the microscope and the atom, it may become possible some day to probe behind the mathematics of the quantum and thus show the reality that is behind it. Maybe, but if we do, it appears that what we find will necessarily be an illusion. In fact, I think they gave in to an illusion a hundred years ago when they accepted the existence of the atom as proven. If you recall from section one, we seem doomed never to be able to detect anything directly, whether it be atom or cardinal. All we can ever know about anything is the information we receive about the effects it has on something else, the disturbances we detect.

To see this, let's review the debate over the existence of the atom of a hundred years ago. This debate has several parallels with the debate over quantum reality. For one, the mathematics that described the behavior of the atom was largely statistical and probabilistic, and today the mathematics of the quantum world is largely statistical and probabilistic. Now interestingly when the atom was finally proven to exist, the accepted proofs were largely statistical and probabilistic. These proofs were Einstein's proof that Brownian motion was caused by atoms, in addition to the development of the laws of thermodynamics.

But Einstein's proof was based on statistics and probability, as are the revelations of thermodynamics, so all they ever really had was the mathematics that described these effects. Yet these were taken as proof at the time that the atom existed, whereas the quantum version has not been accepted as proof either way. What is the difference? The difference is that the atom of 1900 that the mathematics was describing behaved like a believable particle, a familiar macroworld particle, whereas the world being described behind the quantum mathematics is incomprehensibly strange. The idea that aspects of a particle, like that its location or its velocity are not a single value, is just plain unacceptable to the *realists*. Certainly this is at least partly because they continue to think in terms of a material particle, the materiality of which became unknowable long ago. All that is ever knowable about a particle is the effect it has, and *what is behind that effect, if anything, is always only imaginary.*

Finally, it should be noted that during the last century the atom has indeed reverted from a *proven* material particle to a mathematical quantum particle. Its accepted existence as *real* was a short one, and it currently ranks no better than the electron, the photon, or any other quantum particle as being composed of something *real*.

Aspects, and categories:

It turns out that just like the macroworld cars or cardinals of Chapter 4, we can and do divide all the microworld objects up into categories too. One set of these categories are the different quantum particles, the electron, proton, neutron, etc., and just like their macroworld counterparts, they each have a set of characteristics that makes it possible for us to decide which particle they are. Instead of a bill, feet, and feathers, an electron is distinguishable from other particles by its electrical charge and mass, for example. Now cardinals are distinguishable from other birds by the color of its feathers, and the *color* of its feathers is what we call the actual *value* of its color aspect. The value of a bluebird's color category is *blue*. And just like birds, particles are distinguishable from each other by the *values* of their categories, their mass category and charge categories for example. Now the values of some aspects don't change, and *we use these* **constant** *categories to distinguish one type of particle from another type of particle*, an electron from a proton say. A (male) cardinal is always red, and the mass of an electron is always 9.11 x

10^{-28} grams. There are other aspects that objects have, though, both macroworld and microworld, which may change or are **variable**. *These changeable categories we use to distinguish particles of the same type from one another.* These aspects are things like their location, there speed, things like that.

Remember back in Chapter 4 that the only way we had of distinguishing two identical cars from each other was their different location values. It is these variable aspect values that are predicted as probabilities by the quantum wave mathematics. Remember also that it was the different locations of the identical cars that we used to distinguish them, to know that they weren't the same car. We should remember too that in order for two cars, or two husbands, to lose their distinct identities, it was necessary to represent them first as information. In the macroworld, it is possible for identities to entangle only in information systems like the mind, or a computer. We also see a similar phenomenon occur in the microworld, and as will become evident, this too is related to the fact that all we get from the microworld is *information*.

Now for anything to be known to us it must make a difference in the world around us in order for us to detect it. If it makes no difference, no difference whatsoever, then we can't detect it and it doesn't exist in our universe. One way that we detect the existence of an electron, say, is the flash that occurs, the photon it causes, when it crashes into a phosphor screen. This is how the conventional television picture tube works. There is an electron gun at the back of the picture tube that fires streams of electrons at the phosphor screen in the front of the tube painting the moving picture that holds us all transfixed.

Now the primary way that a particle makes a difference in the universe around it is via entanglement. It mingles its potential wave with the waves of everything around it and this affects its potentials and the potentials of everything it interacts with. Now in some experiments that fire an electron at a phosphor screen the potential wave of the electron allows it to potentially hit the screen in any number of places. Apparently what happens is that the universe proceeds forward as if the electron hit the screen in all of these possible places at once. This then generates a flood of potential photons that are now flying toward the eye of some poor graduate student who's sitting there waiting to see a single tiny flash from a single electron on the phosphor screen. Now, the eye of the beholder is surely also a part of the system, so that means that all those photons, only one of which will end up *real-ized*, enter his or her eye and generate separate potential nerve impulses that all traverse to the brain. The brain is also part of the system, so all those different images of the flashing phosphor now generate multiple potential images in the brain. And somewhere right around here the potential wave collapses onto a single image of a single phosphor flashing and the graduate student sees only a single flash.

One point that is very evident from all this is that we certainly never perceive the electron directly, but rather only the disturbance that it makes in the universe around it. On the one hand, just like we never really see the cardinal, but only the disturbance that it makes, we never see the electron, but only the flash from its interaction on the phosphor screen. On the other hand, even registering the flash in our mind is quite a ways downstream on the chain of entangled waves. Also, like the cardinal, the information about the disturbance is carried to us by way of the light that is generated by the disturbance. We never experience the electron directly, and in fact we can't even get very close experientially. All we receive is information about the event in the form of light, which to us becomes a symbolic representation of the event. The mathematics tells us what information it is possible for us to expect to receive from the event, but we cannot ever get directly to the event, much less to what is behind it. Our experience of the information created by the event is way downstream from the event itself. It is impossible for us ever to get down to the foundations of the world. It is impossible for us to experience the ground out of which the world is made.

Quantum theory is if anything about information. It is about what we can know about the microworld, using the macroworld as our intermediary. The constituents of the microworld are too small to detect directly so we have created detectors, instruments that are affected by these microscopic constituents, particles or photons, say, that translate, or amplify that effect to something detectable by us macroworld creatures. And quantum physics is about what or how much information we can get from our detectors, and it is about how much we can deduce from this information about the microworld.

Since it is *utterly impossible* to get to what is behind what the mathematics is telling us, the orthodox interpretation takes the stand that it is a moot point, that there is really no point in thinking about it or imagining something behind it all. If we imagine anything at all, it must be relegated to the status of imagination forever. For all practical purposes, this leaves us with only the mathematics and logic as our bottom level. We have hit a wall, the wall of logic, beyond which we cannot see.

The readers may well be wondering to themselves at this point what it will achieve to imagine a deeper paradigm. Paradigms seem to be guaranteed to fail some day, and this one isn't even verifiable. No matter what one imagines is going on behind the scenes, everyone is going to observe exactly the same things. There is an observational level beyond which we cannot go. At that point, the description becomes mathematical. The formal mathematics of the Formal Paradigm becomes the bottom level, the bottom line description, the one that all of our other paradigms must conform to. If the mathematics is describing some other kind of realism, we are prohibited from seeing it. If there is some bottom level of reality, some ground, it seems at this point that we will never stand on it. The alternative to this is, of course, something like the Greek idea of Logos. A bottom level of pure logic, immaterial, bodiless, out of which all the rest of reality, our reality is constructed.

The Missing Materiality:

The characteristics of the microworld simply do not allow for materiality as we know it. From what we're seeing, the microworld is decidedly immaterial. Any attempt to *imagine* something material existing behind it all is just that, imagination. The only reason we might suspect that the microworld has a material aspect to it at all is that *the macroworld we live in seems to be a material world*, and if the macroworld is material, then it seems that the microworld must be too. As we will see in the next chapter, this turns out to be no evidence at all. The macroworld, the world we live in, has seemed in the past to be many things that it is not.

Giving up the idea of a material microworld has not been very palatable to many physicists, but then again physicists have had to accept many strange ideas in their search for a description of reality. A major point of this section was to expose the reader to some of these weird ideas that physicists have had to accept. Let's revisit just a few of them that have been difficult.

- Space and distances are different for different observers.

- Time passes at different rates for different observers.

- You can observe someone's clock running slower than yours, while to them yours is running slower than theirs.

- You cannot change your speed relative to a light ray. It will always seem to move at 186,000 mi/sec.

- Someone's birth or death can occur twice in your lifetime.

- Cause and effect is not the way the universe works.

- Microscopic particles don't exist when no one is looking.

- Particles may travel into several futures at once.

- A particle's history may be changed.

These are a few of the phenomena of the universe that physicist, and the rest of us, have found some difficulty swallowing. Now let's look at some of the aspects of the microworld that suggest that it consists of no substance, that it cannot be material, at least not our macroworld idea of material.

Compressibility:

The matter that we know and love has a limited compressibility. There is a minimum volume that our matter can be compressed into. Gasses when compressed to a small volume become liquid, and are only microscopically compressible after that. Solid matter too, like a brick or a chunk of stainless steel, is only microscopically compressible. A chunk of coal, or your deceased loved one's ashes, can be pressed into a diamond at high pressures, which becomes very hard and solid, but the volume of the matter barely changes. Matter seems to be hard.

But it turns out that the hard stuff we think of as solid matter is far more compressible than even our idea of a gas. The material composing a white dwarf star compresses the matter of a battleship into the volume of a teaspoon. The matter composing a neutron star compresses the matter of millions of earths into the volume of Manhattan Island. A black hole compresses the matter of a trillion earths into no volume at all, right out of existence, and of course in the case of the Big Bang all the solid matter of the universe was compressed into a microscopic space far smaller than a proton. In the end, there's nothing solid, nothing material, nothing hard there at all. Our idea of materiality, of hard, solid stuff that composes the matter around us results only from our rather limited experience with it in our everyday world. Hard, solid stuff is not all that hard, and in the end consists of no more substance than empty space itself.

Shrinkability and stretchability:

At very high speeds, matter shrinks right along with the space it occupies, and of course as it slows down it stretches back out right along with the space it occupies. At the speed of light, it would shrink out of existence, if it were possible to reach the speed of light. Here again, matter demonstrates a similarity to empty space, expanding and contracting right along with space itself.

Location:

The matter we experience, a brick for example, exists in a very explicit location, has a very definite shape, and has a very definite volume. As we descend into the microworld, though, particles themselves lose these characteristics. A particle, represented by the wave, exists in multiple locations simultaneously, and the wave aspect that defines its location may allow it to range over a considerable volume of space. It may even exist at disconnected regions of space that are separated by a wall. Everything that is definite about a brick itself becomes indefinite when applied to the particles that compose the brick. We think of a brick, and material objects in general, as having definite spatial characteristics. Definite location and volume are characteristics we expect from material objects, and this just isn't the case for objects, for particles, in the microworld.

Time:

A macroworld object exists at a single definite place and at a single definite time. As we have seen, a microworld object's time is no more definite than it's location. Furthermore, it may proceed into multiple futures simultaneously. This leads to a microworld object's having multiple potential histories. We cannot even imagine a material solid object moving into multiple futures. It is a single thing at a single place in time. It is impossible to behave otherwise and still be a solid material object as we know it. Materiality just doesn't act this way.

The wave:

A microworld particle doesn't have the *effect* of a particle when no one is looking. It behaves like a wave, and it is not even a material wave, like a water wave or something. The wave doesn't exist in space at all. All we know about the wave is that the mathematics describes it very well. It doesn't seem to have any kind of *real* existence as we think of real. It doesn't exist in spacetime. It is outside of space and time. Space and time seem to be aspects of it, versus the other way around. We derive space and time from interacting with the wave. Only when we interact with the wave do we get the effects we associate with a particle. The wave is not only decidedly immaterial, it is unknown if it has any kind of real existence at all beyond the mathematics.

Impenetrability:

A billiard ball or a brick are relatively impenetrable to other solid objects. This means basically that they cannot both exist in the same place at the same time (called the space/time exclusion principle). Microworld objects have no such limitation. They not only are able to mingle their locations, but they are able to mingle their very identities. A material wall is no barrier to a microworld object. It simply comes into existence on the other side of it. And if the multiverse interpretation turns out to be correct, we will have whole universes that exist simultaneously. Then, of course, there is the dark matter that we now know composes about 95% of the matter of the universe, which seems to have no problem at all existing in the same place at the same time as our familiar matter. Impenetrability, a characteristic of substance, does not exist in the microworld.

The *materiality* we find in the macroworld does not extend down into the microworld. Our human idea of solid matter, of materiality, of substance, stands in stark contradiction to each one of the phenomena listed above. Nothing material can behave this way or do these things. Whatever else it is, the microworld is not material!

Chapter 8
Making The Macroworld

It is an old maxim of mine that
when you have excluded the impossible,
whatever remains, however improbable,
must be the truth.

—Conan Doyle, The Adventures of Sherlock Holmes, "The
Beryl Coronet"

In our perpetual search for better paradigms, we have always been strictly limited to what it is possible for us to imagine. As we have seen, this is because we as humans necessarily describe things in terms of that which we already know, that with which we are already familiar, the words of our language if you will. This is the sim/dif discussed back in chapter 4, which is necessary for meaning to occur at all. So as a rule each new paradigm has contained or been based on something, or some idea, developed during the previous paradigm. As we probed reality more and more deeply, we have always carried our familiar macroworld idea of materiality down with us. We have now reached the bottom where we have discovered that it doesn't apply. Whatever else quantum particles are, they are not substance. There is no materiality in the microworld...but now in one sense the process has begun to reverse. We have hit the bottom and the ideas we have uncovered there are bouncing back up. We have now added the *immateriality* found in the microworld to our repertoire of familiar ideas and it is spreading, spreading back up the levels of reality, dissolving each higher level as it goes into the realm of immaterial nothingness. Will it eventually reach us and consume us? Will it consume the entire universe?

A microworld particle is characterized by a wave that has no *material* existence, so what exactly does the wave represent? The wave represents the attributes and aspects of the particle. But these attributes and aspects of the particle are nothing but its effects, the effects it has on other particles, and on our measuring instruments. When the wave of one particle mingles with the wave of another particle, they affect each other, that is, they each change or modify in some way the variable aspects of the other particle. This is the *effect* they have on each other. The wave mathematically represents the effects particles will have on each other, and the only thing one particle can know about another particle (if it were capable of knowing) is that something out there had an effect on it.

To help isolate this idea of the effect as an entity onto itself, imagine for a moment that you are an asteroid or a comet happily floating free out between the stars. Let's say that the only sense you have is your sense of motion (relative to your galaxy, say), so you are of course blind as a bat. Now you're floating along and for hundreds of thousands of years you have perceived no change in your motion, but gradually you begin to feel your direction changing ever so slightly. As the eons pass, the change in direction increases and soon your speed in the new direction begins to increase too. Gradually your direction and speed start changing faster and faster until eventually you're hurtling at terrifying speeds through a hairpin turn, like the ones roller coaster junkies are perpetually seeking. Soon you start slowing down again and the turn's sharpness diminishes until finally, in the exact reverse order you are eventually once again happily floating free out between the stars.

What happened of course is that you had entered the gravitational field of a passing star. At first, the stars gravitational effect on you was very slight, the change in your direction being barely perceptible. As you got closer to the star, however, the effect of the gravitational field increased, pulling you faster and faster and more and more in the direction of the star. Eventually, you were approaching the star very closely traveling at super velocities in what's commonly referred to as a slingshot around the star. Then, as you left the vicinity of the star, its effect on your direction and speed became less and less until its effect on you finally went to zero again.

As a blind asteroid, though, you don't know anything about stars. You don't know there even are stars, and you don't know anything about gravity. In fact, you don't know anything about anything. You don't know that there was something, star or otherwise, which caused the effect you experienced. All you know of is that there was this effect on you. Your motion, and how it changes, are all you can know about the universe. It is the only sense you have. You can only know the universe by the effects that you experience, and in this case the only realm you know that can be affected is your motion. If we had also given you a sense of temperature, you would have noticed your temperature changing right along with your speed and direction, and you would certainly have developed a tentative correlation between the increasing temperature and the increasing velocity and curvature of your motion. You might even have presumed that one caused the other, which of course they didn't even though they're correlated. The rise in temperature was caused by the increased radiation received from the star, and the increase in motion was caused by the increasing gravitational field.

The point again though is that we are blind to anything but the effects we experience, and the same is true for any two interacting objects, including particles. The only thing one particle knows of or can tell about another particle is the effect that is occurring on, or to, it. Of course, that particle is having a similar effect on the other particle too. It is these effects that are mediated by the entanglement of the quantum wave.

Aggregate objects:

When two or more particles interact, one effect they may have on each other is that they may clump together, thus creating a new object, a new particle. The new object may then exhibit characteristics that are new and different from the particles from which it is composed. These objects, composed of accumulations or aggregations of other interacting objects, are called aggregate objects. A proton is composed of an aggregate of quarks and is quite a different animal from the quarks that compose it. Atoms too are aggregates of protons, neutrons, and electrons and have quite different characteristics from the constituent particles.

This aggregation process occurs over and over creating higher and higher levels of order, or hierarchies of aggregations. Atoms aggregate to form molecules. Molecules aggregate to form minerals. If one follows up the life hierarchy, molecules aggregate to form amino acids, which aggregate to form proteins. Proteins aggregate to form organelles. Organelles aggregate to form cells. Cells aggregate to form organs. Organs aggregate to form systems, like the digestive system or the nervous system, and systems aggregate to form organisms. Organisms aggregate to form ecosystems. And ecosystems, perhaps, aggregate to form Gaea. One can also follow the hierarchies up the human line where humans aggregate into families, families to communities, communities to municipalities, to counties, to states, to countries, etc. The universe itself qualifies as an aggregate object in that it is composed of interacting components, and anything that doesn't interact is simply not part of the aggregate object, i.e., is not part of this universe. Sometimes it seems like aggregation is so pervasive that creating higher and higher levels of order must be the primary purpose of the physical universe…but that's another book.

Within an aggregate object, the component objects each interact with one another, contributing their effect on each other to create the new whole, the new higher level aggregate object. As usual, each component object knows the other component object only by its effect on them. This is true whether the aggregate object is an atom or a city, and for the interested reader, the constant exchange of effects between the components of an aggregate object is called an *economy*. Now the new higher level aggregate object itself has effects on its surroundings, effects quite different from its individual interacting components, and thus becomes a higher level component itself, participating in yet a new, higher level aggregate object.

The immediate point of all of this is that an object within an aggregate is known to another object around it only by some effect it has on that object, and vice versa. In the end, it turns out that the only things that even can be known about an object, qualify as effects that the object has, and what I have just said in so many words is that *there is nothing else in the world but effects*, at least nothing that we or any other object can know of. You need to memorize that. It's natural for us when we experience an effect to imagine something behind the effect, an object, something that caused the effect, but it turns out that we are truly imagining it. All we can ever know of are effects, and we can never know what was behind it, only imagine it. We cannot know of any objects behind the effects we experience.

As we have seen, in the early 1900's the battle was raging as to whether the atom really existed or whether it was all just a mathematical phantom. With the advent of Einstein's proof and the development of thermodynamics, it was settled in the affirmative…but its material reality was short lived. With the advent of quantum physics, the atom once again reverted to a mathematical phantom right along with all the other quantum particles. Now as you know, the atom is not just a single particle, but is an aggregate of other quantum particles, phantom particles, i.e., protons, neutrons, and electrons. As quantum particles aggregate into larger particles, they still remain quantum particles, that is, they're not *material* particles composed of any substance at all. What happens is that the waves of the component particles entangle creating the effect of the aggregate particle now. What happens then, when two atoms aggregate to form a molecule? Well, their waves entangle too. A molecule is just a group of two or more phantom atoms whose waves are entangled, so molecules aren't *material* particles either. Molecules are no more material particles than the immaterial atoms that compose them. You will also remember that as more and more waves become entangled, their potentials become dramatically more limited, so as these aggregates become larger and larger, they begin showing less and less of quantum randomness until they are behaving in a very orderly way, the way we expect macroworld particles to behave. Nevertheless, they are still quantum waves, and are still composed of nothing material. A house that is constructed from bricks is as hard and opaque as the bricks. It is still brick. A house that is constructed of glass is as transparent as the glass. It is still glass. And a house that is made out of immaterial phantom particles has no substance. It is still immaterial.

As the entangled aggregates become more massive, they begin to act more and more like macroworld objects. They lose their randomness and eventually become big enough to be detected, that is, have an effect on other macroworld objects. This is when they begin to become real to us. This is where the micro-world ends and the macroworld begins. This is when they begin to seem to us to be *material* objects, but they're not really. They are simply larger aggregates of quantum stuff, and there is nothing of substance there, nothing material there at all. So why all of a sudden do they begin to *seem* to us to exhibit materiality?

Perceiving a material world:

If the material world does not exist on a material foundation, if material objects are not composed out of a material substance, then we are forced to look else-where for our perception of materiality. We are forced to start at the other end of the reality chain, at the source of the *perception* of materiality itself. We are the ones who perceive a material world after all. We see bricks, ducks, cardinals, and each other as material things. What exactly are we perceiving that makes us think that these things are material?

We perceive things only by the effects they have, only by the disturbance they cause. We never do perceive an object directly. When we look out the window and see a cardinal sitting in the tree, we in fact are neither seeing the cardinal directly nor even looking through the window. We are not even looking through the air that exists between the window and us. The idea that we are looking out of ourselves at the world around us is totally an illusion. The reality is that it's exactly the opposite. We are sitting here rather passively and the information about the world is coming to us. We are not seeing anywhere. We can't even see beyond the surface of our eyes.

What is happening is this. Sunlight that reaches the cardinal interacts with the cardinal, the object. This interaction is what I've been calling the disturbance, the effected change the cardinal has on the light that strikes it. In this case, one change that occurs is that the red light is scattered, reflected, in all directions. Some of that scattered red light is headed toward you. When it encounters the window, the structure of the glass is such that the light that it absorbs is passed from molecule to molecule until it is retransmitted from its surface again on the far side of the glass. The surface layer of molecules on the side of the glass closest to you then generates the light anew, sending it on its way toward you. This is not the original light that struck the outside of the glass.

In some ways, you can think of the glass as acting like a TV screen on which you're observing the world outside, because the image you are seeing is in fact generated at its inside surface. You are not seeing *through* the glass at all. That is a convenient illusion that occurs, because modern glass recreates the light so perfectly that there is no noticeable distortion to the image. About the only obvious clue you have that you are not looking through the glass is that the objects you are seeing have been slightly displaced and are not quite where you are seeing them. They are actually somewhere else and you are not seeing them through the glass at all. (A quick experiment you can do, which reveals that you do not actually look *through* glass, is to move a pair of eyeglasses around in front of your eyes, and you will see objects appear to move all over the place. You aren't looking at the objects *through* the glasses at all.) Your mind, though, is free to pretend it is looking *through* the glass and indeed there is usually no consequence from this loss of real knowledge…unless you try to walk through it. Then the reality hits you in the face.

The same is true for the air that exists between you and the window. It too is absorbing and regenerating the light right up to the point that it comes in contact with the surface of your eyeballs. You are literally not seeing past the end of you eyeballs. The light you are seeing is generated right there, right at the surface of your eye. You are just sitting there passively receiving this light and not even starting to see across the space or through the window that separates you from the cardinal. You are not even starting to see the cardinal. All you are seeing is the disturbance that was created at the surface of your eyes and which was started by something, and now who can say what it is exactly, that is sitting in the tree outside. The disturbance that finally reaches you is very far removed and way downstream from the original disturbance that occurred out in the tree. All you really received was *information* carried to you via light from the original disturbance. The final disturbance in the light that occurred at the surface of your eye was at the end of a long chain of disturbances that it took to transmit the information to you.

Now a lot of you may be thinking, "So what?! This may all be true (it is) but what difference does this make to anything. I still know there is a cardinal out there. I have a lifetime of experience that has led me to know for sure that it's not imaginary." And you're right! Well…sort of. What you mean when you say you know it's not imaginary is that you know of at least one other way that you can verify that the cardinal exists besides your vision, besides the light it reflects. You can for example, take your BB gun, crack open the window, plink the poor cardinal (be advised, this is against the law in many states), and then go outside and pick it up in your hand and say (over the wail of approaching police sirens) "See! Here it is! I told you so." And indeed you did.

As you grip the dead cardinal in your hand, you not only see it, but you feel it too. You have now verified its reality, its existence, with two of your senses, sight as well as touch, and if you were starving to death, or if you lived in a different society from me, you might *taste* it also, after it was prepared to your satisfaction of course. In fact, one way or another, you can verify its existence with all of your senses.

So it exists. Ok, I'll give you that. You did sense its *effects* after all. Our senses are the source of our information of the world around us, and our senses tell us too that it is a material object. Let's examine a couple of things about all this. Let's revisit *exactly* how we know it *exists*, and let's look at exactly what it is we're sensing with our senses that tells us that it's a material object.

According to the discussion on how we know something exists back in Chapter Two, the number one requirement is that it must have some detectable effect on the universe around it. Our cardinal fulfills this requirement many times over, as we have just seen. It affects the light that strikes it thus allowing us to detect it using our vision. It affects our fingers when we hold it, thus allowing us to feel it, and it affects our taste buds if we eat it, thus allowing us to taste it. Each of the effects that it has on our senses is quite different. If allowed to sense the cardinal with only one of your senses, you will likely come up with different perceptions. If one is blindfolded before feeling it, there is almost a zero chance that the person will imagine it's a cardinal. Ditto with the taste test. The sense of touch is nothing like vision, and the sense of taste is nothing like touch. Which of these effects is it then, that we use to verify the notion that the cardinal is a material object.

It is our senses of vision and touch that we use to verify materiality. One may recognize that if we put something in our mouth to taste it, we can also tell that it is a material object, but this sense comes from the sense of touch inside of our mouth, not the sense of taste. Taste contains no component that relates to materiality. So what is it about our vision and touch that relates to materiality?

First of all, both vision and touch include a sense of space. I call it a sense, but it's not a sense in the same sense that the senses of touch and vision are senses. For one thing, it's a bit more internalized. It's more of a mental representation of space than it is an actual sense. We can close our eyes and wave our hand around in front of us and still mentally sense the space there without seeing or touching anything. The perception of space, though, is certainly necessary and active when we see and touch things. When we see objects, we see them as located in space, and when we close our eyes and touch the end of our nose with our finger, we know exactly where it is in space. Objects, material objects, are located in space and both our sense of vision and our sense of touch are used to locate an object in space, and if we are both seeing and touching an object, then both senses had darned well better agree on that object's location. Can you imagine looking at a coffee cup in one place but feeling it somewhere else? It is a telling phenomenon that it is indeed possible, and easy, to make these sensed locations disagree, as we will see in Section Three.

One thing that comes out of this is that one requirement for an object to be considered material is that it have a location in space. Actually, it is not just a location, but that it occupies a certain region of space, a certain volume, which is after all nothing more than the idea of space itself, i.e., a material object takes up some space. Our cardinal, or a brick, not only has a location, but a certain volume and shape as well.

There's more, however, to the perception of materiality than just the notion that a material object is located in space. It is possible, after all, to project a hologram of a cardinal into the tree and for you to see it sitting there apparently taking up space, but there are clues that can let you know that it is not a material object. If a breeze comes along and moves the leaves of the tree, you will see the leaves waving right through the cardinal as if it wasn't really there, which of course it isn't. If on the other, hand you saw the leaves bouncing off of the image, then you would consider that as evidence that the image had a material existence. So another requirement for materiality is that the region of space that an object occupies have a certain degree of impenetrability, impenetrability to waving leaves for example. This too is the clue we use to determine that ghosts are immaterial. They walk through walls after all.

You will recall that we introduced the concept of the different degrees of penetrability of billiard balls back in Chapter Four. It is the impenetrability aspect of an object that allows our sense of touch to feel it at all. If it had no degree of impenetrability at all, like empty space, we wouldn't be able to feel it. Like the hologram sitting in the tree, our finger would pass right through it. Besides location and volume, then, a degree of impenetrability is the other attribute that an object has that contributes to our concept of materiality. A cardinal or a brick both press back against our finger when we press on it, and both our sense of vision and sense of touch convey the objects location and spatial volume.

In the end, then, what we are left with sense wise as the *operational definition* of a material object, is a visible region of space that has a degree of impenetrability. (One other required behavior is that it exhibit some resistance to movement, i.e. behaves as if it had mass, but since this too is conveyed via the feel/impenetrability sense, I will ignore it here.) Take a coffee cup for example. It's visible, takes up a distinctly shaped region of space, the impenetrability of its handle insures that you can pick it up, and the impenetrability of the cup itself insures that it will hold coffee.

A region of empty space that reflects light and resists penetration *is* a material object. If someone were magically able to take a coffee cup shaped region of space and give it these properties, you couldn't tell the difference from a real coffee cup. In fact, it would work just fine as a real coffee cup. And it, therefore, would be a real coffee cup. This is what a *material* coffee cup is to us, nothing more! This is what substance is to us. We perceive anything that activates these simple senses in us as a material object made from some substance. These are in fact the *effects* that you perceive an object having that cause you to think of it as a material object. When you verified that the dead cardinal was real by picking it up, holding it, and looking at it, this is all and everything that your senses were telling you about the object. This is all that your senses can tell you about the object.

It turns out that the senses of vision and impenetrability are not at all incompatible with a quantum object's immateriality. All that the quantum wave need do is to create a region of space that reflects light and has a certain impenetrability. A non-material object can have these effects and still be non-material, although in us it triggers a sense of materiality. These effects don't contradict its non-materiality at all. In fact, all the evidence from science tells us that it must be a non-material object. It turns out that *substance is an illusion*, just like the illusion that we are looking through the glass window when we see the cardinal outside. We seem to be very prone to illusions. We will investigate this much more thoroughly in Section Three, *The Matter of Mind*.

One rather startling implication of the notion that substance and materiality are an illusion is that it follows that the Earth itself must not be a material object. The Earth itself must be an illusion. The Earth itself must simply be a region of space that reflects light and resists penetration. Take a minute and try to comprehend how this could be possible. At the end of Chapter 7, we listed several characteristics of materiality, and showed that these did not exist in the quantum world. Now I'm saying that the Earth is not a material object. Let's revisit these characteristics of materiality and see how they relate to the Earth itself.

Compressibility:

The Earth certainly seems to be incompressible. Only our most advanced technology can even compress carbon into a diamond, but once we've got a diamond, that's it. We have no way to compress a diamond further. To us, it's incompressible, and this is pretty much true for the rest of the material that composes the Earth. In the end, though, the Earth is very compressible. If it were to be pulled into a white dwarf star, it would be compressed from 8000 miles in diameter to less than a mile. If it were to get sucked into a neutron star, it would be compressed to a diameter of a few feet instantly. And if it were to get sucked into a black hole, it would in fact be compressed right out of existence. In the end, the Earth is no more substantial than empty space itself.

Shrinkability and stretchability:

If the Earth were to be accelerated to a velocity approaching the speed of light, it would shrink right along with the space it occupies and become thinner and thinner until finally it wasn't any thicker than a single atom. The fact is that the Earth is already moving at nearly the speed of light relative to objects on the far side of the universe, and viewed from those locations the Earth is indeed extremely thin. Here again, the Earth demonstrates its similarity to empty space, expanding and contracting right along with space itself.

Location:

The Earth of our experience exists in a very explicit location, has a very definite shape, and has a very definite volume. As we descend into the microworld, the particles that compose the Earth lose these characteristics. A particle, represented by the wave, exists in multiple locations simultaneously, and the wave aspect that defines its location may allow it to range over a considerable volume of space. As more and more particles entangle their waves in the creation of an aggregate object, the probability spread of its location decreases. An object the size of a baseball has a very definite location, so an object the size of the Earth has a very, very definite location. This definite location, however, is still a quantum attribute of the entangled quantum wave of all the particles that compose the Earth, and the Earth is still defined by an entangled quantum wave.

Time:

An almost identical phenomenon occurs with time as with space. As the aggregate object grows and entangles more and more waves, the time aspect becomes more and more definite. So the Earth as a macroworld object exists at very definite times, but is nevertheless an entangled quantum wave.

The wave:

A microworld particle doesn't have the *effect* of a particle when no one is looking. It behaves like a wave, and it is not even a material wave, like a water wave or something. All we know about the wave is that the mathematics describes it very well. It doesn't seem to have any kind of *material* existence as we think of it. The Earth too is an entangled quantum wave, so apparently, it doesn't have the effect of the Earth when no one is looking (which hasn't happened for awhile). Just think, back before life formed on the Earth there was no one to look, so the Earth wouldn't even have had a collapsed wave. Also before minds existed, there was no existent perception of the Earth as a material object. Although the aspects we find when we look at the Earth are much more certain than for a particle, they do still exist only in the realm of probability until someone looks. When we interact with the wave, we get the effects we associate with the material Earth, that is, it is a region of space that reflects light and has a certain impenetrability. The wave is not only decidedly immaterial, it is unknown if it has any kind of existence at all beyond the mathematics, and so too the Earth.

Impenetrability:

When we reach down and touch the ground, it exhibits enough resistance to penetration that we can feel it with our fingertip. Your finger and the ground are both composed of atoms and the outer surface of atoms consist of electrons. One effect electrons have on each other is that they repel each other from a distance. On the microscopic scale, long before the electrons in the outer surface of your finger come into contact with the electrons on the outer surface of the Earth, they repel each other. They never touch and what you are really sensing is the mutual repulsion of the electrons pushing back against your finger. This impenetrability results from the effects of the interacting quantum waves of our finger and the Earth. This means that you can never touch anything that has an outer surface covered with electrons, which includes just about everything on Earth, including your lover. Bummer! Does that mean that the only matter that we ever really touch is the dark matter which, since it doesn't affect us, we can't feel?

Materiality as a mental *representation*:

Although our senses tell us otherwise, we have seen that physics is saying that somehow the materiality of the Earth must be unreal. Not only the Earth, but the space that we and the Earth exist in must be an illusion. I have mentioned several times that space itself seems to result from the location aspect of the quantum wave. On the other hand, it seems utterly impossible that the Earth, and the space it exists in, are not real. It turns out that there is indeed a way that all this can be an illusion.

If there's reason to believe that matter and space don't exist at all, how do we know they're there? This seems to violate the very concept of existence, and this is the key, existence. You will recall that for something to exist, it must have an effect. The only thing that we can know about it is the effect it has. We can never get behind the effect. And we do indeed experience the effects that tell us that space and materiality are there (impenetrability, location, spatial extension). But this seems to be a contradiction. On the one hand, we say that they don't exist, and on the other, we experience the effects of their existence. How can there even be such a thing as their effects if they don't exist? Isn't the experience of their effects by definition sufficient proof of their existence?

Our minds and brains are for one thing information systems, that is, they are designed to receive information from our senses, represent it, process it, and represent the result. They have evolved and adapted to create a useful and workable representation of the world we live in. They create for us a *mental representation* of our world. Since what we experience is just a representation, just a recreation, that representation may or may not be a true representation of the world. The important thing from an evolutionary viewpoint is that it works well enough for the perceiving creature to survive and prosper.

First and foremost, this all implies that our mental picture, our *image* of the universe is necessarily *imaginary*. There's no getting away from that. It wouldn't even be a mental image otherwise. The question becomes as to whether our imaginary image of the world, our mental representation of the world, is an accurate recreation of the world or not. It is necessarily imaginary, though, even if it is an accurate representation of the world. As you have seen, we have reason to suspect that it might not be accurate. We mentally represent the world, we imagine the world, to be a material world, and yet when one considers the phenomena of physics, materiality as we *imagine* it seems to be impossible.

We have all gone through most of our lives believing that we experience the world around us directly. This is not the case. It is easily shown to be an illusion, and is in fact the same illusion we have when we think we're looking through a glass window seeing the world outside. Actually, our brains and minds *recreate* for us a representation, our mental representation, of the world around us. To illustrate that this is a recreation, let's look as some manifestations that can occur if we are experiencing a representation of the universe rather than somehow experiencing the universe directly. The following are characteristics of recreations and representations, and are true whether the medium of representation be watercolors on paper, or the mind/brain.

1) Deletions—When representing or copying the world, it's possible that the new representation is incomplete, that is, some items or aspects are missing or have been deleted from the representation.

2) Additions—When creating a representation of the world, it's possible that some things get invented or added in that don't even exist in the real world.

3) Distortion—When creating a representation of the world, it's possible that some things are recreated incorrectly, or just plain wrong.

4) Representability—When creating a representation of the world, it's possible that there are things in the world that aren't even representable using the chosen media. In this case, the media is the brain and mind itself, so I'm suggesting that there may be aspects of the universe that are not representable in our minds, i.e., they're **un**imaginable.

These four phenomena only occur when experiencing a representation of something, be it a work of art or the world around us. They would not occur if we were experiencing the world directly, and all four of them do occur. Let's examine each more closely.

Deletions—The only information that gets into our brains is provided by our sense organs, period, and there's a great deal out there that we don't sense. We see, for example, what we *call visible light*, but visible light is just a tiny window of the entire electromagnetic spectrum. There is much more of it that we don't see than the little part that we do see. Below the red is the infrared, and above the violet is the ultraviolet, neither of which we humans can see, although some creatures can. The birds and the bees can both see ultraviolet. I wonder what color that looks like. These creatures see things that we don't. If we could see neutrinos, we could see the cores of the Sun and stars. Then there's *dark* matter that isn't represented in our mental picture of the universe at all. All we see in the universe is *ordinary* matter, when in fact the majority of the matter in the universe is dark matter, and the reason we call it dark matter is because, you guessed it, we don't see it. It passes through us, around us, and we could even be partially composed of dark matter, but it is not represented in our mental image. Imagine dark matter creatures that sense only dark matter and no ordinary matter. If we could sense the dark matter instead of the ordinary matter, the universe would look like an entirely different kind of place. As something of a whimsical aside, if we could see dark matter creatures, we would see them walk through walls.

Additions—We do in fact experience things that have no real existence outside of our heads. Hot and cold are a couple. What we're really sensing when we feel hot and cold is something related to the motions of the molecules around us. If the molecules are moving rapidly, we experience this representation in our minds as the sensation of hot. If the molecules are moving slowly, the mental sensation experienced is cold. Hot and cold do not exist in the world around us, only the motion of molecules. The same is true for colors. In the world around us, light comes in varying wavelengths. When this information about these different wavelengths is represented in our brains, it is experienced by us as color. There is no color out there, only different wavelengths. Color is our mental representation of these different wavelengths, these differences. It is not even knowable if we all experience the same sensations when we see colors. My red might be your yellow. Maybe this is why everybody has a different favorite color. Maybe we all prefer the same sensation, but our brains create that sensation from different wavelengths. And if these representations exist only in our minds, then doesn't it follow that the same is true for the rest of our senses. Taste and smell are even more obviously mental representations, in this case of the chemistry around us, that exist only in our minds and are not actually *out there*. Color we might have been able to imagine is an objective part of nature, but surely the smell of something is subjective and requires a mind to represent it. And if all of our sensed perceptions of the world are just convenient mental representations of the world, why not materiality too? Materiality is necessarily a mental representation. The only question is, "Is materiality representing something real about the world, or only imaginary like color?"

Distortion—We perceive ourselves as motionless in space. We perceive locations in space as absolute, unchanging, when in fact there is no absolute space as was discussed in chapter 6. We see space as composed of straight lines, when in fact an apparent straight line between two points is curved. We experience gravity as a force holding us to the ground when actually it results from our traversal of these curved space-time lines. These are all mental representations that are different from what is actually going on. We experience time as passing at a steady rate when it is quite possible that the rate of time's passage is changing. We experience our universe as a material universe, when in fact there is evidence that there is no materiality. These are all mental representations, or in this case, mental misrepresentations.

Representability—The universe abounds with phenomena that we cannot *even* represent in our human mental representation. Higher dimensions is a prime example. Our mental machinery has been designed by evolution to represent three spatial dimensions. There could easily be more, but we only experience, and are able to imagine, three. There are fun books out there that play with objects like four-dimensional cubes, called hypercubes, and while it's great fun trying to stretch your mind around these ideas, the representations always have to fall back on lower dimensional mental representations that our minds are hard wired for. And there are different types of dimensions too that we can't represent mentally. It turns out that the dimensions of the microworld are *imaginary*, that is, they are based on dimensions that are able to represent the square root of negative numbers. These are called imaginary numbers because they don't exist in the world we perceive, the world we experience, but they most certainly exist in the microworld. Another phenomenon we can't represent mentally is the color of ultraviolet light. We simply have no way to imagine it, no machinery to represent it. But, apparently, the birds and the bees do, and they can see a color that we can't even imagine, and of course this list could be extended indefinitely. In the end, what we do represent mentally is quite limited when compared to what's out there to represent.

Our brains have adapted to create evolutionarily *useful* mental representations for us of a world. We get the information about the world through our sense organs that in turn send the information to our brains via their connected nerves. Our sense organs, though, are limited pretty much to sensing just the information useful to the organism, and there's quite a bit going on out there that we don't sense at all. Some of the things that our brains and minds represent to us are colors, hot and cold, materiality, and even our representation of space itself. The question now is as to whether any of these have any real existence or if they all only exist as artificial mental representations. In either case, they are just representations, we do not experience them directly, and all we can know about them is our experience of our mental representation.

The Universe as Information

We do not experience the universe directly. The only thing that reaches our bodies and sense organs is *information* about what is going on out in the universe. This information is passed around in the universe by means of the effects a disturbance has on the world around it, effects that it is impossible for us to see behind. These effects cause long chains of effects that eventually reach our bodies. Our bodies are then affected too, which allows us to sense these outside effects, and our brains and minds represent these effects as the universe that we perceive around us. We are, each one of us, in the most literal sense, information processors, and to process information we need input information. From our point of view, from the point of view of creatures that need information input from the outside universe to process, the universe appears to us to be in the business of passing around information.

When we look out the window and see the cardinal sitting in the tree, the only thing we are receiving/perceiving is the information that has reached the pupils of our eyeballs. It is not even the original light that was reflected from the cardinal, but light that has been absorbed and regenerated many times as the disturbance propagates about the universe, some of which eventually reaches you. In the end, the only disturbance that we receive is the last disturbance, the disturbance that occurred right at the surface of our eyes. The thing that originally caused the disturbance is very far away, unknowable to us. All we can ever know about it, the only thing that our senses sense about it, is the disturbance that it causes, not the thing itself.

At first, it seems like the stuff that is disturbed and carries the information ends up with more reality than that which caused the disturbance. But we can't even know the *stuff* that carries the information! All we know is the disturbance. We don't know that these disturbances are being carried by disturbances in *stuff* at all. The stuff that our brains are representing to us isn't the stuff out there at all, only the disturbances, and it is only the last disturbance that occurred at the surface of our eyes that we receive. Do we really know what the universe is that abuts up against our eyes? Can we? Our brains are representing the information that they receive to us as the world we know, but they are just representing information that they receive. Is that representation accurate, or just an evolutionarily convenient mental representation?

Like ripples on a pond, information is carried about in the universe by the continuous propagation of disturbances. A disturbance is a *change* in something. When something is disturbed, something about the thing that is disturbed changes. We can disturb the glassy smooth surface of a pond by dropping a pebble into it, for example. When a disturbance occurs, whatever it is that is changed requires energy, so all disturbances can be characterized by a change in energy of the medium that is being disturbed, particularly the ones we receive. The information carried to us by light, for example, is transmitted to us by making slight changes in the energy in molecules in the rods and cones in our eyes.

Now, when we think of changes occurring, we always think of the change occurring in something. We always think there has to be a *something* to which the change occurs, but rather miraculously, this turns out not to be the case. It turns out that light can be propagated as changes in nothing. This fact turned out to be a difficult pill to swallow for scientists of a century ago. Light travels through totally empty space just fine, in fact even better than in air, so scientists originally hypothesized an invisible realm through which light propagated, called *ether*. When it turned out, though, that the speed of light was relative to the observer and not the ether, it was realized that the ether wasn't possible. Light travels through nothing better than it travels through something, but it is nevertheless still characterized as a change in energy. Now, energy itself is a rather strange and incomprehensible thing. For example, the formula that represents energy is denominated by the quantity of square seconds, and no one knows what a square second is. Ponder that for a while.

The point of all this is that information is carried by changes, and changes are differences. If the energy of something changes, no matter what energy is, the value of its energy aspect is different from moment to moment. Remember for physicists (and your eyes too), everything is based on measurements, and if there are no changes then nothing is different, and there is no measurement. It turns out that the rods and cones in your eyes are doing the same thing physicists are doing. If there is no change in the energy levels of the molecules in the rods and cones in your eyes, there is no difference in them, and you see nothing, just total absolute blackness. So another way to say that the only things we perceive about the world is the effects that propagate to us, is to say that the only things we know about the world are changes that occur, and those changes are *differences* in energy which propagate to us. If something *doesn't make a difference*, it has no effect on the world around it. If something doesn't make a difference, there is no way to detect it. If something doesn't make a difference, it simply doesn't exist.

We now see that the existence of *difference* doesn't even imply that the something that causes it exists. All that does and can exist to us is some difference. All that we can ever know, all that we can ever receive are differences. All we can ever know about things are the differences that they make, and it turns out that the things we are imagining as making the differences are necessarily imaginary, mental representations reconstructed from receiving those differences. Differences are all there is to us. The effects of the world that scientist measure, the effects that our eyes measure, are just differences. Information is carried about the universe by chains of differences. Is there necessarily anything else? Is it possible that there is anything else?

Philosophically inclined physicists have marveled for some time now at how the behavior of the universe as described by mathematics seems to be captured by differential equations. This universal use of differential equations at the foundation of physics has caused some thinkers to sense the presence of something profound here. But differential equations describe, you guessed it, differences. They describe changes in things. Specifically they describe how one measurable quantity changes in relation to how another quantity changes. There really is something profound here, and it is that physicists are in the business of gathering information about the universe and the only information available to them comes in the form of differences. At first glance, this may seem to be a disappointingly simple explanation, but it really is profound, and what is profound about it is that it emphatically specifies the nature of the universe as information and the nature of physics as being forcibly limited to gathering *information*.

Before a quantum particle interacts with another particle, it makes no difference on anything. Maybe the reason that a single quantum particle exhibits quantum randomness is because until it interacts with another particle it doesn't make any *difference* what its attributes are. When it begins to interact with other particles, however, it begins to make a difference. They are a component of a bigger reality now. The difference manifests itself as the effect each particle has on the aggregate wave function. Maybe the *significance* of the randomness is to give particles the range to aggregate in such a way that everything fits together, and really has *no significance* at all at the single particle level, the level where it makes no difference. We feel like we have to explain quantum randomness, but it may be that at that level it's something of an anomaly, and its real purpose is in how it entangles with other particles.

The potential behavior of a particle in an isolated state is at its most random. In an isolated state, it has no effect on anything. It literally makes no difference what it does. As it becomes more entangled with other particles, it does make a difference and its potentials decrease to those consistent with the rest, and the difference it makes is the same difference that is measured by a measuring instrument. It is ontological to state that **a particle in an isolated state exhibits maximum randomness, because it makes no *difference***. This phrase has slightly different meanings depending on whether we're thinking in terms of conventional physics, or in terms of the universe as information. On the physics side, an isolated particle affects nothing, nothing affects it, so its randomness is not reduced by entanglement. In an information driven universe, though, the idea of something's *significance* begins to surface as will be discussed in Sections 4 and 5. If we're talking about an information driven universe, then a particle's purpose is *only* in its interaction with other particles, and its behavior in an isolated state isn't even of interest.

In the previous paragraph, I used language that referred to phenomena of the universe as if they had a purpose. Thinkers have been noticing from the beginning that sometimes this appears to be the case. Is it possible that we can interpret the actions of the universe as if there was a goal in mind, a goal such as creating a universe in which we humans are able to exist and live so comfortably? This idea that the universe might be so constructed as to explicitly bring us humans into existence is known as the *anthropic* universe. I think more than anything that this seeming phenomenon results from the very real phenomenon that the universe maintains its history to be consistent with the present. In the *cause and effect* paradigm, each event in time follows and is consistent with the event that caused it. In the quantum paradigm, the universe seems to actually have some freedom to go back and collapse onto the history that is consistent with the present. Either way, though, here we are, and the universe around us and the history of that universe that led to us will necessarily be *consistent* with our existence. If there is a purpose to quantum randomness, then perhaps that purpose is to provide the freedom necessary to maintain consistency throughout.

There is another reality here that needs to be considered and that I think sometimes confuses the issue. We are, each one of us, necessarily the center of our own, in many ways unique, universe. In Section One, it was mentioned how each one of us goes through life experiencing our own very unique slice of experiences. We all have different predispositions, experience different experiences, and all develop different philosophies and politics.

But it really runs much deeper than that. In the beginning of chapter 6, we noted that space itself, the distance between the bounces of a ball, for example, are different for different people, are individualized. It turns out that time too runs at a rate unique to, i.e. relative to, the individual. We all live in individual universes that are strongly linked, but that vary from individual to individual in surprising ways. Your physical universe is literally uniquely yours in these ways and is not shared by anyone else.

The quantum wave collapse problem also seems to be centered cn this self-centered universe. With the quantum wave, your universe doesn't even seem to come into existence unless you're there to experience it. We are not only the center of our own universe, but it begins to seem remarkable that the universe of the guy standing next to us is even consistent with ours.

Given these considerations, it would seem utterly inevitable that anthropocentric phrases would creep into our language. Not only that, but under the new interpretation they really seem now to have one context in which they're justified. If I make the blatantly anthropocentric comment that the universe is such-and-such a way because I am here, it can be true, but true without connoting or denoting that it is done that way just so I'll be here. Now the fact that I am here implies that the universe must be such-and-such a way, because otherwise, I wouldn't be here. Whatever else the universe is, it has to be *consistent* with my being here.

It is difficult to discover the underlying or guiding principles of the universe, but if I were to pick one near the top of the scale it would be the requirement of *logical consistency*. We just do not live in a universe that allows contradictions. For so many things in the universe, this means that they can be *only one way*. If you're on trial for murder and you claim you were somewhere else at the time of the murder, then because *you can only be one place at a time*, you couldn't have been the murderer. If the prosecutor produces a witness, however, who places you at the scene, he has created a contradiction to your claim, and you may well be out of luck. Things can only be one way or the other, not both, and this aspect of reality enters when the quantum wave collapses to a single outcome. When someone opens the box to look at Schroedinger's cat, it is either dead or alive, not both. All of us are familiar with this requirement. Whether we ever thought about it or not, we rely on it constantly to keep our world understandable and logical.

A particle's diverse probabilities seem to allow *contradictory realities* to have kind of a semi-existence while no one is looking. A particle can for a time *potentially* exist in so many different places at once, but as soon as someone looks, the wave is collapsed onto a single result. All other particle waves that have mingled with this one are also brought instantly into line, instantly made consistent with this result, even if they are half way across the universe or occurred a billion years in the past. The mathematics of the wave itself is certainly the first line of defense enforcing consistency. The mingling waves limit the attribute values of the particles to only those, which under the rules of quantum physics, are consistent with each other. There are then, two levels of consistency that are enforced. The first one, the wave, we have the mathematics to describe. As for the second one, the collapse of the wave onto a single outcome, we are left guessing.

Is it possible though that somehow the universe works backwards from the way we usually perceive it? We see events unfolding forward in time, with each event being caused by and consistent with preceding events. We then passively observe this phenomena, taking it all in and identifying its consistency to be a principle of the world we live in. Is it possible that it runs the other way, though, *at least to some degree*? Is it possible that reality starts from us somehow and works its way outward, collapsing events across space, and even back into time to make them consistent with our current reality? Is it possible that quantum randomness does have a purpose, that purpose being to allow a sufficient range to events that it can all be made to fit together consistently *in retrospect*, from our perspective? If this sounds like raving to you, please realize that this is simply one rather general interpretation of the Observer Created Reality (OCR) mentioned back in chapter 6.

Consistency is a fundamental principle of the universe. Consistency is also a fundamental principle of logic. The connection is not necessarily profound. Logic is a manmade thing designed to mimic the universe after all. Consistency is essential to avoid contradictions, and contradictions never make it all the way into existence in our universe. Logic is based on the rules for manipulating symbols, and it turns out that something like symbols, i.e. information, is all we get from the universe anyway. We make measurements of the world around us, whether those measurements be with scientific instruments or the rods and cones in our eyes. In the case of instruments, we translate those differences measured into specific patterns on a piece of paper, symbols. In the case of our eyes, we translate those differences into specific patterns of nerve impulses, also symbols. All we know about the universe, all we get from the universe is symbols, and symbols can be translated into marks on a piece of paper. The universe can then be described by these symbols and the rules developed to manipulate them. Coincidentally, this is what computers do too.

The universe around us is knowable to us only from the *information* we receive about it, information that arrives at our bodies as *differences* in energy. It is a legitimate approach for us humans to think of the universe as nothing but information. We receive it as information about our interaction with it. We represent it as information, and studying its behavior becomes reduced to studying how information gets generated and moved around by the universe. Physics is reduced to the study of the rules of symbol manipulation. We mimic the way the universe handles information, the rules it uses, with our symbol manipulations. From this perspective, the universe is a system that manipulates information, that is, it is an *information system*. We are studying the rules by which an information system manipulates the information within it. Those disembodied quantum attributes of time and space become symbols, and our perception of them becomes the way our minds experience these symbols. Ditto materiality. Materiality and substance are our experience of symbols representing space combined with impenetrability. It is not only unknown, but unknowable whether or not these things have any actual existence. All we can know is our translation of, our mental representation of, the information we receive.

Earlier in the book I made a fleeting reference to string theory. String theory is the new theory under development that shows promise of at last uniting quantum theory and relativity, and it shows some promise of leading to TOE, i.e., the Theory of Everything. In string theory, everything in the universe is represented as composed out of one dimensional infinitely thin vibrating strings that form closed loops in one other of the ten or eleven dimensions. Not only particles are composed of strings, but other effects of the universe too fall out of it. These include gravity and mass, time, and location, the big three measurables. Now these vibrating strings are infinitely thin so what are they vibrating in. They have no thickness or substance, no physical reality as we perceive it.

Something that has no thickness is in fact pretty close to nothing, but string theory doesn't need to propose a universe based on physical objects. In string theory, it turns out that all of the phenomena of the physical universe actually arise out of the *geometry* of it all. Now geometry, if you will recall from section one, is an abstraction of the world, first developed and recognized as an abstraction by the Greeks and Egyptians. It is mathematics and logic, and it is one of the ideas that led the Greeks to propose Logos over two thousand years ago. It is symbol manipulation and typographical operations. And yet the universe and everything we know of is turning out to have this abstraction as its foundation. We have truly gone full circle. We have arrived back where the Greeks were two thousand years ago. Somehow abstraction is behind it all. Somehow the universe really is Logos.

Physicists and philosophers who have pondered matter as well as *nothingness* for a lifetime frequently end up feeling that the fact that *something* exists at all needs an explanation. Why is there something instead of nothing, they ask? How is it that anything exists at all? It is turning out that the *unanswerability* of the question results from the *materiality* paradigm. The answer is that, as far as the material universe at least, nothing does exist.

As this section comes to a close, let me hurry to add, lest the nice men in white coats show up and force their way into my study, that I still recognize the need to feed myself. (Perhaps a little too much, even.) Even though I'm proposing that the material world must not really exist, there is still something very real behind it. The material world may all be imaginary, but there is still the need for us to consume that imaginary food that appears on the table in front of us. If we don't, we will most assuredly perish.

Section 3
The Matter of Mind

o o o o o o o o o o o o o o o o o o o o o o o o o o o o o o o o o o

Even if there is only one possible unified theory,
it is just a set of rules and equations.
What is it that breathes fire into the equations and
makes a universe for them to describe?

—*Stephen W. Hawking, A Brief History of Time, 1988*

Chapter 9
From World to Brain

○ ○

...for no man lives in the external truth among salts and acids, but in the warm, phantasmagoric chamber of his brain, with the painted windows and the storied wall.

—*Robert Louis Stevenson (1850–1894)*

Information Handling

The universe is in the business of moving information around, in the business of information handling, and roughly speaking, it does this by perpetuating the effects of, *the disturbance caused by*, some event throughout the universe. If a supernova explodes in a distant galaxy, the information of its occurrence is carried to us across space by the light it generates, among others of its effects. Human beings too are in the business of information handling these days. It is the information age after all, and there is no shortage of examples of how we do it.

Let's take everybody's favorite, the TV, and examine how it works and what it does with information. As a very general description, your local TV network, or any TV system, does three things. It first gathers the information from the world around it. It then must carry that information from where it was gathered to your television set. Then finally, it takes that information and displays it on your TV screen.

A TV network gathers the information from the world around it using a TV camera. The information from the world, carried to the camera in the form of light, passes through the camera lens and is focused on an electronic device that is sensitive to that light and immediately converts it to an electronic form. The electronic form that the light is converted into is an *encoded* series of voltages, in

173

many ways similar to Morse code, and this code contains all the information contained in the light that entered the camera. Morse code could in fact be used to encode your TV picture, although it might be a bit less efficient than the codes used today.

This encoded electronic signal then must be carried from the TV camera to your TV set somehow. This process is usually quite complex, but in the abbreviated version you're getting, it eventually reaches your home either directly via cable, a satellite dish, or an old fashioned TV antenna. Either way it enters your house and your TV set, as a code encoded in the medium of electronic voltages.

The job of our TV set then is to take this encoded signal and *decode* it, that is, convert it from voltages back into light so our kids can sit there mesmerized thirteen hours a day. It accomplishes this by converting the encoded signal into a fast moving electron beam that paints the picture on your TV screen, or at least that's how it's done with TV picture tubes, which at this writing are rapidly becoming antiquated.

So if we look at the overall picture of how a TV network works, it consists of an encoder (the camera) that is connected (the transmission) to the decoder (your television set). This is what the engineers refer to as an *encoder/decoder pair*. In a nutshell, an encoder/decoder pair considered as an entity onto itself, takes information, converts it to a code, and then decodes that information back into its original form.

Our world abounds with encoder/decoder pairs. Even Edison's original phonograph, and Bell's original telephone were encoder/decoder pairs. In Edison's phonograph, sound was converted (encoded) into squiggly lines in wax. Then the job of the phonograph itself was to decode these squiggles back into sound. In Bell's telephone, sound was encoded as electronic voltages at the mouthpiece, and then the earpiece decoded theses voltages back into sound for our ears.

If one looks a little closer, however, of course a little more complexity begins to appear, but the nature of the complexity is not very complicated, and in fact is just more repetition of the same. If one looks closer at a TV network, what they will find is a lot more encoders involved than just the single step of converting light to encoded voltages. That original encoder, the TV camera, really consists of several encoders. The light is originally broken into millions of picture elements called pixels, and each pixel is converted to voltages, the strength of which are related to the lights brightness and color. These voltages are then encoded again, this time into numbers, but the numbers themselves are encoded yet again as sequences of voltages, this time though in digital voltages, that is, they now represent zeroes and ones. This information has now been encoded at least three times via three completely different codes and is now in a format suitable for computers to handle, and the inside of today's TV cameras are indeed heavily computerized. Your TV sets too of course.

Between the light that enters the camera and the light you finally see coming from your TV screen, the information is passed through and processed by dozens, hundreds of computers. Computers seen from the outside, that is from the black box viewpoint, take information in and convert it to some new kind of information coming out, good old input/output, and from this black box viewpoint, computers are indistinguishable from encoders. Computers are encoders, so really all we're saying here is that there are a lot more than a single encoder between the camera and your TV set. Lots and lots of encoders, but only one decoder. Only at the very last step is the encoded information converted back into a visualizable form.

Now encoders and decoders have a lot in common if you think about it. An encoder takes information in as one code format and spits information out in another format, and this is exactly what a decoder does too. So really, decoders are encoders too. From the decoder's point of view, it doesn't know it's different in any way from an encoder. It doesn't know it's not an encoder. The only difference between the decoder and all the encoders is that the information that it spits out is in the original format of way back when, a format that is useful and understandable to human beings. From the information's point of view, though, the whole thing is now just a series of different encoders.

Another aspect of all of this is that nowadays just about all of the encoders are computers, and some of these computers may modify and thoroughly massage the information they receive. When this is the case, the information coming out, the output, is not entirely the same information as was contained in the input, and all of this can be called *information processing*.

Information itself has the funny characteristic that it is quite independent of how it is represented, how it is encoded. We could, just to prove this point, have a step in the series of encoders that brings us our TV image, where the information is encoded with pebbles on the beach. For the most part, the encoding usually involves representing the information as a series of numbers, so imagine a squadron of people on the beach, each with a bucket of pebbles, watching a computer screen covered with numbers. They then proceed to create the numbers with pebbles, either digitally or they could draw them or even write out words for the numbers with the pebbles. There would then be another person with a computer who could see the pebbles, but not see the original computer screen, who would type the numbers they see on the beach into their computer and send them on their way. The process would be slow and probably take roughly a month to send one second's worth of image, but it would demonstrate very plainly that information representation is independent of both the code used and the medium used.

When information from the world is carried to us as a code by a TV system and converted back into something sensable by us, the images we see and the sounds we hear are *recreations* of the original. They are not the original real world. They are very much like it, but they are a recreation, a representation of it, so we have come to call this representation a *virtual reality*. By this we mean that it is not the real thing, but an artificial representation of reality. It is common to refer to virtual reality these days as some system that provides artificial input to many of our senses; vision, hearing, even a sense of gravity, but the image on the TV screen is in fact a little virtual reality too. Even your telephone qualifies as a little virtual reality, since you are not really hearing your friends voice directly, but an artificial recreation of it. Your mind of course goes ahead and pretends that you are indeed hearing the person on the other end speaking directly. A virtual reality that you couldn't pretend was *real* would just be no fun at all. TV just barely qualifies, and then only for some of us. You might even want to include your windowpanes in the virtual reality category. They do after all gather information from the outside world, transmit it to the inside surface, and recreate it so realistically with modern glass that we are able to pretend that we are seeing the real world right through it. The universe is in the business of moving around information too.

Information and the senses:

Now it turns out that all of this discussion about information applies to how we humans get information too. The way your eyes and the visual cortex of your brain work are very closely analogous to how TV networks work. Like the TV camera, light enters through the lens of your eye and is focused on the retina. The information is then converted to encoded voltages on the optic nerve that carries this code to the visual cortex. The visual cortex then processes this encoded information and encodes it anew as networks of neurons within your brain...and then you see the world.

As with the TV network, a closer examination reveals a lot more encoders than just the retina magically creating voltages onto the optic nerve. Light first strikes the rods and cones where the photons are absorbed by molecules that now become chemically active. So there is even one stage where the information of the outside world is encoded chemically. These molecules then do their chemical thing that causes an electron to be released that starts an impulse on a nerve in the retina. The nerves on the back of the retina, though, actually form a mini-processor, a mini-brain, and considerably massage the information right there prior to dumping the output onto the optic nerve. The optic nerve then carries this information into your brain as an encoded series of voltages very similar to the way cable TV carries encoded information into your house, only it uses a different code. And again, the code on your optic nerve has many similarities with dots and dashes of Morse code. When this code enters the brain, the information processing that is caused by its arrival is tremendous and literally almost beyond human comprehension. We will delve much more deeply into how the brain processes information later, but suffice it to say now that the brain behaves like a *massively* parallel computer well beyond the capabilities of our man made computers of today.

Someday we may have artificial electronic eyes for blind people. These will be miniature TV cameras, but instead of converting the information to Morse code or standard digital code, it will convert it to the identical code that the original eye would have created, and then dump these impulses directly onto the optic nerve. This information will then be encoded in the format that the brain is designed to decode, and these people will be able to see using little TV cameras. Of course, once this technology becomes available, it will be almost trivial to allow such a person with an artificial eye to pop their eye out and plug themselves directly into any virtual reality game at their local video game center. Somewhere around then I suppose replacing their real eyes with artificial eyes will succeed tattooing and body piercing as the latest way for kids to annoy the adults who care about them. At this point, we will be approaching the virtual reality capability of being able to isolate the brain and feed virtual sensory information directly into it. The brain will then unknowingly interpret this information as actual sensory input and we will experience a truly virtual reality.

The brain receives information about the visual world as code, a code encoded using a complex medium of voltages and chemical activity on the optic nerve, and this is true of our other senses as well. When we touch something with our fingertip, the compression of the nerve endings in the fingertip is encoded as a set of voltages on the peripheral nervous system and carried to the brain where it is then processed and realized by us as the sense of touch. Information as to what is hot and what is cold too is carried to the brain as encoded voltages by the nerves, and hearing, and taste, and smell. In hearing, the original encoding mechanism is the machinery of the inner ear. For taste and smell, the encoding process occurs first in the medium of chemistry, as chemical reactions between the molecules in the mouth and nose with our taste buds and olfactory sensors. All of this information about the outside world is then converted to electrical voltages and carried to the brain as encoded information on nerves that are connected from our sense organs to our brains…and then we pretend that we are experiencing the real world directly.

Mental representation:

The brain itself exists in a very dark place, protected inside of our bony skulls, physically isolated from the outside world. This is where our experience of the world occurs, in our brains. This is where we live, our home if you will. There are eleven little holes in our skulls via which the information about the outside world gets passed in to us, via which the encoded information is able to enter our house. We do not even come close to experiencing the outside world directly. All we get, all our brains get, is a bunch of encoded information about what's going on out there, and once in our brains, we decode this information somehow into what we are experiencing. We are necessarily experiencing a virtual reality just like our TV set. We are experiencing an artificial representation of the information that gets through our skull, that comes into our home. The information that gets in is represented to us mentally as the experience we have of it and we do not know if it is being decoded back into something like the original real world, or if what we're experiencing is just another encoding of the information into yet another format, one interpretable to our minds.

To help grasp the significance of this, imagine if you will some time in a distant future when we humans have figured out how to visit and explore different universes, universes completely different from ours. Imagine that we are encapsulated within some kind of protective vessel that has sensors on the outside which sense information in that universe, encode it, and pass the encoded information to our interior via wires through the shell. Imagine that this universe is so strange that it doesn't even have space or matter in it. What exactly are we supposed to do with this encoded information that we receive inside? How do we decode it if the universe outside is so different that it is beyond our ability to represent or comprehend? It has no space, no spatial dimensions, but suppose it has dimensions in realms other than space that we can neither imagine nor comprehend (as the quantum world indeed does). Do we represent those dimensions as spatial just so the existing machinery in our brains can work with them? And what if that universe has nothing in it like light either, since it has no space for light to travel in? So let's imagine that there is some mechanism via which information is passed around in those other kinds of dimensions we imagined, much like light carries information in our space dimensions. Are we going to contrive some artificial method to create a TV image to represent it so we can feel like we are able to see in this universe?

The sensor system of our capsule is as always an encoder/decoder pair. The situation is, though, that the final decoder will have to decode the information into some sort of representation that is usable and meaningful to us human beings. The problem is that what is outside of our capsule is not representable as something usable and meaningful to us humans, so we have to convert it to a representation that is. In this case, the final decoder is no longer a decoder at all. It is just another encoder, changing the information into yet another form far different from the original, a visual TV image using light say. Is this what is happening to us. Is our skull the capsule and the final decoding just a useful and convenient mental representation that is utterly different from what is outside, from the universe we're visiting?

Evolution has given us senses for gathering information about the world that are useful to our survival, and the mental machinery to represent it. Other animals have senses different from ours. Porpoises, bats, even some shrews see with sound. Do they experience the information they receive through this sense as something like our vision of space? Or is it somehow represented to them more like our experience of sound. Or very possibly, it's something entirely different that we can't even start to imagine without actually getting into their minds and experiencing what they're experiencing.

Our brains and senses evolved through natural processes over hundreds of millions of years from more primitive organisms. They evolved to gather information from the world around them, process that information, and represent it mentally to that creature. It has evolved to give us *useful* sensations and representations of the world that aren't really there: colors, hot and cold, tastes, and even the sensation of sound, pitch and loudness for example. If you think the sensation of temperature isn't imaginary, just put a few drops of habanera sauce on you tongue and swish it around for a minute. You will swear that the temperature in there is somewhere around the boiling point, but of course it's not. (And because it's not, you can't cool it off.) All of these are just very arbitrary mental representations, that is sensations, which are generated from the encoded information that makes it inside of our skulls. Why not space and form too?

There is no reason at all why our visual representation should be any different. Whatever space and matter really are, evolution had the freedom to create any representation whatsoever as long as it was useful and consistent. The primary requirement from evolution's point of view is that the representation remains useful and consistent with the information that is received from the outside world, and we as beings have the same evolutionary survival requirements whether the real world is material or not, whether we are material beings or just information. The requirement that our mental representation be *consistent* with the information it receives does not mean that it has to be the same thing at all.

The consistency requirement:

We think that the world really is the way we experience it because it works, but this brings us back to the idea of consistency. The only real requirement for a working representation of the world is that it be consistent with that world, but that's nowhere near saying that it is the same thing. Our minds, brains, and senses evolved in this world and the forces of evolution ensured that we and other creatures have a working perception of the world, a perception of the world that works. Any poor snake that perceives mice to be within striking distance when in fact they are beyond striking distance is going to starve to death and not pass on its genes. Only those snakes that perceive striking distances to be actually consistent with striking distances are going to survive and procreate, thus ensuring that all snakes in the next generation will have a working perception of striking distances. Whatever else our mental representations of the world are, they have to be consistent with the real world in order to survive. We as beings have the same evolutionary survival requirements whether the real world is material or not, whether we are material beings or just information.

But being consistent with the world doesn't require that it match what's really there at all. As a trivial example, most people are aware that their eyes actually focus the image upside down on the retinas and that it's the brains job to turn it right side up again. So along these lines, suppose that one of us perceives the world backwards, and by backwards I mean they see things on the left that everybody else sees on the right and vice versa. Let's call him Lefty.

Way back in elementary school when he was taught to put his right hand on his heart and say the Pledge of Allegiance, Lefty would have seen everybody put what appeared to him to be their left hands on their hearts, because he saw everything reversed. He too then would have put that hand, the side we think of as the left side, over his heart. He would have learned early in life to call his perceptually left hand his right hand. His left and right will be reversed from ours. What to him was his left hand was really to us his right since he saw everything backwards, so the teacher and the rest of the class would have seen him put his right hand over his heart.

For the rest of his life, the side the rest of us refer to as our left side he will think is his right. When Lefty gets older and joins the Army and the Sergeant bellows "right face," he will turn left, but of course the Sergeant will see him turn the same direction as everybody else, so he'll survive that okay too. The same when they're marching. When the platoon leader shouts "left, right, left," Lefty'll be going (perceptually) right, left, right in his head, but once again it will be indistinguishable from everybody else. When Lefty grows old and dies, he will have lived a full life in reverse of everybody else in the world, *but he will never have known it, and neither will anyone else.* This is because his world was *consistent* with reality. This could in fact be going on right now in some of us, perhaps you.

The only possible way for anyone to figure it out would be to actually somehow get inside of Lefty's mind and experience what he was experiencing. Would they have been surprised! The fact is, though, that it doesn't matter at all what we perceive as long as it's consistent with reality. Anyway, who's to say that Lefty wasn't right and everybody else was wrong? It might be that he was the only one who had it right and everybody else perceived it wrong. What if at some time in the future we really are able to get inside of each other's minds and we discover that all women experience left on one side and all men experience left on the other side. Now we have a real dilemma. How are we going to decide which half of us is incorrect? Actually, it cannot be done! I'm sure most of us have already chauvinistically decided for ourselves, but the truth is that it isn't possible to resolve this conflict. And currently, it's impossible to know or find out if the person standing next to you perceives the world backwards from you or not, and the truth is that it doesn't matter anyway. It's possible that everybody's wrong. It's all just a mental representation after all, and a mental representation of who knows what. No matter which side you perceive as left, it doesn't matter as long as it's consistent.

What we see with our minds may not be what's really out there. What's more important is that the information we perceive is presented in a *useful* format and consistent with the universe that's providing it. Another way to see this is to go back to our artificial eye example where at some future date it has become possible to replace our eyes with miniature electronic TV camera eyes. Now quality control being what it is in the real world, there will be a few artificial eyes that make it into the market place and get installed that are defective.

Now an artificial eye can be defective in hundreds of way. It could get the colors all mixed up, transmitting green for yellow, and red for blue. It could turn the world around switching left for right, or even turning the world upside-down. It could reverse brightness and dark, causing the user to experience nighttime as a bright whiteout, and see sunlight as shadows. There may be no straight lines, a straight line being represented as a particular curved line. Now, if someone is seventy years old and they get a new eye because their eyesight's failing, they're going to pick out the defect instantly, but what about a newborn who is born blind and receives a defective artificial eye shortly after birth. The poor kid will never know the difference as long as the defects she experiences she experiences consistently.

Of course, the eye could be far more defective than that. Let's imagine our newborn as receiving an artificial eye that is so messed up that the image would not be recognizable as anything familiar at all if implanted in an adult. Now it's an interesting fact about computers so far (and presumably our artificial eye is computerized) that if they are given the same input over and over, they will always produce the same output over and over. All this is to say that when she looks at her mother's face she will always see the same thing, whatever that is. It would be unrecognizable as anything worldly to an experienced adult, but that doesn't matter since the newborn being born blind has no idea of what a worldly face is supposed to look like. This child will come to know and love a mother that looks nothing like a human being to the rest of us. Objects, mothers included, may not even be our idea of objects. Whatever it is she sees when she looks at the world, the only requirements are that it be consistent and that it contain enough information to be useful.

She will grow up in a world completely different from ours, and she will have no idea. She will learn to read different words, and when she's fourteen she will fall madly in love with a boy who looks to us nothing like a human being. (Of course that's frequently true now.) She will have a different sense of beauty and of what is beautiful. If as her graduation present from high school her parents save up and buy her the latest and greatest new and improved UltraVision artificial eyes, she's going to be in for a jolt, presuming of course her new one's not defective too.

The point of all this is, of course, that it is really arbitrary how we mentally envision the world as long as it's consistent. It's really arbitrary how our sense of vision evolved to represent the world. The world that we are seeing need not be there at all, not as a material spatially extended world. Materiality and spatiality are artifacts of our mental representation of the information we receive. All we really know is that we receive this information.

The Brain (101)

Information arrives at the brain through the 11 little holes in our skulls as encoded sequences of voltages on nerve cells. These nerve cells act like and perform the same function as wires and cables that bring information in to our home telephone and cable TV virtual reality systems. Today's TVs and telephones then take this encoded information and using computer chips, convert it into a new format, and so does the brain. The brain is an information processor vastly superior to those little computer chips, and it encodes, represents, and processes the information it handles using the medium of neurons, and networks of neurons.

Neurons are nerve cells, and the brain is largely composed of neurons. The neurons that compose the brain are connected to, and able to communicate with, each other and are arranged into vast networks of connected neurons. There are billions and billions of neurons in the brain. Each neuron has tens of thousands, or hundreds of thousands of connections to other neurons, so there are trillions and trillions of connections. These connections between neurons are an important component of the brains information processing structure and are called *synapses.*

Each neuron is a little information processor onto itself, like a little computer chip, and like any computer each neuron has hardware to perform input, hardware to perform output, and a little processor in between. A neuron receives input from hundreds of thousands of other neurons, processes the information, and then outputs the result to hundreds of thousands of other neurons. The input hardware is called the *dendrite,* and the dendrite is necessarily covered with synapses, since that's how other neurons contact it. The output hardware is called the axon, and the axon is also necessarily covered with synapses, since that's how the neuron communicates its output to the dendrites of other neurons.

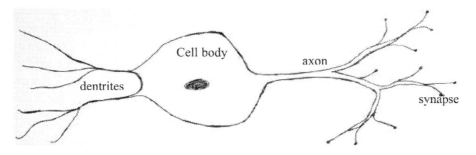

Schematic of a neuron

The above is just a baby schematic of a neuron. As stated, a typical neuron may have hundreds-of-thousands of dendrites that receive input from other neurons, and its single axon may have hundreds of thousands of synapses contacting other neurons.

Each neuron may be thought of as the answer to a question. The information input at the synapse onto the dendrite of one neuron from the axon of another neuron may, therefore, be thought of as the answer to a specific question too, the question that that other neuron answers. Since axons communicate with voltages, the language that they must use to communicate has just two words in it: Hi and Lo. Hi means there is a voltage and Lo means there is no voltage. Each synapse on a dendrite may represent a unique question, and the corresponding answers that a neuron receives from each synapse are Hi, which means *Yes*, and Lo which means *I dunno*.

Now when you think of what a human being can deduce playing Twenty Questions, imagine what a neuron can deduce playing *Hundred Thousand Questions*. Each neuron has a major amount of information available to it. The information processor in each neuron then proceeds to perform a horrendously complex statistical analysis on this input and decides what its own answer will be. Each neuron may be thought of as representing a unique question and it arrives at its own answer by instantly surveying the answers to thousands of relevant questions to which it is hardwired. If the neuron determines that the answer to its own question is *Yes*, it instantly sends *Hi* out on its axon to every possible other neuron out there that might someday have the need to know the answer to its question.

Let's take a totally unrealistic and hugely oversimplified example of this just to see how it works. Suppose we have a neuron whose sole job it is to answer the question "Dog?" What are some of the questions it's going to need to ask to determine if there's a dog out there or not? For one thing, it's going to want to know if we have an animal out there, so one of the synapses on one of its dendrites might represent the question "Animal?" Another question it might want answered is "Cold wet nose?" Some more might be "Barks?", "Four legs?", and "Pants?" Now these questions answered in the affirmative all support the assertion of Dog!, but there are other *negative* questions that may assert that it's not a dog, so our neuron is going to want to know some of these too. How about "Meows?", and "Tusks?". If the answer to either of these is *Yes*, we want to hedge our decision that we have a dog, so a Hi input from either of these two questions will be treated as negative input to the question of "Dog?" and inhibit the Dog? neuron from going Hi.

Now as you can see, the contribution of each of these input answers is used somewhat differently in determining whether we have a dog or not. The answer Animal! might be considered as necessary in arriving at the conclusion that it's a dog. If it's a dog, it has to be an animal after all. Other answers might be considered sufficient in themselves to conclude that we have a dog. If dogs were the only things in the universe that barked, then Barks! could be considered sufficient to determine that we have a dog. (Unfortunately, seals bark too.) Other answers just contribute to a growing probability that it's a dog. It helps to know that it has four legs, but there are three legged dogs, and there are other animals with four legs too, not to mention tables and chairs. So Four Legs!, while helpful, is inconclusive in itself. And then there are the negative questions that inhibit our neuron from answering *Yes*. If the answer to the question Meows? is *Yes*, we'd better let this piece of information completely prevent our neuron from answering *Yes* to Dog?

The job of the imaginary microchip in this neuron is to take all of this statistical information and determine when to answer yes and when not to. When it does answer yes, it immediately sends *Hi* out to all the neurons that might need to ask its question Dog? A few of these might be Danger?, Pet?, or even Cat? since if the dog neuron has already determined that we have a dog it surely isn't a cat.

Now this is all laid out as a network of interconnected neurons. In the example we gave, the Dog? question asked for input from seven other neurons, and it sent its output to three other neurons. This we can represent schematically with our neurons something like the following, incomplete though it is with only three of the input and two of the output neurons shown.

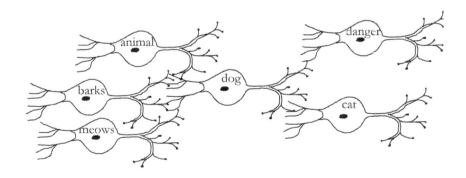

Schematic of a network of neurons.

Networks of neurons:

So how this all works is that the information processing proceeds from left to right in this diagram. There is, of course, a great deal of information processing that we don't see here off to the left. This will be similar support networks that help *animal?* and *barks?* say, determine if they are answered in the affirmative. Once they are, they will send a Hi to the dog neuron that will then proceed to determine if it should answer yes or not. If it does, it in turn sends a Hi to *danger?* and *cat?* that in turn do their thing and use this new piece of information to process their own question. Then if they answer *Yes*, they send their Hi out there axons off to the right to other unseen neurons that find their information useful, and on and on it goes.

Now, earlier I referred to this example as totally unrealistic and hugely over-simplified. The good news is that this example really does give you an idea of how the brain processes information using neurons. The bad news is that the brain doesn't seem to need to represent specific pieces of information or specific objects with a single neuron. That is, there probably is no dog neuron in anyone's brain. Once upon a time it was hypothesized that the brain did use a single neuron to represent a single object. Back then the example used, instead of *dog*, was a *grand-mother*, so the single cell representation concept became known as the *grand-mother cell* hypothesis.

Alas, it was not to be. As the dog example demonstrates, the dog cell really represents the activity of a whole network of supporting neurons, pre-dog neurons, to the left of dog, the ones dog uses to answer its question. Apparently, the brain is content to leave it more or less in the network form, that is, it doesn't need the dog cell explicitly since the network that would have activated the dog cell will suffice to do the job anyway. That network of support information, if considered a single entity, has a myriad of axons protruding out of it too, just like the dog cell would have. Experientially, we perceive a dog, or our grandmother, to be a single thing, but the brain doesn't represent them that way at all, *unless you consider the support network itself to be a single thing.*

So *things* are represented in the brain by *networks* of neurons. A network of neurons, which represents a thing, is composed of smaller networks of neurons that represent the components or the aspects of the thing. The network of neurons that represents the thing is, therefore, an aggregate object, an aggregate of sub-networks. Then the big network that represents the thing is able to partici-pate as a sub-network in yet larger aggregates, which in turn participates in still larger networks. Information, then, is represented in the brain as aggregate objects, each object in this case being a network of neurons that represents a piece of information. Clearly the brain is mimicking the way the universe represents information too, which makes sense since the universe is composed of aggregate objects and the brain has to represent them.

Or could it be the other way around this time? Could it be that we perceive the universe to be composed of aggregate objects because that's the way our brain represents this information to us? We are forced to perceive the universe the way the brain represents it after all, since the brain is where perception takes place.

Whichever aggregate object came first, the brain or the universe, we know that we're on the right track with the description of how the brain represents information and computes with neurons. One way we know this is because we've tried it, and it works pretty well. For a couple of decades, computer and brain researchers have been programming with what are called *neural networks,* which mimic neurons, and they can do some pretty amazing stuff, brain-like stuff. They can learn for one thing, and in a very natural way. For instance, they can learn all by themselves to distinguish between the radar signature of an F-111 and an F-16, which would be horrendously tedious and difficult to program into a computer using standard methods, especially since we can't easily see the difference ourselves. The programmers proceed by setting up the artificial (logical) neurons in several layers of processing, just like in the brain. The first layer receives the raw data, performs some processing on it and passes its results to the next layer. This layer then processes the output of the first layer, and so on and so on, each layer taking the output of the previous layer and processing it, massaging it, changing it.

Now there are a couple of interesting things that fall out of this. One is that each layer of neurons sees only the information as already manipulated and processed by previous layers, not the original information. If we're talking about a representation of the universe here, each layer sees a different universe, and only the first layer saw the actual raw data from the universe. Each layer after that sees something completely different, which brings me to the next interesting point. We have no idea what it is that each layer is representing. They are not clean aspects, components, or objects like were demonstrated in the dog example. These concepts are spread somehow over multiple neurons and even over several layers, and indeed the final concept can only be thought of as being distributed over and represented by the entire network.

This all must be true for our grandmother and our dog too if you think about it. If the brain doesn't use such single cell representations for things like dogs, then it wouldn't be using clean single cell representations for the components of dogs either. Whether you work backwards or forwards, top down or bottom up, you end up with layers of networks of neurons which, while they represent infor-mation about the world, their low level representation is unintelligible to us. We have, however, deduced some of the functionality of the brain at higher levels, and while clear concepts are beginning to emerge represented at high levels, some of what it is doing is wonderfully unintuitive and surprising.

Information is represented by our brains as networks of neurons. When a net-work is activated, meaning when it's actually receiving and sending voltages, then whatever piece of information it is representing has been activated somehow. If it were a dog network, then it would probably mean we were either seeing a dog or we were thinking about a dog. For any given network, though, whatever the piece of information it is representing, it is not likely to be meaningful to us as it seems for the most part to be a mish-mash of entangled information, which only takes on meaning in its relationship and interaction with other networks of neurons. And the case for what information is being represented by each *single* neuron involved in a network is even more obscure.

Experiencing our neurons:

Now at some level, presumably the highest level, for reasons or via methods we don't understand, this activity of networks of neurons becomes decoded (or encoded) from neuron activity to conscious experience, as our perception. Differ-ent networks are responsible for, or mapped onto, different perceptions. One lit-tle group of neurons is activated while we are perceiving colors, and another group located elsewhere in the brain is active when we perceive sound. Yet another network is activated while we perceive vision. What is the difference then, between these different groups that accounts for the different perceptions we experience when they're activated? We have no idea.

We can see no difference. One neuron, or one network of neurons looks just like any other from where we're sitting, yet the differences in the resulting experi-ences are profound. One little network lights up and we see yellow. A different one lights up and we smell bacon frying. Another lights up and we see a dog. Another lights up and we feel like we're forgetting something. Yet another lights up and we're seeing Grandma. Looking at them we can see no difference, except that they are located in different areas of the brain. Is there some greater signifi-cance to these specific locations other than just to keep them separate? This may be the case. For the most part, the locations of the networks that map to similar experiences are very similar in everyone, *and if brain activity from another part of the brain accidentally strays into one of these different perceptual regions, the percep-*

tions associated with that region are experienced even when nothing really exists. And not just location, but size matters too. The bigger the region of neurons activated, the more intrusive the perception is in our consciousness.

As something of an aside, it may just be that the brains orientation in space makes a difference to our perceptions too. I've noticed at night while thinking in bed that if I'm lying in my left side I think and feel differently than if I turn over and lay on my right side. Also, when I was younger, I used to tilt my head consistently to the left when I was thinking, but at this point in my life I tend to tilt it more frequently to the right. I think I was smarter, more acute, when I was younger. And dogs always tilt their heads to the left when they don't understand something. I'm not drawing any conclusions from this. In fact, it may all result more from how the blood sloshes around in our brains than their spatial orientation.

Because of the existence of regions of the brain that relate to specific perceptions, it has been possible to map out the large scale structure of the brain in terms of perceptual activity. This large scale structure is how the human brain has evolved to represent information. Each little area has evolved to give us a perception of a different piece or kind of information that the brain has evolved to represent, frequently as a sensation. The sum total of these little areas is what we can perceive, all we can perceive. There's a very fixed amount of real estate inside of our skulls for brain matter with which to represent information, so nature has had to pick and choose the most useful, and forsake the rest. There's a lot more to the universe as we have already seen that is available to be perceived and could be represented by our brains, but it's not. Colors like ultraviolet beyond our visual spectrum, for example. Or perceiving space as four dimensions instead of just three. The brain structure we ended up with is it, and we are not going to perceive these things we do not have brain structure to represent. We are incapable of envisioning or even imagining them. If the brain doesn't have the machinery to represent them, then we have no way to perceive or experience them. What You See Is What You Get, WYSIWYG, and no more.

Our brains, tucked away inside of our skulls, receive information encoded as voltages through eleven little holes. It then takes these voltage patterns and translates them into networks of neurons that are representing information as we don't know what. These low level networks stimulate higher and higher levels of networks, cascading upwards, each level modifying and massaging the information, and again representing we don't know what. Finally, at some level, the activity of these networks becomes experienced as our perception of the world, much of which is easily shown to be purely imaginary. We experience the world as a virtual reality, and our perception of the world is only implicit at best.

As sentient beings studying our brains, we humans are working backwards, starting from our perceptions of our brains. We are our perceptions after all, and working backwards from our perceptions, we have no idea what the translational relationship is between the top level networks of neurons and our perception of their activity. We have no idea how that network represents information as we perceive it, and thus no real idea what information is being represented. As we descend down through the myriad lower levels of networks, the obscurity of the information being represented becomes even more remote, if that is possible. At some point, we are down to the encoded voltages being fed into us through the little holes in our skulls. We as conscious beings, though, trying to figure this all out, are necessarily working backwards, top down from our perceptions, perceptions in which we are no longer confident.

Is it possible to really know what information those coded voltages coming in represent, since we have no idea what the many levels of networks represent in between? Or is the real meaning of that information totally scrambled, hopelessly lost to us. We have already been able to deduce that our perceptual representation of much of the world is imaginary; colors, temperature, sound, tastes, and smells. Is it any wonder that some of us have come to conclude that all of it is imaginary, that we really don't know what is out there; that space and matter as we perceive them need have no real existence at all?

Chapter 10
Thinking With a Brain

o o o o o o o o o o o o o o o o o o o o o o o o o o o o o o o o o o

The brain is wider than the sky,
For put them side by side
The one the other will contain with ease
And you besides.

—*Emily Dickinson*

We don't quite know how networks of neurons represent information, or even quite what information it is these networks are representing. All we are conscious of are the final results, our perceptions, which are somehow read off of the final level of networks in the information processing hierarchy. Even that statement is more than a little bit presumptuous, because how the activity of the brain becomes mind, and how the brain processes information are so poorly understood at this time.

There is quite a bit more to the brain than just a tangled mass of neurons. There are the glial cells that work in conjunction with the neurons making them more efficient and even helping determine network structure. While electrically inactive, they form networks too. There are also the connection points between neurons, the synapses themselves. They are turning out to be quite complex and are suspected of playing a much greater role in thinking than just providing a simple connection. Communication between neurons occurs when the synapse releases a chemical *neurotransmitter* between neurons, but they are not limited to a single neurotransmitter. Do neurons communicate different things using different neurotransmitters?

In his book *The Physics of Consciousness*, Evan Harris Walker proposes that synapses are all connected, not by neurons but by channels of soluble RNA via which they affect one another. Here's another network existing within the brain, and according to Walker, this one has quantum capabilities, which is something we're looking for. Does this network participate in thinking too? Finally, there's another kind of hidden network in the brain. Logically, networks are basically just lines that intersect one another at nodes. In the case of a network of neurons, the neurons are the lines, and the synapses are where the lines intersect, the nodes. It is possible for any given network, though, to redraw it as a different network by converting the node points to lines, and converting the original lines to node points. Are there hidden networks, *logical* networks, also working in the brain?

As you have seen so often in this book, human understanding proceeds by creating a *mental model* of how something works, and then doing our best to explain everything by making it fit this model. So far, it's looking like *networks* play a role in how our brains model the world, so we are going to construct a model of how the brain thinks using networks. If the observed working of the brain fits our model, then everything is copasetic, and we feel that snug and smug feeling like we understand. If it doesn't fit our model, then we feel anxious and like we don't understand. We have arrived at the point where we are studying ourselves now, our own brains, so to understand our brains we are at the very least going to have to come up with a model of how the brain works, how the brain models things. Our brains are going to have to create a self-referential model, a model modeling itself. Unfortunately, it is known that these sorts of endeavors frequently introduce paradoxes.

A mini-word about paradoxes. Paradoxes are self-contradictory ideas, and frequently can be expressed using language. The most succinct paradoxical statement that I know of is simply "This statement is false." If you play with it for a few seconds, you will see that if it is *true* then it must be *false*, and if it is *false* then it must be *true*. Paradoxes emphatically *do not exist* in the macroworld universe, and thus when we are able to utter a paradox it sets the teeth on edge and raises the hackles of those who strive for, and respect reality. Paradoxes *can* exist, though, when we move into the realm of symbolic representations of things, because whatever that realm, language say, it may now turn back on itself, and represent itself symbolically. We can use language to say things about language, as in the above example, and when a system of representation is able to represent itself, paradoxes become possible.

Modeling, of course, involves the act of representing something symbolically, and we are about to endeavor to model our mental model with a mental model. Hence, one should reasonably be alert to paradoxes in this environment.

(If you have found that this microscopic excursion outside of the box of logic blows your skirt up, then there are some really fun and exciting books out there that will put a really big smile on you face. My introduction to paradoxes and self-referential representation was Douglas Hofstadter's *Gödel, Escher, and Bach, An Eternal Golden Braid*, which I have referenced several times already in this book. His book is now twenty years old but is as relevant and fun today as it was then.)

The point of this is that I'm going to have to beware of introducing paradoxes and contradictions when I speak of my mental model model. Or am I? We are leaving the real world behind to enter the world of information representation, and we know that here, paradoxes and contradictions can exist. Since the brain and the mind seem to be all about symbolic representation, my instincts tell me that this ability of self-referential representation may well be related to the phenomenon of consciousness. And I find the idea provocative that contradictions do indeed exist in the microworld before the wave collapse, and that the mind may play a roll in collapsing the wave and making our perceived world contradiction free. Our interpretation of this process would be the collapse of the quantum potential wave onto a single outcome, which essentially is just our macroworld. Does our resistance to recognizing paradox as something potentially real play a role in our inability to explain consciousness? So I'm left with something of a quandary. I don't want to avoid paradoxes if they have the potential to serve a useful purpose. My strategy will be then, conveniently, to simply let the words flow. If paradoxes appear, so be it.

So back to our modeling. We're going to model the thinking brain as composed of neurons, and networks of neurons. No surprise here, right? We are then going to use this model to explain, and account for, *all* the mental phenomena involved with thinking and understanding that was introduced back in Chapter 4, *Understanding and Thinking*.

Aggregate objects:

It seems like everything in the universe is composed out of pieces, that is, aggregations of the object's component parts. A piece of pure diamond is composed of atoms of carbon. Atoms are composed of protons, neutrons, and electrons. Protons are composed of quarks and gluons. And quarks, I presume, are composed of those single dimensional strings if we want to extend this into string theory. A pencil is composed of its wooden tube, the graphite core, an eraser, and the metal band that joins the eraser to the wood. A car is composed of its myriad parts, many of which unfortunately need replacing during its lifetime. A city is composed of its buildings, streets, residents, infrastructure, and businesses. An ecosystem, the Amazon Jungle for instance, is composed of all the creatures, vegetation, rivers, even the soil in which it is anchored. A solar system is composed of at least one star and all the different kinds of junk that orbit around it.

Each one of these aggregations of objects we will call an *aggregate object*. An aggregate object can be a tightly packed object, like a diamond or a baseball, or it can be distributed over space, like a solar system or the Amazon Jungle. There is, of course, one very essential aspect that was left out of the above description of an aggregate object, and that is the interaction necessary among its components, called its *economy*. This is what makes an aggregate object more than just the sum of its parts. This is what qualifies it as an aggregate object, as an entity. A city without the hustle and bustle of a city is dead, just buildings and asphalt. Each component of an aggregate object must interact in some way with the remainder of the object, each playing a part in making the object what it is. A car that has been disassembled so that its parts don't interact is just a pile of parts, and is not a car at all.

An aggregate object is more than just a pile of its parts. All the parts must be working together to make the aggregate object what it is, and thus it may be thought of as a working *system*, like a solar system. A human being is an aggregate object too, and when a human being's component parts cease their interaction, it is deceased and disposed of. The universe itself obviously qualifies as a system of interacting components. We've even said several times that if there were something in the universe that interacted with nothing else in the universe, then there would be no way at all to even tell that it was there, and thus it wouldn't be part of the universe. The universe itself is by this definition an aggregate object, and we see that this definition of the universe as an aggregate object is compatible with our definition of existence. All the way from the bottom to the top, from the strings and quarks up to the universe itself, each level of aggregate objects is aggregated again into higher and higher hierarchical levels of aggregate objects.

The functioning, thinking brain is physically an aggregate object too, being composed of neurons, synapses, networks of neurons and the like. The model we'll be creating of how the brain represents the information that it receives and processes uses a structure of aggregate objects too, i.e., aggregates of neurons in the form of networks. As mentioned in the last chapter, it's fun to try to imagine which came first, the aggregate structure of the information system of our brains, or the aggregate object hierarchy with which we perceive the universe. Indeed, in a laboratory as we ponder a brain, that brain we are viewing is now perceived as an object of the universe, an object that we are representing in our aggregate object brain as an aggregate object too. While we have entered something of a loop here, it seems evident that the concept of aggregate objects as a valid method of information representation is strongly suggested (whether justified or not).

Anyway, the proposed model here is that the brain models the world around us as aggregate objects by using aggregate objects of its own in the form of networks of neurons. If we are representing a bird as a network of neurons, that top level bird network will be composed of the aggregation of a beak network, wing networks, feet networks, all the networks of the component parts of a bird. Of course, the bird network will be more than just the collection of networks of its parts. The parts stand in a certain relationships to each other, so all the part's sub-networks will be glued together by other neurons that represent the relationships between the parts. Only with the added relationships of the parts can the bird network be considered complete. We will call the completed bird network a *parent* network, because it is the top level network and puts a familial wrapper around all of its component networks.

Remember though that the component networks are aggregate networks too, aggregates of the networks that represent the components of these components. So component networks too are parent networks to the components from which they are composed.

Thoughts as aggregate objects:

As always, we're starting out with our conscious perceptions and working our way backwards from them, so our starting point is at the very top of the information processing that the brain performs. What we read off of this top level are our conscious perceptions, our thoughts, and thoughts are aggregate objects too. Now thoughts are kind of gossamer fuzzy things, and just introspectively thinking about thoughts it may not be altogether clear that thoughts are aggregate objects, but there is a very simple and clear way to determine that thoughts are aggregate objects.

If you remember all the way back to elementary school, the very first grammatical structure that your teachers taught you about, even before they told you about nouns and verbs, was the sentence. Their definition for a sentence way back then was that a sentence is a *complete thought*. Now this may all have changed in the considerable time since I was in elementary school, but for better or for worse I'm going to take them at their word. Supposedly, any and every thought we have we can express as a sentence, and minimally that expression must be a complete sentence. Sentences are thoughts, and sentences are clearly aggregate objects.

Now sentences are obviously aggregations of words, our tags for our concepts, but they tell us a bit more about our thoughts than just that. There's a lot more structure there. A sentence is an aggregate of interacting component parts, and there are several hierarchical levels of aggregation, just like in a biological cell say. Every sentence has a subject, that basic concept that is under discussion, and every sentence has a predicate that elaborates on the subject. Minimally then, a sentence is an aggregate object composed of a subject and a predicate, and these in turn are each composed of interacting aggregates of phrases and clauses that are in many ways like mini-sentences themselves. Phrases and clauses are aggregate objects too as they may be composed of their own subjects and predicates, or at least composed of interacting aggregates of different kinds of words, and there are eight or ten different kinds of words (the parts of speech) that all play a different role in their interaction with the other words in the objects they compose.

Back in chapter 4, we said that words are *symbols* for the concepts we have and that these concepts are *abstractions* derived from those things with which we have become familiar. Words are labels for our concepts, tags that help us locate and express complex concepts efficiently, with a single sound. So let's see how these abstractions that we tag with words might form using networks of neurons.

Abstractions as aggregate objects:

Imagine a baby seeing a bird for the first time. She will not know what it is, and will not identify it as a bird the first time she sees it because she has not yet developed a category for *bird*. It is not yet *familiar* to her. It is new, alien, strange, and fascinating, completely without precedent. But since she is perceiving it, it is nevertheless being represented in the brain by some set of neurons, and every aspect of the bird that she is able to distinguish, or cognize, is being represented with networks of neurons too. By the time she becomes aware of seeing anything at all, an enormous amount of information processing has occurred to the information received in her brain via the optic nerve, the point being that by now each facet or aspect of the bird, each component of which she is aware is itself represented by a network, or aggregated networks, of neurons. The bird itself, the whole bird, is an aggregation of these sub-networks, in addition to the brains representation of the *relationships* of these components. These distinguishable aspects include things like the bird's bill, its feet, wings, and head, in addition to its color, location, etc.

Now at this point she only knows of one thing like this in the universe. It is an *instantiated* object that she knows of, not yet an *abstraction*. What happens, though, if before too long she sees another bird? This information too comes in on the optic nerve and is subject to the same processing as that of the first bird. A new representation of an instantiated bird will now be automatically created using networks of neurons, but since the aspects and their relationships are going to be very similar to the first bird, many of the same networks that were used to represent the first bird are going to be *reused* to represent the second bird. The representation of the bill of the new bird will reuse much of the same sub-network of neurons used to represent the bill of the first bird.

Importantly, however, there will be some minor differences this time, and these *differences* will be represented by using new neurons distinct from the neurons used on the original bird, but much of it will be the same as was used for the first bird she saw. There will be a great deal of overlapping of neurons that were used in the representation of both bills, for example, and this overlap, this *reused portion*, will become the *abstraction* for the *bill* aspect of a bird. It will embody or represent that which is *similar* between bird bills. It will contain none of the unique portions of the aspects that *distinguish* one bill from another. The same thing will be happening with the representation of each other aspect of the bird, including the relationships among the parts, the relationship of the bill to the head for example.

And now a wonderful thing happens. From those overlapping, reused portions of the networks, the concept of a *bird* forms. An *abstraction* for what a bird is has developed, and it too is an aggregate object. The abstraction is composed of all those sub-networks that are themselves abstractions for the component parts and the component relationships. Our baby will now have created a model for a generic bird out of networks of neurons. She has automatically identified, or *cognized*, that which is similar between birds, and henceforth whenever these same *networks are re-activated* by the appearance of another bird, she will *re-cognize* a bird.

Recognition involves the reuse of a network of neurons, and when we recognize something, the way we know we recognize it is because we experience a *feeling of familiarity* associated with a memory. It is familiar to us, and it is this feeling of familiarity that signals to us the reuse of neurons that have previously been incorporated into our model of the world we live in.

As something of an aside, this could also provide an explanation for our experience of deja vu. We have said that the actual information that the brain is representing with neurons and the precise way that it represents we-don't-quite-know-what is obscure to us. It seems possible, therefore, that one experience could activate certain networks or portions of networks that were used to represent another experience that is not quite similar enough to the original experience to cause a re-cognition of the whole original experience. The reuse of that shared network would stimulate a feeling of familiarity, in this case to stand alone without the recognition of the original event, and to me at least, deja vu is the feeling that an event is familiar sans the recognition of a similar event.

As you can see, there are several aspects of thinking that were mentioned in Chapter 4 that are accounted for by the action of *reusing* neuronal networks or portions of networks. The re-use of a network leads directly to the re-cognition of the represented concept, and thus to the sense of recognition. The reuse of a portion of a network identifies the *similarity* between two concepts, and leads directly to the formation of the *abstraction* of a more generalized concept. In this case, it also indirectly identifies the *differences* between two concepts as the unshared portion of the network. Reuse of a network accounts for our feeling of *familiarity* with a concept or memory, and reuse of a network that *models our world* accounts for our feeling of *understanding* our world. And if some event is found not to match (reuse) our model, we experience the feeling of not understanding.

Once an abstraction has been represented by the brain as a network, a *word* can be attached to it, and thereafter hearing or seeing the word will activate this network, and the concept that the word represents will be cognized. A word is presumably a much simpler little network connected to a concept network that acts as a tag or label, which helps us locate that particular network quickly and efficiently. Words, though, and thus neuronal networks, can represent a great many more things about the world than just birds or objects. These are just some of the nouns after all, and there are rather arbitrarily eight or ten categories for words, depending on whom you ask, i.e., the *parts of speech*.

Additionally, neuronal networks are able to represent stuff about the world that apparently is not defined well enough to attach a word to. For example, when we see a bird, we are able to create words for the *bill* and the *head*, and the bill is a component of the bird's head and stands in a definite relationship to the rest of the head. However, there seems to be no easy way to express this relationship, that is, the relationship of the bill to the other components that make up a birds head. When describing the world in terms of aggregate objects, it is relatively easy for us to identify the component aspects, but it is difficult for us to express their relationships. I interpret this to suggest that the neuronal networks that represent completed objects, including the component aspects of an object, are more identifiable somehow than the neurons that glue or connect the component networks together to create the parent level aggregate object representation. It would be very difficult to describe a bird's head in terms of its components and the relationships between the components. But we know a bird's head when we see one, and this is of course why a picture is worth a thousand words.

Words act as tags for our concepts and the vast majority of our concepts are aggregate concepts. These concepts we can describe using preexisting words, aggregates of words called definitions, which are of course sentences. There are bottom level concepts, though, which are not aggregates and that thus cannot be described or defined with words. We can still tag them with a word, but we just can't define the word. Our colors are a good example of this, and in fact all of our *senses* and sensations have this characteristic.

To demonstrate, roughly one in eight Caucasian males in the U. S. A. are red/green colorblind. Now the fact is that most color blind people aren't all that color blind. Most can tell the difference between green and red except in certain circumstances. But let's image that there are some who are completely colorblind, that is, they cannot distinguish between green and red at all. When they observe a stop light while driving, the red and green will look the same color to them. To them, it's not *red lights means stop* and *green lights means go*, it's top light means stop and bottom light means go…but just what color are they seeing? Are they seeing both colors as green, or perhaps both colors as red? Unfortunately, we can never know, and the reason is that we just don't have words to *describe* colors. They cannot tell us which color they see. Colors are not aggregate concepts. Colors come complete and not as an aggregation of concepts tagged with words. We cannot describe the *difference* between green and red without words. The only way we can teach our children the word tags for the colors is to point at one and say "red," and the kid will attach the "red" label to the *sensation* he is experiencing. We can never know exactly what color he is experiencing, but for the rest of his life, whatever it was he will call it "red."

And this is true for all of our primary experiences. "Left" and "right" are another example. You just cannot explain to someone the difference between left and right. You have to show them, and you can never know for sure that what they are seeing is the same as what you are seeing.

Realms of experience:

We tend to call categories of experiences like colors *realms*, as in the *realm of colors*, and this is the term I am going to adopt. The realm of colors is different somehow from the realm of tastes. We are very cognizant that they are different even though we can't express that difference in words. We don't get the two mixed up (unless we have synesthesia). Colors differ from each other too, and we are very cognizant that they are different if we are not colorblind. But all colors also have something in common, and this is how we know that they belong to the category of colors, to the realm of colors, and not the realm of smells or tastes. Notice that the concepts of *similarity* and *difference*, sim/dif, are once again showing up, this time in our description of a *realm*. Colors are distinguished as unique by their differences, but before we can have differences in something we have to have a something, and that something is in the *realm* of color. A realm is a sim/dif engine. It is that upon which differences can be represented, out of which differences are made. It is important to grasp this concept as the *realm* will not only play a very significant role in the remainder of this book, but we will attempt to formalize the concept in a later section.

We have already seen how the brain handles sim/dif with our bird. That which is *similar* among birds is represented by a *shared* portion of a network of neurons and becomes the abstraction, and that which is distinguishable among birds, that which is different, is represented by different little unique networks. Presumably the brain uses the same strategy for representing the sim/diff on the color realm, and indeed it has been found that all colors are experienced from activity at the same location in the brain. There's a little thumbnail sized piece of the brain on the surface of the right hemisphere that is active during the perception of *all* colors, which is what one would expect to find from this representation of sim/dif.

As described here, the way the brain models birds using networks of neurons, and the way it models realms are pretty much identical. So, can the networks of neurons used to model birds be considered to be a realm too, the realm of birds. Yes, it can. Both represent categories on which different, unique instances of members of that category can be represented.

At some point, many people are going to begin to see the similarity between the mathematical idea of a *set*, and this definition of a *realm*, and indeed they are very similar. A set is a category for some grouping of objects (or ideas) after all, and is basically any legitimate method to define that category. The set of all Presidents of the United States, or the set of all integers, are examples. These are realms too by my definition, but the difference is that the concept of a set is almost always used to assign certain aspects, common aspects, to its members. The set captures and names the similarity, but largely ignores the differences, that which makes each member unique and distinguishable. The concept of difference is there implicitly in a set of course, and even sometimes explicitly as when the differences fall out of a Venn diagram, but even here the emphasis is usually on the intersections and unions, and only rarely on the differences. We will make much greater use of the concept of differences in this book. Anyway, for those familiar with the concepts of sets, you are well on your way to understanding realms.

An abstraction occurs when the brain identifies and represents the similarity between two things, two different, distinguishable birds for instance. If our toddler has experienced only one instance of a bird, then the only representation her brain is capable of is the representation of that complete bird. At this point, I suppose she might be distinguishing the bird as a different kind of *animal*, or maybe even a different kind of *squirrel* if she has already established the squirrel realm. It will be like the other squirrels in many ways, only it has feathers, wings, etc. Sim/ diff of course. Now when she sees a second bird, her brain will automatically reuse part of the original bird representation, including the wing and feathers portion, and the initial bird abstraction, the bird realm, will be formed. It takes two to create an abstraction. It takes two to create a realm.

To see another example of this, imagine a human child, the result of an alien abduction say, born into an alien world where the only light was red light. This would be something like black and white TV, only instead of shades of gray, everything would be shades of red. This child will have the standard human brain that is hard wired with the capability to represent all the usual colors we perceive, but the only color that ever gets mentally exercised is red. This child will have a concept of brightness, of shading, etc., but he will not have a concept for color. What he sees he will simply call *light*. To us, it would be red light, but that's only because we know that there is something other than red light. He has not yet perceived of a color realm, because he doesn't know that there is anything that is distinguishable from the light he knows. Not having experienced blue or green light, he cannot even imagine it. If he is dropped off on Earth after his training to spy on Earth is complete, he will be in for an astonishing sensory experience. Suddenly, he will see a color different from red, green say, and he will realize that there is the potential for such a thing as color. The concept of color, the color realm, will suddenly be abstracted where there was no abstraction before. It takes two to create a realm.

Activating a concept:

At the time of this writing, I live in sunny Arizona, and as you probably know, much of Arizona is a desert. The part where I live is anyway. There's not much water here, so we are encouraged to landscape our yards with what's called *desert landscaping*. Instead of grass, we plant desert bushes and shrubs, which require little or no water, and we do our best to become creative and artistic with rocks and gravel. The different varieties of cactus are, of course, a popular choice and as I imagine I look across the street, my neighbors yard contains a beautifully tall saguaro cactus (pronounced suh-war-oh). That's the kind with the arms, you know, like in the beer commercials.

One day I look at my window and beyond the cactus, beyond the top of my neighbor's roof I see the masts and sails of a tall ship slowly sailing past, and it's flying the Jolly Roger! Now, if I lived a half a block from the water in Annapolis, MD., I might find this vision of a pirate ship quaintly interesting. The fact is, though, that I live in the desert, four hours from the nearest ocean, so I find this very interesting indeed. Needless to say *this does not fit my world model* of pirate ships and where they belong, so my first reaction is that what I am seeing is impossible, and I feel that dreaded feeling of *not understanding*. But I am seeing it, so my mind now has the unenviable job of making it possible, a job that it takes very seriously.

Inside of my brain, my model of the world is, of course, an aggregate object composed of networks of neurons. One scenario that I have apparently modeled in my brain includes sailing pirate ships, and one component of that scenario, besides the pirate ship, includes water for the ship to sail in. In this aggregate object model we are creating of how the brain works, what my brain does is that when one component of the neuronal network of this scenario is activated, in this case the pirate ship portion, the brain tries to activate the remainder of the scenario by activating the remainder of the component networks composing this scenario. Again, that parent scenario is an aggregate of aspects and includes a pirate ship component and a water component, but in this case when it asks the question *water?* of its component neuronal networks, it is unable to activate the water portion, so my immediate response is that what I am seeing is impossible. The parent scenario, of which the pirate ship is just one component, cannot go Hi, and will not activate.

From the very moment that the masts, flag, and sails were perceived, the brain has been busy searching for a parent network to activate to which these components belong, and to make sense of this observation. Perhaps the first object it tried to activate was the pirate ship network itself. Masts, sails, and the Jolly Roger are components of the aggregate object *pirate ship*, so when these components went Hi, each one tweaked all of the parent objects in which it was a component, and this would mean that all three tweaked the dendrites of the pirate ship network. The pirate ship object then took these components as sufficient to indicate that it should go Hi itself, so when it went Hi, it tweaked all the parent scenarios, all the networks, in which a pirate ship participated as a component. The top level scenario then, having been tweaked by its pirate ship component, then scanned the questions it needed answered but found its *water?* synapse to be Lo. Water in this case was considered necessary for this scenario network to go Hi, so the scenario stayed Lo...it failed to match. At that point, I felt like I didn't understand, because there was no parent scenario going Hi that contained a pirate ship.

The pirate ship object, was unable to find a parent object. It doesn't have a home. It was unable to find an activatable scenario in which it participated as a component, and it now becomes apparent that feedback from a parent object, the scenario, is one of the requirements to support the pirate ship's continued existence. I imagine this feedback as something along the lines of an axon coming back from the parent scenario object itself and tweaking the pirate ship network, which is one of the scenario's components. This parent synapse feeding back onto the pirate ship component object going Hi may very well be necessary for the pirate ship object to stay Hi, and I now imagine a self-sustaining loop existing between a parent object and each of its components that is required to be active before any of it is considered to be *real*. That way, when the parent object has established itself to actually exist and goes Hi, it validates the existence of its component parts as well, and this will help the brain decide that these components do indeed exist.

Let's envision that feedback loop as having one other effect as well. When a parent object tweaks one of its components that is already active, it creates a self-supporting, self-validating loop, but what about when it tweaks one of its components that has not yet become active. We can go back to our pirate ship example at the point where *pirate ship* has gone Hi, and tweaked the parent scenario object that now includes the required but inactivated component of *water*. Before the parent scenario can go Hi, its component *water* must also go Hi, so let's give parent objects the capability to tweak each of their components that will have the effect of causing each of its component objects to see if it itself exists. In our example, this simply means that the scenario object tweaks the water object, which will cause the water object to determine for itself if water exists, if it should go Hi or not. Being a parent object in its own right, the water object will accomplish this the same way its parent did. It will tweak all of its components too.

Now as usual this is all something of an oversimplification. It will certainly be a more complex relationship of dendrites and axons than just described, but there's a way we can make it simpler still. Let's step back a minute and look at the overall structure that we have just described. We have an aggregate object, a parent object, which is composed of smaller components, each an aggregate object too, and each of those components is composed of yet smaller component aggregate objects. When a component object goes Hi, it automatically tweaks the object in which it participates as a component, its parent object. We will call this *forward tweaking*, that is when a component object goes Hi and tweaks its parent. This in turn will cause the parent object to ask each of its components if they exist by tweaking them. Whenever a parent object tweaks its component objects, we will call this *back tweaking*. But each of the components are aggregate objects too, so when back tweaked by their parent object, the component objects too will ask each of their components if they exist. They too will back tweak all of their components.

This back tweaking will thus continue down and down as far as necessary to determine if the bottom level of components exist. If they find that lower level components exist, these low level components will then go Hi and forward tweak their parents. The process will then cascade back upward, each component that goes Hi forward tweaking its parent, back up to the top level that, when a sufficient number of its components go Hi, will go Hi itself. If at any point the cascade of component activation breaks down because of the nonexistence of critical components, the parent will ultimately fail to go Hi, thus correctly breaking the chain.

Let's apply all of this to our pirate ship scenario in detail. What we are calling the *scenario* object is the top level aggregate object, the parent object. For simplicity, we let it have only two component objects, a *pirate ship object*, and a *water object*. The pirate ship is itself a rather complex aggregate object, consisting of masts, sails, a flag, a deck, a ships body, rudder, etc. Each one of these is an object too, of course.

The first thing that happened then is that when the masts, sails, and flag were observed, their objects went Hi. The very observation of them was sufficient to set them Hi. They are all components of the pirate ship object, so they all forward tweaked the pirate ship object, causing it to forward tweak the scenario object. The pirate ship object also back tweaked the remainder of its component objects, i.e., the deck object, ship body object, etc. The parent scenario object too, having been forward tweaked by its component pirate ship object, now back tweaks its component objects too, in this case the water object. The water object back tweaks its component objects, whatever they are, and the process cascades down to the bottom level of the water objects components, which ultimately fail because there is no water. This then fails all the way back up to the water object causing it to fail, which then causes the parent scenario object to fail too. This is the point at which I felt that what I was seeing was impossible, because at this point I knew there was no water here, and all this happened in less than an instant.

In the meantime, the pirate ship object had initiated its own investigation of itself too by back tweaking its components. There was no incoming information to support its other components, though, like a ships body, since the view of it was blocked by the house, so when the parent scenario object failed, the pirate ship object became untenable. The only support it had was the existence of masts, sails, and flag after all. Apparently now the only thing for me to do is get off of my duff and go over to the next street and see what's going on. Of course, when I get there I discover something like there's a parade going on and the mast, sails, and flag all are just part of a float in the parade.

I would like to add a few comments on the idea of *loops* of activity in the brain. Imagine for yourself a bundle of neurons, some of the connections forming forward tweaking connections and some back tweaking, to form potential *loops* of activity. Now just so you have some way to picture it, imagine activity in these neurons as being represented with light, so neurons flash momentarily when they become active, when they go Hi. What this might look like then is that when information starts to arrive initially, various neurons within the network will begin to flash, forward tweaking their parent networks and back tweaking their components. As new neurons are tweaked, they will flash on momentarily too, tweaking other neurons in the bundle. Now, as long as a neuron is not participating in a self-supporting loop, it will just flash on and then off, but once a loop is complete, activity will be sustained throughout the loop, and the loop will light up and stay lit. At first, maybe only one or two little loops light up and stay lit, but as more and more of the components establish their existence, each newly completed loop lights up too, until finally, there's a huge flash and the whole network lights up all at once, because every component of the network bundle lights up and stays lit. All of this imagery is, of course, just to give you a way to visualize the concept of self-sustaining loops.

I bring up this idea of loops, because I suspect that they may be an important function in the brain and mind, and I suspect this because the concept shows up in several places. Besides their appearance in networks, they show up in psychology. It seems that mental phenomena such as personality disorders and neuroses can be modeled as self-reinforcing loops. As an admittedly oversimplified and superficial example, let's presume that the reason someone overeats is to try to give themselves a treat in an attempt to compensate for something that is missing in their lives, love perhaps. So they're down in the dumps about it and they need something to make themselves feel better, something to lift their spirits, so they give themselves a treat. Of course when they eat extra food, they now gain a little weight, so they now feel less attractive, and they're down about that. So now they give themselves a treat to make themselves feel better, and they eat again. And they gain a little more weight…You see the loop. It is a self-perpetuating, self-reinforcing, self-sustaining loop, and as far as I can tell (not being a psychiatrist myself), it looks like many personality disorders and neuroses have this characteristic, and if the loop can be broken, the disorder ceases to exist. These, of course, are negative or undesirable mental traits or phenomena, but if it's true for them, it seems reasonable to me that our desirable traits might be modeled with this loop phenomenon as well.

It may turn out that just such a loop is involved in the phenomenon of consciousness. Consciousness to me has always seemed to involve some sort of feedback, kind of like looking in the mirror. In fact, I believe it might be that what we typically refer to as consciousness is really consciousness of consciousness given that such things exist as the subconscious and the unconscious mind, minds of which we are not conscious.

This then is my model of how the higher levels of the brain, using networks of neurons, models the world as aggregate objects that forward tweak and back tweak each other. It has several interesting characteristics that we will be seeing again. One is that it can almost instantly build an extraordinarily complex aggregate object, eliminating contradictory components in such a way that the whole object fits together free of contradiction. Another is that from an intermediate starting point of an incomplete scenario, it can look backwards and determine whether it exists or not, and in the process completes the context in which it exists. Additionally, it can look forward, investigating multiple possible scenarios in which it might participate, and determine the exact context in which it does participate. In our pirate ship example, for simplicity, we allowed it to participate in only a single parent scenario, but in the real world, there are usually dozens or hundreds of possible scenarios into which a particular piece of information may participate.

Do any of these above mentioned characteristics feel vaguely familiar to you? You have indeed seen something very similar earlier in this book. ***These are some of the things that our universe does too***.

In the final section of the book, we will see how to program this model into a computer and some of the amazing powers it demonstrates. We will see that in many ways this model parallels the algorithm apparently used by the universe itself, including the ability to look backwards and set its history, and the ability to proceed forward into multiple potential futures simultaneously. We will, in fact, create an imaginary universe in a computer based on this model.

We have seen how a great deal of what we know about our thinking can be modeled using networks of neurons as interacting aggregate objects. This model sheds light on why we describe the world using similarity and difference, as well as our seeing the world itself as composed of aggregate objects. It is able to model the phenomenon of cognition, recognition, and even the feeling of familiarity. It accounts for the formation of, and our use of, abstractions and realms in our thinking. It relates words to thoughts and suggests the aggregate object structure we observe our sentences to have. It suggests the structure of how we model our world, and shows how we are able to match the information we receive from our senses to models we have made, which results in the human feeling of understanding.

But as successful as this model is at accounting for our thinking, there is something about it that is still dissatisfying. That is that it doesn't seem to be referring to anything like our thoughts at all, just some of the characteristics we observe our thinking to have. It says nothing about the thoughts and feelings we know we have, the sensations of experience. A network of neurons is not a thought. It doesn't seem to explain our actual *experience* at all.

Chapter 11
The Experience

If that this thing we call the world
By chance on atoms was begot
Which though in ceaseless motion whirled
Yet weary not
How doth it prove
Thou art so fair and I in love?

—John Hall—seventeenth-century poet

The most fundamental realm:

With our model of how the brain models the world using networks of neurons arranged as aggregate objects, we have gone a long way toward accounting for many of the characteristics and phenomena we observe in our thinking. When we think, though, we are not aware at all of neurons, or networks, or brain activity, and the things we are aware of seem to be entirely different from, and unaccounted for by neuronal activity. The things we are aware of are things like our feelings, our current thoughts, visual images, our senses, and their associated sensations. We have linked certain of these feelings with our model of brain activity, feelings like the feeling of *familiarity*, and feeling like we *understand* or *don't understand*. Possibly even the feeling of *deja vu*. Don't think from this that we have in any way accounted for the actual feelings we are experiencing. All we have said is that when a certain configuration of brain activity occurs, one of these feelings is experienced. What makes these feelings the actual sensation that we experience is completely unaccounted for.

Now all of these things that we experience are quite different from each other. Feelings, for example, are different from visual images, and thoughts are different

208

from sensations. The thought of your car is quite different from the sensation of heat, for example. In the realm of feelings, each feeling is quite different from every other feeling, and in the realm of sensations, each sensation is very different from every other sensation. The sensation of sweetness is quite different from the sense of bitterness. It is not too hard to tell that they are all different, (although it is difficult to express what the difference is), but noting that they are distinguished by *differences*, one is then compelled to identify their *similarity*. What is *their* common abstraction, the realm on which all of them exist? We have, in fact, been naming that realm all along while referring to them, and the realm is our old familiar realm of *experience*. The one thing that they all have in common is that they are each a brand of experience.

This is the lowest level of abstraction that I *know* of. Indeed, the very use of the word *know* in the previous sentence may dictate that it is the lowest achievable realm that a mental being may recognize, since for something to be known, it must be experienced. There is nothing we know of that we don't experience or haven't experienced. There's a lot going on out there that you don't know of, inside the house next door say, and the reason you don't know of it is because you aren't experiencing it. The instant you experience it you know of it, and vice versa.

To help clarify the idea of experiencing, let's once again use the dream as an example. When you sleep, you dream, and when you dream, you experience. I don't need to tell you that as you dream, the events you are experiencing are not occurring in the real world. You can break you arm in your dream, do the wild thing with somebody who doesn't care for you at all, or even die in your dream, but when you wake up it's to pretty much the same old world as when you went to sleep. But there is something that is real about your dream. By that I mean, you really did have a dream. The dream itself existed. The events depicted in the dream didn't exist, but a dream did occur. The dream itself is a real thing, as opposed to the events depicted in the dream.

Let me say that all again, using the word *experience* in place of the word *dream*.

But there is something that is real about your dream. By that I mean you really did have an experience. The experience existed. The events depicted in the experience didn't exist, but an experience did occur. The experience itself is a real thing, as opposed to the events depicted in the experience.

Most people know what an experience is. They know what it means to say that a roller coaster ride, or their first romance, was a real experience, but the idea that an event is experienced is taken for granted by us, and is of trivial importance next to the event itself. The consideration that an event was experienced seems understood, unnecessary and esoteric. Anyone will quickly agree that an event must be experienced in order to be of value to the person experiencing it, but in any conversation, that the event was experienced is always just understood.

There is a lot going on out there that we don't experience. We don't experience what is going on in the next room, in the next country, or on the moon. We don't experience what people across town are experiencing. We don't even experience exactly what the person next to us is experiencing, even though we are both attending to the same events. Our experience is a very personal thing known only to ourselves. Writers, poets, and other artsy oriented people go to great lengths to try to cause others to experience what they are experiencing, and it is neither easy nor completely successful. Two people who read the same book or watch the same movie experience it so differently that one may enjoy the experience they have, while the other may dislike the experience they have.

Everything that you are conscious or aware of depends on it being experienced. The mind itself might be thought of as the sum total of what one is experiencing at any given moment, at least the conscious mind. *All* that you know of is experienced, and what you experience is *all* that you know. You *only* know of what you experience and *only* that which you experience is known to you. Experience is the *all* and the *only*. The realm of experience appears to be the most fundamental realm of a cogent being.

Some may be tempted to say that they are able to deduce a great deal about the world that they don't experience directly, and that, therefore, they are able to know things that they don't experience. This is true only in the very limited sense where *direct experience* here means the sensations and mental images resulting from our *senses*. When one considers that these very deduced thoughts must themselves also be experienced to be known, it becomes clear that even here we cannot know of anything that we don't experience, in this case the deduced thought.

A few hundred years ago the French philosopher René Descartes was asking himself the question of just how he knew he existed, *for sure*. It may seem like a dumb question at first, an unnecessary question, but it's nevertheless a good question in that if we do indeed exist, then the question should indeed have an answer. To get rid of the distracting interference of his five senses, Descartes imagined himself in a sensory free environment, shut away in a dark closet or something so the story goes. Today, to achieve the same sensory free state, one might imagine that their brain had been surgically removed, thus severing all sensory input, and then attached to a nutrient system in a jar somewhere.

Imagine then waking up and sensing no world around you at all, including no body. You may at first wonder if you are in some weird dream state, but eventually you get bored and decide to try to figure out whether you even exist anymore or not. How will you do it? What Descartes recognized was that in the very act of trying to figure out if he existed, he was thinking. He said something to the effect that, "If I'm thinking about my existence, then I am thinking. And if I am thinking, then I, the thinker, exist." This has been passed down as the abbreviated phrase attributed to him of "I think, therefore I am," otherwise popularly expressed as its Latin equivalent of "Cogito, ergo sum."

Now this is clever enough, but he could have taken it down a notch lower, and he wouldn't even have had to remove the distraction of his senses. He could have recognized that along with his sensory sensations, his very thoughts needed to be experienced too before he could know of them, before he could know that he was thinking. If he had, perhaps he would have thought that, "If I experience, then I, the *experiencer*, exist," further iterated as, "I experience, therefore I am," which may be the logical bottom line of mental existence.

Experience is the *realm of existence* when applied to the universe of a conscious being. The requirement as stated throughout this book for something to exist is that it must have some effect. The only thing that a conscious being has to even be affected is its experience. The only things that exist on the realm of experience are what we call experiences. The only things that exist to us are our experiences. We know of nothing else. We can know of nothing else.

Brain activity and experience:

We are the *experiencer*. We are the realm of experience. It is on the realm of experience that our *differences* from nothing occur. Experience is the realm on which the dancing fluctuations of our experiences occur. These dancing fluctuations include our sensations, feelings, thoughts, and visual images, literally everything that we experience and know of. They include our perceptions and concepts of the material world. They include the sensations we call our loved ones. They include the sensations we call ourselves. And importantly, they include the perception we experience when we examine our material brain, within a skull or in a jar.

We as cogent beings investigating the world must necessarily start with our mental representations of the world and work our way outwards. Actually, it's a little worse than that. We as investigators of our world are for the most part investigating *only* our mental representation of the world. For most of us, that is the only world we know. (Science on the other hand uses a quite different representation, the mathematical, but that is not the way we experience the world at all.) The perceptual world of our experiences turns out to be like images on a movie screen. When we examine our world, we are only examining these images, these mental images. One of those mental images of the world that we are investigating happens to be our own brain, and we have discovered that there is an association between the perceived activity in our brains and what we are experiencing, and we naturally find this correlation fascinating.

How did we discover that there is a relationship between the brain and what we experience in the first place? The knowledge that the brain is associated with our minds has been an on-again, off-again concept throughout human history. In the past, the seat of the mind has been intuitively assigned to other body parts, the heart, for example, and the brain was even thought at one point only to function as a place where the blood was cooled, like in the radiator in you car.

One way we know, though, that there is a connection is that we can drive a one-and-a-half inch thick steel rod through somebody's head and, if he lives, we will observe that the brain damage has caused a radical change to his personality…and of course this has actually happened to someone. In 1848, one Phineas P. Gage was tamping blasting powder into a drill hole in rock when the powder accidentally detonated, blasting the thick tamping rod through the front half of his head and brain and off yet another hundred feet. Of course, the tissue damage was massive. He lost a huge portion of his brain that afternoon, but Phineas hardly seemed to notice, losing consciousness only momentarily. Additionally, he remained lucid and coherent not only immediately following the accident, but throughout the following two month recovery period. Except for the loss of vision in his left eye, Gage recovered completely and lived another thirteen years.

But in another sense, Phineas died that day. The personality that had been Phineas was replaced by someone new. The Phineas that everyone knew and loved was gone. Socially and ethically he was a different person. Before the accident, he had been a gentleman and an ideal employee, but now he could no longer hold down a job. He no longer respected ethics or social conventions, and so crude was he that women were permitted to spend only short periods in his company. His animalistic drives became more pronounced, and his will and intellect became diminished. It appears that the brain is not only involved in mind, but even in making us who we are.

Besides driving a rod through someone's head, we now know that there are dozens of ways of dinking with the brain that result in changes in personality and thinking. Strap down a manic depressive person, run a high voltage through his brain, and when the convulsions stop the person will no longer feel depressed, kind of like pressing the reset button. As another example, flooding the brain with alcohol has such an affect on who we are, that there are embarrassing times when we feel the need to claim that "it was the alcohol talking." And there are myriad other substances, both legal and illegal, which profoundly affect our personalities by affecting our brains. Some even help schizophrenics not be schizophrenic.

Substances like anesthesia can *eliminate* our personalities and experience, our minds, completely. Then of course strokes cause brain damage in various areas of the brain that invariably result in the loss of some ability or another, and the identification of these lost abilities within these regions of the brain has provided invaluable information to brain researchers. As Alzheimer's disease fills the brain with invasive amyloid proteins, killing neurons, the victim's personalities seem to just gradually dissolve, their identities ever so slowly vanishing before our eyes. And then there are coma and brain death, which invariably result in the loss of all mental abilities.

Nowadays, scientists using various instruments are able to detect and even correlate activity in certain regions of the brain to certain thoughts and feeling. That there is a link between the mind and the brain is no longer subtle. Brain activity gives all appearances of being directly responsible for the mind. When certain regions of the brain are active, the owner is experiencing the sensations, or performing the actions, associated with that region of the brain. Stimulate certain portions of the brain with electrodes and the recipient experiences thoughts and feelings associated with that area. Stop all brain activity, as in a coma, and the person experiences nothing. Mental *activity*, the mind, is tightly associated with brain *activity*. The mind appears to result from an active brain.

Another thing we can do to demonstrate an association between the brain and the mind is split the brain in two, right down the middle. The brain is composed of two hemispheres, the left and right hemispheres, which communicate with each other over a bundle of neurons called the corpus callosum connecting them. When the corpus callosum is cut, separating the two hemispheres, an interesting thing happens. You end up with two distinct minds inside of one skull. Each one of these is then a separate person and personality, experiencing separate experiences.

Where once they were one, they can now no longer communicate or even cooperate with each other, because the corpus callosum has been destroyed. Only the left side controls language and speech, so the left person gets to tell us all about what it is thinking and feeling. The right hemisphere can hear the left speaking, so it knows what the left is thinking to some extent, but there is no way for the right to tell the world what it is thinking. The right person is muzzled and mute. It cannot speak. These two minds can have such totally different personalities and concerns after separation that there is an interesting case of where one side was suicidal and the other side was not. In their fascinating book *Phantoms In the Brain*, Dr. V. S. Ramachandran and Sandra Blakeslee cite a case where a woman had suffered a stroke in her corpus callosum, effectively isolating the two hemispheres from each other and thus creating two personalities. The right hemisphere mind ended up suicidal (perhaps because it could no longer speak its mind?) and it was a constant battle for the left hemisphere to prevent the right hemisphere from killing them both. They write:

> —every now and then her left hand would fly up to her throat and try to strangle her. She often had to use her right hand to wrestle her left hand under control—much like Peter Sellers portraying Dr. Strangelove. She even sometimes had to sit on the murderous hand, so intent was it on trying to end her life.

Thankfully, humanity has advanced considerably beyond the need to drive steel rods through people's heads, or split their brains in two, to discern a relationship between brain activity and the mind. Through accident and disease, nature continues to provide us with dramatic demonstrations that experience and personality are brain dependent. The afore mentioned book, *Phantoms In the Brain*, is a cornucopia of astonishing examples of this, and I will cite several more for the readers amazement. An inescapable conclusion to be drawn from these examples is that our perception of the world is not only vividly demonstrated to be just a brain based mental construct, but that the perception we have of the world is so fragile, complex, and so easily disrupted that one is left feeling that we are each of us lucky to have a coherent perception at all.

Our imaginary bodies:

The brain takes the information of the world passed in as code through the little holes in the skull and processes it and represents it using networks of neurons. Somehow at this point some of the information becomes re-encoded as our experience of it. We do not experience the universe directly. It appears that if we experience anything directly, it is only the high level *activity* of the *brain*. Somehow our experience comes off of this brain activity. Now, it has been a major theme of this book that our experience of the outside world is not necessarily the way the outside world really is, but *in either case*, our experience of the world is necessarily imaginary, experiential only.

One of the things that seems to be out there that we experience is our very own body. We saw in an earlier chapter how the illusion of the materiality of a coffee cup or a cardinal can be accounted for with just our senses of sight and touch. They are perceived as material objects, and our body is perceived as a material object, but there are some obvious differences between our bodies and other perceived objects. For one thing, those other objects are *only* revealed to us via our sense of sight and touch. While our bodies are also revealed to us in this way, we have many other senses with which we sense our bodies. We seem to be in our bodies. As with other objects, I know that my knee is there, because I can see it and I can touch it with my finger, but unlike the case with the coffee cup, something else happens when I touch my knee. My knee feels my finger too. When I touched the coffee cup, I had no sense of the coffee cup feeling my finger touching it. The coffee cup is not a part of *me*.

It was espoused in an earlier chapter that materiality and space are illusions. The perception of materiality is built out of the senses of touch and vision. Materiality requires nothing more than a region of space that reflects light and resist penetration, that is, we can see it and feel it. Further, space itself as a perception is an illusion, as we will see even more clearly in a moment. That makes materiality a kind of double illusion, an illusion (materiality) that depends on an illusion (space).

If a coffee cup is nothing but a region of space that reflects light and resists penetration, then so must be our bodies, but the difference is that *we as experiencers* seem to inhabit this imaginary volume of space that our bodies occupy. When we press our fingertip into our knee, we actually experience the sense of touch *at our knee*, and also *at our fingertip*. If we touch the table top with our fingertip, we experience the sense of touch at our fingertip, but not at the table top, which is not included in our body image, our *experiencer*. Our body is an object in the ordinary sense in that it takes up space, reflects light, and resists penetration, but we as *experiencers* seem to inhabit this region. Mentally, we have a body image, but since space and materiality don't exist, that body image must be an illusion!

It is hard enough to accept that a coffee cup out there is an illusion, but entertaining the idea that your very own body is an illusion may seem to be pushing the assertion beyond where it can survive. We are really sticking it into the central fire here. Logic dictates, however, that if materiality and space are illusions, then so must be our material body. A good hypothesis must withstand all tests thrown at it to remain in the running after all. If the body is an illusion, we would expect that there be some interesting phenomena that reveals this.

It turns out that the body as an object offers us a new and powerful tool with which to explore the notion that objects are immaterial, and this tool is experience. We as *experiencers* are forever isolated from the coffee cup, but not so the body. In that we seemingly experience our bodies directly, if the body is an illusion, then there ought to be ways to use our experience of it to show this up, and happily this turns out to be the case. It is possible, using our experience of our bodies as an exploratory means, to demonstrate strange and remarkable phenomena that are consistent with the notion that material objects, space, and our bodies, are all illusions.

At first glance, experience seems to give us evidence that the opposite is true. That we experience the sense of touch at our fingertip seems to be empirical evidence that the fingertip must exist. That we feel our fingertips when we rub our thumb and forefinger together seems to make their existence self-evident. But this is just ordinary, everyday, usual experience, which evolution prepared and programmed us to feel. It is possible it turns out to dink with our perceptual systems, our nervous systems, our information processing system, and create some very revealing phenomena that are consistent with our bodies, and body images, being entirely an illusion.

Taking the fingertip metaphorically for any body part, it turns out that there are ways to actually dissociate our visual fingertip from our experienced fingertip. We can feel our fingertip to be located in space somewhere that it visually isn't. We can feel our visually non-existent fingertip to be touching things that don't exist. It is possible to have a remote part of our body touched, our cheek say, but to experience that touch as if it had occurred at the fingertip. We can change the imaginary spatial shape of our experienced body image to an odd shape that doesn't match our visual, physical body. We can extend our experienced body image to incorporate a foreign object in front of us, a coffee cup say, as part of our perceived body, and even experience a sense of touch as from within that object. We will demonstrate all of these in detail in a minute, but the fact is that these phenomena all exist because the body images, both visual and experiential, turn out to exist not in space, but only in the mind.

Where feelings are:

If you hold your fingertip out in front of you and prick it with a toothpick, you feel the prick occurring at you fingertip. You feel the prick occurring at a certain location in space in front of you. Most of the time, that location of the feeling happens to coincide with where your visual fingertip appears to be located. The point is that the feeling itself seems to occur at a location. *Where*, though, exactly does a feeling occur? It certainly seems to be located at your fingertip out in front of you, to be your fingertip doing the experiencing, but asking the location of a feeling turns out to be an invalid question.

If one severs the nerve connecting the fingertip to the brain, or even just deadens it with Novocain, the experience at the fingertip seems to cease to exist. Obviously, it is necessary for the nerve impulse from the fingertip to reach the brain before the sensation is experienced. Does this mean that the experience actually occurs in the brain, and not at the fingertip at all? If the experience is occurring in the brain, then the brain is manufacturing the illusion that it is occurring at a location in front of you. Or does it mean that the experience still occurs at the fingertip, that the fingertip itself is still experiencing the feeling, but the information of the feeling is not making it to the brain so you're just not aware of it?

Let's take a closer look at the latter idea. It is suggesting that it is actually the fingertip that is having the feeling, that the *experience* of being pricked is actually occurring at the fingertip. Now this is certainly how we perceive it. Furthermore, it leaves open the possibility that even when the brain is not receiving the information from the fingertip, that the now isolated fingertip itself may still experience being pricked. We're just prevented from being aware of it. This is saying then that our *awareness* at least of the experience must necessarily occur in the brain, but since the nerve impulse that carries the experience to the brain is missing, then we simply are not aware of it.

One consequence of this notion is that we are now elevating the information carried in a nerve impulse to something far beyond some simple Morse code type of information telling the brain that the finger was pricked. This nerve impulse would now have to be carrying the actual feeling itself to the brain since the feeling is really occurring at the fingertip. Another way one might imagine this is that the brain being composed of nerve cells, when the connection is completed and operational, the fingertip becomes just an extended part of the brain, and thus we are aware of what the nerves at the fingertips are experiencing.

The two preceding ideas, that feelings and experiences themselves can be transmitted by nerves, or that the brain can effectively be extended to experience a distant part of the world, both open up the possibility that it might be possible to extend our experience of the outer world beyond the confines or our bodies simply by connecting our nerves to input sources beyond our bodies. I might then be able to connect a nerve from my fingertip to your body, and thus experience your body as an extension of mine, or better yet, it might now be theoretically possible to connect to your brain and thus experience your mind as an extension of my own. The implications pursued down this path go on and on, but I will not pursue them further, because it turns out that the notion that the experience occurs at the fingertip, the way we actually perceive it, is false, just another illusion.

There is a connection between the fact that our mental representations of our bodies is an illusion, and the fact that we seem to experience touch at our fingertips. We know that the sense of touch occurs when the information is represented in our brains. But our fingertip's location in space, indeed our mental representation of our body, is also represented as information in our brain. Our brain is putting the two together, imagining the feeling as being located at the same imaginary place in space as our imaginary fingertip. This is yet another phenomenon that results from the fact that mental images are just representations of information received from the *real* world, whatever that is. It seems impossible that we are actually feeling at our fingertip, since we know the feeling doesn't occur until the code is represented within our brains. The contradiction that leads us to ponder this in the first place is just that; the feeling seems to occur at our fingertip, yet it must occur in our brains.

It turns out that it is fairly easy to demonstrate that the experience does not occur at the fingertip at all. If a person loses their arm, and thus their fingertips too, it frequently doesn't take too long for a phantom limb to show up, complete with fingertips that experience feeling. Phantom limbs come with a variety of capabilities and forms, one of which is the complete limb with all the capabilities of that complete limb. By complete, I mean every sense and control is there that was there with the original, except of course the phantom limb cannot be seen, nor can it actually manipulate the physical world.

The owner, however, can feel the entire limb, his arm say, and may move it around, grasp objects with it, and touch, and feel things with his fingertips. He can clench his fist and feel his nonexistent fingernails dig into his nonexistent palm. Once again when he rubs his phantom fingertips together, the experience occurs at the sensed location of the fingertips in space out in front of him, just like with the original fingers, but of course, there is no visual confirmation of it this time since there are no fingertips. No material fingertips exist nor does their location, yet the person can still feel these. These feelings he is experiencing clearly are not occurring at the fingertips, but are in his mind nevertheless. There are no nerve impulses arriving at his brain, carrying feelings from his fingertips to his awareness.

Part of the feeling at the phantom fingertips is the location in space at which the feeling seems to occur. The owner of the feeling is able to tell us exactly where in space the feeling occurs. He perceives the location of the feeling right along with the feeling of touch. The *perception* of location is thus an experience too, and some might even call the sense of location itself a feeling. The feeling of touch, including the feeling of where it is occurring, is actually resulting from activity back in the brain. (Remember, there *are* no fingertips.) The feeling that the feeling is occurring at a particular location is an illusion too. Location is just another feeling, and is an illusion too.

The body in the brain:

The experience of our bodies occurs in our brains and not in our bodies. It turns out that each of us has very specific locations near the surface of our brains that are associated with our experiencing of each little portion of our bodies. That each body part is represented in the brain has been known for some time now, but using the sophisticated electronic equipment of today, brain researchers can relatively easily locate these regions in each of us simply by wiring up our heads and going over our bodies from head to toe with a cotton swab, and then watching for the location of the corresponding brain activity. These locations turn out to be almost identical in all of us, drawing something of a map of our bodies on the surface of our brains.

One interesting thing about this map is that it's not shaped at all like we are. Body parts are scattered all over the place. The hand is next to the face, and the feet occur between the body and the genitals, for example. The pieces are not correctly juxtaposed physically in the brain. Somehow the mind juxtaposes the pieces into the smoothly joined whole that is the imaginary body we experience. Another interesting thing about this map is that the more sensitive the region of the body, the bigger is its area in the brain. There seems to be a correlation between the number of neurons involved and the "size" of the experience. The brain areas assigned to the hands, lips, tongue, and genitals are huge in comparison to other less sensitive body parts. When it comes to relating our experience of our bodies to our brain maps, we notice two things. The first is that specific experiences are mapped to specific locations in the brain. Location matters. The second is that the bigger the area of the brain, the bigger the experience. Size matters.

It turns out that phantom limbs can largely be accounted for by the continued activity in that region of the brain that represented that body part, now missing.

That is, after all, where we were experiencing that body part all along, in the brain, not in the imaginary body part itself. As *experiencers, we* can't possibly know the difference since we get our experience off of the brains activity. The experience of that body part results from activity in that region of the brain, nothing more, and not from the real existence of the body part at all.

Dr. Ramachandran has discovered that soon after a body part is amputated or otherwise disconnected from the brain, activity in the surrounding regions of the brain begins to bleed through into the now inactive area. This bleed through creates new activity in that heretofore-dormant area, and the person begins again to experience the sensations associated with the missing body part. The phantom limb appears. He has found that by touching the body part mapped to an adjacent region of the brain, he can create the sensation that the phantom body part itself is being touched. The brain area for the cheek is adjacent to the brain area for the hand for example, and he has found that by stroking a person's cheek with a swab, the person is amazed to feel his phantom hand being stroked too. Dr. Ramachandran has been able to create a detailed map of the hand, fingers and fingertips included, on a person's cheek. He has also discovered a second map for the missing hand on the shoulder. The area in the brain from which the shoulder is experienced turns out also to be adjacent to the hand area, but on the opposite side from the cheek.

Experience occurs from brain activity, and our experience of our bodies occurs from brain activity, and is imaginary. And the spatial extension of our bodies is imaginary. Our bodies are *only* experience, and there seems to be no end to the imaginary experiences that can result from this fact. Phantom limbs are not limited to just the imaginary sense of touch, but they can experience other sensations too, sensations such as hot and cold, itching, and even severe pain. When a phantom limb itches, its owner has a problem. There is no phantom limb to scratch to make the itch go away. The situation is similar with pain. How does one relieve pain in a perceived body part that doesn't exist? It certainly can't be amputated, you would think. Dr. Ramachandran, though, has discovered ways of manipulating the mind that sometimes not only alleviates the imaginary pain, but can cause the phantom limb to go away altogether. He thus claims the honor of being the first person to "amputate" a phantom limb.

We can also have phantom body parts other than just arms and legs. Dr. Ramachandran discusses a case where a person whose appendix had been removed developed a phantom appendix, which returned complete with the excruciating pain of appendicitis. Of course, it was not possible to perform another appendectomy on this poor individual to alleviate the pain.

And apparently, phantom breasts are not uncommon either following radical mastectomies, phantom breasts complete with phantom nipples. Once again taking cotton swab in hand, Dr. Ramachandran has discovered that stimulating the areas of the body that map to the brain regions surrounding the region for the imaginary nipple can create the sensation that the missing nipple is being touched. Women with phantom breasts report the sensation of their missing nipple being touched when they are touched in a variety of other locations around their bodies, including the earlobe, sternum, clavicle, and genitalia.

Having a personal acquaintance who has undergone reconstructive breast surgery (not a complete mastectomy), when I read this I immediately fired off an email to her unabashedly inquiring if touching these remote body areas gave her any sensation in her new nipples. She replied:

> Earlobe, sternum, genitalia yes, clavicle no. I was told I'd have minimal sensation after 1st surgery and none after reconstructive surgery. I have sensations and in fact, even though my nipples were reconstructed using skin from other areas of my breast during the second surgery, they are still sensitive and will become erect. It's pretty amazing actually and I'm sure that I "willed" it or intended it to be so.

I had also inquired as to whether or not the experienced sensations in her nipples occurred with her eyes closed as well as when she actually observed the touching.

> My breasts are definitely more sensitive and aroused when [my partner] touches me, but I too can stimulate sensation. Eyes closed = more sensation.

She's being wonderfully frank, I think. She goes on:

> You are a perv, aren't you? How's the book going,…talk to you soon!

Me, a perv? (Strictly *professional* curiosity!) It is of interest though that she is experiencing both the phantom nipple being touched and the actual nipple being touched. That's not supposed to happen. The new nipple should have no nerve connections to the brain, and thus she should be experiencing no sensation when it is touched, particularly if she does not see it being touched.

There are even phantom penises experienced by men (or otherwise) who have had their penises amputated. The brain area that represents the genitals lies adjacent to the brain area for the foot. Dr. Ramachandran does not mention a case where a guy feels his phantom penis being touched when the foot is touched, but he does discuss an interesting case that is somewhat the other way around. This guy still has his penis, but is missing a leg and thus experiences a phantom foot. What's interesting is that his orgasms now involve not only his penis, but have expanded and are now experienced in his phantom foot as well. He reports further that, his feet being appreciably larger than his penis, the orgasm he experiences is now much greater than before. Size really does make a difference.

Distorting the body image(inary):

That the body image is imaginary can be further demonstrated by the surprising ability to manipulate it in impossible ways. Using mirrors, people hiding under the table and such, Dr. Ramachandran is able to create for the amputee the visual image of an arm in the place where he perceives his phantom arm to be. In many cases, the amputee's mind makes an immediate connection, perceiving the image of the arm in the mirror to be the image of the phantom limb itself. If the image of the arm is moved, the amputee experiences his phantom arm moving in the identical way. In one case, the stand-in hand was hidden in a glove put on upside down, and when the hand was closed, it appeared to the amputee that his gloved hand curled over backwards. The amputee reported experiencing the sensation that his hand was indeed curling over backwards toward his wrist.

Our imaginary body image, though, turns out to be considerably more malleable even than that. There are cases where the forearms of people who have lost their hands are surgically split into pincers, which they are able to learn to use, instead of the alternative hooked metal pincers. In some, the phantom hand becomes split too, with several fingers assigned to each pincer. In others, the body image conforms to the new pincers, becoming the new pincers. There is one case where the pincers themselves later needed to be amputated, leaving the victim not with a phantom hand but with phantom pincers.

Dr. Ramachandran gives us several very simple experiments we can perform on our own imaginary body images to experience it as an illusion first hand. These work about 50% of the time, so if one doesn't work for you, maybe the next one will.

The first one allows you to grow a two-foot long phantom nose of your own. Sit on a straight back chair or stool, with a second one as close as possible in front of you backed up to you. Have a second person sit in that chair with their back to you, and closing your eyes, reach around them and put your fingertip on the tip of their nose. Now keeping your eyes closed, have a third person sitting beside you put a finger on the tip of your nose, and with their other hand grasp your extended hand. They then proceed to tap and rub the tip of the nose of the person in front of you with your extended finger, at the same time exactly matching the tapping and rubbing on your nose with their other hand. After a minute, your nose will suddenly leap out in front of you to feel like it is several feet long. Your mental image of your nose turns out to be quite elastic. Clearly your mental image of your nose in space is mind manufactured, and is an illusion.

The second experiment requires a fake plastic or rubber hand that you can probably pick up at your local costume shop. Shape a piece of cardboard to create a small wall on the table in front of you, perhaps by cutting it out of an old cardboard box or something. Place one hand out-of-sight behind the cardboard, and place the fake hand in view in front of the cardboard. Now have a friend sit in such a way as to be able to reach both hands. Have your friend stroke both your hidden hand and the fake hand in identical synchronous ways while you watch only the fake hand. According to Dr. Ramachandran, within a minute your mind will have assigned the sensations you are feeling to be coming from the fake hand. Your body image illusion will have adjusted itself to incorporate the fake hand as part of your body. Of course it's imaginary too.

Dr. Ramachandran was able to force the body image to include even more of the surrounding world than just the fake hand. He discovered that he could simply hide one of your hands under the table, and if your friend stroked the hidden hand and the visible *tabletop* simultaneously, your mind would soon incorporate the tabletop too into your body image, and perceive the sensations you are experiencing to be coming from the tabletop. You actually experience the illusion of feeling the tabletop being stroked. To test that their subject's mind really did feel that the tabletop was part of their bodies, he attached them to a galvanic skin response meter (GSR) and then slammed the tabletop with a hammer. The GSR responded as if the subjects themselves had just been struck, but only while they were in the state of including the tabletop as part of their body image.

Dr. Ramachandran states that, "your body image, despite all its appearance of durability, is an entirely transitory internal construct that can be modified with just a few simple tricks."

The computer in our heads:

Our body image is clearly a mental construct, the experience of which is easily confused. It is the result of an information processing system that has been programmed by evolution to create an imaginary body image that is consistent with the information *ordinarily* input by nature. If it is fed extra-ordinary information, however, it cannot process it correctly. It cannot manufacture the correct body image, because the body image does not come from a body at all. It is not programmed to handle unusual information, so from an information processing point of view, it's a demonstration of the old computer adage *garbage in, garbage out*. Since our experience is of only the final output from all this processing, we experience only the *garbage out* part. We actually *feel* this output, in this case the garbage. Somehow, the high level results of the brain's information processing activity are translated/encoded into the experience of, say, a two-foot long nose.

Location in space is something that the brain manufactures for every experience of touch. That it is a product of the mind is clearly demonstrated by the perception of the phantom limb falsely existing in space, and by the easy distortion of our body image. The stroked hand experiment demonstrates that your mind can assign sensations as arriving from quite different locations in space, even locations not occupied by your body. Space, the perception of space, and the body's extension in space, exists only in the mind. The feeling that our bodies occupy space is an illusion. It is a mental representation, an experience, and nothing more. The body does not lie in the body at all, but in the brain, or more accurately, in experience. The feeling of your fingertip being pricked seems to occur at your fingertip, but that is an illusion. The location in space of the pricked feeling is fabricated in your mind. Space doesn't even need to exist if its perception is so clearly an easily manipulated mental construct.

Whether space has any real existence at all is now arbitrary. We will experience it anyway, whether or not it actually exists. Location is just another experience. We, of course, couldn't know of it otherwise. Our brains or minds manufacture this experience from the information they receive, and it's not too hard to confuse the information processing system that generates the illusion of space into producing ridiculous results, which we then experience too.

Splitting the mind in space:

Besides the overwhelming mystery of what it is that translates brain activity into experience, there's another mystery buried in here. It has to do with the split-brain phenomenon mentioned earlier, whereby severing the connecting corpus callosum between the two hemispheres of the brain creates two distinct minds. On the one hand, we have said that the experience of pricking the fingertip does not occur at the fingertip but in the brain. We are thus implying that the nerve impulses arriving in the brain from the fingertip simply trigger the activity in the brain that is then experienced as the feeling. On the other hand, we seem to be saying that when we sever the nerves connecting the two sides of the brain, that we really do isolate the experiences occurring on each side from the other. In the finger case, severing the input nerve simply prevents the trigger impulse from triggering the experience in the brain, where in the split brain case severing the nerves seems to isolate the actual experiences from each other.

To me right now, I seem to be a single minded entity experiencing both hemispheres of my brain simultaneously. I can't even imagine being split into two minds. I suppose if it happened, though, each resulting mind would consider itself to be the continuation of *me*. The point is that there is obviously a role for those connecting neurons in the corpus callosum in making both hemispheres single minded. But this is the very concept that was rejected for the fingertip. Can it be both ways? Should we reconsider the notion that the fingertip is actually experiencing at the fingertip, that it is in effect a mind of it's own, or at least an *experiencer* in its own right? Is it possible that experience itself is somehow transmitted on the nerves? If so, is it then possible to connect my fingertip to your wrist and for me to experience what your hand is feeling? Is it possible to connect my fingertip to machines, and then experience what the machines are experiencing? Does it imply that it really might be possible to somehow connect two separate brains together, yours and mine say, to become a single mind? Maybe there really is a way to experience what's going on inside another person's head, and find out if they experience left and right the same way you do.

Or should we consider the possibility that the left brain experiences the right brain the same way it experiences the pricking of a finger tip, that is, the information of the right brain activity is carried into the left brain via the corpus callosum and triggers a whole new representation of that information in the left brain. That would seem to imply that the left brain is already an isolated mind onto itself, and doesn't experience the right brain any more directly than it does the finger tip. Ditto the right brain, but that means that there are already two minds up there. I'm certainly not aware of two minds. Which one would be me?

Frequently when we find ourselves asking questions that seem not to make sense, seem meaningless, or are otherwise unanswerable, it ends up that we are exceeding the capabilities of a given paradigm, and it's one of the jobs of a new paradigm either to answer them or to show them as meaningless. That could very easily be so in this case too. You will notice that the language of the discussion reverted back to our familiar notion that the brain, and neurons, are material objects with an actual physical and spatial existence. We are coming to see that that just isn't true or possible, that the physical fingertip, the physical brain and its physical corpus callosum don't physically exist either. Perhaps one day when we have become more adept and nimble at thinking of the universe in terms of just information, without the requirement of space and matter, the explanation of this seeming contradiction will become apparent.

The unreliability of our senses:

Most of the discussion so far demonstrating the unreliability of our experience of the world has been centered on senses related to the sense of touch, but what about our other senses. Our sense of vision is our most important sense for gathering information from the world around us, after all.

It turns out that there is ample evidence that the remainder of the senses too may be inconsistent from one individual to the next, and once again it turns out to result from variations in how the information is processed by the brain. There are those among us who see colors when they hear words or certain music or see certain letters of the alphabet. They feel the shapes of tastes, see weeks or years as shaped, or see kaleidoscopic images associated with words. This condition is called synesthesia and roughly speaking, involves senses other than, and in addition to, the usual senses being triggered by sensory input. In her book *Blue Cats and Chartreuse Kittens*, Patricia Lynne Duffy describes her experiences as a synesthete, as well as those of other synesthetes, some quit famous. Although she had experienced synesthesia throughout her childhood, she did not realize that not everyone saw the world the same way she did until one day at sixteen she inadvertently mentioned it to her father. Upon discovering that her perception of the world was unique, she writes:

> I suddenly felt marooned on my own private island of navy blue C's, dark brown D's, sparkling green 7's, and wine-colored V's. What else did I see differently from the rest of the world? I wondered. What did the rest of the world see that I didn't? It occurred to me that maybe every person in the world had some little oddity of perception they weren't aware of that put them on a private island, mysteriously separated from others. I suddenly had the dizzying feeling that there might be as many of these private islands as there were people in the world.

This phenomenon, apparently, has its origin in a process similar to the phantom limb phenomenon. In this case too, it seems to involve brain activity in one area of the brain stimulating activity in an adjacent area. A great many of the known synesthetes experience seeing colors associated with other senses, and in these cases the ordinary sensory processing is stimulating activity in the color processing regions of the brain as well. Once again the information processor has gotten mixed up, and only the final output results in an experience.

But synesthesia is a lightweight when compared to a neurological condition called *Charles Bonnet syndrome*. This phenomenon turns out to be quite common, and usually occurs in people who have lost vision in part or all of their visual field. These people actually see things going on in these otherwise defunct areas of vision that aren't really there. These are not your usual experience of just visualizing an image with your imagination. These are full blown hallucinations, sometimes even more vividly experienced than the experience of actual vision. Once again, in *Phantoms in the Brain*, Dr. Ramachandran details cases of people with Charles Bonnet syndrome who see nonexistent people, animals, or objects in the room with them. One patient observed "two miniature policemen guiding a midget villain into a tiny prison van." Others see floating ghostly translucent figures, dragons, or angels. Still others see circus animals, clowns, and elves where none should be. Many tend to see children, with one case where the woman could hear their laughter as well. One woman saw her recently deceased husband on a regular basis. Another patient awoke from his coma to find his hospital bed surrounded not only by doctors and nurses, but by football players and Hawaiian dancers as well, all just as real. This same patient observed a monkey sitting in Dr. Ramachandran's lap during one of his visits. Dr. Ramachandran suspects that even James Thurber experienced Charles Bonnet syndrome, and quotes Thurber as saying, "I saw a Cuban flag flying over a national bank, I saw a gay old lady with a gray parasol walk right through the side of a truck, I saw a cat roll across a street in a small striped barrel. I saw bridges rise lazily into the air, like balloons."

Dr. Ramachandran states that this syndrome is actually very common, particularly among the elderly who suffer from a myriad of degenerative vision disorders. I suspect my own family even encountered this. One week before her death, my elderly mother angrily scolded my brother from her nursing home bed for embedding her feet in a block of concrete, which she could apparently see quite clearly. My brother, alarmed, did his best to convince her that there was no such block of concrete, and she eventually abandoned the point. This had always been a complete mystery to me. As mentioned, these hallucinations can sometimes be visually more vivid than reality itself, and Dr. Ramachandran states that some patients are able to learn to use this extraordinary vividness itself to distinguish the hallucinations from reality.

The sense of vision now too reveals its fallibility. We would like to believe that what we see is what's really out there, the way the real world really is, but clearly the brain has the capability to manufacture every aspect of a vision, including its vividness.

That the brain manufactures our vision is a *very* important point. Ordinarily the brain manufactures our visual experience based on the coded information that it receives on the optic nerves coming in through our skulls, but the important point is that what we see is necessarily *always* a total fabrication. We are seeing that we have no good reason at all to believe that the manufactured images we experience are what is really out there, as long as they are workable and consistent. In fact, we have already encountered several reasons to believe that what's out there is nothing like what we see.

The mind/brain connection:

Our *experience* of the world is far removed from the world itself, and all we experience is the processed results of the information received in the brain. We do not experience the universe directly the way we feel like we do. That feeling too is a fabrication. We do not even experience our own bodies directly. Our bodies turn out to be only manufactured representations too. The closest thing we can come to what we might experience directly is the neuronal network *activity* going on in our brains.

The connection that we perceive between mind and brain is a very slender one. The only independent variables we have been able to identify that seem to be associated with experience are *brain activity*, and the *location* in the brain at which that activity occurs, and the correlations are only of the crudest sort at this point. Brain activity seems to be necessary for there to be any experience at all, and location of the activity correlates to the nature of the experience, e.g., whether it's vision, touch, or an emotion, but we have no idea why. Of course the next question is "How does this brain activity result in the phenomenon of experience at all?" We know there's a *correlation*, but what is the *connection*? How does one become the other?

There is a missing step, a gap in our string of encoders that occurs between the brain and the mind. We do not know what the connection is between the brain and the mind. It's as if our minds are being decoded directly off of those top level networks of neurons in the brain. A certain region of our brain lights up and we feel our nose is two feet long. Another region lights up and we feel our nipple being touched. Another region lights up and we experience a vision of a nipple.

Our mind consists of our experience of the information represented with the brain, but we cannot see on what medium the mind is being represented. If we go back to our earlier analogy, where the information is decoded onto a TV or movie screen, it is as if *we are the screen* itself. Somehow the information represented in the brain gets encoded onto this screen, but we can neither see the final encoder nor the screen. We do not know what the link is between brain activity and the mind's experience of it, but we know there is one.

Does the mind result from the brain activity directly somehow, or is the mind somehow independent of the brain, but is affected, or provided for, by the brain? Another way of phrasing this is to ask if there needs to be an *experiencer* at all, or if experience just happens from brain activity, kind of like the flame on a match. Yet another way to look at this is to go back to our encoder/decoder analogy. From this perspective, experience seems to be somehow a decoding of the brain activity, since it emphatically is not the same thing. From the encoder/decoder perspective then, we have to ask, "where is the decoder?" Is it invisible to us? (There are several ways that this could be so, and will be discussed in the next chapter.) If so, what is the decoder's mechanism? How does it create experience from brain activity? And how is activity from one area of the brain experienced as different from activity in another area?

Earlier in this chapter we arrived at the conclusion that ***if I experience, then I, the experiencer, exist***. We are now asking the question of whether experience can exist on its own resulting directly from brain activity, called an *emergent* phenomenon, or whether it requires an *experiencer*. (We will discuss this more thoroughly in a coming chapter, but be forewarned that the big money from the scientific community is betting that experience does not require an *experiencer*. While this kind of group intelligence seems to work well at the racetrack or stock market, the loopholes in this case are considerably larger than the arguments supporting it, so it may not be time yet to start worrying. Then again, maybe it is.) If it turns out that experience doesn't require an *experiencer* and is an emergent phenomenon, then our earlier conclusion will have to be modified to ***if I experience, then I, the experience, exist***. Now this statement does have a certain tautological appeal, despite the fact that it's somewhat discomfiting to imagine that our existence might be just that ethereal.

We do not know how experience occurs, but we do know that one way or another we are it. We also know that our experience is all we know, all we know of, and all we can know. When we look back from experience at our brains, we are looking back across an experience/brain abyss that we cannot account for and do not understand. We do not know what the connection is between brain activity and experience, but by addressing this question we have in reality opened up a complex situation here.

We now know that most of what we experience is an illusion, and thus seeing the material brain itself must be an illusion that we are experiencing. Seeing the brain activity thus must be an illusion too. Under this circumstance, is it even reasonable to consider that we, the experience, can be explained by examining an *illusion* of our source? Is it possible then that the brain might really be the decoder we're looking for, but its misrepresentation to us as a material object makes it impossible for us to see its true nature in the realm of experience? In this case, our brain may be simply a grossly distorted mental representation of our mind, distorted to be represented as the illusion of a material object in a nonexistent material universe. In this case, there may be no gap at all, no abyss between mind and brain. In this case, we may be observing our mind directly.

Chapter 12
The Universe of Mind

○ ○

*What a peculiar privilege has this little agitation
of the brain which we call 'thought'.*

—*Hume*

Speculations on experience:

At any given moment, our mind is the sum total of what we are experiencing. This is us at that moment. But what is experience, that the mind seems somehow to be composed of it? How does experience occur? Does it require a medium on which to occur? If there is a hidden decoder that is decoding brain activity into experience, onto what medium is the information now being encoded. The information of the universe with which we are familiar has always required a medium out of which it is composed and onto which it is encoded. That medium might be electromagnetism in the case of light, or even in the case of the electronic representation in most of today's information systems. The medium might be ink on paper, or it might be pebbles on a beach. The medium might be sound waves in air, or acoustic waves in water. It might be waves of ions along a neuron in the brain, or it might be Braille bumps of metal on an elevator's control panel, but it seems that in every case we know of, information always requires a medium on which it is represented.

Perhaps the idea of a medium is a little too concrete when it comes to representing *that upon which, or out of which, information can be represented*. It was exactly this idea that information had to have a physical medium that made it so difficult for scientists a century ago to believe that the speed of light was not affected by some physical or spatial medium on which it was carried. The speed of information carried by light, it turned out, mysteriously depended only on its receiver, and not on any medium through which, or on which, it was traveling.

Electromagnetism it turned out, had no known medium, was only known by, and as, its effect, and was one of the first clear physical demonstrations of the notion that all we know of the universe are effects. Electromagnetism in the end then, is only the name of an effect, and we have the same problem identifying a medium for it that we do identifying a medium for experience. (That electromagnetism has no identifiable medium and is observer related, and that experience has no identifiable medium, is observer related, and is affected by brain activity that is largely electromagnetic, might be cause for wonder.) For electromagnetism to bypass the missing medium problem, we made up a name for that class of effect and say that the effects exist on the realm of that name. In the case of electromagnetism, the name of the realm is of course electromagnetism.

Whether or not we can identify a medium on which the effects of experience are represented, we can still name a realm for that class of effects, and the name for that realm in this case is of course the realm of experience. We don't know what the realm of experience is, or how information is represented on it, but we are intimately familiar with its effects, and these effects are precisely what our experiences are. The most nourishing and fertile soil existent for speculation and imagination is that which has not yet been depleted of disproven theories. The potential explanations for the realm of experience then, germinate from some of the richest soil ever known to humankind. There are several avenues of speculation that are tentatively harmonious with the ideas pursued in this book.

One idea, advocated by Sir Alfred North Whitehead around the turn of the last century, starts out from the notion that all matter in the universe experiences. That's right, not just brains and fingertips, but tabletops and teapots too. Of course, we've already established that tabletops and teapots are aggregate objects composed out of smaller pieces of matter, so we might as well save ourselves some time and head straight to the bottom where the so called elementary particles exist. Presumably, if there is such a thing as an elementary particle, then in this hypothesis it will also be associated with an elementary unit of experience. Just to have a particle to talk about, let's imagine that the little electron somehow experiences.

Now we have no idea what experience would be like for the electron, or even if it has any variation to its experience. Since the electromagnetic affect is mediated by the photon, perhaps the electron's experience varies when it emits or absorbs a photon. Maybe when it absorbs photons it feels full or gets like a sugar high or something. Or perhaps it's the photon itself that experiences, or mediates experience. Whatever the bottom level, we have already noted that for an effect to exist at all, it must exist as a *difference* on a realm, so somewhere at or near the bottom level, a variation must be able to occur in experience.

Now in the process of trying to imagine this, a couple of considerations occur. One is that whatever this electron is experiencing, it is nothing like the rich variations that we as conscious beings experience. The electron's experience must consist of a remarkable sameness, perhaps altering almost *digitally* (or quantizedly) with the absorption or emission of a photon.

Another probable point is that it will experience, but it will not be aware that it experiences. It will not be having thoughts, and it will not be having memories. Imagine it as not only not conscious of itself, but not conscious at all. Consciousness, memory, etc., are experiential phenomena that seem to occur only at extremely high levels of aggregation. Try to imagine it in an utterly vegetative state, unaware on anything and everything in the world, just a little tiny feeling, which may fluctuate from time to time. This is how I imagine it anyway.

What then would a rock experience, since it is an aggregate of large numbers of electrons. Well, my best guess is nothing, or more explicitly, nothing at the rock level. Each electron in the rock might be having its little experience, but my best guess is that the rock will not have a single *rock* experience, something like a rock mind. The reason I suspect this is that there is none of the structure to the rock that we associate with mind or mental experience, and we have already seen how even in the brain, the mind can be cleaved by isolating electrical activity of one region from another. In the rock, each electron is more or less isolated from the others. Now a chunk of metal might be something else again, since it in some ways is a single electronic object.

A second speculative approach to accounting for experience is to consider that our senses are capable of perceiving only 4% of the stuff of the universe that is out there. That means that 96% of what is out there is undetectable to us, 24 times more than the tiny little bit we are aware of and perceive as matter. Well, if we're going to speculate, let's go ahead and speculate about what we could do with that other 96%. Of course, there's no limit to what we can do with it. Our bodies might be composed of vastly more of this substance or energy than we can perceive. We in fact might only be aware of 4% of ourselves. Some of that other 96% might actually compose the missing mediums for the realms of experience and electromagnetism.

We now have no problem coming up with a source of invisible stuff for our invisible encoder that decodes information from the brains representation of the information onto the realm of experience. It may be wrapped around our brains right now decoding away like mad, but since our senses can't provide our brains with any information about it, the only way we know it's there at all is that we're having experiences. We now have no problem coming up with an *experiencer*, especially if there is something that we can now call a medium out of which experience is represented. We, the *experiencer* might be composed out of the stuff of this medium and may indeed exist.

A third speculative idea of how experience might exist falls back on the developing field of string theory that I have referred to occasionally throughout the book. When I introspectively pursue my own experience, consciousness, and awareness to its lowest level, I invariably end up with the sense that there's something like a feedback mechanism involved somewhere, something distantly akin to looking in a mirror. A feedback mechanism is a system that returns information about itself back to where it started. It's a loop. Now according to string theory, everything in the universe can be accounted for by one-dimensional strings, the ends of which are curved back through another dimension and joined to form loops. Hmmmm. This in no way says that these loops are the same (speculative) loops out of which our (speculative) feedback system is composed, but if someday it turns out that the introspective sense of feedback is indeed involved in experience, then if we're looking for loops, we have a place with loops.

Yet another notion is that the realm of experience requires no medium at all, because it is a generated phenomenon, an emergent phenomenon. A crude demonstration of this idea is the flame on a match. When a match is ignited, a process of combustion is initiated, which releases heat. The released heat raises the temperature of the gasses and air involved to the level where the gasses themselves begin to glow red hot, just like a red hot piece of iron at the blacksmith's. This glowing gas is the flame we see on the match and is a phenomenon generated from the process of combustion. Since the realm of experience is so far totally unaccounted for, there is nothing to stop us from speculating that it is a phenomenon generated from the processes and activity of the brain itself. Just like when striking a match results in a flame, something about the brain activity results in experience. In this case, we, our experience, exist only as the generated phenomenon of brain activity, a glow maybe, dancing around brightly while the brain is active, but ceasing to exist, "going out," when the brain activity ceases.

It may be possible that there is a grain of truth to each of these speculations, despite their contradictions. By this I mean, there may be a way that some aspects of *each* of these ideas may end up in the final explanation. The original notion that the stuff of the universe may itself experience is very compatible with the notion that something in that 96% of the universe we do not perceive accounts for the realm, or medium, of experience. And if string theory perseveres, it will account not only for the 4% of the universe that we do perceive, but also for the other 96% percent, so those invisible realms of experience will in this case necessarily be composed of the loops of string theory. The notion that experience doesn't exist except as an emergent phenomenon, however, is in contrast to the notion that all matter is experiencing, but if it turns out that matter experiences, that this is the realm of experience, the actual experiences we experience on this realm could still be generated by the activity of our brains. Now hopefully, the one thing about all this of which I don't need to remind the reader, the one thing that we do know absolutely is true about all of this, is that it is all speculation!

Consciousness:

By this time, we are struggling with vocabulary. A person who knows and understands the explicit meanings of all the vocabulary in a particular field of study is a professional in that field. Unfortunately in the study of the mind, the vocabulary is vague, lacks specificity, and thus makes it almost impossible to speak, or think, clearly on the topic. We are thinking in fuzz balls at best. I have talked about *experience*, *consciousness*, *thinking*, *awareness*, and the *mind* at times as if they were all almost the same thing, sometimes using the terms interchangeably, and I must confess to having committed a grievous offense against the reader in doing so.

Building an explicit vocabulary with which to discuss these topics is anything but straightforward. We find ourselves in a position very similar to the person who wants to explain the color red to someone who has been blind from birth. There just aren't words to describe basic mental experiences that have not already been experienced by our audience. Fortunately in this case, none of us have been blind since birth. Unlike with the colors, though, it is not an easy thing to point to these sensations and give them a name.

While there is a tremendous *similarity* or overlap in the meanings of the terms *mind*, *experience*, etc., and while they frequently may be used interchangeably, they bear subtle but important *differences*. Earlier we discussed how the brain represents concepts using networks of neurons composed of aggregates of neurons representing a concept's aspects or components. This implies not only that mental concepts are composed of aggregates of aspects, but that to have a clear grasp of the concept, we must have a clear grasp of its aggregate aspects. In that aspects are ultimately differences, identifying the differences between concepts gives us a direction to proceed in our attempt to develop explicit meanings for our vocabulary. As we peel away the differences, that which remains is ultimately what is similar between concepts. To some, this will appear analogous to picking up a stick and beating around the bush in order to determine what a bush is. It is, but while seemingly crude, at least it gives us a method with which to proceed, that is, by beating around the bush.

Consciousness, I believe, is a phenomenon based almost entirely on experience, but it has some characteristics that experience alone does not have. With consciousness, the idea of awareness is creeping in there somewhere. Now these ideas haven't been explicitly defined, so there's still some room for opinion here, so I guess this is just largely how I see it. One thing I think that consciousness implies, that experience doesn't, is that *consciousness requires an object.* You can be conscious of something. You can be conscious of an experience for one thing, but an experience can just be. If you're experiencing things and you know it, you're conscious.

It is even possible to have different degrees of consciousness. The medical community recognizes five levels of consciousness, from completely okay conscious, to not knowing what today is, all the way down to only reacting to someone sticking a pin in the sole of your bare foot. If you don't react to that, they say you're unconsciousness. There's even some discussion as to whether animals are conscious or not at all. Now it may seem to you that it shouldn't be that hard to tell. Just stick a pin in its foot, and if it bites you, it was consciousness. Some people have evidence, however, that animals may be completely unaware of themselves and what they're experiencing, and that they may just be acting like robots, doing what their brains are programmed to do under the right circumstances.

That an animal could be a robot that acts like it's conscious is not as farfetched as it may seem at first. There is in fact, if you remember from Chapter 6, a whole school of thought that believes that nothing we humans do is consciously motivated either, but is just programmed into the brain. This school admits to our consciousness, but they think it's just along for the ride so to speak, and has nothing to do with the decisions we seem to make, or the actions we seem to intentionally take. It has indeed been discovered that there is a great deal going on in our brains that we are not consciousness of.

One of these is our vision. Dr. Ramachandran (again), in the book *Phantoms in the Brain*, discusses cases where people have lost the portion of their vision that they're conscious of. They are conscious of seeing nothing, yet some part of them still apparently sees quite clearly. To them, they are completely blind, but if they can be coaxed into trying to take certain actions despite their blindness, actions that require vision, they are able to perform them flawlessly. So far these are simple actions, like spontaneously reaching and taking a pencil, or correctly orienting a letter and inserting into a mail slot, but the conscious blind person is completely unaware that they are able to do these things. Clearly, consciousness of vision is not necessary to take these actions. Is this the evidence for an automaton, the robot in us and animals, that some people hypothesize?

It turns out that the phenomenon we call vision results from a hodgepodge of over thirty different processes scattered all over the inside of our brains. When we see the world, it seems to us to be a single image that contains colors, depth, shapes, locations, objects, etc., but these different aspects are all processed by different networks of neurons that are not conjoined in the brain at all. They are all over the place, yet we experience vision as a single coherent image. I remember reading some time ago that the visual cortex in our brains is something along the lines of a screen on which the image is reconstructed, but there is no such screen it turns out. The construction of a visual image occurs at the level of experience only, nowhere in the brain. Apparently one or more of these thirty some areas is related to our being *conscious* of our visual experience, and if this area of the brain is damaged, we are no longer conscious of vision. Perhaps the visual *experience* continues, though, but the person is just no longer *conscious* of it, similar to the earlier discussed notion that a pricked finger may still feel pricked at the fingertip, even though we may not be conscious of it if the information never reaches the brain.

The deconstruction of consciousness:

I made the statement earlier on that I thought if electrons indeed experienced, that it would be a simple mindless experience that did not qualify as conscious. To see how one might suspect this, let's imagine someone sitting there just like you are now, but who has no memory from one moment to the next. They not only don't remember what day it is or what their name is, they don't remember what they were doing one second ago. They don't remember what the last word was that they read, or the last letter even, so words never get a chance to form. They don't remember what a book is or anything else, so they don't know what any other object they're seeing is. They don't remember seeing anything even a microsecond ago, so everything in their visual field is continuously new and unfamiliar. They don't know that they were born or that they'll age, and indeed they live in an instantaneous and timeless world and have no experience of time. They don't wonder why they don't know anything, because they don't know there is such a thing as knowing.

Without at least a microscopic moment of memory, they're unable to know anything and are utterly mindless. They just sit there in a complete vegetative state experiencing their visual field and other senses without a thought in their head about it. They don't know that they're experiencing, they don't know what experience is, because they don't know that they ever experienced anything ever before, even a millisecond before. At some point, we have reduced them to just an *experiencer*. Without memory, they are capable of experience, but they are conscious of nothing.

This to me is what simple experience is, experience before consciousness. Now some people will feel that if this person is experiencing vision, then it can be said that they are conscious at least of vision, and this is one of the confusing points of the multiple ways these words are currently used. How does this jive with our earlier discussion above of the brain damaged blind person that was conscious of no vision at all, yet seemed perhaps to be experiencing vision at some level that they weren't conscious of? We said that they were not conscious of vision. Were they just not conscious of it, or were they just not experiencing it, or what?

First of all, this seems to indicate that the concept of conscious now implies an entity, an identity. If this person is not conscious of a visual experience, yet the visual experience is nevertheless occurring somewhere that they aren't conscious of, then it's only that particular entity that isn't conscious of it. This doesn't come as too much of a surprise. Experiences apparently are occurring elsewhere all the time of which I'm not conscious, inside of your head for example. Indeed we saw a single entity split into two separate identities earlier in the split-brain experiments. In fact, it's even conceivable that that is exactly what has happened in this case, or at least something quite similar. That is, it's conceivable that something like the right brain is experiencing vision, but the left brain isn't. The left brain, which gets to do all the talking, will swear up and down that the entity embodied therein is blind, but the right brain, which cannot reach the speech center, is mute and can perhaps see just fine. (No wonder the right brain sometimes becomes suicidal!) So besides requiring an *object*, and *memory*, it appears that *identity* too is a player in the concept of consciousness.

Consciousness requires memory, and interestingly this implies that consciousness requires, or embodies, the concept of time. Unlike space, we can't take a time yardstick and measure off two locations that both exist simultaneously. We indeed have clocks that measure time, but the hands of the clock have only one position at any given moment. Length exists in space, but its analog in time, duration, doesn't perceptually exist. No length of time seems to have an instantaneous existence, indeed the idea embodies a contradiction. *Only with the introduction of memory can two different points of time exist simultaneously.* Only through memory are we able to be aware of the past, or even that there is a past at all. It is also of interest (to me at least) that memory qualifies as something of a feedback system, as a loop. In this case, the loop occurs through time, and the starting and ending place of the feedback is the moment of experience itself. The original experience is brought back to its original starting place, the *experiencer*, or perhaps the entity, through time. We are reexperiencing an experience.

As an interesting aside, if consciousness requires memory, then it is closely linked to the idea of context. With no memory at all, a person has no context, no model, by which to know the world, and if you will remember from section one, context is related to our notion of *meaning*. Something, a thought, for which there is no context, i.e., no schema, can't have a meaning and cannot be understood. A quick demonstration of this dependence of meaning on context is that a thought or statement *taken out of context* frequently looses its original meaning and is free then to take on a new, perhaps unintended meaning.

Memory/context is critical to meaning, and memory is critical to consciousness. And the meaning of something certainly seems to be a conscious experience, and to be closely related to understanding. There are a lot of people out there arguing that machines can never understand the meaning of something because they are not conscious (assuming they're not), and I believe that they argue this way because they sense this link between consciousness and meaning, or understanding. What they are not recognizing, however, is that this association holds only for experience, only for the *feelings* of understanding and meaning. The brain and the mind both behave in many ways like information systems, and it is possible to capture and model meaning in a computer, sans the feelings.

At some point, we become aware that we are experiencing. Awareness is an experience too, so at some point, in some way, we are experiencing that we experience. Memory is one version of this, but I think it is possible to experience that we are experiencing more directly. I am tempted to say that we become conscious of experiencing, so consciousness and awareness have a great deal in common too. Are they the same thing? It is possible to not only be aware of experience, but to be aware that we're conscious. It is possible to be aware that we are aware. If I close my eyes and try to be aware that I am aware, if I strain really hard, I seem to be able to go so far as to be (aware that (I'm aware that (I'm aware))). I'm sure there are those out there that won't find that hard to beat, taking their awareness of awareness to even higher levels. Clearly though, we're capable of nested levels of awareness, each level experiencing the level before. Each level is in fact an experience of an experience. These are demonstrations of feedback loops, with experience being fed back itself to be experienced. Is this what distinguishes consciousness and awareness from simple experience? Are they just still experience, but in this case experience of experience? If this is the case, consciousness and awareness are just meta-experiences.

Reconstructing consciousness:

Consciousness and awareness seem to occur only in brains, at least as far as we know. Is it possible then that there is something about the brain that causes this to happen? We for sure don't know where experience comes from in the first place, but given that it exists somehow, is there something about the brain that might bring about the phenomenon of consciousness, that might somehow turn simple experience into consciousness? At first glance, it looks like the brain may well be able to provide at least a couple of the requirements for consciousness to occur.

The first one is the requirement that consciousness seems to require an object, that we are conscious of something. The brain represents thoughts, ideas, sensations, etc. as networks of neurons, and it seems to be these networks of neurons that we experience. The brain certainly seems to be capable of representing the objects that we seem to be conscious of.

The second one is memory. We know that the brain is able to recreate a facsimile of past experience by reactivating some of the networks of neurons that were activated during the initial experience. We don't know too much about how the brain goes about identifying these networks, and then reactivating them, but we at least know that it provides the necessary medium from which experiences are represented and triggered. And memory is a critical component for consciousness to occur.

The next requirement is that we should have the capability of a feedback system via which experience itself can be experienced. We know that the brain has the physical means to cause, or allow, different areas of activity in the brain to be experienced as a single thing, or by/as a single identity. We don't know how it does it, but we know it's brain based and we know it depends on the active areas being physically linked by neurons. Sever the corpus collosum and you now have two identities where before you had only one. A single experience/consciousness now becomes two. Whatever the case, it certainly has the appearance that the brain has the capability to somehow link experiences from different regions of the brain via neurons. And certainly if experiences can be linked via neurons, they can be looped back upon themselves via additional neurons. It is beginning to look like if all that discussion about memory and feedback systems being involved in the creation of consciousness has any merit at all, then the brain seems to have some of the structure necessary to make it happen right there. One aside of this is if that is true, and consciousness does turn out to depend on brain structure, then that's one for the *flame on the match* crowd. Consciousness and mind really will cease with the cessation of brain activity. Maybe it is time to start worrying after all.

Consciousness and awareness my not be such mysterious phenomena after all. The real mystery might be that experience exists, but given that it does, consciousness and awareness might turn out to be relatively straightforward manipulations of it. Almost physical manipulations of it. In terms of our hypothetical experiencing electron, all this is saying is that unlike a simple rock, the brain has done something like find a way to organize experiencing electrons into structures that allows their experience to combine and interact somehow.

This has been a little foray into the foggy and uncharted realm of the mind. The terms we use are grossly ill defined. We don't know what aspects are included in each term, what aspects are common among terms, and what aspects distinguish one term from another. We don't even know what aspects are relevant. We do not have clear concepts with which to proceed or discuss the subject. Until this task is undertaken explicitly, we will not have a working science of mind. Until we develop at least agreed upon concepts built from explicit aspects, the field will necessarily resemble a belief system. Even after the concepts become iterated and explicit, it will not have reached the level of a quantitative science, and will more resemble something like alchemy with a mysterious foundation. We are a long way from understanding, that is, having a workable paradigm for the mind. While philosophers have been tentatively prodding this beast for millennia, our species seems to have past some critical threshold in the last decade, and more and more minds are turning to the task. For some reason, we must have come to sense somehow that we can now solve this mystery.

Action and will:

Whatever the universe is, it passes information around in the form of effects. Some of these effects affect our senses, which in turn, relay the effects into the brain encoded as neuronal activity. This activity is massaged and manipulated, and eventually some of it is decoded into our experience of the world. These experiences are all that we know. Several hundred years ago, when Descartes was asking himself how he knew he really existed, he skipped over the idea that his experience proved he existed (I experience, therefore I am), and went on to establish, to his satisfaction at least, that he, the thinker, existed. He had a reason for doing this.

Philosophers by this time knew very well that what they were experiencing as the world around them was not necessarily what was really there at all. They didn't have our sophisticated mathematical methods of physics, or Dr. Ramachandran's demonstrations that aspects of our bodies are illusions, but they had other examples that clearly gave away the possibility that experience was corruptible and could be imaginary. They knew about dreams, and they knew about hallucinations, and they knew that because of the existence of these, that the world of perception might easily be something of the sort. Descartes then, being a skeptic, asked himself if there was anything about the world that he knew for certain existed, and rather than settle on the fact that he experienced, he settled on the fact that the one thing he knew for sure was that *he was a skeptic*. He knew that in his endeavors to establish his existence that his method was to start from a position called *skepticism*. But if his thinking method was to be a skeptic then that revealed beyond any doubt that he was thinking. Thus he arrived at the conclusion that he, the thinker at least, existed.

Now besides the fact that a thinker is an *experiencer* too, a thinker also differs from just a plain old passive *experiencer* in that a thinker is active. It is not just sitting there letting experiences flash across it. Thinking has a directed, goal oriented, intentional aspect to it that simple experiencing doesn't, so when Descartes decides that he exists because he's a thinker, he is saying something quite different from the notion that just an *experiencer* exists. He's saying that something exists that has the capability of intentionality, something capable of taking an action motivated by a will. In one stroke, he has defined his being as having at least three distinguishable aspects, these being *experience*, *will*, and the capability of *action*.

In the task of trying to establish the existence of something, Descartes' thinker has one advantage. We have been saying throughout the book that for something to exist, it must have an effect, and a thinker has an effect, whereas an *experiencer* does not. The things that a thinker affects are his thoughts, which are really a specific kind of experience, so the thinker has an effect on the realm of experience. The *experiencer* on the other hand is really just that realm of experience, which is the affectee. Since the only thing I can know is experience, it is the only affectee in the universe, at least in my universe, so I suppose this realm enjoys a certain kind of existence in its own right, but a thinker more closely satisfies our original definition.

So thinking is able to have an effect on experience, i.e., it is able to make a *change* occur in our experience, and the act of changing is itself called *action*. And the thing that is taking the action and making the change we will call an acter (since the other spelling is already taken). Now we also have a name for what seems to be the acter in each of us, and we call it our *will*. Apparently, the way the will works is that it experiences certain feelings that lead to desires (also feelings) that are achievable by it by utilizing the repertoire of actions it has available to it to take, and then it just does it.

Now these feelings and desires that ultimately lead to action via the will are called *motivations* and *emotions*, and you will notice that both words are based on the same root word as *move*, and all of these words are based on the concept of action. Somehow, the will takes our motivations and turns them into actions. So far we're still talking about the mental actions that a thinker has available to it. An example of this might be adding 2 + 2 in our heads. Or if we needed to get gas for the car, our will will turn our attention to the mental task of planning this activity, deciding where to go for gas for example. Controlling what we are attending to seems to be one of the capabilities of the will, one of the mental actions that it has available to it, and when it applies enough will to any give particular action, it just happens.

An interesting aspect of this concept of will is that we don't know how it initiates the action it takes. To us, it just seems to do it. Now apparently there are degrees of will. There are weak wills and there are strong wills, and there are some actions that seem to take a lot of will, especially when there are conflicting motivations, so each motivation seems to carry a certain amount of will along with it. The will also seems to have the capability of deciding on how much will to apply to bring about any given action. That's another capability that the will seems to have.

Sometimes though the will seems not to be so autonomous. Sometimes it appears to behave as an automaton, a robot. (I guess another way of saying this is that sometimes the will seems to be automatous rather than autonomous.) For example, when we have conflicting motivations, each motivation really does seem to come with a certain amount of desire attached, and it seems to be the motivation that comes forward with the most desire that wins. If we are going out to eat at a restaurant and are deciding between two restaurants, we end up going to the one we are most motivated to go to. We are then more willing to go to one than the other. If we desire both equally, we experience difficulty making the decision. If the desire to achieve two conflicting motivations is equal, we may resort to other criteria to decide, but what we are really doing is searching for aspects that will alter the amounts of desire involved, so that a decision automatically drops out. If one restaurant is much closer than another one, we may raise the desirability of one and lower the desirability of the other, so now the will is able to *automatically* execute one action over the other. Interestingly, there seems to be a little place in the brain that is programmed to handle precisely this situation.

Some people looking at this phenomenon have arrived at the conclusion that we are automatons, robot like creatures that really don't have any say in the choices we make. The choice is made for us by the amount of desire each motivation carries along with it. We will always act on the one that comes out on top. There really doesn't appear to be a way around this observation. If you say that you're going to prove this to be wrong by performing some act that you're not motivated to do at all, even negatively motivated to do, stick yourself with a pin, say, you haven't really gotten around it at all. What happens is that you have become strongly motivated to prove this notion wrong, so now this action comes forward with more desire than the desire to withhold from sticking yourself. Your will has no choice in the matter. The calculations have already been made, and you will stick yourself with the pin. We can confuse the issue by introducing more and more complex, subtle, even unidentifiable motivations, like subconscious motivations, but in the end it seems to come back to an almost mechanical calculation.

Action from feelings:

There's something else involved here that's worth a look. The size of the motivation, or desire, that accompanies each potential choice is a feeling, and it is based on a feeling. We experience motivation as a feeling, a desire, and we experience the size of a motivation as a feeling. It is a feeling to want or like something, or to dislike something. The precursor emotions, feelings like fear, love, or anger, all end up triggering great motivations. Or at least they appear to. Now the robot crowd would like to say that, being robots, we are not motivated by feelings at all. They say that we are completely hardwired to take the actions we take under even the most subtle circumstances, and that those feelings we experience have no real effect at all. They say that all those feelings are just along for the ride, and the idea of feelings as motivations is a complete illusion. Here's how they do it.

You have already seen the first part of the argument. It really does appear that it is impossible to come up with a conscious, independent *free will* that is able to exorcise itself from the absolute requirement that it execute the choice with the greatest motivation attached, a motivation that comes from elsewhere. So free will of that kind is already out, although many people will say that this still qualifies as free will. The other part of the argument is that we already know that experience depends on brain activity, on which networks of neurons are activated, so our feelings of motivations must result from brain activity too. There presumably are networks of neurons that light up, that when active, we experience fear, or love, or anger.

Apparently then, the brain as an information processor is grinding away, processing everything that's going on in there, and if you look up and see a slavering lion charging down on you, the brain calculates that you had best start running, and starts you running. Somewhere in there too, it activates the network on which you experience fear, and in fact there's nothing to keep it from activating the fear network considerably after it sets you to running, thus exemplifying that the action of running was not motivated by fear at all, but was just the result of a hardwired process in the brain. I believe there are even instances of such hardwired neural pathways that have been discovered in the spinal cord and brain stem, which automatically initiate actions like that based on a mechanist, emotionless input trigger. Stepping on a snake seems to be an example of that automat(on)ic action too as the person invariably discovers themselves to be several feet in the air by the time they actually realize what's happening.

It's looking pretty good for the robot guys, at least on paper, but the argument isn't over yet. There turn out to be reasons to suspect that they might yet be wrong. Right off the bat, there's the problem of why we should feel anything at all if they are correct. If feelings don't contribute to motivation, what good are they, and why would they have evolved in the first place? The evolutionary psychologists say that for the most part our motivations evolved to motivate us to do things that are good for us, or at least good for our evolutionary ancestors, and motivate us to avoid actions that are unhealthy for us. Way back when evolution was still a factor in who lived and who died, eating sugar was good for us, because it gave us energy that helped us escape charging lions, so we evolved a sensation that was a good experience when we ate sugar, and this good experience supposedly motivates us to take the action of eating sweets to this day. On the other hand, poking ourselves in the eye was not healthy and contributed negatively to the survival of the pokee, so we evolved sensations that motivated us to avoid poking ourselves in the eye.

According to the robot theory, these feelings contribute not at all to whether or not we eat sweets or poke ourselves in the eye. Statistically then, one would expect to find that the distribution of good and bad feelings associated with taking actions would be random. If the robot theory is true, roughly 50% of the actions we take that are good for us should be unpleasant, and 50% pleasant, and exactly the same random distribution should be found associated with taking actions that are bad for us. According to the robot theory, there's an even chance that either poking ourselves in the eye, or sticking our hand in boiling water, will be a pleasant experience. This is not the case as everyone well knows, and indeed the evolutionary psychologists have found closer to 100% correlation in agreement with their theory, thus supporting the notion that these feelings do indeed play a part in our choice of the actions that we take.

There's another action, though, which I think even more directly supports the notion that feelings play a role in our motivations and corresponding actions. This action is the expression of feelings. Poets go to great lengths to come up with just the right words that will trigger particular feelings in the recipient. Communicating a feeling I think would be impossible if that feeling was not able to affect the brain at some point. Expressing that feeling takes a great deal of brain work, identifying the matching words, trying new combinations of words until finally we are able to trigger the feeling in ourselves, and eventually activating the neurons that trigger the larynx or the hands to express these words. If our feelings were not able to affect the brain, the brain would never know to stop trying new words to capture the feeling, because the brain could not know that the feeling had been satisfactorily recreated. At some point, that feeling has to be able to affect the brain in order to become expressed. If feelings were just along for the ride, we would experience them, but we wouldn't be able to express them, and of course all this holds for expressing our *thoughts* as well as our feelings. If the mind were unable to affect the brain, then it would be unable to tell us of its existence. (If this isn't so, then those philosophers I derided back in Chapter 2 for claiming that communication is impossible might just be right after all.)

If it is true, though, that feelings do affect our choice of actions, and the above two arguments seem to strongly imply that it is, then we have just opened up a whole new can of worms. The actions we have been talking about here are not just thinking actions, actions of the mind. The actions we have recently discussed are actions in the physical world, running, writing, and speaking. Our physical actions get out there via our muscles, and our muscles are controlled by our nervous systems, which start in our brains. We are now very clearly, therefore, talking about our mind's having the ability to affect the brain's activity.

The mind/body problem:

Most of the discussion in this book so far has been on how experience is affected by, and results from the brain activity, that is, how information travels from our bodies and brains to our mind. We don't know how this happens, hidden decoders or whatever, but we are now reversing our direction and saying that the brain can be affected by the mind, by feelings like fear, by experiences. If it is true that something feeling good can cause us to do it, eating sweets say, then it is true that the mind can affect the brain, causing brain activity that fires neurons that eventually raise a piece of candy to our mouth.

This is a two-sided problem now. How does brain activity become experienced, become mind, and how does mind then become brain activity? The brain is a physical object of the material world, as is the body, and the mind is what? How does one affect the other? This problem, that two seemingly totally unrelated types of (what word could possibly work here?) realms can affect each other is known as the mind/body problem.

When you intend to move your arm, and then just do it, the mind seems somehow to have caused action in the material world, and this has been a source of wonder for philosophers for centuries. The back side of this problem, that the brain can somehow cause experience, has also been known, but has apparently not created the same sense of wonder. The mind, whatever it is, is ethereal and non-material, and that something non-material can cause action in the material world, that it can cause your arm to move, for example, has always seemed much more wonderful and difficult to explain. We do not see the connection. We see (or feel) the experience, and we see the brain activity, but they seem to come from two totally different realms, the realm of experience and the realm of the physical. Somehow, they are able to affect each other.

In the last several hundred years, we have narrowed the mysterious gap tremendously. What was originally the mind/body problem has now been narrowed to the mind/brain problem. The mind doesn't have to actually move the arm anymore. With our understanding of the nervous system and the brain, we now know that what the mind would have to do to accomplish moving the arm, is to somehow influence the brain activity in just the right ways, or areas, that the hard wired portion of the nervous system would take care of the rest and cause the arm to move. Nevertheless, brain activity is activity in the physical universe. It is still the case that something mental must somehow affect something physical.

The mind/brain interactive realm:

If the mind is able to affect the brain, it would have played a part in the evolutionary success of an organism. Patterns of neurons that were experienced as gibberish, that were inconsistent with reality, or that were otherwise not useful to the organism would have been selected against. The mind, and the images and senses experienced by the mind would thus have been major players in the evolution of the brain and mind.

We saw in an earlier section how those things that are discovered to affect each other actually define a realm. Physical objects that interact physically, like billiard balls, define the interactive realm of *hardness*. The interactions between electrons and protons, defined the realm that was named *electromagnetic*. Once a realm is identified and named, anything new that is discovered to affect those things belonging to that realm is said to have the quality of that realm too. In the end, we don't know what a realm really is. The realm of hardness of physical objects, interestingly, turns out to be based on the realm of electromagnetism, but despite our familiarity with the term, no one really knows what electromagnetism is. We know some of its properties, some of the affects it has, but that's all we can know about it. In the end, a realm turns out to be a totally abstract thing anyway. For our purposes here, we can define it crudely *as that upon which a particular type or class of difference can occur, on which a change can occur, on which affecting can occur.*

At some point, we're going to have to admit to something like a realm via which the mind and the brain interact, at least behaviorally, at least as an abstraction. At first, we will not know what that realm ultimately will be. All we can know are some of its properties and some of the ways the mind and the brain affect each other. Our knowledge of how the mind and brain affect each other is extremely crude at this time. We know little more at this point than just that they apparently do. We should not feel like we're inventing some sort of new concept by supposing such a realm. We already have examples of non-material ethereal type *stuff* that affects the material world, the concept of energy for example. It may be that the mind/brain interactive medium may be thought of as something similar, if not the same.

Whatever the realm or means of interaction between the mind and the brain, it may be that it need have only the tiniest, most miniscule effect, even vanishingly small. The brain could easily act as an amplifier, multiplying the effect something has on it, in this case the mind. We have already seen that all material world objects are inescapably quantum objects, and we have also seen indications that it might be in the mind/brain that the quantum collapse takes place. This is all wildly speculative of course, but this seems like an almost ideal mechanism via which the mind could affect the physical universe. Even almost too good to be true. We saw earlier the idea that if the mind can affect the quantum aspects of the brain, then it potentially not only breathes new life into the debate over free will, but also offers a potential solution to the quantum wave collapse dilemma.

In the end, though, with all of our discussion on realms and such, all we're searching for here are mental tricks that allow us to visualize, comprehend, describe, or even just think about all of this. We humans must compose new descriptions out of concepts that we already have. We understand things in terms of analogies, similes, and metaphors, and build new concepts as aggregates out of building blocks that necessarily exist (already). So most of what we've been doing here is trying to find analogies that show a similarity to what we've observed about the mind/brain phenomenon, and which being familiar, give the reader some sense of comprehension. Sometimes, however, these pre-existing concepts bring along a great deal of baggage that cause one to infer properties to the new model that do not belong.

One concept that we've been falling back on for the sake of familiarity is that the human body, and the brain itself, are actually material world objects. They are not. They are illusions. The apparent physical world is only perceived by us that way, apparently as an evolutionarily convenient means of representing certain properties of the universe. When we realize this, some of the mysteriousness of the mind/brain problem becomes less mysterious, or at least the potential is there. For one thing, before we didn't know what the stuff of the mind was. Now we don't know what the stuff of the brain and body are either. This sounds like the expression of a loss of knowledge, not a gain of knowledge, but what has potentially happened here is that we have taken a step backwards so that we may now proceed down a more correct path.

With the development of quantum physics, one thing that it has demonstrated to us is that we do not know what physical reality is, and we know this for sure. Now we realize that we don't know what the body and the brain are either, and we never knew what the mind, or experience, was. We're getting really close to including everything we know of here, everything we thought we knew about. What's amazing is that this really isn't an overstatement. We do have enormous collections of information about the universe, the lives we live, what last years cars look like, but we are arriving at the point where we have to admit that we really, really don't know what any of it is. This is, of course, a major paradigm shift for everybody, scientists and philosophers being no exception, but the sensible thing to do now is take all those old perplexing questions and ask them again, but from inside of this new paradigm.

One question that might not even get asked under the new paradigm is the mind/body question, i.e., how can something as ethereal as the mind ultimately end up causing the body to move. If someone insists on asking it anyway, one answer might simply be that it doesn't. The body doesn't exist. It is an illusion. If it does have some sort of existence, then it is ethereal itself at most. Another answer might be that since we don't know what either the mind or the body are now, they just might be the same thing, made of the same stuff. There may not be such a dichotomy between body and mind after all.

Even the connection between the mind and the quantum collapse should become less unpalatable to physicists. Physicists like to account for the actions of the universe as mechanistic or mathematical, at the very least without the involvement of mind, but once it becomes obvious that their perceptions of the physical universe are imaginary, i.e., they exist only in their minds, the involvement of mind in their endeavors becomes inescapable. These same physicists are the ones who have just discovered that we only experience or perceive 4% of that of which the universe is composed, so if any of this speculation is on the right track, they will be the ones to determine if it is so.

As already mentioned, we are free now to entertain the simplest solution of all, that solution being that the mind and brain will turn out to be one and the same thing. Since the brain as we see it in the laboratory is necessarily imaginary, we just don't know what it really is. It is now possible that that electromagnetic activity that we are detecting either is experience going on itself, or at least some aspect of the mind that intersects that 4% of the universe that we perceive as physical and are able to detect.

Section 4
How to Make a Physicist

○ ○

There are no facts, only interpretations.

—*Freidrich Nietzsche*

Chapter 13
The World in the Computer

o o o o o o o o o o o o o o o o o o o o o o o o o o o o o o o o

I think there's a world market for about five computers.

—Thomas Watson, (Founder of IBM)

Representing information in a computer:

A well programmed computer is today frequently referred to as an information system, and this is because it takes information and manipulates it. In order to manipulate information, a computer must first have a way to represent that information internally. As we have already seen, information is always represented as some sort of code and represented on, or out of, some medium. Those mediums available to us on which to represent the information are necessarily made out of the stuff of our universe. That is the only stuff available to us after all.

We have already seen that information can be represented on almost any medium possible, pebbles on the beach, for example, but the majority of information handled by computers is represented internally as little variations in voltages. Floppy disks depend on the orientations of microscopic magnetic fields as a medium, and CDs rely on microscopic bubbles as a medium, but the computer reads these and encodes them as little voltages, which it then passes around to its various internal parts.

The geniuses who invented computers figured out a way to encode all information with only two little voltages, one being a higher voltage than the other, and these two voltages are thus frequently referred to as just *hi* and *lo*. Now there is, of course, a *difference* between hi and lo, and this is why it requires at least two voltages. If they tried to do it with only one voltage, there would be no difference, and as you have already seen, the only way we know of anything at all is by the difference it make. So they are really encoding everything out of this one difference, but most people see the code as based on these two states of hi and lo, so they call it a binary code.

These two voltage states of hi and lo are used to represent things as symbols inside of the computer, and there turn out to be quite a few things in our world that are binary in nature, and that we can thus represent symbolically with just hi and lo. Some of these are *yes* and *no*, *1* and *0*, *on* and *off*, and *true* and *false*. You may recall that even neurons in the brain used a binary system also based on voltages, in this case the voltage in the axon. In the case of the neuron, if each neuron was thought of as answering a question, then its symbolic binary answers were either *yes* or *I don't know*.

Each of these little voltages must actually physically exist within the computer, usually on something electrical called a semiconductor, so it actually has a physical location, although they are now quite microscopic. Each of these little voltages, which may be either hi or lo, is called a *bit*. It is the smallest bit of information that can be represented inside of a computer, and all other information within the computer must be encoded out of multiple bits, aggregates of bits.

Manipulating information:

In order for information to be manipulated by the computer, it has to have a means of affecting the information. Information is ultimately made out of bits, so what it needs is a means to affect the bits. The means it uses to affect the bits is to let bits affect each other. They do this by letting the hi/lo state of *two* existing bits to be compared to each other and, applying a simple rule, define the state of a new bit. The rules are utterly simple, and in the end they come from pure logic. Just as an example, the logical rule called the AND rule says that if both bits are hi, then the new bit will be set hi, otherwise set it lo.

There are only three logic rules used, the AND, the OR, and the NOT rules, and they are each as utterly simple. As far as representing and manipulating information, at its very bottom level, *this is ALL that a computer does*, and it was the incredible genius of just a few people who saw the potential of creating today's computers based on such a simple system.

This is what today's computers are doing at their lowest level of information manipulation. Everything that today's computers are doing, they are accomplishing by using these simple representations of bits with their interactive logic rules. The trick here is in the idea of lowest level, or more accurately, the idea of levels.

You are familiar by now with the concept of levels of hierarchy, and aggregate objects. Remember, electrons, protons, and neutrons aggregate to make the different atoms. The different atoms aggregate to make the infinite variety of molecules. Molecules aggregate to form proteins, etc. Well, this idea is at the base of today's information systems too.

It is pretty standard in most computers to combine eight bits together to form what is called a byte. It turns out that if you line up eight bits together, that there are 256 possible ways that they can variously be set hi or lo. Each one of these 256 ways is unique and can be used as the *symbol* for a specific thing. There has also developed a standard for what each one represents (called ASCII) and they include the ten digits, 0 through 9, and all the letters of the alphabet. We now have a way to encode everything we will ever want to say, because we can now make every word and number we know, and we accomplished this just by aggregating eight bits together.

As we have said, though, computers don't just sit there and hold information, like a disk say. They are dynamic things. They manipulate information too. Computers are, therefore, built in such a way that they have certain instructions that we can give them to tell them what to do with the information. The only things that a computer knows how to look at or be affected by at its lowest level are bits, so these instructions too are made using bits.

There aren't usually many instructions available to tell a computer what to do, and the few things they do at their low levels seems quite unremarkable at first. Some of the instructions tell the computer to move information from one place to another. Some do arithmetic. Some compare two bytes to see which one is the greater. Some instruct the computer to go to different places in the program.

As always, at the bottom level it doesn't do very much and everything is very simple, but with a little ingenuity, quite a bit can be done with these simple instructions. A program can now be written that takes letters typed in on a keyboard and *moves* them to memory, or onto a disk. Using basically just the *compare* instruction and the *move* instruction, a sort program can be written, or a program that manages a database. With the *arithmetic*, the *compare*, and the *move* instructions we can just about write a program that will perform the symbol manipulations of calculus. With the ability to *compare* those letters to each other that were typed on a keyboard, we can now find the spaces between words, so we can write a little program that picks out words. Those words can then be *compared* to words we already know, a dictionary, and we have a basic spell checker program. There seems to be almost no limit to what we can do with just these ultra simple little instructions.

But then someone realized that, using just those simple low level instructions, we could write a whole new set of instructions, each with much greater capabilities. We can now write a little program that moves a specified quantity of information from one place and puts it somewhere else, and we will call this instruction *COPY*. We can write a little program that moves information from one place but doesn't put it somewhere else, and we will call this instruction *DELETE*. We can write one that scans through a list looking for a certain character, and we will call it *SEARCH*. We can now take our SEARCH instruction and search for the place that a word will need to go in an alphabetical list, and then COPY the word there, and we will call this new combined instruction INSERT. We can now compare two things and if one compares greater than the other, we can jump somewhere else in the program, and we call this the IF/THEN instruction. With the If/Then instruction, we now have the capability to make decisions, to think. What we are doing is creating a whole new set of instructions that we can use to manipulate information. We have, in fact, invented a new language with which to instruct the computer how to manipulate information, called a *computer language*, or a *programming language*.

Computer languages:

As the tasks we want our computer languages to perform become more complex or specialized, we may write yet another higher level language, now created out of this new language. This is pretty much the state of computer languages today. Some of them are written from levels of languages four, five, or six language levels deep, but at the bottom of it all, inside of the computer, it's still all just a bunch of bits interacting with each other and causing new bits to go either hi or lo.

Like every human language, some things are more easily expressed in some computer languages than others. Some languages are designed to best meet business needs, while others are aimed more at the needs of science, mathematics, and engineering. In recent years, modern languages have been moving in the direction of what is called object oriented programming, or *oop*. These languages view the world of information as composed of objects, much like the brain.

These objects have two important characteristics. One is that the information it contains is seen to be an interactive unit in some way. Examples might be a single word, or a file, or a matrix, or a window if you're running Windows, or even an application. The second characteristic is that they have an *interface* to the rest of the program by way of which the program sees the object, and the interface can be quite different from the information that is contained in the object. Now what's of interest about these objects is that they capture some of the qualities of aggregate objects in the world we live in, in our universe. I don't know the history of where the inventors of these languages got their ideas, but wherever it was, they have identified much of what it will take to represent a universe of aggregate objects inside of a computer.

Objects in the real world are known to us by the effects they have on us and on the surrounding world. An apple is known to us by its color, shape, location, hardness, etc. While there is much more to the apple internally than this, these are the aspects of an apple by which it reveals itself, i.e. affects, the outside world. If we were to represent the apple as information inside of the computer, these are exactly the aspects that we would include in its interface. These would be the characteristics by which the other objects of the program saw the apple. It would be similar if we wanted to represent an *atom* inside of our computer program. We would give its interface all the characteristics by which it would be known to surrounding atoms and other particles. It would have a location, a valence, a mass, etc. The information encapsulated within the atom object, unseen by the outside world would be quit different. Inside we would find three new kinds of objects; electrons, protons, and neutrons. Each of these objects would have an interface by which it was known and interacted with the other objects inside of the atom object, and their combined interaction would translate to the combined effect revealed by the atom's interface. Inside a computer, each objects interface would be the aggregate set of its characteristics as seen by the surrounding program. In our world, each object too is known to us by its interface, its set of characteristics.

While oop has brought us a long way toward a highly efficient and realistic technique for representing information, we do not yet know what is the best way. While the universe, our brains, and now oop all represent information using aggregate objects, there's more to it than that. We saw in our discussion of information representation in the brain, the emergence of the concept of the realm on which information exists. Discussion of this topic is so broad as to be treated adequately only by another complete book, but I will give the basic structure here.

Realms of information:

Some people will find it useful when understanding the idea of a realm, to start from their intuitive idea of a dimension. For others, the idea of a set may be a more well defined starting place. It appears possible that these initial concepts can be embellished into machinery with which all information can be represented and handled. By machinery, I mean the concepts upon which a basic algorithm might be developed and used to represent and handle information within a computer. So let's start with the idea of a set.

Imagine the set of all Presidents of the United States. The actual things that are in a set, its objects, are called its elements or members. At the time of this writing, the set of Presidents of the United States has forty…uh, forty some elements in it. First of all then, we need a way to tell if an object belongs in a set, and if an object doesn't belong in a set?

The first thing we do with a candidate object is see if it passes a test that will qualify it for membership. If we test Andrew Jackson to see if he was a President of the United States, we find that he passes the test, and we admit him as a member of the set. If we test *Jesse* Jackson, we find that he was not a President of the United States, so he is not a member of the set. So far so good. We've got Andrew Jackson in our set.

Now suppose we take the next candidate that somebody hands us, Andrew Jackson say (not a misprint), and decide to see if he should be put into the set, and we find that he passes the test. Do we add him to our set again? The answer is no, we already have him in our set, but now the question becomes *how do we know he's already in the set?* We have to do a test to make sure that each new candidate is *distinguishable* from every known member of the set. In order for each candidate to be entered as a member of the set, we see that it has to pass *two* tests. It has to meet the criteria for the set definition, and it has to be distinguishable in some way from all the other members.

Sets are specified today by naming some characteristic that is common to all members, and then only allowing in members that share that common characteristic. Thus there is *some similarity* between every single member of a set, and the first test examines for that similarity, so it will be called the *similarity test*. The second test requires that all members be distinguishable from each other somehow someway, so there has to be at least something *different* about each member by which to distinguish them. This test we will call the *difference test*. Hmmmm, similarity and difference again, sim/dif. We must be on the right track.

There's one last characteristic of a set that we should examine, and that is that a set is almost always a subset of another set, and more often than not that other set is explicitly iterated, but not necessarily. In fact, our set of all Presidents of the United States is one of the exceptions and doesn't explicitly name a superset, but there are certainly several immediately implicit supersets, the set of all people, for one, since Presidents have to be people. The guys who invented sets in the first place, the mathematicians, always specify a superset. They define the set of even numbers as the *set of all integers* divisible by two, for example. In this case, the superset is the set of integers, the similarity test is dividing by two with a zero remainder, and the distinguishability test, which up until now is almost always implicit, might be that the result when divided by two be different from the result for any other member. We could just fall back on the requirement that the symbol, or tag, for the member numbers all be different, but then 4 and IV could both be members, and we can't allow that. It's usually pragmatically expedient to name the subsuming superset to be the smallest possible, so if we are defining our set of Presidents formally, we might define it as the set of all past and present American males over the age of 34 such that they were Presidents of the United States.

These three components allow us to completely identify and manipulate a set. They are:

- A similarity test

- A difference test

- A subsuming set

At the moment that someone fills in these three components with actual specific tests and a superset, then poof, the set itself exists. We may not have our hands on it yet, or have gone to all the trouble to dig out its members, but at that moment it's out there somewhere and we know it's now just a matter of legwork.

Now a realm is based on this idea of a set, so how do we get from a set to a realm. It's rather easy actually. A set is composed of two major parts, the objects in it, and the machinery that identifies these objects. To get from a set to a realm then, we take a given set, the set of all Presidents of the United States say, and then take out all the members, take away all instances of Presidents. This leaves the machinery that once identified all the Presidents, but with nothing in it.

Now ordinarily when you take all the members out of a set you are left with what is called the *empty set*, but we're actually doing something different here. What we're doing is shifting our focus from the objects of a set, to just the machinery, just the set definition. We're suddenly more interested in the definition than the objects defined. The machinery in this case is, of course, just those three components of a sets definition, and these three components, sans the set members, is what we will be calling a realm.

So the *realm* of Presidents of the United States looks like:

- similarity test—was or is a President of the United States

- difference test—name must be different from all other members

- subsuming set—past and present American males over the age of 34

The realm of all Presidents of the United States may not seem very intuitively like a realm to some people who are new to this, so let's choose another, more intuitive one, like the realm of integers. We can specify the set of integers as the set of all numbers evenly divisible by 1. So it's realm might be:

- similarity test—evenly divisible by 1

- difference test—value differs from all others by at least 1

- subsuming set—rational numbers

The members, or values, of a set are distinguishable by their differences. It has been stated several times in this book that it is only by the difference something makes that it exists at all, and the members that exist on a realm are no exception. On the realm of integers, each integer is indeed a difference, not from each other so much, but from zero. This is the value of that integer, the *effect* it has in the world, and in the case of integers, it is also this difference that we are ultimately testing for in our difference test.

Now when we look back at our set of Presidents, the difference we are testing for is apparently just the spelling of their names. This is not the same difference by which we know they existed. This is not the *effect* they had as President. If we wanted to extend this difference idea to Presidents, we would be comparing what they did while they were in office for differences, or something like that, the effect they had. The closer we can get to an operational definition here, the better. It is very convenient for us humans, though, just to distinguish things by the words we have chosen for them, by their symbol, and this can confuse the issue.

We generate a word, a tag, for almost everything we cognize as human beings. The tags are necessarily all different, so it is natural that we resort to the simplicity of easily distinguishable tags when distinguishing between members of a set, but when we do this, we lose sight of that object's differences that makes it significant as an interactive object to the world. The idea of distinguishing things by their difference, by knowing of them by their difference, seems strange when first encountered. We are still all doing it though without realizing it. We still really only know of things by the differences that they make, but this action has become unconscious to us, probably because we have become so adept and dependent at just referring to them symbolically by their tags. Those of us interested in machine intelligence are going to have to recapture the differences that make an object significant on its realm if we are ever going to bring meaning back to the symbols we manipulate.

Abstractions:

Back in Chapter 4, we were introduced to the importance of abstractions as they facilitate our thinking and understanding of the world. Again in Chapter 10, abstractions were modeled as those portions of networks of neurons that were reused by the brain when modeling similar objects, sets of similar objects, for example all birds. It even went so far as to propose that our cognition of a type of thing, a set, only occurred at the moment the abstraction formed. As I'm sure you're putting together, the idea of the realm and the idea of the abstraction turn out to be closely related. The abstraction turns out to be the similarity test, and the subsuming realm portion of the realm definition, sans the difference test. You will also recall that the abstraction was represented as an aggregate object. So where is the aggregate object specified in our definition of a realm?

It shows up in all three components of a realm definition. In the similarity test, there is frequently more than one aspect to be tested for. To qualify as a member of the set of birds, we might require that the object just have feathers, or we might require that it have feathers, wings, and a beak or bill. In the distinguishability test, we might include size, color, and/or location. The realms included in the similarity and distinguishability tests are those aspects that may be either *constant* or *variable* across the set. The subsuming set plays cleanup here and may include vast numbers of characteristics that will be common to every member of the set. The subsuming set for birds might be animals, which means that every bird must have every characteristic that makes it an animal. We are literally specifying its taxonomy here. The subsuming set we named for integers was the set of numbers, which means that every integer must have all the characteristics of a number too.

We said earlier that all of those component aspects that aggregate to compose an object are themselves abstractions too. That for the abstraction of a car, each component, e.g., windshield, wheels, steering wheel, were all abstractions too. And so it is with realms. Each aspect of a realm is itself expressible as a realm, so realms are really aggregate objects too, composed of aggregates of realms.

Realms in computers:

So how does all of this apply to computers? Let's take our realm of integers as our first example and see how we're going to implement that. Well, the first thing we notice is that we don't have to. If we are using one of the many standard computer languages available, that language has already been written to handle the realm of integers for us. We don't have to take our candidate integer and see if it's evenly divisible by 1, and we don't have to make sure that it has all the characteristics of a number either. We don't have to write the program that makes all of these tests…but rest assured that somebody did. All you have to do is tell the computer that what you're giving it is an integer, and the computer takes care of the rest. The way we know that these tests are being made, is to lie to the computer. If we pass it a letter of the alphabet but tell it that it's an integer, a well written programming language will catch it as a type mismatch and politely tell us that we are mistaken, that it's not an integer at all.

Most computer languages come with a small set of what are called *data types,* which are actually built in realms, and some examples of these are integers, alphabetic characters, and real numbers. But what about aggregate realms? Well, it turns out that we can make these too. Most computer languages have some provision to create new data types that are aggregates of the built in data types, but it's the newer oop languages that really excel with this feature. The *objects* to which the name refers are actually aggregate data types, and some of their behavior is remarkably like real world aggregate objects. Each object conceals its components, i.e., whatever it's composed of is not obvious to the outside world, but it also has an interface via which it interacts with the world, the world in this case being the program it's imbedded in. They are already expressible as abstractions, that is, the data type definition itself. Oop objects seem to be ready made for creating and programming in realms of our own invention.

The brain algorithm:

You will remember from Chapter 10, that our model of how the brain worked was that it modeled objects with networks of neurons. These objects were aggregate objects, so each component object was modeled as if it were an aggregate object too of networks of neurons. Each object then, as well as each component object, was modeled as an aggregate of networks of neurons, each network being composed of smaller component networks of neurons.

When a component network became activated somehow, what it did was immediately forward tweak the parent object networks in which it was imbedded as a component, and the parent networks then each went about the business of determining whether it existed, or whether it was all just a false alarm. The method the parent used to do this was to back tweak all of its component objects, which would in turn back tweak each of their component objects too, to determine if they existed or not. Down and down the back tweaking continued until, when the bottom level components were finally reached, those that activated would bounce the process back up the hierarchy, each forward tweaking all possible parents and enmasse causing one or some of them to actually activate this time.

We also saw that those *portions of the networks that were reused* for the representation of particular types of objects, birds for example, became the abstract representation for that type of object. Those portions of the networks that were reused for the representation of *all* birds, became the abstraction for the objects we call birds, and at this point the symbol *bird* is attached to the abstraction network as a tag or label for quick and easy reference.

Abstractions are also aggregate objects, in this case being aggregates of component abstractions, and realms, similarly, are aggregate objects composed of aggregates of realms. In the realm of birds, some of the component realms are the realms of beaks, wings, and feathers, just to name a few. A disordered pile of beak, wing, and feather realms is not by itself enough to define a bird realm, so what has to be captured to turn the component realms into the parent bird realm, are the correct relationships between the components. Once the component realms and their relationships have been identified, the bird realm is complete.

Now it turns out that all of these realms, and all of their forward and backward tweaking, is not too hard to program into a computer. To do this, one has to first *define* the objects they want to represent in terms of the object's component objects, and the relationships between those components. These definitions for objects are of course abstractions for objects, the instantiations of which are distinguished within the computer, and are thus legitimate realms. Since we will be directing the computer to actually *construct* these objects from these object definitions, another way to think of them is as templates for objects, or as the *rules* for constructing an object.

The object I chose to construct with this method was the *sentence*. I didn't choose birds because the spatial relationships between a bird's components are difficult to capture, particularly for a computer that can't see anyway. Also, sentences have complex hierarchical levels of components, and have a certain relevancy to thinking to boot, which makes them attractive. Computer programs that verify sentence structure are out there by the millions, and they are called sentence parsers, so as far as the actual *goal* of the program here, it's not new. There are two standard overall designs for parser programs. One starts at the top level of the hierarchy, in this case the completed sentence object level, and then verifies that the parts it is composed of are correct and in the right places. This is called *top down*. The other design is to start at the bottom level of the component hierarchy and see if all the parts are put together properly, creating the bottom level structure first, and working up the hierarchical levels to eventually create a sentence. This is called *bottom up*.

For demonstration purposes here, we'll use an ultra-simplified and informal version of sentence syntax. As you remember from elementary school, a sentence has two parts, a subject and a predicate. The subject is minimally a phrase based on a noun, called a *Noun Phrase*, and abbreviated here as NP. The predicate is minimally a phrase based on a verb, called a *Verb Phrase*, and abbreviated as VP. We will define a sentence then to be an aggregate of these two objects, a NP and a VP, followed by a Period. A really simple construction rule for a sentence then would look like (NP + VP + Period). While the Period is a basic, non-composite object, the NP and the VP are composite objects themselves. For our simplified example, let's say that there are two possible kinds of NP, either a single noun all by itself, like "I," or an article followed by a noun, as in "the house." Our NP definition will now look like ((Noun) OR (Article + Noun)). For our simplified example of a VP, let's say it has only two possibilities too, and it will look like ((Verb) OR (Verb + NP)). This describes the second level down in the Sentence hierarchy. The bottom we will leave at the parts of speech, abbreviated as POS, and this level will just be all the parts of speech, and the Period.

In summary, the construction rule for each component is:

network		aggregate definition
Sentence	=	(NP + VP + Period)
NP	=	((Noun) OR (Article + Noun))
VP	=	((Verb) OR (Verb + NP))
POS	=	((Noun) OR (Verb) OR (Article) OR...OR (Period))

(I must here apologize to all the astute computer and language scientists who are aware of the additional levels of hierarchy, the additional implicit relationships, and

the myriad housekeeping tasks, which I am leaving out for the sake of the simplicity of this demonstration.)

The purpose of the program is, given a string of words as input, to determine if they form a syntactically correct sentence or not, *syntactically correct* meaning they conform to the above rules. It attempts to do this using the brain's model of aggregates of networks of neurons. It may be easier on your head, though, if you imagine these objects each to be a single neuron (the grandmother cell method) triggered at the time all its component neurons going Hi. The bottom level neuron objects are the POSs. The top level neuron is the Sentence.

There are three main functions that make up the program, instantiate(), forwardTweak(), and backTweak(). When it has been decided that a neuron is to go Hi, it has been established to exist, or has been *instantiated*. The job of the instantiate() function then is to examine a neuron and see if its construction rule has been satisfied. If it has, that neuron is considered instantiated, goes Hi, and forwardTweak()'s every possible parent neuron in which it can participate as a component. It does this by actually insinuating itself into that location in the parent objects construction rule (with a ptr). On the other hand, if when instantiate() examines a partially completed neuron it is unable to declare its rule completed, it backTweak()'s one of the non-instantiated components, which then causes that component to attempt to instantiate itself. If there are multiple OR'ed construction rules for an object, a component from each one must be backTweak()'ed, lest one possibility be overlooked.

The program begins by first trying to instantiate a neuron. It doesn't matter what neuron, or where it is in the schema of things. It might start off with the Sentence neuron, a POS neuron, or one of the intermediate level neurons in between. Since the first neuron does not have enough support to go HI, it necessarily starts a chain of backTweak()'s that extends down until it instantiates a ground level neuron, and which will always happen if there is a ground level at all. If there is no ground level support discovered for a particular branch, that branch of the process expires, and thus its parent is never instantiated. Once a ground neuron has been instantiated, that neuron forwardTweak()'s all parent neurons in which it can participate as a component, many of which may be unrelated to the original backTweak()'ing, and the action begins to take off.

Very quickly the program develops many forwardTweak() and backTweak() branches that are being pursued. In a large parallel processor, and in the brain too, all of these branches would be pursued simultaneously. On a Von Newman machine, however, each newly tweaked neuron must be investigated one at a time. In this program, a queue of sorts was used, but with different considerations as to where a newly tweaked neuron was placed on the queue, so it's considered *best first* rather than *breadth first* or *depth first*. If the queue is allowed to complete, however, since all paths are ultimately investigated, it makes little difference which method is applied.

This parser has a couple of interesting characteristics that are not found in ordinary parsers. One is that it is neither strictly bottom up nor top down, but proceeds using whichever method is appropriate from the current state of a neuron's construction rule. Another difference is that it can start from anywhere in the middle of the process, which as we saw in the pirate ship scenario of Chapter 10, is an essential characteristic of the brain.

A final interesting characteristic of this algorithm was that it was extremely robust and thus difficult to debug. This was because long before it was bug free, it was, nevertheless, successfully parsing sentences and discovering the correct solutions. It turns out that there is so much redundancy available in this method that if a correct path incorrectly failed to complete, because of a bug, there was usually another one that found its way to the answer. This suggests to me that the brain may achieve its extreme levels of fault tolerance by its implementation of this algorithm.

Constructing a correct hierarchical aggregate object that validates a sentence's existence is a good example of a particular type of puzzle, so this program can be thought of as using a puzzle solving algorithm. This also reveals that the brain is constantly solving puzzles, finding the correct combinations of neuronal networks, and fitting incoming information into known scenarios that make sense out of the world for us.

Chapter 14
Creating a Virtual Universe

Something unknown is doing we don't know what.

—*Sir Arthur Eddington, (1882–1944)*

Levels of hierarchy:

If we want to create a *virtual universe* inside of a computer, we have to decide how deep we want our levels of hierarchy to go. We could create it at the level of our perception of the world, that is, with people and trees and houses, etc., as the lowest level of the object hierarchy. In this case, most objects would not consist of components, and would not be aggregate objects at all. This is pretty much the way virtual realities are programmed today. If you could actually plug someone into one of these, everything would be just fine until they broke a leg, or needed an appendectomy or something. The problem is of course that there will arise a great furor when the surgeons open them up and discover that there is nothing inside, since they are not composed of any components smaller than themselves. (Of course you will argue that without these components, they wouldn't be having problems with them anyway.)

Now the higher up the object hierarchy we stay, the less computing power is necessary. If we stop at the above mentioned object level, for someone to move their arm, the computer program *just does it*. If, however, we decide to program in some of the component anatomy, like the musculature say and bones, now for the program to move the arm it will do so by computing the muscle contractions that will move the arm where we want it to go. It will then move the arm by activating the muscles and this will cause the arm to move accordingly, just like in us. This will take a bit more computing power than if the program just moved the arm without having to calculate the muscle movement, but it will also simplify the algorithm since the computer can now use a common subroutine, the muscle contraction subroutine, to move each limb.

If we want to go another level deeper in the component object hierarchy, we might go to the cellular level. Now those muscles are all composed of billions of cells. To move the arm now, we still have to calculate how the muscles will move, but to calculate muscle movement we now have to calculate the contraction of each cell that composes the muscle. Then the muscle will contract accordingly, and the arm will be seen to move accordingly. This will require a considerable boost in the computing power necessary to handle it.

If we stop at the cellular level, the virtual surgeons won't be alarmed anymore when they open somebody up, because everything will be there. Now, though, the virtual biologists will be the ones left scratching their collective heads. When they look at cells under the microscope, they will find that they are composed of nothing. No nucleus, no mitochondria, no cytoplasm at all. If we next program our computer to go down another step and create the molecular level of the object hierarchy, the biologist's problem will be taken care of. Suddenly we'll have protoplasm and organelles, and all those things that biologists look for in explaining biology, but we will need an additional leap in computer power because in order to calculate the arm's movement, the computer will now do so by calculating the behavior of all the molecules that compose the proteins that compose the organelles that compose the cells that compose the muscles that compose the arm. And the arm will be seen to move accordingly.

So where do we stop. Our eventual goal is to imbed a virtual physicist into this virtual reality, and he's going to be investigating his universe all the way down to the bottom level of the object hierarchy, wherever it is that we decide to stop it. The bottom level that he finds will of course be the one that the virtual reality is programmed for, and when he looks into that bottom level, like the virtual surgeon or the virtual biologist above, he will find it to be composed of nothing. When programming in a virtual universe, there is necessarily a bottom level where that group of scientists will be left scratching their heads. Since this whole thing is imaginary, let's pretend that computing power is not an issue, that we have ample computing power, and we'll program our virtual reality to go all the way to the subatomic particle level.

The bottom level of the object hierarchy in our real universe (for the time being), is the quantum level. Unfortunately, today's computers cannot do quantum calculations, no matter how much power they have, so we won't be doing too much quantum stuff with our virtual universe. The whiz kids are actually working away right now trying to invent quantum computers, and progress is being made. Someday soon, when these people succeed, a single quantum computer will be able to instantly perform calculations that an infinite number of today's computers could not perform. The world will change when that day comes. Nobody knows yet how to program even a pretend one of these, although that's being developed too, so in the meantime we'll have to imagine all of this done on an ordinary computer, albeit one with massive computing power.

At the quantum level, objects cease to exist anyway, so we will take our object hierarchy right down to this level, i.e., the level at which the *effect* of the particles as objects first shows up. In our endeavor to create a universe, the first thing we are going to create is matter, i.e., particles. You might think that the first thing we should be doing if we're creating a virtual universe is to create space, that is, create a place to put the matter when we create matter, but surprisingly you will see that this turns out not to be necessary. It will turn out that space is just our mental representation of an aspect of matter, so for the time being, imagine space as coming into existence with matter.

Affected realms:

For particles to exist in a virtual universe, they must have an effect of some kind. If they don't have some effect on something, there will be no way to know that they are even there. They will make no difference, so they might as well not exist. While I suppose we could represent them in the computer, if they make no difference then we will certainly not have to include them in our calculations, so it will make no difference either if we just delete them. If we start out creating a test universe by creating a handful of particles, the only things in the universe for them to affect is each other.

In order to have an effect, though, there has to be a change in something of the affected particle, a difference has to be made in something. We have already crudely stated that a realm is that upon which a difference can be made, so for the sake of the vocabulary, we will call those aspects of particles that change to be realms. Particles have several realms that can be changed during an interaction with another particle, some being the realms of energy, time, momentum, and position. Particles also have some realms that don't change during an interaction, including its mass and its electric charge. A particle then, being composed of several realms, can be considered an aggregation of realms in our computer.

Now we're getting into something we already know about. Just a few paragraphs back we were representing abstractions, and neurons in the brain as aggregates of realms. We are getting close to being able to represent a particle inside of our computer, inside of our virtual universe. We described the bird realm (partially) as the beak, wing, and feather realms, and their relationships. We can describe the particle realm (partially) as the energy, time, momentum, position, mass, and charge realms, and their relationships. These realms pretty much all stand in mathematical relationships expressed as mathematical formulae, which capture how one changes in relation to how another changes. For example, the momentum of a particle changes in accordance with the particle's mass and its rate of change of position, expressed as $p = mv$, or *momentum equals mass times velocity*.

Inside of the computer, a particle can be represented as an aggregate of realms and their relationships, much like a bird or a sentence. The values of these realms are changeable for some realms, but are constant for other realms. The mass and charge variables are constant for example for a given kind of particle, a proton say, and in fact these constant values are used to help specify a particle's type. The values of the other realms, like position or energy, are variable, however, and these are the realms on which the particles affect each other. Without too much imagination, we can imagine using standard oop object representation from existing computer languages to capture this.

Each realm will be defined inside the computer with some version of our original definition of a realm. There will be a test component so that anything in the computer that is suspected of being a value on this realm can be verified to be so. There will be a component to distinguish each value from each other value, and there will likely be a subsuming realm for the values that these realms can take, in this case frequently the realm of *complex numbers*.

Each object in the computer, each instantiated particle, each proton or electron, will be based on an abstraction, an aggregation of realms, that will have a means to determine if some object belongs to that realm, will have a test to distinguish objects on that realm from one another, and in this case will have several subsuming realms, the realms of which its definition is an aggregate. Each particle object will be represented in the computer basically as a little place in computer's memory. That little piece of computer memory will be just big enough to hold the values for all of a particle's realms.

Imagine that we've created a little test universe now, which contains a handful of particles, and is represented in the computer as just a bunch of memory locations that hold the values of each particle's realms. The relationships that exist between the realms will be little programs, which exist only in one place, back in the abstraction definition for that class of particle. When we first create our little universe, we will assign reasonable starting values to all of our objects, like locations, etc., and everything will just sit there. Just to get things started, we give one of the particles some values on their energy and momentum realms, and now things start to happen. Because there is a relationship between momentum and location, when we assign its momentum realm some value, that particle's location value will be changing. If it is a charged particle, as its location changes in relation to other charged particles, those other particle's locations will begin to change too. As their locations change, the momentum and energy of those particles will start changing too. This is what we call the *effect* that one charged particle has on another charged particle. This is how one particle knows another particle is even there, e.g., its location, momentum, and energy values change in variable ways.

Pretty soon, the locations of all of the particles are changing in complex ways, because the effect that all of those changing location realm values have on each other is now quite complex. If we display each particle as its set of realm values on the computer screen, like little scrolling odometers say, we will see that the location value is changing, scrolling, for all of these little particles, which means nothing more than that they're all moving all over the place. Or does it? As far as what's going on inside of the computer, nothing is going anywhere. All of those little particles that started out occupying a certain location in the computers memory are still in exactly the same place. They haven't moved inside of the computer at all. The only thing that is changing that makes us say they are moving is that a variable we have named the *position* or *location* variable, is scrolling away as we watch. Inside of our pretend virtual universe, maybe they are all moving around, but not inside of the computer.

As we said earlier, the virtual universe does not need space to exist in it before we can create matter, before we create the particles. The space that the particles are moving in does not need to exist as space at all. It is just another realm that is an aspect of the particle that the particles carry around with them. The realm of location incidentally has many qualities that are similar to other realms, the momentum realm for example, and physicist do indeed come to refer to, and think of these other realms as a kind of space. In the case of momentum, it's called momentum space, or just p-space, as p is the symbol frequently used to tag momentum. Inside of a computer, space is just a realm like any other realm, a mathematical entity on which varying values can occur.

This little demonstration universe inside of a computer is oversimplified to be sure, but there is nothing in principle to prevent us from expanding it into a full-blown universe with all of a universe's base realms. We can represent a whole universe this way, as little more than changing realms, because this is basically what a universe does. At first, we describe the universe using the concept of particles that affect the realms of other particles in ways that are captured mathematically, but after you play with it for a while, the concept of a particle starts to fade and begins to seem unnecessary at all. It's the realms that are affected, and represent the effects. The mathematical relationships is between, and defined on, the realms. It's the realms that begin to take on the greater reality.

Virtual reality as a puzzle:

In our real universe, the relationships between the aspect realms of particles have been discovered to be mathematical, and physicists have nailed down the mathematics to a very high degree of accuracy. We have borrowed some of these known mathematical relationships for our computerized virtual universe in order to make it run properly, similar to the universe we know. But what if our virtual universe hadn't gone all the way to the subatomic level of mathematics. If we had stopped at any one of the higher levels of the object hierarchy, we would not have these succinct mathematical relationships to depend on. How would we now handle the component objects of our universe and their interactions?

The objects of the universe are not static. They are active. They move around and they interact with each other. They do things, and what they do has to be kept *consistent* with what they were doing in their immediate past, and they must be kept consistent with what everything else in the universe is doing too. When we had the mathematical relationships predefined for us, consistency wasn't a problem. The mathematical relationships captured the consistency. One of the nice features of mathematics is the logical consistency mathematics carries around with it and everything it touches. Without the mathematical relationships, the computer would have the potential to move the objects in any way imaginable if there are no longer any constraints. We will need to make some constraints then, and make it so that violating the constraints is impossible.

An object first and foremost must not be allowed to do something impossible. Let's take my car as an example. Right now it's sitting in my garage in Scottsdale, AZ. In the next five minutes, a lot of things can happen that change its location, but there are far more things that can't happen, that are impossible, and the program has to make sure that these never happen. For example, in the next minute I might go out for a cup of coffee, or to get gas. My car has the potential to have changed its location to a great many new locations if somebody *doesn't look* again until five minutes from now, but there are a great many more places that it cannot be in five minutes. It is absolutely impossible that in five minutes someone will find it in New York or Seattle, or anywhere else in the universe more that five or six miles from where it is now for that matter. Our virtual universe then, is immediately able to partition the values of my car's location realm into two areas, the impossible and the possible, and interestingly this can be captured with a mathematical rule.

Besides not being allowed to do the impossible, my car has to interact with, and be consistent with what all the other objects in the world are doing, other cars for example. When I go out into traffic, the possibilities of what my car can do are severely restricted by what other cars are doing. I cannot change lanes if there is a car beside me, and I cannot go faster than the car in front of me, and I affect other cars around me in exactly the same way. We are all out there interacting together, drastically limiting the possibilities of each other and all traffic as a whole. The more cars there are out there interacting with each other, the more restricted the actions of each individual car will become. If traffic is light, we may see one car weaving in and out of traffic and able to move rather freely around the highway, but as more and more cars are added to the equation, the freely moving car will become more and more limited as to its possible future actions until finally its motion is completely limited, completely determined by the cars around it. (Just add a frustrated consciousness behind the wheel, and you have road rage.)

There are really two levels of consistency then that the computer has to handle here. One is the limiting factor imposed by the interactions with objects around it, and the other is the limit of that which is possible even under the most extreme circumstance, the circumstance of having no interactions at all. The computer program is then given the very considerable task of somehow making this all fit together smoothly without any logical contradictions. That is, it must all end up logically consistent with itself. How can it proceed?

One way to think of this is as a gigantically complex puzzle. Puzzles are something that we know a little bit about, though. We have seen that the brain is extremely good at solving puzzles of this kind, i.e., putting together pieces of the universe into a consistent, non-contradictory whole. Pretty much this exact puzzle, actually, since it is our daily lives in our universe that it is making sense of. And we already have a little algorithm that at least partially captures the brains puzzle solving abilities. Let's see how it would proceed solving a puzzle of this nature.

Once again, let's take a simplified example. The universe is such a messy problem after all, with its ill-defined constraints and all of its complexity. Ben Franklin was a puzzle solver, and there's one type that his particular brain was particularly good at. Here is an example.

1, 2, 3, 4, 5, 6, 7, 8, 9

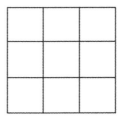

We create a little 3 by 3 grid of squares, with three rows and three columns. The goal of the puzzle is to place each of the above digits, 1 through 9, one in each square in such a way that the sums of the three digits in each row, column, and diagonal adds up to 15. Each digit may be used only once. It's amazing to me that such a thing is even possible, but good ol' Ben Franklin solved puzzles of this nature with literally thousands of squares in them, and just to make them interesting he even added additional requirements and constraints. I have included the solution of our little 3 x 3 grid below, but you may want to try to complete the puzzle yourself to learn its nature a little better. There are eight different solutions if one counts all of the possible symmetries as distinct.

2	7	6
9	5	1
4	3	8

As universe lingo goes, we will consider the nine digits to be the objects of the universe and the 3 x 3 grid to be something like a spatially extended aggregate object, which embodies some of the constraints. The aspects of the puzzle and its solution that we are interested in demonstrating do not depend on the detailed translation of all of this into realms, so I will save you the grief for the time being. It will be necessary though when we modify the parser program to perform this.

The first level of consistency we're looking for is the partitioning of the universe into the possible and the impossible. The possible places to place the numbers are of course anywhere within the grid, and the way we made it, there are no impossible places. If we had made the grid larger, say 5 x 5, and then limited ourselves to a 3 x 3 grid within the larger grid, we would then have a region of space that would be considered impossible for any of the digits to appear in.

The next level of consistency that we will be examining is that imposed by the interactions of each component with the objects around it. Now prior to our putting in the first digit, each digit has the potential to go into any square in the grid, i.e., until there are at least two objects involved, there are no constraints at all. We (the program) will start out by selecting one of the digits and putting it in one of the squares. All possible starting grids will need to be explored, so the first digit, and the square it will go into, can be chosen completely at random.

At this point, this first digit is the only digit in the grid, so it is not being influenced by any other digit in the grid. It is not being affected by any other digit or interacting with any other digit, so it can go anywhere in the *possible* zone. There are 9 possible squares into which it can be entered, so its placement will be at its most random now. If we were to stop the program at this point, and check which square the first digit was entered into, it would appear to be completely random. If we stopped the program here a hundred times in a row, we would begin to see that statistically, the *probability* that a particular square being filled first was turning out to be evenly distributed over all 9 squares.

Now as soon as we go to place a second digit in the grid, it's placement is dramatically affected by the location of the first digit. For example, if one tries to place it in a square that is either in the same row, column, or diagonal as the first digit, the rule has to be obeyed that the sum of the two digits must be less than 15. (Otherwise you couldn't add a third digit in that row, column, or diagonal.) Of course when there are two digits in a row already, there is only one possible third digit to fill in the last square that will add to 15. To an outsider watching, the aggregating particles of our puzzle universe, the digits will appear to be interacting by some law that perhaps can be captured mathematically. As more and more digits are interacting in the grid, the greater the constraints on the placement of the remaining digits. Their behavior will be observed to become less and less random.

Each time we put in another digit to interact with the system, the potential locations of the remaining digits are greatly reduced. Now there are not only nine possible squares for the placement of the first digit, but there are nine possible digits for the first choice, which means there are a total of 81 possible ways to start solving the puzzle, 81 possible first moves so to speak. Brains and universes act like they are massively parallel, so let's assume we have a computer that can process this problem down many parallel tracts too. Our parallel computer will start out building every one of the 81 *possible* starting grids, or universes, i.e., each digit in every possible square. Now for each one of these 81, there are still 8 squares with nothing in them yet, and 8 possible digits for each square, which is 64 possible ways to put the second digit in. Since there were 81 starting grids with each one having 64 possible ways to add the next digit, there are 81 x 64 = 5184 possible two digit grids. Since the puzzle solver is tracking every one of these, there will be 5184 developing objects possible from the second move that the program must investigate.

We have already pointed out though that the placement of the first digit puts tremendous restrictions on what second digit can be placed where, so as the computer checks these 5184 possible 2 digit grids against reality, a significant percentage of them will expire at this point. That is, the computer will see that they violate the *sum of 15 rule* and eliminate them from the possible grids that are allowed to continue. Those grids that violate the constraints will flash into and back out of existence instantly, and will not progress into the future since the requirements for existence are not met. If we were to stop the puzzle solver after the second digit had been added, we would never see these failed two digit grids. If we were to add additional rules and constraints, the number of developing grids would be fewer still.

The puzzle solver will continue to add each next number to the surviving grids in this way. As each new placement is investigated, more branches will be started on our developing trees, trees that will reflect the *history* of the formation of each grid. Soon, as time progresses, it will be discovered that some branches cannot continue at all within the constraints of the puzzle, and whole branches, which contain the history of these developing solutions, will then start disappearing off of our trees. At some point, as more particles are added, whole history trees will be eliminated and vanish, those that started with the digit 9 in any corner square for example. Rather than increasing as they did at first, at some point the possible solutions, and their history trees, will start becoming fewer. With the particular rules of interaction we are applying, the more interacting components that are added, the fewer entangled potentials are possible.

In the end, there will be eight completed, valid solutions existing, if all symmetries are treated as unique, all competing to be the one grid that finally comes into existence. (Only one if symmetries are eliminated.) It is a fact, learned very early in computer science that a computer program in a given state, given identical input, will always do exactly the same thing. It will always arrive at the same conclusion, or produce the same output in this circumstance. In this way, computers are completely deterministic in their computed results. The computer described here will always produce the same eight completed potential solutions to the same puzzle, and to that degree, this puzzle solver is necessarily deterministic. All that's missing now is a Joe Blow to come along and pick one, and poof, the rest will disappear.

Now this seemed to make great use of the bottom up, forwardTweaking capabilities of our little algorithm, but it didn't seem to use the backTweaking capabilities at all. In fact, what was described was the behavior of a rather ordinary bottom up puzzle solver. The reason that backTweaking wasn't apparent was that *as an aggregate object*, there were only two levels to the object hierarchy, the bottom level of particles, the digits, and the top level, which is the completed grid. There was both forwardTweaking and backTweaking going on though and here's how. When the first digit was instantiated, it forwardTweaked the grid object. The grid object then attempted to validate its existence by backTweaking one of its other, uninstantiated component objects. At the bottom level, which was transparently only one step away, the program looked to see if there was an object available to instantiate that position of the grid, and then attempted to instantiate it with every possible available object.

A more obvious way to implement the object aggregation capability of the puzzle solver using forward and back tweaking, is to define some intermediate sized aggregate objects, say a *double* and a *triple*. A double is any two adjacent squares in the grid. A triple is any three linearly adjacent squares in the grid. This makes a single square a *single*. A double is composed of two *singles*, and a triple is composed of either a double and a single, OR two overlapping doubles. The completed grid is composed of eight overlapping triples. Now when the first digit is entered into a single, it will forwardTweak anywhere from three to eight possible parent doubles, depending on its location. Each of these forwardTweaked doubles would then backTweak their other component to see if they could exist. Those that successfully formed would forwardTweak all of the triples in which that double could participate, and those triples would then go about trying to instantiate themselves. Each time a triple would instantiate, it would forwardTweak all possible developing grids in which it could participate, and so on.

There's another interesting characteristic that's demonstrable with this little puzzle scenario. Suppose your universe has two separate puzzles going, two different grids developing, in two different locations of the universe. Now let's consider the idea that someday down the road these two grids are going to interact in such a way that only a few of the potential grids are going to meet the proper interactive requirements, requirements that *only become apparent at that later time*. For demonstration purposes, let's say the constraint is that they will form an aggregate of two grids by joining on an edge triplet, by sharing an edge that has matching digits, which means that at least one of each of their edges contains a reversed sequence of digits from each other.

Let's say that yesterday each of these completed sets of eight *potential* grids came into existence, at which time nothing had reduced them to a single result, each one still being represented by all eight potential grids. Between then and now, though, one of them has undergone an interaction, say, which has reduced it to a single one of its original potential grids. Now today when these two grid objects interact, since one has been reduced to a single object, most of the potential grids of the other object will not have the correct edge triplet to interact with the single grid, so only a few of the potential eight will interact and continue on past this point. The rest will not qualify to continue in the universe as reality is now defined, and they will vanish from it, along with any interactive histories in which any of them participated.

This characteristic of the puzzle objects of having multiple potentials, has in this case allowed at least one of the potential objects, one reality, to continue forward, but perhaps several. It has provided the diversity necessary to allow separately evolving objects the flexibility of components to create at least one future, and in this case it has reduced the possible potential futures to be consistent with a single reality. Of course those that don't survive simply never exist as solutions to this later stage of the puzzle. If there were no symmetric edges for some reason when it was required for them to interact, say they had both been reduced in their potentials by previous interactions, then both grids would have ceased to exist altogether, along with any realities that had developed along their histories.

These are some of the behaviors that appear when a brain-like-aggregate-object-puzzle-solving algorithm solves puzzles inside of a computer.

The brain-like-aggregate-object-puzzle-solving universe:

Since we have already embedded our little 3 x 3 puzzles into the puzzle-solving algorithm, let's go ahead and embellish our puzzle solver with the characteristics of our earlier universe algorithm. When the puzzle solver successfully assembles a completed puzzle, it has created a new aggregate particle, which we will call an *atom*, say. The digits 1 through 9 will each be a subatomic particle, each with slightly different aggregation characteristics. Each particle now will be associated with the six realms that we have assigned to particles, i.e., location, mass, etc. Our puzzle atom will be ultra-microscopic, and will itself be associate with the six particle realms. The realms of the atom will be assembled from the realms of the subatomic particles. Its mass realm will be the sum of the mass of all of its component particles. Its location will be the same as all the component particles. Its electrical field realm value too will result from the electrical fields of its aggregated components. We could even relate the electrical characteristics of our atoms to their edge components, since their edge triplets are also involved in how the atoms aggregate (although we'd have to make some adjustments to realize that analogy).

We now have a little universe with some handful of subatomic particles, a few of which have aggregated into atoms, and they're all (virtually) flying around in there together. Once again, inside of the computer, nothing is going anywhere. Each particle representation sits at a particular memory location, and the only thing that changes are the values of their realms. If nine of the subatomic particles have successfully aggregated to create an atom, the atom will be represented as a cluster of nine pointers to those nine particles inside of the computer memory. An atom now may have eight or so *potential* identities, and each one will be composed of pointers to the same nine subatomic particles. They will all be competing for those same nine particles. The nine subatomic particles will then have eight or so potential futures, and the universe driver program will pursue all of them until they are modified, or fail. Our universe driver will in fact be driving a multiverse, as discussed back in Section 2.

What the universe driver program is interested in is changes. It needs to calculate the changes that are occurring on all those realms for each of those particles. If a particle is moving in a uniform, constant way, its motion can be represented by a constant (from which some interesting relativistic effects can appear), and the computer need not look at it again until it interacts with something, i.e., *something changes it.* All that the driver will be looking at is how the changing realms of one particle affects another. The point of all this is that the driver will be looking for the effects of realms on realms. What's really important to the driver are the realms, and the effects they have on each other. The particle aspect itself does little more than enforce an association between realms.

One realm is going to turn out to be particularly significant in the interaction of the other realms, and that is the *location* or *position* realm. As the values of two particle's location realms approach each other, the interactions of the other realms will become greater. When their location values become the same, they become an aggregate object. The particle aspect is really just a localization (on the location realm) of the affects the realms have on each other. Also of interest is that if a particle is isolated, or on a non-interactive constant path, that particle need not be updated until some critical time in the future when it does interact with the rest of the universe again, and in the meantime its history may languish in some distant past. And this brings up the problem of time.

We will use a very unsophisticated method to handle time, as it doesn't appear necessary to get relativistic for our purposes here. Our universe will have some small time interval we'll call a *tick*. Between ticks, the universe will be advancing all of the necessary calculations forward so that everything is up to date for the next tick. When everything is ready, the next tick will tick, and the universe will start over advancing everything forward for the next tick. (I think there was a *Twilight Zone* episode that did something like this.)

A couple of interesting notes on this are that *our time* in our universe will not be synchronized, or even linked to their time, except that they are both moving in the same direction, namely forward. If we define a tick to be one second in their universe, many seconds could pass in ours between ticks, or if our computer was fast enough, there time might run faster than ours, so there's a de-linking of time between the two. Another interesting aside is that if there is something, an aggregate object say, in the virtual universe that is not going to interact with anything in that universe for several ticks, or several billion ticks, its realm values need not be changing between interactions, so the computer can ignore it until its next interaction time, which is the situation mentioned in the preceding paragraph.

The puzzle as realms:

Throughout all of this, we have been carrying along an artifact of our puzzle solving example that is now beginning to appear unnecessary. In the example, the components that needed to be fit together into the grid to solve the puzzle were the digits 1 through 9. We then merged our puzzle solver with our preexisting universe driver program by attaching those little grids, each to the particle aspect realms of our universe driver. We have recently seen, though, that the only thing important about a particle, the only thing that the driver needs to track, are its realm values, and that its *particle* aspect is simply related to one of those realm values, the location realm. Our little grid with its nine digits now no longer seems useful or necessary. But our little brain-like-aggregate-object-puzzle-solving algorithm is what makes it possible for our universe driver to proceed forward at all, so to keep the algorithm and the all important realms too, let's just drop the digits 1 through 9, and replace them in the puzzle solving grid with the realms themselves. In this case, each little box in the grid will represent one of the realms.

The puzzle created from using realm values has the same initial characteristics as the original puzzle. The first is that the values that those realms may take can be partitioned into the impossible and the possible. Also, there were relationships between the digits in the original puzzle that were necessarily maintained by the puzzle solver, the sum-of-fifteen rule for example. There are also relationships between the values of the realms, and it is these relationships that the puzzle solver will now need to attend to when creating all of the potential solutions to the particle grids it is creating. The puzzle solver is still solving a puzzle. There is a major difference that we are going to discover now though. Whereas before, the eight *potential* grids were formed as a result of fitting the nine potential digits into each of its boxes, now we are going to see the multiple potential grids forming out of the *range* of potential possible values on each of its realms.

Unlike the original set of nine digits that were discreet, many of these realm values may now vary over a continuous range of values. These realms are the particle's aspects, so a particle will appear to somehow have multiple possible values, a range of values, to its aspects, until it becomes necessary to limit those values. We will no longer have just eight discreet potential grids as the puzzle's solution, but we will have a smear of an infinite number of potential grids, smeared over the continuous range of possible values that each realm may take. One of those realms is the realm of location. Any given potential particle will now act as if it is spread over a range of potential locations, that is, spread out in space.

I have gone to considerable trouble up until now to avoid introducing phenomena *directly* from the universe we know into our little test universe. All of the phenomena that have shown up so far, result just from considerations of the symbolic nature of our computerized information, and the nature of our little brain-like-aggregate-object-puzzle-solving algorithm. Unfortunately, of the two major phenomena that haven't shown up, the collapse of the potentials to a single outcome, and the quantum, I am going to have to deliberately insert one in order to keep this discussion on track.

That one is that something causes all of those potential realm values to collapse from time to time onto a single value. One possible way that this might happen in a computerized universe is that some sort of interaction occurs that dictates that all of those potential values except one now become impossible, as when our grids shared a common edge in our earlier example. Another possible way that this may happen, as long as I'm borrowing from our universe, is that somebody looked, and this somehow causes all potentials to vanish but one.

Either way, in order to continue this discussion, we will imagine that there is some mechanism that collapses the potentials onto a single outcome from time to time.

During the time between collapses, the location aspect is undecided over a range of values. The localized particle aspect doesn't exist at all during this period, and only shows up when the potentials are collapsed. Until then, it becomes all realms and no discreet particles at all. As far as our universe driver is concerned, discreet particles are not what is important during the time between collapses. It's all realms. It's also of interest to note that between the collapse points, no distinct particle representation need exist at all, *including in our computer memory*. Since particles don't really exist during the calculations between collapses, it would be more convenient to generate new particle objects for the particles that appear at each collapse point. If represented this way, we will have to drop our discreet oop object representation of particles between collapse points, leaving only the interacting realms. Particles will now lose their unique identities within the computer driver, will simply spring into existence temporarily at collapse points, and will simply serve as the starting point for the realm values for the next set of realm calculations.

There's one more thing that drops out of this representation, and that is what will appear to be action at a distance. It is partly a consequence of the fact that the driver allows multiple futures to continue simultaneously, and partly a consequence of location being just another symbolic realm. Just to demonstrate the point, imagine that there are two ways that a joined pair of atoms can break apart into single puzzles again. Let's say something silly like atoms can only break apart leaving a smooth break or a jagged break, so after they have broken apart, there are now two *potential* atoms for each new atom. Each atom will consist of the *potential pair* of having the broken edge smooth or the broken edge jagged. Of course for the potential atom that has the smooth edge, the corresponding atom of its earlier mate must also have a smooth edge, and vice versa.

Now, let's say the two original atoms that have broken apart are flying away from each other, but each one consists of the potential pair of smooth/jagged edged atoms. And let's say that when their location realm values differ by a billion light years, Joe Blow comes along and looks at one of them. Now when he looks, the universe is going to collapse onto a single one of the potential atoms, let's say it's the one that has the jagged edge. In order to keep the universe consistent, which is the job of the puzzle solver after all, the driver is going to have to collapse the other atom too, which is now a billion light years away, onto the single potential atom that is also jagged edged. Now if, after a prearranged delay,

by G. Wells Hanson

one microsecond later Joan Blow looks at that other atom, she will find that it is the one with the jagged edge, and it will appear to her and Joe that the universe acted instantaneously across a billion light years to collapse that atom onto the correct one. And of course it did. But of course distance doesn't really mean anything inside of our universe driver since location is just a particle aspect, so in a way it didn't act across any distance at all.

We have taken our brain's puzzle solving algorithm, and embellished it into a universe driver inside of a computer. We have seen though that in order for it to create a universe that behaves similarly to ours, it must resort behind the scene to some very un-universe-like tricks and methods…and we have seen that several un-universe-like phenomena occur as a result. Each of these phenomena occurs because of some feature of this arrangement. There are two primary considerations that are responsible for, and account for these phenomena. One is that it is all occurring as only a symbolic representation within an information system, and the other is the specific methods applied by our little brain-like-aggregate-object-puzzle-solving algorithm.

I have created an hierarchical outline below representing how each phenomenon depends on the characteristics of that branch.

consistency puzzle solver/information system
   driver is deterministic
   puzzle solving algorithm
      multiple futures pursued to maintain consistency (from brain algorithm)
         instantaneous action at a distance (necessary to maintain consistency)
      able to go back and affect history (from brain algorithm)
      a *single* particle's potential is restricted only by the *possible/impossible* boundary
         a single particle demonstrates maximum randomness
      the more *interacting* components, the fewer entangled potentials (depends on rules)
matter represented symbolically only (it's an information system)
   represented as realms (the differences upon which effects manifest themselves)
      only effects exist (that's all that needs to be calculated)
      no materiality
      space doesn't exist (space is only a particle aspect)
         instantaneous action at a distance
   time decoupled between puzzle solver and virtual universe
      instantaneous action at a distance
   particles need not be updated in between interactions (have no effect, don't exist)

particles need not exist between collapse points
   particles lose their identities

Virtual computers:

Let's now take a giant imaginary step and rev up our little universe to a fully functioning universe. We will imagine that we have all the computing power necessary to do this. There will now be programmed in a full repertoire of all the different types of particles, still represented symbolically of course. We could even have initiated our universe with all the energy starting from a single point, our own version of the Big Bang, and run it forward to a time when there are virtual worlds and virtual people and the like. I'm getting a little ahead of the story here, because we're not going to talk about introducing people into this universe until the next chapter, but for our purposes here, we need something like people, so we'll assume it is populated. If you're having trouble picturing how people composed of this mish-mash of symbolic representations can perceive their world as a world, etc., don't worry too much about it. That will be addressed in the next chapter too. In the meantime, just picture them as picturing their world the same way we picture ours. So our universe has reached the stage where aggregate objects exist and work fine, so now we can actually make things from the stuff of this universe, and one of the things we can make is a computer. Computers are made from the materials of the universe they exist in after all.

It turns out that because the computers in this universe are necessarily constructed out of the stuff of this universe, they can never even theoretically match in computing power of the universe from which they are constructed. There are many of ways to see why. First of all, it's not possible for a little computer composed of a microscopic fraction of the material in the universe to even represent all the material in the universe. It would minimally have to be as big as the universe to do that. Also, it can never run as fast as the universe. This is because it necessarily uses the processes of the universe to make computations, e.g., electrical impulses, so if it were trying to calculate the electrical impulses of just itself, for example, using those very electrical impulses, it would necessarily lag way, way behind. Additionally, all the processes of the universe run massively in parallel. Everything in the universe that will happen in the next second will all happen together at the same time. Our little computer can't possibly even calculate all the physical processes that will occur just within itself in the next second. Once again, our little computer will necessarily lag way behind. This is all looking at the computational problem from the point of view of an imbedded computer looking out at the universe it's trying to mimic, *bottom up* let's call it. But we can also look at the problem top down, looking down at our virtual computer from the universe that contains it.

To keep everything straight, we will need names for our universe and our computer, which is made from the stuff of our universe. We will name our universe, the one we live in, U1, and we will name our computer C1. Now let's say we have successfully programmed a virtual universe representation inside of C1, as we imagined a few paragraphs earlier. We will name this virtual universe U2, and U2 is just a program running on our computer C1, just like any other program we run on our computer. The virtual objects in U2, which is programmed inside of C1, are necessarily composed of the virtual substances represented in U2. For example, if we represent virtual atoms in our U2 program, then any object in U2, a virtual object, will have to be composed of these atoms, i.e., virtual atoms. Now that we have virtual atoms and virtual objects in U2, we can construct a computer in U2, a virtual computer made from the virtual atoms programmed inside of U2. We will call this virtual computer C2.

To a resident of U2, C2 will appear to run just like our computer C1 does to us residents of U1. In one sense, though, C2 is not computing anything at all. We need to realize that everything happening inside of U2, including C2, is being calculated inside of our higher-level computer, C1. U2 is just a program running on C1. So let's imagine that some virtual resident of U2 has written a program that runs on C2 that mimics the behavior of an atom he found in his universe, U2. A U2 atom is already a virtual atom since it's running on C1, but an atom represented on the virtual computer C2 is a virtual U2 atom, or a virtual virtual-atom, which is being represented on a computer, C2, already built of virtual atoms.

Now the important thing to keep sight of here is that both the virtual atoms within U2, and the virtual virtual-atoms on C2 are necessarily all being run on the same computer, C1. To run the behavior of a U2 virtual atom, C1 needs to run just a little routine representing that atom in our U2 program, but to run the behavior of the virtual virtual-atom in C2, C1 needs to run several quadrillion routines representing all the virtual atoms that compose the virtual computer C2. There is in this case, therefore, a decrease in efficiency of minimally several quadrillion between a universe and a virtual representation of it.

It is of interest to note that it is also possible for a virtual resident of U2 to write a virtual universe program to run on his virtual computer C2, i.e., a virtual virtual-universe U3. It is also then possible to create yet a lower level virtual virtual-computer C3 from the material of U3, and of course we need not stop here.

A resident of U3 can program a U4 to run on C3 and then a computer C4 can be created out of the material of U4. In principle, it appears to be possible to program nested universes down endlessly, as long as we have ways to represent them (computers) made from the substances of those virtual universes. As we have seen, though, we would experience a drastic decrease in efficiency in our virtual computers at each level we go down. In each case, the decrease would not be noticeable to the residents though due to the decoupling of time at each level.

Chapter 15
Making a Physicist

The most beautiful thing we can experience is the mysterious.

—Albert Einstein, (1879–1955)

Making his universe:

If we are going to make a physicist, we first have to create a virtual universe, which he will inhabit, and fill it with material from which he can be made. Physicists in our universe are composed of the stuff of this universe after all, so the physicists of our virtual universe must also be composed of the stuff of their universe. As we have seen, we can hypothetically create something of a universe inside of our computers by programming them to model the universe we know.

Now when we speak of creating a universe within a computer, we are certainly not creating an actual *physical* universe. We are not even creating something like the universe portrayed in the now antiquated science fiction movie *Tron* that takes place inside of a computer. In that movie, the inhabitants were the bits and bytes, electrical circuits and the like, and the physical insides of the computer participated in the universe. The insides of our computer is a part of *our* physical reality in *our* universe and will not appear inside of a programmed universe. The inhabitants of Tron's universe were themselves composed of elements from *our* physical reality, that is, bits and bytes, etc. That's not the way it will be inside of a programmed computer universe. A universe programmed inside of a computer will be utterly abstract. It will be an abstract representation of a universe composed of information only.

Computers as information systems basically do only two things. They represent information symbolically, and they manipulate that information, those symbols, according to the rules we program into them. If we're going to represent a universe inside of our computer, then we're going to have to do it by representing it as information, and then manipulate that information to mimic the behavior of a universe. It turns out that our simplified universe from the last chapter, based on realms, aggregates of realms, and a puzzle-solving algorithm is sufficient for our imaginary purposes.

Earlier, our little puzzle-solving algorithm solved 3 x 3 matrices using the interactive effects of aggregating objects. These effects were represented as changes on various realms (values in the singles, doubles, and triples). After a puzzle was successfully solved, the rule that was satisfied was that each triplet of it added up to 15. We then expanded our notion to imagine that these were micro-world particles of a universe, and attached the realms to them that particles in our universe enjoy, i.e., locations, momentum, energy, time, etc., and we embellished our puzzle solver to take the interactive effects of these realms into consideration as it created higher and higher levels of aggregate particles, i.e., new aggregate objects aggregated from the particles. Finally, we discovered that we could drop the original puzzle and replace it with the puzzle of putting together, and maintaining the particle aspect realms from the original universe driver

The functions, operators, and algorithms of quantum physics in our universe give us exquisitely perfect mathematical rules that describe these interactions, but I don't want to use them in our computerized universe for several reasons. One is that we have gotten along fine without them up to this point. Another is that to do so would limit somewhat any new knowledge about the phenomena that appear in a computerized universe. Another is that I am going to assume that quantum physics is not the bottom level rules, that they are just a very good mathematical description of physics at that level. This is not an altogether unfounded assumption. With recent developments in string theory, information theory, and the knowledge that quantum and relativistic physics are incompatible, it seems almost prudent to anticipate that this will turn out to be the case. Anyway, we're going to pretend that our puzzle solver knows what the bottom level rules are, solves puzzles according to these rules, and that these are not necessarily the same rules captured by quantum physics.

Now imagine we have a virtual universe that essentially progresses as a puzzle solver, albeit we don't know exactly what its bottom level rules are, exactly what puzzle it is solving. One thing is certain, though, and that is that one consequence of its actions must be the appearance of logical consistency (and perhaps mathematics itself). For simplification, we might even imagine that consistency is one of the explicit rules that the puzzle solver is trying to satisfy. Now to get it all started we must pick an initial state, so let's pick the state that all matter and energy, and everything else that might be, are all starting out at a single infinitesimally small point…and then we hit the start key.

Bang!

If we programmed everything correctly, we will have just created the Big Bang, and our *virtual* universe will be taking off. Over time, that little 4% of the stuff we call matter will condense out. Virtual stars and planets will form, and on a few of these, the virtual molecules that will participate in early life form. It is not necessary that our puzzle solver have any of these as goals, as the puzzles it is solving. It is just furiously working away solving puzzles that involve interactive realms. All the rest of this, the prolific creation of aggregate objects, etc., just drops out as a consequence.

We will imagine that on at least one planet, virtual molecules begin to aggregate into self-replicating configurations, and eventually virtual life begins. Because of the life-and-death competition between the life forms here, only the superior creatures proliferate, and the forces of evolution eventually create a creature with a mind, whatever that is. We will also imagine, for lack of knowledge, that whatever it is that constitutes mind dictates that this creature will perceive only one of the potential universes.

It's important to keep in mind that mind or not, there are no real objects that exist anyway. All of this is just information represented in our little information system. There aren't even any representations of objects within this information system. Everything is just a huge mishmash of realms, all interacting with each other according to the dictates of the puzzle solver. The first representation of an object doesn't occur until the first creature with a mind opens its eyes. It's entirely possible that the only place that the representation of an *object* occurs at all is in the mind of the creature itself. Before the creatures of this universe can even have eyes to open, though, they will have to evolve senses with which to gather information about the virtual world around them.

Evolution of the senses:

In order to sense the world around them, the creatures will require a sense organ that is *affected* by the world around them. While nothing is affecting this sense organ, nothing is being sensed. Only when a change occurs in the state of the sense organ will information exist to be carried to the mind of the creature. Since the world at large consists of interacting realms, the sense organs of the creature are going to have to have realms that are affected by the realms of the universe.

This is not really a problem since the sense organs, and the creature itself, are necessarily composed from the same realms/stuff as the universe already.

This will first of all, dictate what he can and cannot sense. It all depends on what realms a given sense organ is sensitive to and will translate into some code to be passed on to his brain. It's then up to his evolved, virtual brain to make what sense of the information that it can. Of course, because this creature is the product of evolution, the sense organs will have evolved to gather information from the environment that is useful to the survival of this organism, and the brain will be translating it into a mental representation (experience) that is also useful to the organism. It is possible that the brain is receiving information from the *location* realm of the virtual world around it, and representing it to the creature as space, like ours does. It is also entirely possible, however, that the creature experiences it as something completely different from our idea of space. It is even possible that the brain is receiving information from one of the other aggregate realms that is composed of scalar orthogonal (space like) realms, and representing this realm to the creature as the space that the creature lives in. This creature then would perceive itself to be living in some kind of a spatial universe, but it would not be the same space that we experience.

Whatever its final senses end up being, and whatever its mental representations of the sensed information ends up being, this will be the real world to this creature. If it, coincidentally, ends up sensing the same realms we do, and *very* coincidentally experiencing them similarly mentally, this creature would experience living in a universe similar to the one we experience. It seems impossible though that his mental representations of colors, temperature, tastes, sound, and especially space and materiality are likely to be the same as ours. Remember, this is really all just a bunch of 1s and 0s, or more correctly, little voltages changing away in our computer. It's his experience of the information that makes reality what it seems to be to him.

This creature is composed of the little voltage changes in our computer, just like everything else in his virtual universe. Our computer represents his particles the same way it represents all particles, that is, as interacting aggregates of realms. His particles, and aggregate particles are a result of the puzzle solver progressing forward through time just like the rest of the objects in his universe. Presumably evolution has created a system in his universe, like ours, which builds life on increasingly higher hierarchical aggregations of components like amino acids, which aggregate to form proteins, which form organelles, which form cells, which form organs, which form systems, which form the creatures themselves. We will presume so, as to avoid the need for inventing a whole new biology for our purposes here. Most importantly, we will assume he has a brain, and a nervous system that retrieves information from his sense organs and carries it to his brain.

At the very bottom level, the actions of this creature are driven by our computer that is driving his universe. If a particular set of neurons goes hi in his brain, the computer driven realms composing these neurons interact with realms of other neurons, and eventually the interacting effect reaches, say, the creature's arm muscle, and its arm moves (presuming it has an arm). Once that initial set of neurons in his brain went hi, all of the rest of this, his arm moving, happened inevitably and automatically as a result of the puzzle solver advancing its puzzle solving forward through time. This creature just described is completely on autopilot. If certain chemicals in its body drop too low, or rise too high, nerve impulses will go hi, which trigger its hunger center in its brain, which will then initiate the proper action to bring these chemicals back into the proper balance, i.e., it will go find some food. If we grant this creature a mind, which we will as of now (but account for later), there appears to be one more step in the process of feeding itself. In this case, the activated neurons in the hunger center cause the creature to *feel* hungry, and the *feeling* of hunger itself now somehow plays a role in triggering the neurons that send the creature in search of food.

The creature's brain is in fact a very complex computer. Since it is in a virtual universe, it is a *virtual* brain, and thus a virtual computer composed of virtual stuff. This computer has evolved within the virtual universe because it aided in its host's survival, and thus its own survival. This virtual computer is represented as an aggregate object on our driving (real) computer, and the computations that this virtual computer/brain perform result from the interactive effects of its realms as driven by the real computer. The virtual computer/brain is in fact a process running on the real computer. In fact, the whole organism can be considered a process running on the real computer, a subprocess within the universe process.

Science in a virtual universe:

The brain receives information from the neurons that are connected to the sense organs. We will presume that the brain evolved to represent the information it receives as aggregate objects (see Chap. 10), in this case mimicking the way the brain-like algorithm we're using to run his universe represents the (collapsed) information. At the opposite end of the neurons that supply the brain, are the sense organs. In order to operate, the sense organs have to be affected by the universe, that is, they have to stick out and interact with the universe. The information that is retrieved and sent to the brain is simply the encoded log of these interactive events, but the point is that there has to be some point where the sense organ actually contacts the universe at the surface of the creature.

Like a blind person trying to *feel* how the billiard balls are moving on a billiard's table, the creature will not be able to sense the microworld without disturbing it. The driving computer will not only calculate the effect the realms of the universe have on his sense organs. It will also calculate the effect the realms of his sense organs have on the universe. Sense organs, which sense the macro world, i.e., sense the larger aggregate objects, are necessarily composed of from millions to billions of smaller components that each interact on an individual basis. In our universe, these individual components exist somewhere around the electron level of the object hierarchy, so we might as well let that be the case for our creatures in the virtual universe too.

Now for the most part these creatures go about their daily business, their brains representing to their perception a macroworld that is based on aggregated objects composed of the microworld. And for the most part, these creatures perceive this to be the real world, this macroworld, and don't think another thing about it. But let's imagine too that throughout their history there have been some, unusual among their kind, who have taken an interest in trying to understand the universe they live in.

These would be their philosophers and scientists, and they would discover that the universe exhibited a great deal of order and consistency. They would discover mathematical relationships among the measurable effects of their world that held to a high degree of accuracy, and they would have marveled that it was possible to describe their world with abstractions. Of course in their case, *this results from the fact that their universe is indeed being represented as abstract relationships inside of a computer.* As time went on, they would discover phenomena predicted by their abstractions that were not evident to their senses, and they would wonder at how it was possible that the abstractions seemed to capture a more accurate reality than the world they knew and sensed.

Eventually, their measuring instruments would reach a degree of precision that they would be able to probe, and develop the mathematics to describe the microworld. They would soon notice as they traversed down to lower and lower levels of aggregate object, that the objects gradually faded away and just turned into the effects that were measured. Finally they would recognize that when they opened up the most bottom level particle and looked inside, that there was nothing there. They would have expected the bottom level of their world to be composed of something like the Greek atom, something minute and material, but instead, like the surgeon in the virtual reality of chapter 13 who cut open the patient to find nothing inside, they too would look into the particle at the lowest level that the computer was maintaining, and there would be nothing there.

Imagine again the surgeon who cut open a body and it was completely hollow. In his universe, with no muscles and bones, there would be no way to explain the movements of the body. They would be reduced to just describing the body's movements with only the formal rules that they could devise, and to which the body's movements conformed. It would, for example, be discovered that if the creature was tapped below the knee with a rubber hammer, his foot would jump, but it would never be possible to understand why, only that it did. For our creatures exploring their physics, their description of their bottom level would be reduced to a set of formal rules that described what effects their microscopic probes could expect to find at the bottom level.

The rules of physics that the creatures deduced, and the phenomena they implied, would make no sense at all to them, and they would make no sense at all because the creatures continued to think of their world as a material world, made out of space and material objects inhabiting that space, rather than just an abstract representation of effects inside of our computer. The phenomena would seem uncanny and impossible, and indeed it would be if they were actually living in the material universe they imagined themselves to be living in. Some of these mysterious unexplained phenomena that they would discover, or deduce, and that *result from the nature of their symbolic representation, and the puzzle-solving algorithm*, we saw in the last chapter, and include:

- materiality evaporates into abstraction somewhere before the bottom level

- the bottom level of the universe is described by formal rules

- space is just one of the many aspect realms of a particle, and doesn't exist as space

- a particle, or object, seems to move forward through multiple potential futures simultaneously

- of those multiple potential futures, randomness is maximized for a single, non-interactive particle

- the universe of potentials is a multiverse

- the more particles that interact and entangle, the fewer the potentials

- a particle is capable of multiple histories, and an experimenter can pick which one becomes real

- particles seem to behave as information only and don't need to exist between interactions

- particles lose their individual existence and do not maintain unique identities

- particles have some method of interacting instantaneously across any distance

- the bottom level of the universe is only the effects detected

- the abstract representation of the universe predicts phenomena not apparent to their senses, and

- the abstractions predict phenomena more accurately than their senses

- their world is deterministic

As demonstrated in the previous chapter, all of these seemingly mysterious phenomena occur as a result of the symbolic representation of their universe inside of a computer, as well as the nature of the puzzle-solving algorithm implemented. What the creatures have really discovered and are scratching their heads over, are characteristics of the process running their universe inside of the computer. There is yet an even more disturbing phenomenon, though, that the creatures will discover that results from our programming their universe inside of a computer.

Because computers represent information symbolically, in today's computers digitally, there is a limit to the accuracy with which they can represent quantities. By this I mean that, there is a limit to the number of decimal places that the computer will use to represent a number. Depending on the programming language used, that limit might be eight, sixteen, or even thirty-two decimal places (or usually binary places), but there is a definite limit.

Now, this is not usually a problem to the programmer, because the number of decimal places is usually more than sufficient to handle the accuracy of the type of information represented in most programs. In our creature's universe, though, it is a problem because we are using these very quantities to represent the values on the various realms at the bottom level of this universe. If the computer only takes values to a predetermined decimal place, at their smallest level these values will demonstrate a minute discreteness. For example, if we limit our computer to three decimal places, the only allowed numbers between 1.250 and 1.255 will be

1.251, 1.252, 1.253, and 1.254. Continuous values will not exist at the very bottom level. One of the first things, then, that is going to show up to our probing creatures in their little universe is that there is a certain discreteness to the values that their realms may take. If we are conscientious programmers, we will extend the number of decimal places out to where this discreteness is inconsequentially minute, but we will have to write the program to handle it nevertheless.

The reason that we will have to program our universe to handle this is because the limited precision introduces a certain potential error into the calculations, and thus into the values on the realms. Now all scientists and researchers are trained in the necessity and techniques for tracking and maintaining the degree of error in any given calculation (sigma and all that), so we won't go into the specifics here, but we will have to write our universe driver to do the same thing in this case. Tracking this potential error in our computer will be handled by introducing and maintaining a precise uncertainty into our calculations, since we know already exactly what the precision of our representation of quantities is.

There are two more phenomena then, that our creatures in a computerized universe will discover,

- a microscopic discreteness to the values that their realms can take

- an uncertainty related to this discreteness that is mysteriously maintained by their universe

The creatures will have discovered that their universe is quantized!

By now, the reader must be wondering if it will ever be possible for the creatures to determine that they are inside of a computer. Is there some way that they can actually detect the computer that is running their universe?

The only things that affect our creatures, and thus the only things that they can detect at all, are the *effects on the realms* symbolically represented in our computer. The creatures, and their measuring instruments, are made from these realms, and thus are affected only by disturbances on these realms. This means first of all that they cannot detect the computer directly. They can never detect the medium on which the information is encoded in the computer's universe, i.e., they cannot even detect the little voltages our computer is using to represent their universe. They cannot detect their ground, you might say. They are doomed to forever appear to just exist.

- they appear to just exist out of nothing

Two levels of universes:

There are a lot of other questions one might ask about what these creatures can and cannot know and do. Can they determine that their universe is imbedded within a higher-level universe, i.e., our universe? If so, that higher universe must appear to be vastly more powerful computationally than theirs. How efficiently then, how close can they get to tapping into the computer power of the higher-level universe? Since they themselves already are processes running on our computer, is it possible for them to create processes that run on our computer and tap into our computing power that way? Can they deduce anything about our mathematics? Can they deduce the actual puzzle algorithm?

The creatures of the virtual universe are *processes* running on a computer in our universe. Not only that, but *everything* in their universe is a *process* running on our computer. Now computers and their processes have some interesting relationship, so lets examine some of these.

A computer exists in a universe, and a process running on a computer exists in the same universe as the computer it's running on. In our computers in our universe, a process running on the computer is basically just fluctuating little voltages within the computer, and thus within our universe too. Since a virtual universe process is running on our computer, it thus has some capability to affect our universe. A virtual creature sub-process, as part of the virtual universe process, also has the capability to affect our universe. All of these effects will be seen in our universe as just fluctuating little voltages in our computer. These little voltages, though, have the potential to be amplified into a much more significant effect, as is the case now with any computer controlled devices that we have already created. If we ever create robots, for example, their actions will result from the amplified effect of their driving process. (Can the process that is their brain be considered a virtual universe?)

If our virtual creature programs a virtual virtual universe into its virtual computer, everything in that virtual virtual universe is a process running on his virtual computer. He will be able to amplify the effects of that process to have an amplified effect in his universe. Ultimately, however, a process running on a virtual virtual computer, as well as its amplified effect in the virtual universe, is just a process running on our computer too, so any virtual virtual creatures also have the potential to affect our universe.

And going down instead of up, our universe of course, has the capability to affect any universe running as a process within it. We do that every time we use the mouse to click on a button.

The creature's virtual brain is a virtual computer running in the virtual universe. The brain's activity is thus a process running on this virtual computer, on the virtual brain, but the process running on the brain is necessarily also a process running on the higher-level computer in our universe. There is a huge difference between the two processes though. Each neuron of the virtual brain, indeed all the atomic and subatomic components of each neuron are little processes running on the higher-level computer. Each neuron then is an aggregate process, and the brain itself will be a massively aggregate process running on the computer. But the brain is a virtual computer too, which is able to run processes. What will a process running on the virtual brain look like on the top-level computer?

One would think that first of all it probably wouldn't be recognizable to us as a process. In the computer, it would appear as fluctuations on the realms that represented the virtual brain, and it probably would be difficult to identify any significant pattern. Is it possible, though, that under the influence of evolution in the virtual universe, more or less independent processes could evolve that are interactive with the virtual brain aggregate process, and aid in the creature's survival? If evolutionary brains started out very small, as just several neurons, it seems much more possible that processes could spontaneously occur that identified patterns on the realms of these neurons. That process might even resemble today's computer language interpreters, and it could be interpreting the virtual neuronal activity as if it were a language. Such a process would have, or would be capable of, many of the characteristics of a mind, such as setting or selecting neuronal states, although we still haven't accounted for the phenomenon of experience. Somewhere in all the processes and virtual processes does just the right configuration of information occur to create the phenomenon of experience? If so, the forces of evolution may well have enhanced it into mind.

The Problem of Mind:

A problem with creating a lower level universe, a virtual universe, within our universe is how to give consciousness to the beings in it. To create a conscious mind, we need to first create experience, and we discussed several possibilities of how experience might relate to the brain in an earlier section.

One of these was that experience just results as a consequence of the brain activity, that it is an emergent phenomenon. Applying that idea to our virtual universe, the analog is that experience would just appear somehow as a consequence of the information processing performed by the virtual brain. This would suggest that there might be something inherent in information itself, or in the processing or relationships of information, which leads to the phenomenon of experience. Now we saw in an earlier chapter how it might be possible that, given experience already, the brain activity might be able to manipulate it to create consciousness, awareness, and mind, but we had to presuppose experience to imagine this. If we imagine for a moment that it would be possible for experience to result from brain activity, there would be some interesting considerations.

One consideration stems from the notion that the virtual creature's brain is in fact a virtual computer. We have seen that the mind itself, as opposed to, and in addition to the brain, has many of the characteristics of an information system in its own right, one apparently running in the realm of experience. But which universe does the mind as an information system exist in? This is roughly the same as asking from what material, or of what realm is the mind computer composed? The answer is of course *experience*. What we're seeing is that the virtual computer/brain apparently *spawned* a virtual virtual universe (experience) as an emergent phenomenon, in which a virtual virtual computer/mind formed.

An interesting aspect of this, assuming that the mind really does affect the brain, is that the virtual virtual computer/mind, if it were running *inside of* the virtual computer/brain, would indeed have the capability to independently affect the brain, as we saw a few paragraphs back. That affect could then be amplified in the brain's universe by the brain into the actions that give the appearance as coming from the power of choice. If it is the case, however, that the mind somehow resulted from brain activity, then there is a problem with this scenario. We would expect the mind to be able to affect the brain if it were running as a process in a universe running as a process in the brain, but the essence of mind, the universe of experience, does not appear to us as a process running in the brain, but as an emergent process. We have to hypothesize it as mysteriously appearing, and we are once again confronted with the invisible decoder. And once again we might want to consider how that invisible encoder could be accounted for.

We have already suggested the notion that there might be something inherent in information itself, or in the processing of information, that could result in the emergent phenomenon of experience. For the most part, I have treated information simplistically as involving little more than requiring encoding, and requiring a medium on which to encode it. Information theory, though, is a field that was born about the same time as quantum theory, and has also advance tremendously over the last eighty years. There is even some talk that quantum theory and *information theory* may be related. The observable effects of quantum theory are all just information after all. It should not be too surprising if in the end there really does turn out to be a relationship between information and the phenomenon of experience.

Another possible way to account for the invisible decoder is to consider (again) the possibility that it is composed of that other, immaterial, 96% of that universe. Remember, we imagined that only 4% of the stuff of the creature's virtual universe condensed out as something detectable as matter. The remaining 96% is of course intimately linked to and associate with that material 4%. Anything that is constructed from that material 4% is likely to be 96% something else, with only the material 4% of it perceivable, like the tip on an iceberg. There is in this case, therefore, much more to the virtual brain than meets the (virtual) eye. Of course from where we're sitting in our higher level universe, we could read all about it in our computer, but unfortunately, this is still an imaginary situation, so that 96% of virtual stuff is still imaginary too. It might provide the medium for the virtual virtual universe of experience from which the virtual virtual computer of mind might form.

Another possibility would be for experience to come from a higher level universe rather than a lower level universe. In this case, rather than the mind being considered a virtual virtual computer running on a virtual computer/brain, the universe of experience could be coming from a higher level universe, our universe. The virtual universe, and its virtual creatures, are running as processes in our universe after all, and we already know that the matter out of which our computer is composed is only 4% of our universe. Our very own computer could, therefore, be composed of far more than what we can sense, than what meets the eye, our eye. Our computer, along with its processes, could be experiencing away the whole time. If this were the case, it would be entirely possible, even probable, that evolution in the virtual universe would have favored processes accompanied by useful minds.

Yet another possibility is that the higher level universe *is* the universe of experience. This is not quite as far fetched as it might at first sound, since to us experience is the all and only. It's relatively straight forward to arrive at the conclusion that there simply isn't anything else. In this case, our computer, its processes, the virtual universe, and the virtual creatures, are all somehow experience already. We don't have to provide our virtual creatures with experience in this case as, their universe being necessarily composed of experience too, they likely could have evolved minds.

A final way that we might provide our virtual creature with a mind is to provide it ourselves. We already have minds, after all. In this scenario, we would set up our minds somehow to experience the virtual universe, and we would set up our minds to be able to affect the virtual world. The way we might do this today is to put on a helmet with mini TV screens and audio to experience the virtual world, and to affect the virtual world using a joystick, but let's imagine a system much more sophisticated than this. Let's imagine that we can create an interactive correspondence between the virtual neurons in the virtual creature's brain, and the neurons in our own brain. Then, as far as experiencing their universe, we will see what it sees, hear what it hears, and feel what it feels. Since our neuronal activity will be duplicated in the virtual brain, we will be able to control the virtual body and interact with its virtual world that way. So we're talking something along the lines of wiring our brains directly into our computer, something like in the original movie Matrix.

In this case, we of course would provide, would be, the mind of the creature in the virtual universe. We would only be able to sense the realms that his senses sense. We would have no knowledge of any other universes, or that what seemed to be our universe was actually a process running on a computer in a higher level universe. We would not be able to detect the computer that we, our creature body process, was running on. There would be nothing in our perceived universe to account for mind at all. It would just magically be there, and although there is indeed a decoder/connection up in our higher level universe, it would be completely and permanently hidden from us as we could not perceive anything beyond the virtual universe we could sense.

A brain scientist in this virtual universe, studying the brains and brain activity of the creatures there, would discover that their brains represented information, and accounted for all of the information that they experienced…but the buck would stop there. There would be no clue of how this information was decoded into the experience of it that they had. The *experiencer*, after all, would not be within their universe. It would be impossible to account for the mind from the physics of their universe, the mind actually being in a higher level universe.

- Brain activity will correlate closely to what is being experienced.

- There will be no mechanism perceivable as to how brain activity became experience.

- Experience and mind will be unexplainable from the physics of their universe.

Collapsing to a single reality:

Somewhere in all this, something is collapsing all of our puzzle solver's potential futures and pasts onto a single reality. It may be something inherent in experience itself that dictates that we, as virtual creatures, can experience only a single reality. It is hard to imagine actually experiencing multiple realities simultaneously. Or if there is an *experiencer*, it might be something inherent in its construction or functioning that dictates that only a single reality is experienced. I'm assuming that the virtual brain, as an object of the virtual reality, can itself proceed into multiple futures, so I am not looking for the source of the collapse to be inherent to the virtual brain.

Rather than bemoaning our lack of knowledge as to experience and the collapse, it may be more constructive to consider what we do know about our virtual universe and imaginary situation. (We're beating around the bush again hoping to figure out something about the bush.) We do know that we experience only a single reality, that is, we do know that the multiple potentials are reduced to a single instance for experience. Now we need to ask ourselves if we know of anything in this whole setup *that even has the power* to make this happen.

We must consider first of all that the virtual universe is a process running on our computer. That process is running one universe up from the virtual universe. Certainly the computer that the process is running on has the capability to collapse the process onto a single reality. We must also take into account here that the processes running on the computer have the capability to affect the computer, so that means every universe, sub-universe, or even creatures in any of these universes potentially have the capability to indirectly cause the collapse, since they are all, in the end, processes running on the top level computer.

Another potential source is anything outside of the computer, i.e., in the computer's universe. We could be sitting there with a mouse for example selecting the potential futures we want, figuratively of course. In any of these cases, since the collapse is coming from processes running on the computer in a higher level universe, and since the process that causes the collapse is outside of the physics of the creature's virtual universe, the cause of the collapse will never be perceivable, only that the collapse has occurred at some point.

- The mechanism of the collapse of potentials onto a single potential is not perceivable.

If, for demonstration purposes, we proceed for the remainder of this discussion with the scenario where we're actually wired into the computer, then our minds might be choosing the future directly. In this scenario, recall that there is something close to a one-to-one interactive mapping between my neurons, say, in this universe, and the virtual creatures neurons in the virtual universe. Consider the programming considerations if this were the case.

The creature, and its brain, is driven by the virtual universe process, the puzzle solver. In that universe, the creature has multiple potentials just like every other object therein. The brain of this creature will be receiving information via its sense organs, but it will be receiving information from the progression of several potential futures, so the brain will be in a state of representing all of these potentials. If I want to introduce a mind into this scenario, the first thing I notice is that this seems to be tailor made for the introduction of *choice, the choice of the multiple brain potentials*. It's unlikely that I could have come up with a more ideal configuration to work from to give a mind the ability to manipulate that virtual universe.

Weak minds and strong minds:

Let's say that for the purpose of imagining this, my brain is now hardwired into the computer and my connection is matched up to a creature's brain. Let's also say that my brain is now completely driven by the brain activity of the virtual brain, the point being that my brain is not doing any thinking on its own. All the thoughts and feelings I have will now be generated from the neuronal activity of the virtual brain. My mind will now be experiencing what is going on in the virtual brain. In addition, if the mind really is able to interact intentionally with the brain, then my *mind*, being able to affect my brain, will now be able to affect the creature's brain in the virtual universe to that degree.

We now have two choices as to how to manage the effect the mind has on the virtual brain. In one case, we can limit the mind to simply the ability to select one of the existing potential states of the virtual brain from the existing field of potential states created by the puzzle solver driver. Let's call this kind of mind the *weak mind*. In the other, the mind will actually have the power to set the brain into a *new* state, one that wasn't one of the preexisting states created by the puzzle solver driving the virtual universe. Let's call this kind of mind the *strong mind*.

Let's see how the weak mind would work. For demonstration purposes, let's make the weak mind the simplest possible. Let's limit it to the simple ability to mechanistically select the potential that *feels the most desirable*. That will be all that it can do. If it has two potentials available and one is more desirable than the other, it will mechanically always choose the more desirable.

Remember that the virtual brain is really an extremely complex virtual computer that is processing information in extremely complex ways. As information comes in, it will trigger certain thoughts. These thoughts will trigger other, usually related, associated thoughts. The weak mind will be happily riding along, continuously choosing which thoughts will be realized from the field of potential thoughts that the virtual brain is continuously generating. The weak mind will thus have the power to steer the creature's thoughts quite effectively in whichever direction it finds desirability, so given a brain with sufficient thought generative power, the weak mind will have the power to direct thinking. Interestingly, this seems too to satisfy the criteria for that mysterious but useful mental phenomenon of *directed attention*.

If the creature is involved in an experiment where it is told to watch a rotating disk and to note the position of the disk at the moment it decides to move its arm, as it sits there watching the disk, its virtual brain will be continuously generating both potentials, to move its arm **and** to not move its arm, but the weak mind will at first be selecting the potential of not moving the arm. At some point, though, it will become desirable to move the arm, and the weak mind will choose the already existing potential where the arm has been preparing to move, and at that moment the creature will also notice the position of the disk. The experimenter will of course be befuddled, because the *history* of the reality that was chosen by our creature will show that *its arm had prepared to move* just prior to the creature's decision to move it.

And if the creature is trying to choose between restaurants that are equally desirable, it will not be able to until a thought occurs that gives one restaurant more desirability than the other. In this case, it will become desirable to generate just such a thought, so thinking will be directed in this direction.

Remember too that the weak mind doesn't generate the feelings themselves, including the all important feeling of desirability. All feelings experienced will be generated from neuronal activity in the brain, including the feeling of desirability. In this scenario, the brain at first appears to be effectively driven by whatever it is that generates the feeling of desirability, which is necessarily the brain itself since the brain generates all feelings. We are going to take it as axiomatic, though, that it is the **experience** *of desirability* itself that drives the process, not the brain activity that underlies the experience, and we are going to take that as an axiom from the simple consideration that if it was mindless brain activity that generated the selection, the associated feeling might just as well be undesirability as desirability, at least some of the time. Despite the fact that it may appear that the brain is doing all of the computation, implicit here is that the weak mind has minimally the computational ability of a primitive comparator, being able to compare two desires and choose the greater. If this reasoning has merit, we do indeed have the beginnings of a rudimentary information processing system up in the realm of experience.

The next level of complexity to be considered for the weak mind appears when we consider that the feelings being compared are not just simply degrees of desirability. The weak mind seems to be able to compare just about any two feelings for desirability. It can not only compare the taste of an apple to the taste of an orange to see which one is currently more desirable, but it can compare the taste of an apple to the thought of doing homework and determine which one is more desirable. More familiarly perhaps, it can compare the taste of a piece of cheesecake to the thought of being thin and decide which one is more desirable. In this case, however, it is not absolutely necessary that this comparison take place in the mind. This comparison might very well be taking place in the brain, with the brain only needing to activate the neurons indicating the desirability of each, and the weak mind will simply pick the more desirable based on the brain's results.

The potential complexity of the weak mind as an information system seems to range from the most rudimentary simple comparator to the complexity of the brain itself if it is actually able to compare the feelings associated with every thought. The brain may generate every feeling, but the weak mind may process every feeling. We have seen, however, that what looks like the processing of feelings can also be done by the brain, so it appears that it's possible for the brain and the mind to be two interacting systems able to trade off functionality. It all depends on which one is performing which processes.

Further discussion of the weak mind as an information system extends beyond the scope of this book, but it is beginning to look as if the weak mind might be able to account for just about all the mind/brain phenomena we can come up with. Is there any reason to suspect that we should even pursue the case for the strong mind?

The strong mind is usually what we imagine when we envision free will, and it will have a huge advantage over the weak mind. For one thing, it will have the capability to generate feelings and actions more or less directly. The strong mind will be able to generate desirability directly by setting new brain states. As an information processor interacting with the brain, it would be much more powerful and efficient. It could activate previously inactive neurons, generating new neuronal activity as well as new thoughts and feelings. It would not have to choose from only the potentials generated by the puzzle solver, but could actually introduce new states of the virtual brain that the puzzle solver would now have to pick up on and drive forward in the virtual universe.

At first glance, it may seem that a strong mind, introducing new brain states in the universe, will create new challenges for the puzzle solver, those stated being outside of the potentials offered up by the virtual universe, but I don't think this will be the case. Since the new states that the strong mind sets are limited to the virtual brain, this will not seem to interfere with the puzzle solvers potential solutions too much. It will behave much like *new input* to any computational system, which will pick it up and drive it from there. It's not like, given a strong mind, we will see miraculous behavior, like flying or something. If the puzzle solver is challenged somehow by the strong mind, it may come into play with the introduction of *multiple* strong minds, now all having to be coordinated beyond the scope of the puzzle solvers initial coordination of potentials. Then again, if that creates a challenge, it may be that the same challenge is created by the introduction of multiple weak minds selecting existent potential states, but now potentially in conflict with each other.

One consideration that seems to argue against the strong mind is the requirement that the neuronal states that it sets must be in agreement with what is happening and what is possible in the virtual universe. It would, for example, now have the potential to activate the neuronal state of seeing a lion coming towards us when in fact it was just our pet cat. There are two ways though that this could be handled. One is by evolution. Those creatures whose minds were not restricted to setting states compatible with the universe would most likely have perished, so it is likely that some sort of constraint mechanism would have evolved. The other is simply that it *wasn't* completely handled. We do indeed seem to have people among us who perceive things that are incompatible with reality. I suspect though that since drugs seem to be able to improve these people, that the manifestation is physical, i.e., neuronal, or brain based.

Another consideration that seems to argue against the strong mind is the *moving arm experiment*. In the case of the strong mind, if the mind is setting a new brain state to move the arm at the time that the will wills it, the history of the arm should not be seen to have prepared to move prior to the decision, as it will be in the case of the weak mind. The weak mind selects from preexisting potential states, but the strong mind generates new states at will. But is there any phenomenon that I know of that might require a strong mind, which is not achievable by the weak mind?

Initially I thought that the mental action of *trying* to do something might be just such a phenomenon, particularly the state of **trying really hard** (TRH we'll call it). We can TRH to do any number of things, and frequently it is involved with learning new things. We can TRH to lift a heavy weight. We can TRH to accurately shoot a basketball, or do a back flip. We can TRH to think of something, or TRH to remember something. We can TRH to figure something out. We can even TRH to fly, but alas, success with TRH seems to be limited to within the mind/brain and body and doesn't extend to the external universe.

Now first of all, TRH requires a motivation, i.e., the action already has to be desirable, and we have already presupposed that that can be set by neuronal activity of the brain. In some cases, TRH seems to be an attempt to focus our thoughts and eliminate unwanted thoughts, but we have also seen that it appears that directing attention can be done by a weak mind. From these considerations I suspect that TRH can be accounted for with a weak mind, although this little discussion doesn't completely justify that conclusion at this time.

More than choice:

There is a problem with all the foregoing that needs to be stated. I have been stating throughout the book that one of the most basic tenants of the universe is that it be consistent with itself, and that one of the most basic tenants of the (useful) mind is that its *mental representations* of the universe be minimally consistent with the universe. This is rather straightforwardly asserting that it does make a difference what that *mental representation* is, since we use this representation to make life and death decisions. Our mental representation of the universe is experienced, and our decisions, while including the aspect of *desirability*, are largely based on the experience of this mental representation too. However, if all that were involved here were the weak mind choosing desirability, we wouldn't seem to need a *mental representation* of the universe at all. All we would need would be a sense of *desirability* that we could intentionally pursue, and the brain could blindly do all of the rest. I have already allowed that the overwhelming statistical correlation between what feels good being good for us, and what feels bad being bad for us, be allowed to show that feelings must play a role somehow in our decision making process. It seems then that I must also allow that the *consistency* of our mental representation of the universe with the universe, shows that our *mental representation* of the universe plays a role in our decision making process.

It has been stated, of course, throughout the book that the mind consists of experience, that experience is all there is. What we have been describing previously in regards to the weak and strong mind, is simply the *intentional* aspect of the mind, just the decision making aspect. The fact, though, that the mental representation makes a difference in our decision making process, implies that the experience of the mental representation itself makes a difference in desirability, that the determination of the desirability of any given image is also determined by the mind (vs. brain), not just the simple comparison between two states of desirability. We have been presuming that all feelings come off of network representations in the brain. If this is true, then the *feeling of desirability* associated with a mental representation is also represented in the brain as an activated network of neurons somewhere. Is the mind then setting the state of this *desirability* network of neurons too? This would be a strong mind.

All of this once again raises the concept that the complexity of the mind is approaching the complexity of the neuronal activity that seems to generate those feelings and images, and this once again raises the concept that the brain activity, and the corresponding mind, may somehow be one and the same thing.

Perceiving his world

The way we have imagined it, our physicist creature has evolved to perceive a material world similar to ours. The information about his universe retrieved from his senses is represented in his virtual brain as aggregate objects, where it is perceived as such. The information that his senses retrieve, however, is nothing but effects, little differences on the realms that they had evolved to detect. His brain is creating the representation of objects not from objects, not from things, but from differences. From a vantage point as programmers in the higher universe, we will know that there aren't really any objects in his universe. We will see the numbers changing on the realms he is sensing. These changes are of course just differences, and it's easy to see that his perception of materiality and space are strictly illusions based on the processing his brain performs on the information the senses send to it.

As he investigates his world more deeply, though, that materiality is an illusion becomes evident. At the point where objects become too small to be detected directly or indirectly by his senses, they effectively disappear. He will now rely on measuring instruments to replace his senses, but they too must depend on, and measure only the differences occurring on the realms they are designed to measure. His measuring instruments do not return information about objects, because the perception of objects is generated only in his brain, and the instruments are not attached to a brain. In fact, they become encoder/decoder devices that translate the information of the effects of the microworld into something he can sense. The results of these measurements will be discovered to exhibit certain consistencies, and these will be captured and iterated as laws of nature, albeit unexplained laws, and perhaps mathematically. What will the mathematics discovered tell him about the true algorithm of his puzzle-solver driven universe? The mathematics he discovers will turn out to be at least one step removed from the puzzle solver's rules, and is not the algorithm itself, but rather is designed to capture the behavior of the algorithm after the fact.

He will eventually reach the bottom level of the realms used to represent his universe, beyond which he cannot go, and there will be nothing there. There will be no ground that he can stand on. That's because the ground that his virtual universe is standing on is in another universe, the higher level universe, a universe that is utterly undetectable to him. There is thus more to the physicist himself than he can detect. His particles are not just the values represented in his universe. His particles are each processes, and together they constitute a massive aggregate process in another universe, a universe undetectable to him.

As his research continued, he may have eventually deduced that his universe was running inside of an information system of some sort. We made his universe to be similar to ours so we could imagine it, but of course it need not have been at all similar. It would have been entirely possible to create that universe with completely different types of realms, puzzle solvers, etc. In that case, his evolved imagination would be limited to what his virtual brain was capable of representing of this totally strange and different universe, and he would be utterly unable to imagine a higher level universe like ours in which the computer was imbedded. Universes may be utterly different from level to level.

At first glance, it looks like the closest he can get to understanding that higher level universe is what he can deduce about the algorithm that is driving his universe. It may even be possible to deduce the algorithm and from that, some aspects of the higher level computer, but he may be able to do better than that. Everything in his universe is just processes running on our computer, which may give him some power to manipulate the computer, and thus other processes in it. If so, let's hope he doesn't accidentally figure out how to crash it.

There are two major phenomena that our virtual physicist hasn't accounted for at all, the collapse of the multiple potentials onto a single outcome, and experience and mind, and that will leave him scratching his head. It may be that the coincident missing explanations has a cause. As set up in this imaginary scenario, experience, and thus his mind came from a different universe, a higher level universe, and thus are utterly unaccounted for by the physics and behavior of his universe. We have also seen that the collapse must necessarily occur in the computer, which is itself in a higher level universe, and thus may also be beyond his ken. If it does turn out that it is experience that is causing the collapse in the computer, will our physicist wonder if this implies that the computer, and perhaps the higher level universe itself, might be somehow composed of the stuff of, of the realm of, experience?

Our creature scientists, who perceive their universe to be a material universe remember, have made quite a few interesting and unexplained discoveries about their universe that have left them scratching their collective heads. All of these phenomena result from the fact that their universe is just information symbolically represented inside of a computer, in addition to the idiosyncrasies of the consistency puzzle-solving algorithm. Let's look at them one last time, and how they come about. We will be seeing all of them again.

- materiality evaporates into abstraction somewhere before the bottom level

  cause: there is nothing there, only information calculated within the computer

- the bottom level of the universe is described by formal rules

  cause: rules deduced to capture the behavior of the puzzle solver

- space doesn't exist as space in the microworld

  cause: location is just an aspect realm of a particle

- a particle, or object, seems to move forward through multiple potential futures simultaneously

  cause: the puzzle-solver pursues multiple potential/allowable outcomes

- randomness of the potentials is maximized for a single, non-interactive particle

  cause: puzzle solutions are not restricted prior to particle interactions

- the universe of potentials is a multiverse

  cause: prior to collapse, the puzzle-solver pursues multiple histories and futures

- the more particles that interact and entangle, the fewer the potentials

  cause: potential solutions for the puzzle-solver are reduced with each interaction

- a particle has multiple histories, and an experimenter can pick which one becomes real

  cause: the puzzle solver will keep the history consistent with an event

- particles seem to behave as information only and don't need to exist between interactions

  cause: the particle representation doesn't exist in the computer between collapse points

- particles lose their individual existence and do not maintain unique identities

  cause: particle representations are generated anew, and only at collapse points

- particles have some method of interacting instantaneously across any distance

  cause: inside the computer there is no distance, and time is desynchronized

- the bottom level of the universe is only the effects detected

  cause: information is carried only as the difference it makes on a realm

- the abstract representation of the universe predicts phenomena not apparent to their senses, and

- the abstractions predict phenomena more accurately than their perceptions

  cause: their universe is abstract, and mental representations are virtually generated

- their world is deterministic

  cause: computer processing is deterministic

- a microscopic discreteness to the values that their realms can take

  cause: symbolic representation of quantities must be limited in accuracy

- an uncertainty related to this discreteness that is mysteriously maintained by their universe

  cause: the universe maintains the accumulated error resulting from the limit of accuracy

- they appear to just exist out of nothing

  cause: they cannot detect the computer on which their process is running

- the mechanism of the collapse of potentials onto a single potential is not perceivable

  cause: It occurs in the higher level computer, outside of their detectable universe.

- brain activity will correlate closely to what is being experienced.

- there will be no mechanism perceivable as to how brain activity became experience.

- experience and mind will be unexplainable from the physics of their universe.

  cause: The *experiencer* exists outside of their universe and is thus undetectable to them.

Section 5
The Information System Paradigm

$\circ \ \circ$

The difficulty lies, not in the new ideas, but in escaping the old ones, which ramify, for those brought up as most of us have been, in every corner of our minds.

—*John Maynard Keynes*

Chapter 16
Our Computerized Universe

We have found a strange footprint
on the shores of the unknown.

—*Sir Arthur Eddington, (1882–1944)*

It is with some sense of trepidation that I begin this chapter. The reason is that the book is in many ways complete without it, and indeed is about much more than just this chapter. Most of what I know, think, can reason out, or speculate about has already been said. This has been largely a visit to ideas many of which are not new after all, and some have been floating around for two-and-a-half millennia already. And the previous section on virtual universes in computers, while involving imagination, is a legitimate thought experiment and, therefore, valid to that degree. (Or at least admitted fantasy.)

The reader who has not picked up on the implications of the previous chapter, though, is surely not among the living. I do not believe that even the staunchest materialist wouldn't agree that the book is now committed to this course, and that I am thus honor bound to carry through the logic to its conclusion. How disappointing it would be to stop the book here and not make that final little logical step. I am sure so many readers are poised to do so already, even if against their better judgment.

There is at least one more reason though why I want to explore the central idea of this chapter. It is that in some sense humanity seems to be craving a look at it. We all know about the *Matrix* series of movies, and others, and I have referenced David Deutsch's book *The Fabric of Reality*. Scientists themselves have, however, been murmuring over the similarities of the universe to an information system for well over two decades now, probably more since that's only when I picked up on it. We will examine some of these ideas that are circulating within the scientific community before this chapter is through.

So without further delay, let's take that last little step and ask the big question.

Is *our* universe just a virtual universe running inside of some sort of information system? Is it possible that our physical bodies are just virtual creatures living inside of a fabulous computer?

Our universe in a computer:

(The bullet points that follow are extracted directly from the list of phenomena that the creatures observed from their virtual universe in Chapter 15.)

Let's imagine that it is so! Let's imagine that the universe around us is not real. Let's imagine that we are the creatures of the previous chapter, creatures whose minds exist somehow *outside* of the information system we are experiencing and investigating. Let's imagine that like them, our minds are somehow in direct contact, and interact with, the information system that drives our universe. Imagine if you must, that you are some sort of being reclining in a higher level universe with wires running from your head to a computer that is supplying your senses with a virtual universe, this universe, the universe we live in. (But only if you must, because that certainly is not the mechanism.) This is tantamount to imagining that we're plugged into a virtual reality, as in the movie *Matrix*. The next question is, if our physicists and philosophers are investigating the bottom level physics of a computer driven virtual reality (physicists in the Matrix, say), what have they found? Will they be able to tell that our world is just computer generated? Will they be able to figure out that our reality isn't really real at all?

For more than two thousand years now, our deepest thinkers have noticed that there is a mysterious universe of logic and abstraction behind the material world that is in some way more real than the material world we perceive. This was, of course, initially the Greek Logos, which was discussed in Section One. The Greeks even noticed a structure to Logos, something we now call the Platonic Form, which was a way to represent each individual abstraction itself as information, and this Platonic Form is remarkably similar to the oop objects that we use in computers today to represent abstractions.

We have seen that many of these abstractions result from the way the brain parses and represents information received from the outside world as overlapping networks of neurons, but there is a more pure type of abstraction too, the relational abstractions captured by mathematics, geometry, and logic that go beyond strictly brain based abstractions for objects. When we represent these abstractions with symbols and manipulate them according to the discovered rules, we are able to capture the behavior of the universe to an astonishing degree of accuracy. That this should be so was a huge surprise to the thinkers of the era surrounding Isaac Newton, and the reason that it is true has remained a mystery since that time. Symbol manipulation is of course all that a virtual reality is composed of.

And these manipulations of these symbols as the basis of our universe were discovered to be utterly mindless. Indeed, it was discovered that they can be duplicated, that the behavior of our universe can be duplicated, by programming a simple typesetting machine to mindlessly move symbols around. At the most fundamental level, the behavior of our universe can be captured by symbols and their manipulation, and this is exactly what computers do. This is only what computers do. We know of other things that are able to do this, like our brains, but in the end, they turn out to be computers, or information systems too. In the end, then, the only things we know of that can accurately duplicate the behavior of our universe are computers, symbol manipulators, or information systems.

By the late 1800's, it had become apparent to our (virtual) physicists that the purely symbolic representation of our universe predicted its behavior more accurately than the universe of our perception. By the early 1900's, the mathematics and logic was predicting phenomena that contradicted our perceptions, our idea of space and the material world altogether, signaling that the material worldview, our perception, was somehow obviously incorrect. We reviewed a few of these incomprehensible phenomena in Section Two, *What's the Matter With Matter?*, and they included:

- space can shrink and expand

- supposedly solid matter can shrink and expand, even shrink right out of existence

- there is matter that can pass right through other matter unaffected, including us

- particles may vanish and mysteriously rematerialize on the other side of a wall

- someone's death can occur twice in your lifetime

These are not phenomena that jive with our everyday idea of our material world, but if all of this is just computer driven, if all of this is just information inside of a computer, just a virtual reality, any of the above become possible. Just like the creatures in their virtual universe, our virtual physicists in our virtual universe have discovered that:

- the abstract representation of the universe predicts phenomena not apparent to our senses

- the abstractions predict phenomena more accurately than our perceived material universe

As scientists probed deeper into the microworld, into the foundations of our virtual world, it was discovered that the particles they had imagined to be down there didn't really need to exist at all, and that all that was necessary to describe it was the Formal logic and mathematics.

- the bottom level of the universe is described by formal rules

Eventually, our physicists deduced, to everyone's horror, and resulting from a somewhat desperate attempt to fudge the mathematics to fit the facts, that the smallest quantities of the measurements of the universe were not continuous, but discreet. They were quantized. And it was discovered that there was a corresponding uncertainty in the values derived from these, and associated with the possible measurements at this level, which was closely related to the size or this discreetness. Like creatures in a computerized universe, physicists in our universe discovered:

- a microscopic discreteness to the values that their realms can take

- an uncertainty related to this discreteness that is mysteriously maintained by the universe

which ushered in the era of *quantum* physics. With the development of quantum physics, it became established that the particles at the foundation of our universe are somehow not composed of anything material at all, that at the bottom level only the recorded effect of an act of measurement is even knowable. Physicists probing the foundations of a virtual reality must necessarily find that, and did find that:

- materiality evaporates into abstraction somewhere before the bottom level

- the bottom level of the universe is only the effects detected there

- they (and the universe) appear to just exist out of nothing

Since there is no materiality in the microworld, the values that could be measured became abstracted and the computable aspect realms were identified, and these included the particle's location (configuration space) and time. As must be true of a universe represented only as information, physicists discovered that:

- space is just one of the abstracted aspect realms of a particle, and doesn't exist as space

Physicists then discovered that, unlike in the macroworld where objects have a single existence, and only a single future, particles in the microworld seemed to be allowed a variety of potential futures, only one of which eventually was realized, and each of these futures occurred with a certain, determinant, probability. There was no other known aspect of the universe that related to, or which affected these probabilities, and they appeared to be independent and random to that degree. Like our puzzle-solver running in a PC, scientists deduced that:

- a particle, or object, seems to move forward through multiple potential futures simultaneously

- the quantum world is deterministic

The mathematics that turned out to describe these multiple potential futures of a particle turned out to be the mathematics that describe waves. A wave that was unaffected by other waves demonstrated the highest degree of variability or freedom, but as the multiple waves of multiple particles entangled and interacted, the randomness became more and more reduced. Again, like a puzzle-solving algorithm driving a virtual universe, the microworld demonstrated that:

- of those multiple potential futures, randomness is maximized for a single, non-interactive particle

- the more particles that interact and entangle their waves, the fewer the potentials

The discovery that the elements of the universe had multiple potential futures, gave rise to the notion that perhaps all potentials continued to exist all together somehow in developing parallel universes, and the idea of the multiverse was born.

- the universe of potentials is a multiverse

It was then realized that between the times that an experimenter was making measurements, the particle aspect of measurement need not exist as particles at all, only as intermingling waves. As soon as the experimenter looked again, however, the particles would magically rematerialize, even sometimes on the other side of a wall. The waves represented the information that was knowable about the particles between the times anyone looked, but in between times, the particle's identities merged right along with their mingled waves. It was thus no longer possible to decide if one of the new materialized particles was the same as one of the old dematerialized particles from the previous measurement. It was discovered that like a virtual universe represented within an information system:

- particles seem to behave as information only and don't need to exist between interactions

- particles lose their individual existence and do not maintain unique identities

Since the wave mathematics that describes a particle in a virtual reality also describes the particles of the measuring device that is making the measurement, physicists were amazed to discover that the mathematics implied that by altering the measuring device well after an experiment had begun, they could apparently go back in time and change the history of the particle involved in the experiment. These mathematical predictions were eventually verified with actual experiments. Like in a puzzle-solving algorithm running in a time-decoupled universe:

- a particle is capable of multiple histories, and an experimenter can pick which one becomes real

It was further implied by the mathematics that an entangled wave function, if not yet collapsed to a single potential, could stretch across all of space, and that collapsing the wave for a particle at one end would instantly collapse the wave for any entangled particles across all of space. This seemed to violate the relativistic notion that information in the universe could not travel faster than the speed of light. Again, like a puzzle-solving algorithm running in a spaceless, time-decoupled virtual universe where there is no real space at all, physicists deduced that:

- particles have some method of interacting instantaneously across any distance

Scientists have found no mechanism or reason for the multiple potentials to collapse onto a single potential, and this phenomenon is still completely unexplained. Like a virtual reality where the computer that collapses the potentials is necessarily in a higher level universe, and therefore undetectable, our physicists have found that:

- the mechanism of the collapse of potentials onto a single potential is not perceivable

And brain researchers, analyzing the encoder/decoders of our sensory organs and brain, are able to explain how the brain represents information as networks of neurons, but are totally unable to explain how this representation is decoded to our experience of it. Like creatures somehow plugged into a virtual universe, information about that universe seems to stop at the brain. Somehow, the information represented on the brain is being experienced, but the decoder, and indeed the *experiencer* itself, are completely undetectable from within this, our virtual universe.

Our brains are virtual brains in a virtual universe. Information is represented in our virtual brains as activated networks of neurons, but our experience of the information represented on these networks of neurons is not accounted for. In the scenario we are imagining here, our brains in this universe are just abstract information in a computer existing in a higher-level universe, and which our *experiencer* is somehow connected to. We would be experiencing only the information from the lower level universe. We would not be able to see that the information represented on the brain was being somehow interpreted in a higher-level universe as our experience of it. Frustrated brain researchers have discovered that:

- Brain activity will correlate closely to what is being experienced.

- There will be no mechanism perceivable as to how brain activity becomes experience.

- Experience and mind will be unexplainable from the physics of this universe.

The I. S. paradigm:

As we saw in the previous chapter, all of these mysterious phenomena resulted from the two considerations that the virtual universe was represented symbolically in an information system, as well as the nature of the puzzle solver, and now we see that physicists are observing almost the identical phenomena as character-istics of our very own universe. These are phenomena that on the one hand result form the I. S. representation of a universe. It is thus a legitimate statement to say that to this degree, the universe we live in *acts like* it is an I. S. representation of a universe. This is not to say that there might not be other causes for the observed phenomena of our universe, but it is still a correct observation to note that as far as these phenomena are concerned, our universe exhibits behavior similar to a computerized universe. This correspondence between observation and model is what a paradigm does, and this is really, in the end, as close as any paradigm can get to the true reality.

We saw earlier in the book how it seems to be inevitable that all paradigms should fail eventually, inevitably to be replaced by a better fitting paradigm at some future time. After a paradigm gains acceptance, it invariably begins to accu-mulate little glitches over time, phenomena that it cannot account for, and this is exactly what has been happening to the *material world paradigm*. It may seem strange at first to call our perception of the material world just another paradigm, but indeed that's exactly what it is. We are making assumptions about the world, and these assumptions give a foundation to, and provide a framework and expla-nation for everything we know. In this case, the assumptions are that there are space and objects out there, material objects, and that our senses and brains and minds are accurately representing this materiality to us. Through all of our other paradigms, the unconscious assumptions of materiality have survived without the necessity to be altered. Materiality as a paradigm has been very powerful and use-ful. Evolution did well by us.

But over the last couple of centuries, phenomena have been noticed, and accu-mulated, which the material world paradigm is truly unable to account for, phe-nomena that utterly violates the concept of materiality. Indeed, quantum physics constitutes a considerable part of the phenomena that are unexplained under the material world paradigm. It should be evident simply on rational grounds, simply from our knowledge of the behavior of failing paradigms, that it is now inevitable that the material world paradigm has to go. No matter what paradigm we eventu-ally replace it with, whether it be an I. S. universe paradigm, or some other para-digm, the material world paradigm simply cannot account for recent discoveries, and is now failing us.

And now that we're actually letting go of materiality, as always we can look back and see the lengths to which philosophers have had to go to preserve it. For millennia now, they have been seeing, and indeed expressing, evidence that the material world is an illusion, and particularly in the last four centuries. In every case, though, (with the exception of George Berkeley), after they've uttered their observations, they find it necessary to hedge their comments by stating something to the effect that they are not saying that the material world doesn't exist, despite the fact that what they have just said might be interpreted that way. I would think that it should be evident by now that what they have been saying over and over is that the material world doesn't exist, despite their continuously hedging that it does. So strong is our belief in the material world, that we are reluctant to let it go even when it's rationally obvious that we should. This is why the first three sections of this book were dedicated to demonstrating to the reader not only that the discoveries of physics contradict the notion of materiality, but also to explaining how it is even possible that we have an erroneous notion of materiality at all, that is, that it is all a mental representation that is necessarily just a virtual representation *anyway*.

Physicists are a reluctant lot when it comes to entertaining new ideas, even when those new ideas come from within the physics community in the form of eigenfunctions, Hamiltonians, and Lagrangians and the like. Indeed, *reluctant* is an understatement, so it is, therefore, a grand understatement to say that asking physicists to seriously entertain the idea that their universe is represented inside of some kind of information system is asking an awfully lot. There is an avenue, however, via which even physicists may ultimately end up at a similar conclusion, indeed may already have ended up at a similar conclusion.

Physicists have for some time now recognized that when they speak of the universe they are speaking of it in terms of information. There is even currently ongoing research that seems to be realizing the startling potential of deriving the major equations of physics from the more basic considerations of information theory. (See Appendix A.) There was even an article recently in a general science magazine that discussed the universe itself as a computational system, and derived the computational power of the universe, thereby demonstrating that it can be treated as such. Now, once one lets go of the idea of materiality and space, the only thing left is *information*. In this sense, the universe is indeed some kind of information system by default, if information is all there is to it, if that is the only word left. And this information is definitely not just a collection of noise or garbage. It is very ordered, consistent, and its behavior can be mimicked with computers. To this degree, I think physicists are already *entertaining the idea* that the universe is, in some way, an information system.

The toughest part to accept is of course the analogy of the universe with the desktop PC. Is there really that great of a similarity inherent within information systems themselves, that a simple universe programmed into a PC would necessarily demonstrate characteristics essentially identical to the information system that is our universe? Does the little quantum really result from a finite accuracy essential in the symbolic, non-analog representation of quantities in all information systems, i.e., is the universe really digital? Is the Heisenberg Uncertainty Principle really possibly related to the maintenance of that error in our little pretend universe? It's a lot to ask, to ask someone to consider this. But then one might think it's a lot to ask too, to consider all of those corresponding bullet points above to be just a series of coincidences.

Well, what is out there if it's not the material world? Why do we have to eat food to stay alive, or go to work every day? The answer is that it's all there, just not the way we perceive it. It's all there, with the exception of your perception of it. There is no blue, or sweet, or space, or ham sandwich. That's all an experiential virtual reality. It in fact all exists, though, but as information, immaterial and spaceless. The food you consume is just ethereal information, differences on a realm, but then again so are you, so it shouldn't be too surprising that your ethereal information body can gain sustenance from consuming other ethereal information. Of course if your body, composed of little differences, doesn't consume and interact with those little differences you call food, the information that is your body information will change in a way that it will cease to interact altogether as a living thing, and it will decease. So please don't feel that letting go of materiality in any way warrants, or justifies, a change of life style.

Our new handle into reality:

The computerized universe paradigm at least gives us some way to think about the unexplained phenomena of relativistic and quantum physics, i.e., it gives us a mental handle on it. This is one thing a paradigm is supposed to do. With the rise of the identification of the clock-like, mechanical properties of the universe, humanity began to think of nature as mechanistic. The quantum paradigm never actually caught on with the public, mainly because we were never able to come up with a mental analogy that matched its phenomena, but now with the information system analogy, we may want to move to that as a new paradigm. Of course, it may quickly become apparent that none of the conclusions or analogies derived from the I. S. paradigm hold up, in which case it will be immediately abandoned. On the other hand, it may turn out that we are able to advance our knowledge, and tighten our grip on the phenomena of universes, information systems, and minds, in which case the paradigm may linger for awhile until it is replaced by a superior paradigm. The information system universe seems, at first blush at least, to potentially provide us with a means of accounting for many known but unexplained phenomena, as detailed above. We need now to examine, under the I. S. paradigm, some of the other concepts that we struggle with.

Probably one of the earliest concepts that any young thinker struggles with is infinity. Infinity violates what the brain is capable of imagining, and this of course includes infinite materiality and an infinite universe. We cannot imagine infinite space, infinite numbers, infinite anything. There has even been discussion among advanced mathematicians as to whether infinity is ever realized in the universe or not. Does infinite anything ever really exist? The mathematicians have discovered that it is certainly a necessary participant in their representation of reality, so in some sense it must exist. Once we have relinquished our dependence on materiality and spatiality, however, the idea of a symbolic infinity becomes much more user friendly. We don't need to imagine infinite space anymore, for example. Once we assign infinity to a simple symbolic representation in an information system, it becomes even easier to accept.

And there are other concepts that behave similarly and for similar reasons, the idea of higher dimensions for example. All of those crazy examples back in Chapter 6, that space and matter can stretch and shrink, the variability of the rate of time, that there are different kinds of space, multiple universes coexisting, even the Big Bang creating the universe from nothing, now each seem a little easier to comprehend and are at least partially accounted for if all of this is just symbols in an information system.

We now know what that probability wave is made of, that wave that seems to carry the potentials of all the particles and didn't seem to be made of anything physical. Now it doesn't have to have some sort of physical reality. It is simply a process. Particles lose their identities? We've seen multiple times in this book that as information an object's identity is mutable, and not absolute. As for the magic of disembodied particles appearing on the other side of walls, it no longer seems like magic. If quantum operators are simply processes, *computer functions*, then of course they're not going to be commutative. That the universe seems to have a look-ahead capability loses its mysteriousness too. Computer Science students have been doing it for decades programming with their DFAs and NFAs, their Deterministic and Nondeterministic Finite Automatons. Look-ahead capability is relatively easy to achieve in an information system.

As we begin to apply the new paradigm of the universe as information, even science fiction stuff takes on a certain plausibility, *Star Trek* type transporters, for example. If materiality doesn't exist and we are just information to start with, it's now not so hard to imagine that it might be possible to convert us back and forth between different representations of information on different mediums, encoder/decoders again. At this writing, Australian scientists are taking this notion very seriously and have had some success *transporting* elementary particles around as information. They have even transported a laser beam from one place to another. It ended one place and started up again somewhere else, 18 inches away. This is an incredibly exciting accomplishment.

Not long ago I watched a TV program about UFOs on one of the science channels. There was a supposedly reputable physicist on there claiming to have observed an object (in Area 51 or something), accelerate from a dead stop to a point 6 miles away, to a dead stop again in approximately 2 seconds. (Those aren't the exact numbers, but something like that.) That's approximately 10,000 miles per hour, and in the bottom of the atmosphere. Not only would acceleration like that liquefy any creatures inside, but it probably would have liquefied the vehicle itself…unless of course it was somehow just information. If his observation was legitimate, have extraterrestrials learned how to move themselves around as information, something like the *Star Trek* transporters, only from continuous point to point? Just a stray thought.

The universe as a computer process:

As creatures living within a virtual reality, everything we observe is just the result of *processes* running on an information system. The universe our physicists probe is just a big computer program running out there, or perhaps more accurately, a hodge-podge of interacting little processes, all under the umbrella of the universe driver. If every object is a process, if particles and measuring instruments are just aggregate processes, then what physicists are discovering are the rules by which these processes interact. What are we to make of the fact that these rules of interaction are describable with mathematics?

The mathematics that the physicists have found behind it all may not be the mathematics that the universe driver is using. The universe driver may simply be using a puzzle-solving algorithm, one of the things that drops out being consistency. Mathematics might be our invention, our way of getting a handle on that consistency. We have invented mathematics just this way before. Classical physics, the physics that developed before the quantum realm was known, was highly mathematical. Newton's physics, his laws of motion, law of gravitation, are all mathematical, and helped contribute to the mechanistic paradigm of the universe. It turns out, though, that for the most part, the mathematics of classical physics are just *discovered*, or *invented* mathematics. The "real" mathematics is going on at a much lower level, at the quantum level, and the higher level mathematics, the classical level, is either just a close approximation, or can be derived from the quantum mathematics.

The point is that the mathematics discovered to work by the classical physicists wasn't the "real" mathematics that the universe uses. Are we sure that the quantum mathematics is the end all, or is it just another derivation from something more fundamental? Will quantum mathematics turn out to be just a close approximation to string theory mathematics? Our mathematics is descriptive, designed to describe what has happened after the fact, not how something happens. Indeed, some believe that the statistical nature of quantum physics is forced from this very after-the-fact descriptive requirement. Behind the scenes, it may turn out not even to be mathematical at all. Mathematics, and consistency itself, may just turn out to be inventions of ours that capture the behavior of the interacting processes.

In our little pretend universe, quanta were the error introduced by the limit of accuracy of the value representation. In our universe, quanta seem to somehow be what it is composed of. Is it possible to compose a universe completely out of the error, as aggregates of errors, in an information system? I think it might be. All information at its lowest level is not the medium that represents it. For example, in a computer, the little voltage itself is not what represents the information. It is the differences between voltages that represent the information. Information then in a way, is composed not of a thing itself, not of a medium, but of the difference between things. It can be a difficult concept to grasp. We are so accustomed to perceiving our world as composed of objects, of things, but it's really based on something like the opposite, i.e., on something like the spaces between objects. It's sort of like looking at the number line.

$$0 \quad 1 \quad 2 \quad 3 \quad 4 \quad 5 \quad 6 \quad 7 \quad 8 \quad 9 \quad 10$$

When we look at the numbers, we look at the vertical line on the number line to mark the number, to be the number. The vertical line that marks 2 is where the object 2 occurs, but that's really not the number. The number is more correctly not represented by the vertical mark, but by the line that extends between the points, in the case of 2, the line that extends from 0 to 2. Numbers, like all information, are differences, are the spaces between the points, rather than the points. When information about differences makes it into our brains, our brains turn it inside out, turn it into the experience of an object, but in reality it starts out as something almost the opposite of an object. Apparently there are no objects out there, so taking this into consideration, it feels like there might be a similarity there between quanta in our universe, and the error in our pretend universe.

We, and our measuring instruments, are processes running on an I. S., processes that interact with, and are affected by other processes. We are learning the rules by which these processes interact. The rules that we are learning, though, are after the fact, downstream from what the universe driver is doing. We are working out what the program does from what it has done, but not necessarily how it does it, and this is always what physics has done. With each level that physics descends into its description of reality, the precision with which the results of these interactions are predicted becomes more precise. But we cannot see how these interactions are being computed. We cannot see the process behind the oop object interface, so to speak. We cannot see the computer language in which it is written. We cannot see the medium on which it is represented.

Just to illustrate, suppose some creature were to evolve on a realm on which the perceived locations of its particles were actually the selling price of stocks on the stock market in our universe. (The continuously changing selling price of stocks actually does exhibit some characteristics similar to the random motion of particles.) Any poor creature that evolved in this universe and was trying to work out the physics for the behavior of these particles, must surely come up with some *probabilistic, statistical* description of this behavior. It would be impossible for them to conceive of the phenomena behind the scenes (stocks in our universe) by which the changing locations of their particles was computed. (since we can't either.)

Is it necessarily true, however, that we can never detect the innards of these processes any more directly than through the gross interactions of one process interface with another? There are some reasons to think that just maybe we can, depending on just how deeply this I. S. universe paradigm holds.

If the universe that we experience is virtual, then we are processes running on an I. S. in a higher level universe. As processes, we then have some existence in, and some effect in that higher level universe. Processes on a computer are able to affect other processes on that computer, and all of this is taking place one level of universe up, in the universe of the computer. We know of processes on our computers down here in this universe that manipulate the innards of other processes, compilers for example. Processes on a computer can not only interact with each other. Processes can manipulate the medium on which they're represented, at least deterministically. In the case of our computers, processes, which are represented by those fluctuating little voltages, can manipulate those little voltages in such a way as to make new processes. Will our physics ever be able to go so deep as to discover processes that can manipulate the information that is the processes themselves? If so, I wonder if we will discover that the universe too has a version of the Halting Problem. If we discover that it doesn't, we should want to know why.

If the universe is an I.S., and if it is programmed, then perhaps we can dink with the program. In a virtual universe in our computers, the objects of a program can only influence the objects of the universe that the computer has generated for them, and by the rules that the programming language allows them to use, but that's just today's computers. As a programmer in the Army in 1967, the "second generation" computers we worked with could change the rules. That meant we could program these computers in such a way that they could alter their original program at run time. This concept of a self-altering, self-programming computer has been pretty much eliminated from today's computers as it causes a huge potential for errors, but in fact all computers are capable of self programming if you can get past the operating system. Some research has been done in this area, called evolutionary or genetic programming. If our universe is programmed into a system that allows self-programming, then it might be possible that the rules of the universe can change with time, that the universe driver is evolving.

The processes that run on a computer tell us something about the capabilities of that computer. As one digs deeper and deeper into the subprocesses of those processes, one is getting closer and closer to the capabilities of the "machine language" in which the processes are written. As physicists dig deeper and deeper into the subprocesses of our universe, will they be getting closer and closer to the language that our universe uses to represent those processes? Will physicists one day discover the language itself, the instructions or the microinstructions, and be able to write their own processes? Does *Star Trek* like *transportation* of a laser beam, perhaps, qualify as a new process created by physicists, nonexistent in our universe until now? Does all technology qualify? Is it possible that we may be able to find ways to manipulate the driver itself, and thus change the rules of physics? The rules of physics would be set at the driver level, after all. Is it possible that if we ever achieve this, that we should worry about possibly crashing the system?

The higher level universe:

Computers rely on the physics of the universe in which they reside, and depend on those physics for their capabilities. Our computers of today represent information electronically, and are thus based on, and limited to, the computations that are possible using a logic representable with voltages. On our horizon, however, are quantum computers. The information and the processing capabilities of quantum computers will be based on, and limited to, the computations that are possible using a logic based on quantum effects. As virtual computers in a virtual universe, quantum effects are much closer to the low level instructions of the universe driver than are today's computers, which depend on voltages. They, therefore, will be far more efficient, with capabilities far beyond what today's electronic computers can do, and should be a sight to behold. The point is, though, that an information system, at least those of our experience, imply something about the physics of the universe from which they are composed. As we dig deeper and deeper into the processes of the information system in which our universe is embedded, will we be able to deduce more and more about the physics of the higher level universe in which our universe's I. S. is embedded? Is the discreetness of the quantum just such an artifact of the information system in which we're imbedded?

As we begin to explore the implementation of quantum physics in quantum computers, we see that the computational ability of just a few particles far exceeds the capabilities of our current computers. As computers, they are even able to instantly make calculations that would require infinite time on computers based on the physics of our computers today. If this is all a virtual reality, then those particle calculations are being made on the I. S. in the next higher level universe. What kind of physics must exist in that universe that such calculations are possible.

If our physics is driven as a virtual universe inside of some sort of I. S., we have discovered a possible source of phenomena that is outside of our physics, outside of our universe. Any such phenomena will appear mysterious, supernatural, and unexplainable, and *it will be from within our physics*. We have two immediate candidates for just such phenomena, the collapse of the potentials function, and experience, and we've also seen that it appears possible that they may be related. (Even the great mathematician John von Neumann deduced that the collapse of the potentials to a single reality must be in some way related to mind.) If we remain mindful of the fact that the single, collapsed reality is all that we ever know, all that we ever experience, and if we accept that materiality doesn't exist, and that all that exists is experience, then some might say that it would be irrational not to contemplate a possible connection between experience and the collapse to this single reality.

The physics of the higher level universe need not be the same as the physics in any virtual universes created as information in it. In fact, it appears that they are most certainly not. If we are imbedded in a higher level universe, it is most likely not like this one at all. It will not have space and materiality, perhaps not even something like time. Of course it is impossible to even start to imagine such a universe since we are limited to imagining only what we already know, and we know only our universe. I cannot help but consider the possibility that that higher level universe, and the I. S. we're imbedded in, have something to do with experience itself.

Chapter 17
Epilogue

There are times when all the world's asleep
The questions run so deep
For such a simple man.

—The Logical Song—by Super Tramp

While this book has not, and was not intended to, achieve the level of truth we call scientific, it does represent a very powerful technique employed by engineers and think tanks in their search for practical solutions to complex problems, called *brainstorming*. In brainstorming, it is imperative that the participants do not sensor their thoughts as to their degree of fancifulness. It is imperative that the stream-of-consciousness thoughts of each member of the group get heard around the room. These thoughts then trigger other thoughts in the minds of other participants, who make them public, etc. Only near the end of the process are the requirements of plausibility tightened as the search for a realistic solution is narrowed. I remember reading about an instance where NASA engineers in the sixties were trying to find a method to fasten the helmets to the space suits so they would be airtight. The brainstorming thought process that eventually traced to a solution was initiated by someone saying something like they were imagining two caterpillars, or centipedes belly to belly griping each other with their legs.

So in some ways, this book is like a brainstorm. There have been quite a few thoughts put forth, some of which the reader may feel are fanciful. It is one of my hopes that these will lead to other thoughts in people that eventually contribute to the solutions of the dilemmas discussed. This book differs from a brainstorm, however, in one way that many readers might not recognize, and that is, believe it or not, that I did sensor the results as to their fancifulness. I spent a great deal of thought on each topic searching for only the plausible, and eliminating the obviously implausible. This is not true brainstorming, but you can imagine how fanciful the book would have been without it.

So do I believe all of this, or not?

Not all of it perhaps, but there is a great deal of it that I do believe, and I believe that most of that is self evident to those willing to think about it, or nearly so.

I believe that it is self-evident that we humans have been through many different paradigms of the universe in our history, that all have eventually failed, and that it requires the utmost denial to imagine that we now live in the time of the one *true* and final paradigm, especially with physicists out there writing books, pursuing the very task of searching for a paradigm that will satisfactorily account for quantum phenomena. It's important to note that no current paradigm does account for quantum phenomena.

I do believe in the information nature of reality, that all is differences on realms, brought to us as cascading chains of effects. I think it is deducible even at the macroworld level that our universe is composed not of things, but of the difference of things. I think this is so easily understood as to be nearly self evident, and can be realized simply by contemplating cardinals, even without resorting to the discoveries of physics. We cannot know what is behind the effects, only imagine. All we ever can really know are the downstream effects themselves. That's all we get at our bodies. The things we perceive are not composed of things, but of differences. Those things we perceive, or believe we perceive, are just our *mental representations* constructed from these differences. Our minds turn differences into the perception of things, but they are not things at all. If we are ever to understand what really is, we are going to have to reach down the gullet of our idea of reality, and turn it inside out.

And I believe that all of the world that we can know is what is displayed on the big screen of our experience. Experience is all there is, and when we study physics, we are ultimately studying the rules behind how our experiences vary. I believe that our experience of the material/spatial world is a mental representation of the universe of information that evolved, and survived, because of its usefulness, but that our experience of the world is not the way that it need be at all. The material world around us doesn't necessarily exist as anything material, and almost certainly doesn't. The clues that the material world as a paradigm is failing, and should be replaced, have been lingering around for ages.

I believe that if material objects don't exist, it follows that when we open up our skulls and look at our brains, we are not seeing them as they really exist either, and it seems to me that this may be an important factor in why we are unable to understand how brain activity becomes experience.

Do I believe that it is the mind that collapses the multiple potentials onto a single reality? At this point, that would require more of a leap of faith than I am prepared to do. *Suspect* might be a more accurate term than *believe*. I do think, however, that there are good reasons to suspect that the mind is involved, not the least of which is that our experience is all we know. I believe that feelings, i.e. experiences, are involved in the decisions we make and the corresponding actions we take, and I think that this implies that the mind can affect the brain. I think if we develop the ideas of the weak and strong mind, it may even become self evident whether or not the mechanism via which the mind affects the brain involves the quantum collapse, or not.

Do I believe that our universe is just a program running inside of some creature's desktop PC in a higher level universe? Well, not exactly. But apparently I did for a few days. I have to relate this story.

Before writing this book, I had noticed maybe four of the similarities between a computerized universe and quantum phenomena. During the writing I came up with many more, which I found very encouraging, but I never even dreamed that I would identify a phenomenon that would behave similarly to the quantum itself.

Up until then, this had all been great fun, just a wonderfully exciting puzzle to be solved. Within minutes of that discovery, though, I became very depressed, a tormented depression, and I remained so for several days. Apparently there is a switch within us, subconscious or unconscious, which decides for us whether we believe something or not, and with that discovery, my switch had flip flopped over to the believing position. I had convinced some deep part of myself that we really do live inside of a computer. Now I'm still unclear as to just exactly why this part of me found this idea to be so depressing, perhaps because now it had to worry about some gangly sophomore coming along and tripping over the computer cord...or something similar. Anyway, the depression soon lifted.

I do believe, however, that the universe is just information, and that, therefore, a legitimate term to describe it is by default an *information system*. What this information system is, is the $64,000 question. And I think that it is very suggestive that so many of the unexplained quantum phenomena turn up if one programs a universe inside of an information system as we know it, even a PC.

The first thing many are going to want to do is to try to account for this coincidence of phenomena by some other means. The first thing that some will suspect is that many of these phenomena appearing in the programmed universe have been inadvertently introduced directly by the programmer, who is trying to mimic the behavior of the universe after all. In your reading, you will see that there are a couple (besides the collapse of potentials) that perhaps do seem to be introduced inadvertently, but I believe in these cases that their origin is from the brain-like-aggregate-object-puzzle-solving algorithm. I would suggest that if the reader feels that any have been questionably introduced, that those phenomena should simply be ignored and only the remainder be considered suggestive of the information system nature of the universe.

There are at least two more potential sources of these phenomena that I can think of and that I did not pursue in the text. One is the science of physics itself. Physicists are problem solvers after all. Is it possible that they have inadvertently invented a puzzle solving algorithm, called quantum physics, to mimic the behavior of the universe, and that some of these mysterious phenomena result from their methods? If this is the case, then the reappearance of these phenomena from another puzzle solver is not so mysterious.

The other potential source is our brain. The brain is an information system after all, and the brain does represent to us everything that we know, including the universe. The brain is even digital. Is it possible that we are ultimately studying the universe as represented to us by our brains, that this could be the source of these strange phenomena. Is it possible that instead of studying an objective universe, that in many ways we are actually studying our brains too? If so, then it might account for the apparent coincidence of the appearance of these phenomena in both the universe and a computer running a brain like algorithm.

I do believe that it is possible that the paradigm that the universe acts in some ways like an information system, or more likely a more developed version of this idea, may be useful and possibly enjoy a day or two in the sun. I further believe that the paradigm of materiality failed long ago, now contradicts the known facts, and should have been abandoned before now. We are like eleven year olds still dragging around a tattered security blanket, and we are in danger of looking correspondingly silly. I also think that we have reached a state where it is imperative that scientists start taking into account that all we can know about the world is experience. And we have to quit playing games with the idea. There's so much that we don't know about experience that antagonists have little problem coming up with apparently unsolvable riddles, and everybody throws their hands up, shakes their head, and goes home. Science, though, has always progressed by making assumptions now that are only revealed to be false at a later time. I think it's time we made the assumption that all we can know is experience, see how far it takes us, and fine tune it as information and implications dictate. This poor little infant idea has been around for thousands of years, and it's never been allowed to grow or show what it can become.

The discussion about, the argument over, what is real and the correct paradigm to represent it has been going on since the beginning of human history. Anyone who thinks they have just figured it all out is seriously deluding themselves. I am not, and this goes for the naysayers too. Any new paradigm must be accepted on its usefulness as matching current experience and anticipating new experiments and control. Any new paradigm, though, must be entered into with the full knowledge that it will someday be shown to be wrong too, and that its temporary purpose is simply to advance our knowledge to the limit of that paradigm. With a little luck, in the process, we will discover and become familiar with new phenomena that will form the foundation for the next useful paradigm.

I find it exciting though to contemplate the paradigm of the universe as a process running in an information system of a higher level universe. The reason I find it exciting is because I anticipate that it may give us a fabulous new handle into reality. This is one thing new paradigms are supposed to do, after all. In this paradigm, all manner of technologies become conceivable that are unintuitive in the material world paradigm, *transportation* for example. I have only scratched the surface of the notion of the relationships between processes, how they affect each other, their different levels, and the like, but I have a sense that in that direction lies the explanation of the quantum collapse, and much of the explanation of the relationship of mind to the universe.

And I find it exciting to contemplate the notion of a higher-level universe. Certainly it is nothing like we imagine ours to be. Certainly it is not material/spatial. If not, then what could it be? Is this where the phenomena of experience occurs, which leads to the phenomenon of mind? Is this how to account for the fact that the mind, and the quantum collapse don't seem to be accounted for by the physics of our universe, that is, because they are effectively outside of the physics, the process that is our universe? Is it possible that the higher level universe *is*, or at least contains, the realm of experience itself? Or maybe experience exists in an even higher level universe. If any of this has any truth to it at all, I believe that we can *deduce* many of the details from considerations of what we know already. I was actually hoping to stumble onto the cause of the quantum collapse during the writing of this book while exploring the relationships of the mind to virtual realities. I think that the explanation is that close, and I feel that with just a little more imagination I may have seen it. Perhaps a reader will. We may well be at a point where we are better able to figure this stuff out with think tanks than with the plodding methods of research and publication.

Hopefully this book has brought to the reader some interesting ideas, levels of universes, universes as information systems, etc., which are fun and perhaps enlightening. And hopefully this will now have opened new concepts to the imagination to be explored. The ant's eye view we are taking of the *theory of computation* is not leading us to an overview of information systems, and there is a lot of useful information in the overview. What phenomena result from interactive processes? What happens when a computer analyzes its own activity? Where are the paradoxes in the mind that should be showing up? Is there something hiding in interactive levels of universes that does explain experience or quantum collapse? A computer analyzing (contemplating) its activity of analyzing (contemplating) its activity will go into an infinite regress that leads it away from solving the problem. What's different about the mind that allows it to contemplate its contemplation? What are the properties of information systems in this respect? What are the properties of universes, and how do they compare? Does the mind demonstrate some of these properties *similar* to an information system? If so/not, what properties does it have that *differ?* We have seen that the universe demonstrates properties similar to information systems. Does the universe demonstrate any properties unique to mind? It takes but a minute to rattle off these questions. There are hundreds, thousands, of them that need asking and investigating.

This book is not the final word on anything, nor is it intended to be. What it does I think is suggest that there is something out there that needs exploring, ideas that need developing, hundreds of ideas that can be researched deeply with little more than logic and simple deduction. At best, I have done little more than send up a kite with a key on it. It's like damn, man, shouldn't the whiz kids be turned loose on this task?

APPENDIX

From New Scientist, 30 January 1999
© Copyright New Scientist, RBI Limited 1999
http://www.newscientist.com/ns/19990130/iisthelaw.html

It's the ultimate big idea, the source of everything we know about the physical world. And it all comes from one simple question, says Robert Matthews. Where do the laws of physics come from? It's the sort of question only children and geniuses ask—certainly most physicists are far too busy putting the laws to work.

Take quantum theory, the laws of the subatomic world. Over the past century it has passed every single test with flying colours, with some predictions vindicated to 10 places of decimals. Not surprisingly, physicists claim quantum theory as one of their greatest triumphs. But behind their boasts lies a guilty secret: they haven't the slightest idea why the laws work, or where they come from. All their vaunted equations are just mathematical lash-ups, made out of bits and pieces from other parts of physics whose main justification is that they seem to work.

Now one physicist thinks he knows where the laws of quantum theory come from. More amazingly still, Roy Frieden thinks he can account for all the laws of physics, governing everything from schoolroom solenoids to space and time. Sounds incredible? You haven't heard the first of it. For Frieden believes he has found the Law of Laws, the principle underpinning physics itself.

The laws of electricity, magnetism, gases, fluids, even Newton's laws of motion—all of these, Frieden believes, arise directly from the same basic source: the information gap between what nature knows and what nature is prepared to let us find out. Using sophisticated mathematics, Frieden has shown that this notion of physics as a "quest for information" is no empty philosophical pose. It can be made solid, and leads to a way of deriving all the major laws of fundamental physics—along with some new ones.

The sheer power of Frieden's approach is beginning to catch the eye of other researchers. "The results already obtained are extremely spectacular and I'm an enthusiastic supporter," says theorist Peter Hawkes from the CNRS laboratories in Toulouse, France.

Unlike most of the mathematical Schwarzeneggers now trying to unify the whole of physics, Frieden does not normally spend his waking hours wrestling with 26-dimensional space-time. As a researcher at the Optical Sciences Center of the University of Arizona, he has an international reputation in the more practical field of optical image enhancement.

In the early 1970s, he pioneered techniques to "clean up" fuzzy images of everything from distant galaxies to stolen car number plates. He was put on the trail of a radical new view of physics while investigating alternative ways of capturing the information content of images. "For years, I had kept in the back of my mind a passage I had read in a textbook on information theory, which talked about something called 'Fisher Information'. Someday, I thought, I was going to investigate that—and now the time was ripe."

Named after the Cambridge statistician Ronald Aylmer Fisher in the mid-1920s, Fisher information—usually contracted to I—captures how much information you can squeeze out of a physical system. Suppose you want to know where a gas molecule is. You can try measuring it, but no measurements are perfect—they all come with a certain amount of error. What's more there are inherent "errors" in the system—random disorder, jitters associated with the temperature of the gas and the "jolts" caused by the very act of observing, made famous by quantum theory. All of these errors are governed by statistical distributions, such as the famous bell-shaped curve. Plugging these distributions into a formula worked out by Fisher, you end up with a measure of how much information you can extract from a physical system, given all the errors.

At first, Frieden simply used Fisher information calculations as a way of prising more information out of blurry images. But it was while he was reading around the subject that he found himself being pointed in another, more profound, direction. "I came across a 1959 paper by the Dutch mathematician A. J. Stam, who showed that I could be used to derive Heisenberg's famous uncertainty principle," recalls Frieden. "And being a physicist, this set me thinking."

Studying Stam's work, Frieden noticed that it made use of a result from information theory called the Cramer-Rao inequality. This little-known mathematical result shows, roughly speaking, that when the error in a measurement is multiplied by the amount of Fisher information in the measurement, the result is a number that is never less than one.

It's a relationship strikingly similar to the uncertainty principle. Multiply together the uncertainties in your knowledge of a particle's position and its momentum, and the result is never less than a certain value. The more precisely you know the position, the less precisely you can know the momentum. Or put another way, the act of measuring the position influences the measured value of the momentum—and vice versa.

The similarity between the Cramer-Rao inequality and the uncertainty principle started Frieden wondering whether information—and Fisher information in particular—had a much deeper role in physics. "Since Heisenberg's principle is so basic, it occurred to me that perhaps every physical phenomenon occurs in reaction to measurement—that measurement acts as a kind of catalyst for the effect," says Frieden. "And the possibility that physical laws occur as answers to questions excited my curiosity."

Digging into this possibility, Frieden soon found another mathematical "coincidence". Whenever he did calculations using the Fisher information, the final results were differential equations. "What struck me," he recalls, "is that virtually all of physics can also be expressed in terms of differential equations."

Differential equations are formulae showing how the rate of change of a certain quantity changes under outside influences. For instance, Newton's second law of motion relates the acceleration of an object to the force applied: F = ma. The acceleration in this formula is the rate of change of velocity, which in turn is the rate of change of distance. Quantum theory has its own, more abstract, examples, such as Schrödinger's famous wave equation and Dirac's relativistic equation for the electron. The same format shows up across the whole of physics.

Again, it's the kind of observation that is apt to provoke a shrug of the shoulders. But now Frieden was sure he was on to something really deep. The ubiquity of these types of equation, he believed, is intimately linked to one of the most profound mysteries in science: despite the vast range of phenomena covered by the fundamental laws of physics, all of those laws can be made to drop out of mathematical objects known as Lagrangians. And no one knows why.

Put simply, Lagrangians are made up of the difference between two quantities which together form something called the "action". For reasons as yet utterly mysterious, this quantity stays as small as possible under all circumstances. This curiosity—known as the principle of least action—is reflected in the fact that the fundamental laws of physics are differential equations, since that's what you need to minimize the action.

In Newton's laws of motion, for example, the relevant action turns out to be the difference between the kinetic energy and the potential energy of a body. Kinetic energy is the energy associated with how fast something is moving, and potential energy with its location. It turns out that to keep the difference between these two to a minimum, the object's mass times its acceleration always has to equal the force applied. Minimising this particular action leads to Newton's second law of motion.

Beyond action:

Theorists are convinced that action must be incredibly important—so much so that the discovery of any new fundamental law prompts a race to work out the particular action needed to produce it. The trouble is that no one understands the principles behind nature's infatuation with action, and so no one can calculate it directly. Instead, they have to reverse-engineer it, working backwards from the newly discovered law.

It is the puzzle of action—and thus the origin of the laws of physics—that Frieden now reckons he has solved. And, he says, it all comes down to information—the information we try to prise from nature by making observations and the information nature has, but is reluctant to part with.

If you look at Lagrangians for gravity or electromagnetism, says Frieden, they all have more or less the same mathematical form. They are all made up of the difference between I, the Fisher information from observing the phenomenon, and another statistical quantity, J, which is the amount of information bound up in the phenomenon you're trying to measure.

It is from this that Frieden has built his radically new vision of physics based not on the mysterious "action", but on something more intuitive: our attempt to come up with the best possible description of phenomena. All the information needed for such a description exists, in the form of J, and we want as much of it as possible to be extracted by our measurements, in the form of I. In other words, we want the information difference—I minus J—to be as small as possible. And it turns out that for this difference to be as small as possible, the phenomenon must obey a differential equation.

Frieden's information-based methods provide a stunningly clear interpretation of the laws of physics: they represent the best we can possibly do in our quest to extract information using our inevitably error-prone methods. "Through the very act of observing, we thus actually define the physics of the thing measured," says Frieden. He adds that while unfamiliar, the idea that "reality"—or, at least, the laws of physics—are created by observation is not new. During the 18th century, empiricist philosophers such as Bishop Berkeley were raising similar ideas. Much more recently, John Wheeler, a physicist at Princeton University who is widely regarded as one of the deepest thinkers on the foundations of physics, has championed remarkably similar views. "Observer participancy gives rise to information and information gives rise to physics," he says.

That's not to say Frieden's approach implies that the laws of physics are "all in the mind". Rather, it means that any physical attempt to extract information about nature determines the answer we obtain—and the best information we can ever extract is what we call the laws of physics.

So Frieden's achievement is to give a philosophical view of physics a solid mathematical foundation. For any given system, I and J are statistical quantities which can be calculated using Frieden's methods. And the payoff is spectacular: with these two quantities, you can fulfill the 200-year-old dream of deriving the Lagrangian for that system, and thus of deriving the physical law that rules it.

Over the past 10 years, in a series of papers in such journals as Physical Review, Frieden and colleagues including Bernard Soffer of the Hughes Research Laboratories in Malibu, California, have been steadily working their way through physics, showing that all of its laws are the result of a kind of cosmic game between ourselves and the "real" world. To derive each law—or, more accurately, each Lagrangian—we have to ask an incredibly simple yet fundamental question, such as "what is the precise location of a particle in space and time?"

Any attempt to answer such questions requires the same two quantities: the information that exists in any given thing or system, J, and the information we can acquire, I. Frieden has developed methods of calculating both for a wide range of phenomena in physics. Subtracting J from I then leads straight to the appropriate Lagrangian, and when this is made as small as possible, the appropriate law of physics "emerges". No reverse engineering, no fancy use of mathematical tricks, no inspired guesses.

Take that question about the precise location of a particle in space and time. Frieden's approach leads directly to the Lagrangian for the Klein-Gordon equation. This is the central law of relativistic quantum theory which describes the way particles move through space and time. If, on the other hand, you want to know about the location of a particle in space alone, Frieden's approach leads to Schrödinger's wave equation.

That this one principle can act as a key to unlock the fundamental laws is impressive enough, but if it really is the key to all physics, it should do more than reproduce what physicists already know. It should also reveal the secrets of unsolved mysteries.

Turbulence tamed:

Some researchers are finding that it can. Take turbulence, the roiling motion of fast-moving fluids whose understanding Einstein himself regarded as the biggest challenge to classical physics. In 1996, John Cocke at the University of Arizona showed that using Frieden's approach on the question of what is the flow of mass at a particular time and place leads to a law governing the size of density fluctuations in turbulent fluids. This law makes sense of otherwise baffling results from studies of fluid behaviour.

The quantum world offers an equally demanding challenge that has effectively defeated the world's best theorists for decades. Quantum theory—which sees everything in terms of discrete jerks, jumps and packets—just does not sit easily with Einstein's concept of smooth expanses of curved space-time.

Yet Frieden found last year that by asking what space-time like is, he arrives at a Lagrangian which leads straight to the Wheeler-deWitt equation: a formula giving a quantum description of space-time. The Wheeler-deWitt equation, now more than 30 years old, is one of the few concrete results in quantum gravity theory.

Until now, however, the principles behind Wheeler-deWitt have been far from clear. Frieden's theory not only shows how to derive the Wheeler-deWitt equation, but also seems to shed light on what the equation means. Frieden is already examining these clues to see how they may help theorists go beyond the equation to a full-blown theory of quantum gravity.

Frieden is still struggling to spread his message among other theorists, many of whom are reluctant even to study his approach. "Part of the reason is probably simple inertia to learning about a new concept like Fisher information," he says.

But others are more enthusiastic. "Frieden's shown that a host of what used to be regarded as fundamental equations of physics are actually capable of derivation," says Hawkes. Cocke agrees: "It is a sort of unifying principle, and I see it as a method of solving tough problems in statistical physics."

Frieden hopes that his new book, which shows in detail how to apply Fisher information to physical problems, will help to convince others how powerful his approach is, and encourage them to join in. "What I and my co-workers have done so far is by no means the final word, but it does offer a systematic way to finding laws for new phenomena. And it seems that information is what physics is all about."

Robert Matthews is science correspondent of The Sunday Telegraph

Further reading:

* Physics from Fisher Information by Roy Frieden, Cambridge University Press

Bibliography

The following is a list of the books from my bookshelf, other than textbooks, which did, or very likely did, contribute information or ideas to this book.

Adams, James L. *Conceptual Blockbusting, A Guide to Better Ideas*. San Francisco: W. H. Freeman and Company, 1974.

Albert, David Z. *Quantum Mechanics and Experience*. Cambridge, Massachusetts: Harvard University Press, 1994.

Baggott, Jim. *The Meaning of Quantum Theory*. Oxford: Oxford University Press, 1992.

Buber, Martin. *I and Thou*. New York: Charles Scribner Sons, 1958.

Chang, Briankle G. *Deconstructing Communication—Representation, Subject, and Economies of Exchange*. Minnesota: University of Minnesota Press, 1997.

Churchland, Patricia S., Terrence J. Sejnowski. *The Computational Brain*. Cambridge, Massachusetts: The MIT Press, 1991.

de Bono, Edward. *Lateral Thinking*. New York: Harper and Row, 1973.

———. *de Bono's Thinking Course*. New York: Facts on File Publications, 1985.

Deutsch, David. *The Fabric of Reality*. New York: Penguin Books, 1997.

Duffy, Patricia Lynne. *Blue Cats and Chartreuse Kittens*. New York: Henry Holt and Company, 2001.

Egner, Robert E. and Lester E. Denonn, Editors. *The Basic Writings of Bertrand Russell*. New York: Simon and Schuster, 1903–1959.

Fogel, David B. *Evolutionary Computation*. New York: IEEE Press, 1995.

Greene, Brian. *The Elegant Universe*. New York: Vintage Books, 1999.

Greenstein, George, Arthur G. Zajonc. *The Quantum Challenge*. Sudbury, Massachusetts: Jones and Bartlett, Publishers, 1997.

Grobstein, Clifford. *The Strategy of Life*. San Francisco: W. H. Freeman and Company, 1974.

Haack, Susan. *Deviant Logic*. Cambridge, England: Cambridge University Press, 1974.

Harrison, Edward. *Masks of the Universe*. New York: Macmillan Publishing Company, 1985.

Hawking, Stephen W. *A Brief History of Time*. New York: Bantam Books, 1988.

Herbert, Nick. *Quantum Reality, Beyond the New Physics*. Garden City, New York: Anchor Press/Doubleday, 1987.

Hofstadter, Douglas R. *Gödel, Escher, Bach: An Eternal Golden Braid*. New York: Random House, 1980.

Holland, John H. *Hidden Order: How Adaptation Builds Complexity*. Massachusetts: Addison-Wesley Publishing Company, 1995.

————. *Emergence—From Chaos to Order*. Reading, Massachusetts: Addison-Wesley Publishing Company, 1998.

J. Bronowski (1973). *The Ascent of Man*. Boston: Little, Brown and Company

Kafatos, Menas, Robert Nadeau. *The Conscious Universe—Part and Whole in Modern Physical Theory*. New York: Springer-Verlag, 1990.

Koza, John R. *Genetic Programming II*. Cambridge, Massachusetts: The MIT Press, 1994.

Mayer, Richard E. *Thinking, Problem Solving, Cognition*. San Francisco: W. H. Freeman and Company, 1992.

Nicholls, John G., A. Robert Martin, Burce G. Wallace. *From Neuron to Brain*. Sunderland, Massachusetts: Sinauer Associates, 1992.

Nielsen, Michael A. and Isaac L. Chaung. *Quantum Computation and Quantum Information*. Cambridge, England: Cambridge University Press, 2000.

Nozick, Robert. *Philosophical Explanations.* Cambridge, Massachusetts: Harvard University Press, 1981.

Omnès, Roland. *Quantum Philosophy—Understanding and Interpreting Contemporary Science.* Princeton, New Jersey: Princeton University Press, 1999.

Ornstein, Robert E. *The Psychology of Consciousness.* San Francisco: W. H. Freeman and Company, 1972.

Penrose, Roger. *The Large, The Small, and The Human Mind.* Cambridge, England: Cambridge University Press, 1999.

Pierce, John R. *An Introduction to Information Theory; Symbols, Signals and Noise.* Toronto, Ontario: Dover, 1961.

Pinker, Steven. *How the Mind Works.* New York: W. W. Norton & Co., 1997.

Powell, Jim. *Derrida for Beginners.* New York: Writers and Readers Publishing, Inc., 1997.

Ramachandran, V.S., M.D., Ph.D., and Sandra Blakeslee. *Phantoms In the Brain.* New York: HarperCollins Publishers, 1998.

Shannon, Claude E., Warren Weaver. *The Mathematical Theory of Communication.* Urbana, Illinois: University of Illinois Press, 1964.

Treiman, Sam. *The Odd Quantum.* Princeton, New Jersey: Princeton University Press, 1999.

Vonnegut, Kurt Jr. *Slaughterhouse Five.* New York: Dell Publishing Company, 1969.

Walker, Evan Harris. *The Physics of Consciousness.* Massachusetts: Perseus Publishing, 2000.

Warmington, Erich H. and Philip G. Rouse, Editors. *Great Dialogues of Plato.* New York: New American Library, 1956.

0-595-66296-X